CA 34.

Normality and Pathology in Cognitive Functions

Normality and Pathology in Cognitive Functions

Edited by

ANDREW W. ELLIS

Department of Psychology
University of Lancaster
England

ACADEMIC PRESS   1982
A Subsidiary of Harcourt Brace Jovanovich, Publishers

London   New York
Paris   San Diego   San Francisco   São Paulo
Sydney   Tokyo   Toronto

ACADEMIC PRESS INC. (LONDON) LTD
24/28 Oval Road
London NW1 7DX

United States Edition published by
ACADEMIC PRESS INC.
111 Fifth Avenue
New York, New York 10003

British Library Cataloguing in Publication Data
Ellis, A. W.
  Normality and pathology in cognitive functions.
  1. Cognition   2. Neuropsychology
  I. Title
  153.4   BF311

  ISBN 0–12–237480–0

Phototypesetting by Oxford Publishing Services, Oxford
Printed in Great Britain by
T.J. Press (Padstow) Ltd., Padstow, Cornwall

List of Contributors

BYRNE, RICHARD W.   Department of Psychology, University of St. Andrews, St. Andrews, Fife, Scotland, KY16 9JU

ELLIS, ANDREW W.   Department of Psychology, University of Lancaster, Lancaster LA1 4YF, England

GARDNER, HOWARD   Psychology Service: 14th Floor, Boston Veterans Administration Hospital, 150 South Huntington Avenue, Boston, Massachusetts 02130, USA

GARRETT, MERRILL F.   Department of Psychology, Massachusetts Institute of Technology, E10–034, 77 Massachusetts Avenue, Cambridge, Massachusetts 02139, USA

HAY, DENNIS C.   Department of Psychology, University of Lancaster, Lancaster LA1 4YF, England

MARSHALL, JOHN C.   Neuropsychology Unit, University Department of Clinical Neurology, The Radcliffe Infirmary, Oxford OX2 6HE, England

MAYES, A.   Department of Psychology, University of Manchester, Manchester M13 9PL, England

MEUDALL, P.   Department of Psychology, University of Manchester, Manchester M13 9PL, England

NEWCOMBE, FREDA   Neuropsychology Unit, University Department of Clinical Neurology, The Radcliffe Infirmary, Oxford OX2 6HE, England

PATTERSON, KARALYN E.   MRC Applied Psychology Unit, 15 Chaucer Road, Cambridge CB2 2EF, England

RATCLIFF, GRAHAM   Western Psychiatric Institute and Clinic, University of Pittsburgh, 3811 O'Hara Street, Pittsburgh, Pennsylvania, PA 15261, USA

ROY, ERIC A.   Department of Kinesiology, Faculty of Human Kinetics and Leisure Studies, University of Waterloo, Waterloo, Ontario N21 3G1, Canada

YOUNG, ANDREW W.   Department of Psychology, University of Lancaster, Lancaster LA1 4YF, England

Introduction

In the past there have been cognitive psychologists working with normal healthy individuals, studying memory, perception, language, or whatever. There have also been clinical neuropsychologists working in hospitals with brain-injured patients, trying to describe and understand the many and varied difficulties which the patients experience with the same cognitive skills of memory, perception, language etc. Recent years, however, have seen a marked change in this picture. Clinical neuropsychologists have increasingly been drawing upon cognitive theories to explain patients' symptoms, and more and more cognitive psychologists are taking either an active or passive interest in the ways that brain injury can impair cognitive skills.

Those who involve themselves in this approach do so in the belief that the flow of information between normal and pathological conditions should be two-way. That is, not only should cognitive psychology illuminate neuropsychological analyses, but the study of neuropsychological syndromes should have direct and specific implications for our theories of normal functioning.

'Psychology', in the memorable words of Marshall and Fryer (1978), 'is not a young science; it is merely a difficult one'. Marshall opens this volume (chapter 1) with an historical and theoretical overview and perspective on the present efforts after an integrated cognitive neuropsychology. In so doing, he provides an important critique of the usual formulation of the 'mind-body problem'. Marshall writes:

Most 20th century philosophical discussion of these issues has been vitiated by the strange assumption that the character of both mind and brain is known, and that therefore the sole issue lies in the nature of the relationship between the two domains. Nothing could be further from the truth.

Marshall goes on to suggest that the traditional two-level approach to the mind-body problem may be inadequate. Following Marr's work, Marshall suggests that as many as (or at least) four descriptive levels may be needed, from a 'theory of computation' at the top to a cellular, neurophysiological level at the bottom. The various levels of explanation must be connected one to another by 'bridging laws'. Some important points emerge from this characterisation. First, no level of representation is more fundamental or more basic than any other. Second, the scientist is left free to operate legitimately at any one of these levels. Thus, for example, it is a viable enterprise to attempt to describe and account for the effects of brain injury on cognitive performance solely and entirely at the cognitive-psychological level of explanation. This approach can be seen in the chapters by Garrett on speech production (chapter 2), Patterson on reading (chapter 3), Ellis on spelling and writing (chapter 4), Ratcliff and Newcombe on object recognition (chapter 5) and Byrne on geographical knowledge and orientation (chapter 8).

Equally legitimate is the endeavour to relate between levels of description. This can be seen, for example, in the discussions of hemispheric specialisation by Hay and Young (chapter 6) with respect to face recognition, or Gardner (chapter 10) with respect to artistic skills. Attempts at more specific 'localisation of function' are made by Meudell and Mayes (chapter 7) regarding the brain structures mediating human memory, and Roy (chapter 9) regarding the organisation and control of action and performance. It must be emphasised, of course, that much of what these latter authors say is couched in purely cognitive terms and is relevant at that level.

A third point arising out of Marshall's opening chapter is that within-level and between-level approaches may permit or demand different *types* of neuropsychological study. As Conrad (1954) noted, localisational studies require large numbers of cases, whereas meaningful cognitive analysis can be carried out on single patients (e.g. Patterson, chapter 3; Ratcliff and Newcombe, chapter 5; Gardner, chapter 10).

The individual chapters require no further introduction from me. They by no means exhaust the areas where a fruitful exchange of ideas between cognitive psychology and neuropsychology has occurred, but they provide a fairly representative sampler, and should be sufficient to allow the reader to decide whether this is a developing field worth keeping an eye on.

References

Conrad, K. (1954). New problems of aphasia. *Brain* 77, 491–509
Marshall, J. C. and Fryer, D. M. (1978). Speak Memory! An introduction to some historic studies of remembering and forgetting. *In* 'Aspects of Memory' (M. M. Gruneberg and P. E. Morris, eds). London: Methuen

October 1981   ANDREW W. ELLIS

Contents

4 Spelling and Writing (and Reading and Speaking)   113

ANDREW W. ELLIS

5 Object Recognition: Some Deductions from the Clinical Evidence   147

GRAHAM RATCLIFF and FREDA NEWCOMBE

6 The Human Face   173

DENNIS C. HAY and ANDREW W. YOUNG

1

Models of the Mind in Health and Disease

JOHN C. MARSHALL

Neuropsychology Unit, The Radcliffe Infirmary, Oxford, England

1 Introduction

In any study of the history of ideas we often discover that propositions taken for granted are more revealing than claims explicitly argued for. Thus in *The Localization of Cerebral Disease* (1878) we find David Ferrier setting the scene for his inquiries in the following manner:

That the brain is the organ of the mind, no one doubts; and that, when mental aberrations, of whatever nature, are manifested, the brain is diseased organically or functionally, we take as an axiom.

The point of the passage lies, of course, in the claim that *all* mental functions have a neuronal correlate. The passage is also an exercise in rhetoric, for Ferrier knew perfectly well that, even in 1878, many scholars were not disposed to accept 'token physicalism' (Fodor, 1975) as axiomatic. And indeed a full century later there are still scholars who appear to believe that the self is distinct from its brain (Popper and Eccles, 1977). Between 1855 and 1888, Ludwig Büchner's *Kraft und Stoff* went through sixteen (German) editions and was translated into thirteen languages. Büchner summarized his materialist outlook on cognition by asserting that:

Thought can and must be regarded as a special form of the general motion of nature, which is as peculiar to the substance of the cerebral nerve-elements as contraction is to the muscles, or the motion of light is to the world-ether.

But many philosophers were so incensed by such views that, like Paulsen (1892), they could only suppose that a conspiracy was afoot:

In its youth the book circulated particularly among the educated middle class who were at outs with the church and its creed; it long since penetrated into the lower strata of society; it is now the working tool of the itinerant social-democratic agitator.

The claim that Ferrier and Büchner were propagating was that, in principle, psychology is (or should be) a natural science, albeit one in which results of any depth are difficult to come by. In its modern form we owe this doctrine to Franz Josef Gall, who, as Young (1970) writes, 'convinced the scientific community once and for all that "the brain is the organ of the mind" ' and that 'both its structure and functions could be concomitantly analysed by observation rather than speculation'. For his pains, Gall was prohibited from lecturing by an 1802 decree of Emperor Francis I and finally expelled from Vienna in 1805; Pius VII excommunicated him in 1817 and placed his books on the *Index*. Yet even Gall's main scientific adversary, Pierre Flourens acknowledged that although 'the proposition that the brain is the exclusive seat of the soul is not a new proposition, and hence does not originate with Gall', nonetheless the principle 'may be said to reign there ever since his appearance' (Young, 1970). The dispute between Gall and the experimental physiologists, led by Flourens, concerned Gall's view that both mind and brain are modular, an issue that is quite distinct from token physicalism.

Although Flourens is correct in his denial of priority to Gall, we have to go back two millenia before we find another physician who was as committed to the proposition as Gall was. We must return to the Hippocratic treatise *On the Sacred Disease* (epilepsy). In health:

Men ought to know that from nothing else but the brain come joy, despondency and lamentation . . . and by this, in an especial manner we acquire wisdom and knowledge, and see and hear. . . .

And likewise in disease:

By the same organ we become mad and delirious and fears and terrors assail us, some by night and some by day; and dreams and untimely wanderings, and cares that are not suitable, and ignorance of present circumstances, desuetude, and unskilfulness. All these things we endure from the brain when it is not healthy.

For Hippocrates, epilepsy is 'in no wise more divine nor more sacred than other diseases; but has a natural cause, from which it originates like other affections'. To some extent, Hippocrates argues on pragmatic grounds: if epilepsy has a purely divine origin it ought to be cured in the temples. But it isn't! More importantly, what links Hippocrates, Gall and Ferrier is precisely the belief that the interpretation and explanation of higher cognitive functions is, in principle, subject to 'natural law'. Special pleading is no more to be admitted when dealing with the mind and its material substrate than it would be when considering the structure and function of (other) organs of the body. I stress the point because it would seem that beliefs of this scope and strength are required in order to convert the vague view that there are some relationships between brain and behaviour into an actual research program. In particular, the mere observation of cooccurrences between disordered brain and disordered behaviour does not suffice to motivate attempts at explanation.

For example, on cuneiform tablets from Assyria we can read that disorders of action, knowledge and consciousness are often found 'when a man's brain holds fire, and his eyes are dim' (Thompson, 1908). Such observations were sufficient to motivate therapeutic intervention, both pharmacological and psychological. Thus it was recommended for such a patient that one 'grind and strain one-third of a ka of Sihlu, knead it in an infusion of cassia, bind it on his head, and do not remove for three days'. This treatment could be augmented by incanting over the patient the prayer: 'O Willow, Willow, dark Willow, come! and come, dark Cloud which the dark rainstorm hath o'erspread!' No doubt some of the patients recovered (at least in the short term), but it appears unlikely that the Assyrian physicians could provide any more detailed account of how and why this was the case beyond simply pointing to the efficacy of the regime itself. Similarly, in the very earliest extant medical documents, Egyptian surgeons recorded on papyrus their observations of language-loss, and its interpretation, namely that 'The breath of an outside god or death' had entered the brains of their patients who henceforth became 'silent in sadness' (Breasted, 1930). Once again the belief-system could licence practical intervention. The Egyptian neurosurgeons practiced trepanning (removal of a bone flap from the skull) in order to provide the gods with a larger exit door. In many instances, such operations would give short-term relief, demonstrating thereby that it is indeed possible to do the right deed for the wrong reason. But it was not the belief in gods and devils *per se* that precluded the further development of Egyptian medicine. If these physicians had taken their gods seriously as causitive agents they would presumably have inquired into their mode of operation: How and under what circumstances does the breath of an outside god enter the patient's head? Which particular parts of the brain is the god partial to? How precisely does the god attack brain tissue? The gods were no less real to the Greeks than they were to the Egyptians; but for Hippocrates the gods of disease were (like everything else) constrained to obey natural laws that it was the physicians' duty to discover. Once this insight into the unlimited scope of natural law had been obtained there would be no further use for purely *metaphysical* speculation on the relationship of body (including brain) to mind. As von Bonin (1950) remarks in his history of the study of the cortex:

We do not, of course, expect a solution of the problem of body and mind. There is no such problem, as has often been shown. But the formal laws of cortical events should be translatable into the formal laws of psychological events.

Much 20th-century philosophical discussion of these issues has been vitiated by the strange assumption that the character of both mind and brain is known, and that therefore the sole issue lies in the nature of the relationship between the two domains. Nothing could be further from the truth. Our preferred forms of interpretation constantly change in psychological, physiological and anatomical theory; as they change, so must the nature of the bridge laws that link the domains. Thus traditional accounts of the 'mind-body problem' only make sense as theory-schemata that carry a commitment (implicit or explicit) to a particular research program. This point has been argued most cogently by Edel (1960) who summarizes the position as follows:

. . . our theory-catagories had a rich content in their origins, though it was a fusion of scientific, metaphysical, and, at many points, valuational material. In sorting out the problems in modern times we have made them bloodless categories. If we want to infuse new life into them, we should consider the possibility that they have a broad material content which involves some configuration of scientific knowledge cutting across many areas – in short, they are concepts geared to the theoretical expression of material truths.

I shall attempt to follow these suggestions when setting out some models of the mind that have guided the interpretation of cognitive functioning over the centuries.

2 Viaducts and ventricles

The earliest formal models of mental life are constrained by two overiding principles. First, that the successive psychological mappings from sensation to cognition (or conversely, from cognition to movement) are to be regarded as a purely linear sequence of operations; second, that the relationship between the function stages isolated in psychological theory are in direct one-to-one correspondence with the anatomical structures that constitute their material substrate. It is convenient to attribute the first hypothesis – the linear succession of progressively more 'abstract' internal representations – to Aristotle (384–322 B.C.). The most general 'fractionation' of the mind that Aristotle and his followers adopted for two-thousand years postulated four primary faculties: The Common Sense; Imagination and Fantasy; Conceptual thought and Reasoning; and Memory:

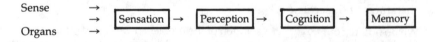

Sense   →
           →   Sensation →   Perception →   Cognition →   Memory
Organs   →

The schema was considerably elaborated over these two millennia – many more meticulous decompositions have been proposed – but the overall picture has continued to dominate Western thought down to the current age. The clearest indication that this is so can be inferred from the fact it is still thought necessary to *attack* the schema. Thus Neisser (1976) has caricatured modern 'information-flow' views of cognition on the grounds that they merely postulate processing, more processing, and still more processing. Wall (1974) spells out the problem:

Behaviour, including mental behaviour, must operate in the context of the body. At a minimum, some medium must exist which allows communication between the periphery of the body and the shape of mental processes. What is the nature of this connecting matrix? Textbooks of physiology and psychology answer the question by a confidence trick. They place chapters on peripheral nerves, sensory mechanisms, perception, and cognition near to each other in sequence, leaving the impression that the chapters are connected by something other than the binding of the book.

For the followers of Aristotle, the 'connecting matrix' was water, or more precisely *pneuma*, a substance found in all living systems and that achieved its most subtle transformation – the animal spirit – when passing through those purportedly hollow tubes that we now refer to as nerves. The physical analogues of the Aristotelian system are accordingly to be found in the viaducts and reservoirs that conducted and stored the other 'vital spirit' so essential to health and civilization (Marshall, 1977).

At this point Aristotle's abstract theory of information-flow can be turned over to the anatomists. One of the more obvious structures within the brain is a set of large fluid-filled cavities. Detectable with relatively crude dissection techniques, these structures – the ventricles – provided the ideal substrate onto which a unilinear theory could be mapped. From the time of Herophilus (*ca* 300 B.C.), throughout the medieval period, and extending into the eighteenth century (Soemmering, 1796), the Aristotelian components of the soul were assigned to the ventricles (or cells, as they were termed by the Early Church Fathers). By the nineteenth century the soul had finally migrated to the cerebral convolutions, a position prefigured in the writings of Erasistratus (335–280 B.C.), and the ventricles had become the mere repository of cerebro-spinal fluid. Yet the overall structure of Greek doctrine persists. 'Sensation' is still regarded as the input to 'perception' which in turn is input to 'cognition'. Disorders of *higher* mental functioning are only diagnosed when impairment at lower levels (sensori-motor deficits) can be ruled out. Similarly, much nineteenth- and early twentieth-century brain anatomy (and physiology) preserves, albeit in a new medium, the direct mapping of psychological levels onto discrete, linearly-ordered material levels. The roles of the linked ventricles are transferred to the succession of cortical tissue – primary receiving areas, association areas, and association areas of association areas. It is difficult to see that any progress could be made in unravelling brain-behaviour relationships without admitting the twin notions of psychological and anatomical decomposition; but it is not so obvious that the particular decompositions and mappings characterized in Alexandrian theory should continue to dominate our thoughts.

3 Logics and libraries

Once decomposition or fractionation had become *the* mode of psychological and anatomical analysis, the way forward for a productive
research program would be to push the idea to its limits. Aristotle
accordingly applied this strategy to the internal structure of memory. The
proud owner of the largest library in private hands, Aristotle realized the
crucial importance of systematic organization if his collection was to
function effectively as an external memory. The library had to be filed and
catalogued. Aristotle took over the terminology of Simonides' place
(*topoi*) theory of memory (Marshall and Fryer, 1978) to refer to general
patterns of argument, subject headings (or topics) under which a variety
of instances fall. The structure of a physical library thus became the model
for a mental library that constituted the internal decomposition of the
faculty of memory. Kant (1798) summarizes the new theory:

Most of all, the use of topics – that is, of a framework for universal concepts, called
general headings (*loci topici*) – makes remembering easier, by dividing the material
into classes, as when we arrange the books in a library on shelves with different
labels.

The virtue of the model lay in directing the attention of clinicians to the
existence and importance of relatively circumscribed deficits that could
plausibly be regarded as 'loss of memory' for examplars under one of the
general headings in the 'psychological library'. So it is that Pliny (A.D.
23–79) can interpret a selective deficit in face recognition in a patient who
fell from a high roof and could no longer recognize his mother, other
relatives, and friends. Similarly, Maximus (*ca* A.D. 30) reported on a case
of isolated traumatic dyslexia in which an Athenian scholar who suffered
a closed head injury lost 'the memory of letters' while apparently retain-
ing intact the rest of his knowledge and skills (Kempf, 1888). The library
metaphor permits both total destruction of a section, and local peturba-
tion within a section. Thomson (1907) illustrates this latter interpretation:

. . . after some brain shock, a person may be able to speak, but the wrong word
often vexatiously comes to his lips, just as if his Broca shelves had been jumbled.

And once more, when the posterior cell of the ventricular system had
long ceased to be the locus of the library, the notion of direct mapping to
an alternative anatomy persisted. Carus (1903) writes:

If we could take out of . . . a brain the living substance without destroying the
membranes in which the cells have enveloped themselves, it would afford an
aspect of divisions and subdivisions not unlike that of the departments, shelves,
and pigeon holes of a library from which the books are removed, and we would
have an anatomical representation of a system of formal thought.

Stated so forthrightly, Carus' hypothesis does seem somewhat extreme,
although his general strategy of following a metaphor through to its

conclusion is invaluable. In particular, it enables Carus to draw a very firm distinction between the library *qua* books (= knowledge), and the library *qua* index system or catalogue. Carus is supremely explicit. He introduces the idea quite baldly: 'Let us suppose that the chief librarian of the library of our brains for the sake of arranging a catalogue takes an inventory of all the books. . .'. And the catalogue, he suggests, is then held in a separate area, the reference room, where it constitutes a 'meta-memory'.

This reference room in our brain is called logical ability . . . and its establishment marks another important step in the development of reason; it is formal thought. It is the beginning of scientific thought by the help of which we gain information about the methodical arrangement of our conceptions.

Few more recent accounts of cognitive functioning have subdivided the faculty of memory with quite the anatomical precision that Carus required, although grandmother cells and Volkswagen detectors are easy to find in the current technical literature, although more difficult to find in the brain. And most scholars retain a number of broader divisions derived in part from the consequences of local damage. Few would deny that deficits of verbal memory are correlated with left hemisphere (and perhaps more specifically left temporal) damage while maximal impairment to non-verbal memory is typically seen after right hemisphere injury (Milner, 1958). And the much more extreme 'mosaic' maps of cortical function produced by Kleist (1934) and Nielsen (1946) have never quite disappeared from contemporary neuropsychology. Despite such excesses, fractionation of memory has played an important role in showing just how circumscribed the deficits consequent upon brain damage can be. The major deleterious effect of the 'memory theory' was that it concentrated attention on 'loss of knowledge' thereby deflecting interest away from the *processes* that underly the ability to, say, recognise faces, engage in skilled action, or comprehend speech. In a sense, the memory-theory attempted to reduce the aphasias, agnosias, and apraxias to material or task-specific amnesias. In the second half of the twentieth century the argument re-emerges in the form of controversy over whether the aphasias, for example, should be regarded as impairments of competence or of performance (Weigl and Bierwisch, 1970).

4 Atoms and associations

By the eighteenth century it had become clear that fractionation, both psychological and anatomical, could be carried a good deal further than even the most enthusiastic medieval proponents of the memory-theory had suggested. One could, as it were, go down a level to the 'ultimate constituents' of the mind and brain. A picture of the peripheral and central nervous system was beginning to arise in which the crucial primitive *functional* elements were nerve cells, their axonal and dendritic arborization, and their synaptic interconnections. Interest in the physiology of nerves dominated nineteenth- (and late eighteenth-) century experimentation, although, as Young (1970) notes, the fundamental notion of a functional division of nerves into those subserving sensation and motion goes back to Vesalius, Galen, and Hippocrates. The novelty of the emerging synthesis lay in the grafting of an associationist psychology onto a sensori-motor physiology. Atomic sensations and movements could be linked to afferent and efferent nerve tracts, and 'ideation' was interpreted as a more central representation constructed by the laws of association out of the same kind of psychological, physiological and anatomical elements. The nerves transmitted information by 'vibrating', thus joining one sensation with another. Hartley (1749) provides a particularly clear account of the enterprise:

The doctrine of *vibrations* may appear at first sight to have no connection with that of *association*; however, if these doctrines be found in fact to contain the laws of the bodily and mental powers respectively, they must be related to each other, since the body and mind are. One may expect that vibrations should infer association as their effect, and association points to vibrations as its cause.

The upshot was an attempt to destroy the ghost within the machine of the brain. The sensory keyboard was a physical part of the brain, as was the motor keyboard. They were henceforth to be linked together by principles no less 'mechanistic', albeit perhaps more complex, than those that determined nervous transmission from the senses and to the muscles. In a famous footnote, Jackson (1870) summarizes the new paradigm:

It is asserted by some that the cerebrum is the organ of mind, and that it is not a *motor* organ. Some think that the cerebrum is to be linked to an instrumentalist, and the motor centres to the instrument; One part is for ideas, and the other for movements. It may then be asked, How can discharge of part of a *mental* organ produce *motor* symptoms only? (. . .) But of what 'substance' can the organ of mind be composed, unless of processes representing movements and impressions; and how can the convolutions differ from the inferior centres, except as parts representing *more* intricate co-ordinations of impression and movements in time and space than they do? (. . .) What can an 'idea', say of a ball be, except a process representing certain impressions of surface and particular muscular adjustments? (. . .) Surely the conclusion is irresistible, that 'mental' symptoms from disease of the hemisphere are fundamentally like hemiplegia, chorea, and convulsions, however specially different. They must all be due to lack, or to disorderly development, of sensori-motor processes.

In short, for Jackson the 'higher' centres of the brain are built on a plan that is not 'fundamentally different' from that of 'lower centres and of the peripheral nervous system'. Associationist neuropsychology enabled scholars to downplay somewhat the notion of the 'contents' of memory and emphasize rather the nature of retrieval processes. For example, when Crichton (1798) discusses the specific word-finding difficulties in 'anomic aphasia' that had previously been interpreted as 'loss of memory for words *tout court*', he writes:

. . . this very singular defect of memory ought rather to be regarded as a defect of that principle, by which ideas, and their proper expressions, are associated, than memory.

A further advantage of 'physiological associationalism' was that it eventually enabled clinicians to break away from the doctrine of 'punctate' localization. If a 'complex idea' can be decomposed into sensory and motor primitives linked by 'association tracts' there is little reason to expect the effects of circumscribed lesions to fractionate behaviour into the categories postulated by psychological theory. And indeed when behaviour did break down into psychologically meaningful categories, associationists were rather put out. Thus Gesner (1770) reported that in some of his patients comprehension was impaired 'with respect to only certain classes of ideas'; the deficit was disproportionately severe for particular abstract concepts. But he now has some difficulty in reconciling the phenomena with the theoretical stance that he has taken against punctate localization and an orderly mapping between the elements of anatomy and of ideation:

The vessels of the brain are surely not arranged in accordance with categories of . . . ideas and therefore it is incomprehensible that these categories should correspond to areas of destruction.

The passage marks a watershed in interpretation of the effects of lesions. What has become 'incomprehensible' to Gesner is precisely a result that would have seemed so obvious to an earlier memory theorist who could easily have arranged the internal library into abstract *vs* concrete topics.

Yet the associationists could not fully escape from a theoretically direct mapping between their physiology and their psychology. All that has happened is that the anatomical substrate for cognition has been allowed to scatter itself widely across the brain. Only a *geometrical* constraint has been relaxed. William James (1891) remained sceptical that this sufficed:

If we make a symbolic diagram on the blackboard of the laws of association between ideas, we are inevitably led to draw circles, or closed figures of some kind, and to connect them by lines. When we hear that the nerve centres contain cells which send off fibres, we say that Nature has realised our diagram for us, and that the mechanical substratum of thought is plain. In some way, it is true our diagram must be realised in the brain, but surely in no such visible and palpable way as we at first suppose.

5   Organs and embryos

The interpretation of cognitive disorders as failures of association between the elements of a vast associative net did not hold undisputed sway
over nineteenth-century theory. An alternative framework was provided
by Franz Joseph Gall's revival, albeit in much modified form, of 'faculty'
psychology. Gall (1791, 1810) grouped together into underlying faculties
those talents, skills, propensities and capacities that seemed to give an
intuitively satisfying account of the individual differences that characterize man in society. He then argued that each faculty has a responsible
cortical organ, the activity of which varies according to the organ's size.
Gall's own work was so varied, extensive and original that it is still
somewhat premature to attempt a final accounting. A very preliminary
balance sheet would, however, include the following credits and debits.
Modern neuroanatomy starts with Gall; yet although Gall unravelled
much of the brain's fine structure he never succeeded in linking his purely
anatomical studies with his psychological theory (Marshall, 1980b). Gall
was largely responsible for the rise of the notion that the seat of higher
mental functions is to be found in columns descending from the cortical
convolutions; modern interest in the cytoarchitectonics of cortical regions
thus results from Gall's work, although few, if any, of his functional
localizations have proved correct. Gall emphasized the crucial importance of the *size* of different cortical areas, although his method for
estimating size *in vivo* – measurement of cranial prominences over the
lobes of the brain – does not provide very reliable estimates of underlying
volume. Nonetheless, the notion that size is one assay of functional
efficiency is still with us. Geschwind (1972) writes:

What happens to the child whose brain shows a bilateral right-sided pattern of the
planum temporale? What is that child like as compared to one who has a huge left
planum and a small one on the right side? In other words, there are many different
variations here which may well correspond to differences in talent.

It has also been suggested recently (Galaburda, Sanides and Geschwind,
1978) that the extent and direction of cortical asymmetries may correlate
with individual differences in recovery from brain damage and with the
nature of some childhood learning disorders.

   The most striking difference between Gall and his 'associationist'
contemporaries lay however in Gall's choice of a guiding metaphor for his
life's work. Gall's anatomical studies had included numerous ontogenetic
and phylogenetic comparisons of brain structure. This background in
embryology determined Gall's approach to the mind. For Gall (1810):

. . . the development of the mind of the child, far from being a mere moulding of it
by the impression made upon it by its environment . . . is an unfolding of latent
potentialities.

Thus the primary powers (the Language Faculty, the Number Faculty, the Faculty of Place and Space, the Music Faculty) simply 'grow' in the mind as the embryological maturation of their cerebral organs takes its basically predetermined course. Gall perceived no conflict between the claim that the 'elementary qualities of the mind are innate' and the fact that environmental stimulation was required to 'draw out and cultivate' the faculties. But, by contrast with the associationists' position, he argued that the principle role of the environment was to trigger and direct innate dispositions, not to build or shape the formal character of the mind (Marshall, 1980b). Viewpoints that are not dissimilar to Gall's can be found in current physiology (Purves and Lichtman, 1980) and psychology (Chomsky, 1980).

Gall had few ideas concerning the internal structure (either anatomical or functional) of the faculties he postulated, and this led many critics to attack the faculties on the grounds that they were non-explanatory. The criticism was not entirely fair to Gall, who willingly conceded that the best he could manage was a gross decomposition into psychological and anatomical domains. But it was no part of his doctrine to rule out the possibility that later workers would succeed in elucidating the structure of the principles at work *within* each domain. A more serious objection was that Gall had simply got the functional decomposition wrong. Thus Beneke (1845) writes:

That the brain is the chief and central organ for the support of our physical activities no one will deny, nor need it be disputed that therefore something depends on the size of it . . . As to the phrenologists, they really ought to see into what palpable contradictions they fall with the strange mental powers which they invent, such as 'philoprogenitiveness', 'love of unity', 'combativeness', 'secretiveness', 'acquisitiveness', 'love of praise', etc. Our physical forms may, without being changed, form part of groups and series of the most diverse kinds; and by so doing they become interwoven and crossed one with another, so as to form a kind of variegated web. From this it unquestionably follows that one and the same form may take part in philoprogenitiveness, in combativeness, acquisitiveness, etc.; for everything is capable of becoming a constituent part of that with which it fits, and by which it is required.

Beneke's point is well taken. Postulation of a discrete faculty is justified only to the extent that the principles operating within that faculty are distinct from those of some other hypothesized domain.

6   Diagrams then and now

Gall's success rate in localizing the cortical substrate of his faculties was not high. He did, however, locate the organ of verbal memory in the frontal lobes after noticing at school that classmates with large, protruding eyes were particularly adept at verbal learning. And Gall, and many later phrenologists, confirmed the speculation by noting disorders of expression after injury to the (left) frontal lobe. It was this localization that encouraged Paul Broca (1861) to demonstrate at autopsy that one of his patients with severe expressive aphasia had a lesion apparently centered on the posterior part of the third frontal convolution of the left hemisphere. Thus did 'Broca's area' become the seat of the faculty of articulate speech. Against a background of associationism and organology, Broca's success enabled other scholars to attempt an extensive *psychological study of language on an anatomical basis*, as the subtitle of Carl Wernicke's 1874 monograph reads. Despite his protestations to the contrary, Wernicke (1874, 1906) tried to form a unified framework from Gall's concept of computational centres and Hartley's notion of complex connections between sensation and motor response. The idea was to decompose language abilities into functional subsystems whose internal structure and pattern of interconnection could be anatomically interpreted. Wernicke (1874) writes:

There is a significant difference between the invention of various theoretic centres (co-ordination centre, concept centre) – with complete neglect of their anatomic substrates . . . and an attempt, based on an exhaustive study of brain anatomy and the commonly-recognized laws of experimental psychology, to translate such anatomic findings into psychological data, seeking in this way to formulate a theory by use of the same kind of material.

The anatomy to which Wernicke refers is that of Meynert (1867) in which a distinction is drawn between 'projection tracts', 'association tracts' and cells with short processes. In the Meynert-Wernicke system, clusters of cells interconnected by short fibres are regarded as computational or storage centres, the centres being linked (associated) by long association tracts that are the cortico-cortical analogues of the efferent and afferent projection tracts that connect the brain with its body. And the psychology in question is associationism translated directly into cellular terms.

In the cortex there are ganglion cells invested with the feature of permanent modification of transient stimuli, of which persisting residuals remain, which we describe as memory images . . . The stability of all associations of such memory imagery is maintained by repetition of the same or similar stimuli. The simultaneous and contiguous occurence of a number of sensory impressions results in the permanent association of such memory associations.   (Wernicke, 1900)

Broca's area accordingly becomes a higher-order motor area in which the articulatory images of words are represented; Wernicke's area (part of the temporal lobe, damage to which results in severe disorder of speech comprehension) becomes a higher-order sensory area containing the auditory images of words. The two centres are linked by the arcuate fasciculus that serves to associate auditory with articulatory images. It was crucial, then, for Wernicke himself that diagrams of the fractionation of the language faculty should be drawn on the surface of the brain; a reflection once more of the direct correspondence that was demanded between the terms of the psychological and anatomical aspects of the theory. But one of the diagram-makers, Ludwig Lichtheim, seems to have realized that the bond could be broken. In his 1885 paper he agrees with Wernicke that ultimately 'Our task is to determine the connections and localization of the paths of innervation subservient to language and its correlated functions'; however, he takes the important step forward of removing diagrams from the brain's surface and presenting them as abstract psychological theories. The effect is to make it clear that an inadequate functional analysis cannot be strengthened by mapping it onto some simple anatomy. In part, of course, nineteenth-century diagram-making was motivated by the concern to provide a taxonomy of the aphasias, agnosias, and apraxias that would have practical localizing significance; that is, the constellation of symptoms displayed by the patient should enable the physician to predict the site of the responsible lesion. Critiques of the diagram-makers' efforts, while supporting the medical value of symptom-localization, noted that the direct mapping hypothesis frequently led to a confusion of symptoms with functions (Jackson, 1874; Freud, 1891). If theory is to make progress, we should at very least insist that the functions postulated in psychological models fit together formally as part of a computational system that can demonstrably perform what is claimed of it (Fryer and Marshall, 1979; Arbib and Caplan, 1979). It is not clear that this constraint is met by either nineteenth-century diagram-making or its modern descendents (Coltheart, Patterson and Marshall, 1980). There is furthermore no guarantee that the signs and symptoms that cluster together subsequent to focal brain damage will be diagnostic of unified mechanisms. To force them together by insisting upon punctate localization of functions in centres and tracts is likely to lead to both bad psychology and bad anatomy, and to the invention of purely imaginary physiologies of 'anatomies in motion'.

If we are eventually to reach beyond the diagram-makers' achievements, we shall have to answer Kurt Goldstein's rewording of the traditional question posed in neuropsychology:

The question of the relationship between the symptom complex and a definitely localized lesion again became a problem, no longer, however, in the form: where is a definite function or symptom localized? but: *how does a definite lesion modify the function of the brain so that a definite symptom comes to the fore?*　(Goldstein, 1948)

7 Where next?

The most striking characteristic of all the models we have considered is that they postulate only two defined levels of representation – a psychology and an 'interpreted' anatomy. The 'grain' of the psychology may be more or less fine, ranging between global functions (the faculty of melody, for example, in Gall's theory) and relatively atomic elements (letters of the alphabet, in the case of Maximus). In a similar fashion, the grain of the relevant anatomy has ranged between grossly delineated areas (the temporal lobe) and atomic elements (a specific cell in striate cortex, for example). The 'two-level' assumption naturally lends itself to accounts in which a one-to-one mapping is postulated between the levels. On occasion, some scholars have relaxed this constraint at the anatomical end, thereby allowing a one-to-many mapping in which there are multiple neuronal representations of the same psychological function or item of stored knowledge (Piercy, 1964). Conversely, other scholars have relaxed the constraint at the psychological end, proposing a many-to-one mapping in which multiple psychological functions are sub-served by the same neuronal hardware, consequent upon the overall 'position' of the function within some wider system. This latter hypothesis is prefigured in Beneke's critique of Gall; it then emerges in a particularly clear form in Jackson's (1870) speculation that each and every part of the corpus striatum contains representations of the movement potentialities for each body part, albeit 'in different degrees' and 'grouped in different order'. More recently, the notion has been restated by Lashley (1950):

. . . all of the cells of the brain are constantly active and are participating, by a sort of algebraic summation, in every activity.

In an important simulation study, Wood (1978, 1980) has shown that systems of the type envisaged by Lashley can respond to damage by appearing to show classical, punctate localization of function. Specifically:
.

. . . a neuronal model whose function (in this case association) is distributed across all its neural elements can, under certain conditions, produce lesion effects that would generally be interpreted as evidence for the participation of specific elements in specific associations. (Wood, 1980)

The absolutely homogenous 'neural' substrate found in Wood's simulation is not compatible with current views on the structure of the central nervous system, although the idea of *multiple* maps that differ in representational style has recently gained ground (Kaas, Nelson, Sur, Lin and Merzenich, 1979; Diamond, 1979) in neurophysiological investigations. In a peculiarly resonant phrase, Bogen (1976) refers to this 'new' concept of neuronal instantiation as 'Jackson's heterogeneous hologram'. Bogen interprets the notion as:

. . . a generalization of which the optical hologram and a system of compartmentalized 'centers' are boundary (that is, oppositely extreme) cases. Because it is more general, it can be expected to accommodate a much greater variety of facts. What it cannot do is to tell us what it is that is represented in the heterogram.

The last line of the quotation is crucial: The problem is that it is extra-ordinarily difficult to see how one could individuate a psychology of higher mental functions within such a physiology (Marshall, 1980a). Relevant generalizations simply seem to disappear when the mapping between psychology and anatomy is many-to-many. In short, 'Modern neurophysiology has learned much about the operations of the individual nerve cell, but disconcertingly little about the meaning of the circuits that they compose in the brain' (Marr, 1980).

The first step toward remedying this state of affairs is to disavow explicitly a theoretical style in which there are only *two* defined levels of representation – psychology and anatomy/physiology. The most incisive exponent of the new philosophy has been David Marr:

The core of the problem is that a system as complex as a nervous system or a developing embryo must be analysed and understood at several different levels. [. . .] At the lowest level, there is basic component and circuit analysis: how do transitors (or neurons) or diodes (or synapses) work? The second level is the study of particular mechanisms: adders, multipliers and memories, these being assemblies made from basic components. The third level is that of the algorithm, the schema for a computation; and the top level contains the *theory* of the computation.   (Marr, 1980)

Marr illustrates the four levels by considering the 'function' of addition. Here the theory of the computation is a 'competence' account of the meaning and formal structure of addition that is independent of the particular representation of the numbers involved, arabic or roman, say. At level three we have an algorithm, that is, a specific procedure by which numbers may be added. On this level the exact representation of the numbers is important; an algorithm that works on arabic numerals will certainly not work on roman. At level two, we find the particular arrange-ment of mechanisms that implement the algorithm in a particular calcu-lating device. And at the bottom level we have a characterization of the physical elements, with their mechanical, electrical and chemical properties, out of which the basic mechanisms are built.

By insisting upon four-level theories, Marr's group (Marr and Nishihara, 1978; Ullman, 1979) have deepened very considerably our understanding of visual information processing. One may have, I believe, reasonable confidence that other aspects of higher mental func-tioning will yield to the same strategy. In particular, the language faculty is a promising candidate for analysis (Marshall, 1980a). At the top level – the theory of the computation – we are already beginning to see deductive theories with a relatively small number of principles and parameters that define the form of species – and task-specific representations (Chomsky, 1981). At level three, interesting algorithms are becoming available for the on-line assignment of appropriate structural descriptions in both perception (Marcus, 1980) and production (McDonald, 1980). At level two, rigorous adoption of the traditional fractionation approach to the aphasias can reveal the existence of independent mechanisms, provided that we do not confuse these mechanisms with either the more complex functions in which they participate, or with the elements of which they are composed (Wood, 1980). Finally, at the lowest level of basic component and circuit analysis, the architectonic analysis of cortical tissue does, at very least, show that the classical 'language areas' are structurally distinct from their surrounding regions (Braak, 1980; Galaburda and Sanides, 1980). In principle, then, there is a specialized anatomy for language functions to 'inhabit'.

It is true, of course, that no current analysis of language even approaches the full four-tiered account that is required. Nonetheless, we are, I believe, much clearer about the nature of the game that we should be playing than was the case even a decade ago. If the temptation to conflate the top three levels is resisted, it may be possible to construct a theoretical neuropsychology.

In his critique of neuropsychology, Kant (1766) argued that:

My soul as a whole is everywhere in my body and in its entirety in each of its parts.

Yet while denying any 'local seat' of the soul, the evidence forced him to admit that the soul did indeed have a 'virtual seat'. That is, its presence could be made felt 'through activity displayed at a region where in fact the soul does not reside' (Riese, 1959). The spurious conflict between holism and localizationism may yet be dissolved by adoption of multilevel theories. One may find cells and circuits in the brain; one may even seek there the mechanisms formed from cells and circuits. But we are unlikely to achieve much by looking for a direct physiological instantiation of either a theory of a computation or an algorithm. There is a sense in which the behaviour of a system is more than the sum of its parts, although nothing has been 'added' to the parts. Theories of a computation and algorithms for implementing them describe that 'something more'.

References

Arbib, M. and Caplan, D. (1979). Neurolinguistics must be computational. *The Behavioural and Brain Sciences* **2**, 449–483
Beneke, F. E. (1845). *Lehrbuch der Psychologie als Naturwissenschaft*. Berlin: Dummler
Bogen, J. (1976). Hughlings Jackson's heterogram. *In* D. O. Walter, L. Rogers and J. M. Finzi-Friied (eds), *BIS Conference Report 42*. Los Angeles: University of California
Bonin, G. von (1950). *Essay on the Cerebral Cortex*. Springfield, Illinois: C. C. Thomas
Braak, H. (1980). *Architectonics of the Human Telencephalic Cortex*. Berlin: Springer
Breasted, J. H. (1930). *The Edwin Smith Surgical Papyrus*. Chicago: University of Chicago Press

Broca, P. (1861). Remarques sur le siège de la faculté du langage articulé, suivies d'une observation d'aphemie, *Bulletin de la Société Antomique* **36**, 330—357

Buchner, L. (1855). *Kraft und Stoff*. Leipzig: Voss

Carus, P. (1903). *Fundamental Problems*. Chicago: Open Court

Chomsky, N. (1980). *Rules and Representations*. New York: Columbia University Press

Chomsky, N. (1981). Principles and parameters in syntactic theory. *In* N. Hornstein and D. Lightfoot (eds), *Explanation in Linguistics*. London: Longmans

Coltheart, M., Patterson, K. and Marshall, J. C. (eds) (1980). *Deep Dyslexia*. London: Routledge and Kegan Paul

Crighton, A. (1798). *An Inquiry into the Nature and Origin of Mental Derangement*. London: Cadel and Davies

Diamond, I. T. (1979). The subdivisions of the neocortex: A proposal to revise the traditional view of sensory, motor and association areas. *Progress in Psychobiology and Physiological Psychology* **8**, 1–43

Edel, A. (1960). Theory categories in the mind—body problem. *In* S. Hook, (ed.), *Dimension of Mind*. New York: New York University Press

Ferrier, D. (1878). *The Localisation of Cerebral Disease*. London: Smith, Elder and Co.

Fodor, J. A. (1975). *The Language of Thought*. New York: Thomas Y. Crowell

Freud, S. (1891). *Zur Auffassung der Aphasien*. Vienna: Deuticke

Fryer, D. and Marshall, J. C. (1979). The motives of Jacques de Vaucanson. *Technology and Culture* **20**, 257–269

Galaburda, A. M. and Sanides, F. (1980). Cytoarchitectonic organization of the human auditory cortex. *Journal of Comparative Neurology* **190**, 597–610

Galaburda, A. M., Sanides, F. and Geschwind, N. (1978). Human brain: Cytoarchitectonic left-right asymmetries in the temporal speech region. *Archives of Neurology* **35**, 812–817

Gall, F.-J. (1791). *Philosophisch-medicinische Untersuchungen*. Vienna: Gräffer

Gall, F.-J. (1810). *Anatomie et Physiologie du System Nerveux*. Paris: Schoell

Geschwind, N. (1972). Disorders of higher cortical function in children. *Clinical Proceedings, Children's Hospital National Medical Center* **28**, 261–272

Gesner, J. A. P. (1770). *Die Sprachamnesie*. Nordlingen: Beck

Goldstein, K. (1948). *Language and Language Disturbances*. New York: Grune and Stratton

Hartley, D. (1749). *Observations on Man*. London: Hall

Jackson, J. H. (1870). A study of convulsions. *Transactions of the St. Andrews Medical Graduates Association* **3**, 162–191

Jackson, J. H. (1874). On the nature and duality of the brain. *Medical Press and Circular* **1**, 19–41

James, W. (1891). *The Principles of Psychology*. London: Macmillan

Kaas, J. H., Nelson, R. J., Sur, M., Lin, C.-S. and Merzenich, M. M. (1979). Multiple representations of the body within the primary somatosensory cortex of primates. *Science* **204**, 521–523

Kant, I. (1766). *Die Träume eines Geistersehers*. Leipzig: Hirzel

Kant, I. (1789). *Anthropologie in pragmatischer Hinsicht*. Köningsberg: Nicolovius

Kempf, K. (1888). *Valerii maximi factorum et dictorum memorabilium*. Leipzig: Teubner

Kleist, K. (1934). *Gehirnpathologie*. Leipzig: Barth

Lashley, K. S. (1950). In search of the engram. *Symposia of the Society for Experimental Biology* **4**, 454–482

Lichtheim, L. (1885). On aphasia. *Brain* **7**, 433–484

Marcus, M. (1980). *A Theory of Syntactic Recognition for Natural Languages*. Cambridge, Mass: MIT Press

Marr, D. (1980). Visual information processing: The structure and creation of visual representations. *Philosophical Transactions of the Royal Society of London*, Series B **290**, 199–218

Marr, D. and Nishihara, H. K. (1978). Representation and recognition of the spatial organization of three-dimensional shapes. *Proceedings of the Royal Society of London*, Series B **200**, 269–294

Marshall, J. C. (1977). Minds, machines and metaphors. *Social Studies of Science* **7**, 474–488
Marshall, J. C. (1980a). On the biology of language acquisition. *In* D. Caplan (ed.), *Biological Studies of Mental Processes*. Cambridge, Mass.: MIT Press
Marshall, J. C. (1980b). The new organology. *The Behavioral and Brain Sciences* **3**, 23–25
Marshall, J. C. and Fryer, D. (1978). Speak, Memory! An introduction to some historic studies of remembering and forgetting. *In* M. Gruneberg and P. Morris (eds), *Aspects of Memory*. London: Methuen
McDonald, D. (1980). *Natural Language Production as a Process of Decision Making under Constraint*. Unpublished Ph.D. thesis, MIT, Cambridge, Mass.
Meynert, T. (1867). Der Bau der Grosshirnrinde und seine örtlichen Verschiedenheiten. *Vierteljahrschrift für Psychiatrie* **1**, 77–93
Milner, B. (1958). Psychological defects produced by temporal-lobe excision. *Research Publications, Association for Research in Nervous and Mental Disease* **36**, 244–257
Neisser, U. (1976). *Cognition and Reality*. San Francisco: W. H. Freeman
Nielsen, J. M. (1946). *Agnosia, Apraxia, Aphasia*. New York: Hafner
Paulsen, F. (1892). *Introduction to Philosophy*. New York: Holt
Piercy, M. (1964). The effects of cerebral lesions on intellectual functions: a review of current research trends. *British Journal of Psychiatry* **110**, 310–352
Popper, K. and Eccles, J. (1977). *The Self and Its Brain*. Heidelberg: Springer
Purves, D. and Lichtman, J. W. (1980). Elimination of synapses in the developing nervous system. *Science* **210**, 153–157
Riese, W. (1959). *A History of Neurology*. New York: MD Publications
Soemmerring, S. T. (1796). *Über das Organ der Seele*. Königsberg: Nicolovius
Thompson, R. C. (1908). Assyrian prescriptions for diseases of the head. *American Journal of Semitic Languages* **24**, 323–353
Thomson, W. H. (1907). *Brain and Personality*. New York: Dodd, Mead & Co.
Ullman, S. (1979). *The Interpretation of Visual Motion*. Cambridge, Mass.: MIT Press
Wall, P. D. (1974). My foot hurts me: An analysis of a sentence. *In* R. Bellairs and E. G. Gray (eds), *Essays on the Nervous System*. Oxford: Clarendon Press
Weigl, E. and Bierwisch, M. (1970). Neuropsychology and Linguistics: Topics of common concern. *Foundations of Language* **6**, 1–18
Wernicke, C. (1874). *Der aphasische Symptomenkomplex*. Breslau: Cohn and Weigart
Wernicke, C. (1900). *Grunzüge der Psychiatrie*. Leipzig: Thieme
Wernicke, C. (1906). Der Aphasie Symptomenkomplex. *Deutsche Klinik* **6**, 487–556
Wood, C. C. (1978). Variations on a theme of Lashley: Lesion experiments on the neural model of Anderson, Silverstein, Ritz and Jones. *Psychological Review* **85**, 582–591
Wood, C. C. (1980). Interpretation of real and simulated lesion experiments. *Psychological Review* **87**, 474–476
Young, R. M. (1970). *Mind, Brain and Adaption in the Nineteenth Century*. Oxford: Clarendon Press

2

Production of Speech: Observations from Normal and Pathological Language Use

MERRILL F. GARRETT
Department of Psychology, Massachusetts Institute of Technology, USA

1 Introduction

A SETTING THE PROBLEM

If one construes the problem of language production solely as one of explaining how we decide *what* to say, then this chapter is not about language production. It is, rather, about how we recruit our knowledge of language structure in order to build sentences, given some rather specific representation of message content. Thus, many significant issues are untouched – those dealing with articulatory control at one extreme and those which determine message formulation at the other. My assumption is that this decomposition of the production process is warranted – i.e. that the mental processes of lexical selection and phrasal construction are not so dependent upon either articulatory function or semantic and pragmatic intention as to render the attempt at description of specifically syntactic and phonological processes pointless. This general view requires brief comment before we proceed to more particular matters.

When we talk or listen, we do something very specific in terms of behavior – i.e. we engage an intricately organized, internally coherent motor and perceptual system; but, we do it in aid of something very general in terms of cognition – i.e. the encyclopedic knowledge which gives rise to our communicative intentions. Query: how far beyond the motor and sensory systems that instantiate their surface form does the independent organization of language processes extend? That the articulatory portion of the production system has a language base, we know in diverse ways, ranging from the existence of apraxic disorders of speech to the existence of language specific phonological constraints whose violation we perceive as 'accented' or 'foreign' speech. In each case, there are just certain sounds or sequences that, either through accident of birth and training or through insult to the central nervous

19

system, one cannot produce, even though one's motor system is demonstrably capable of executing the appropriate articulatory movements. The system for controlling speech relevant movement uses, but is distinct from, the more general system for motor control of articulatory structures.

One may raise the same question *vis-à-vis* the more abstract functions of our language capacity – as, those involving the morphological, phonological, syntactic and logical aspects of sentence organization. Are these features of sentence structure, some or all, the consequence of a processing system distinct from our more general cognitive apparatus? There is more than a little reason to answer, 'yes', not the least of which is the empirical success of formal linguistic and logical analyses of language. There, after all, does exist an enormous range of psychological phenomena (e.g. the distributional facts of grammatical utterance; the determinants of valid inference) which may be captured solely by appeal to the form of sentences.

Against this, we must array the detail of evidence that utterance structure is penetrated by our general knowledge of the world. Although, for example, the syntax of sentences is accountable in terms of systems of rules which do not consider the attitudes, emotional states, social status, or beliefs of language users, each of these factors and more can be shown to affect the uttered form of sentences – their prosody, their lexical content, their syntax (for some illustration, see Cutler and Isard, 1980; Gazdar, 1980). The theory of the human mental processes which determine language use in real time must provide for this, while permitting a rational reconstruction of the formal linguistic and formal logical systems immanent in sentence form.

The most promising approach to this accommodation lies in models which represent language processing as the product of a set of independent processing systems, each of which has determinate internal structure; it is the principled interaction of these component systems which permits the generation of a single complex object – the uttered form of a sentence – bearing their joint influences (for one recent discussion of such systems see Arbib and Caplan, 1980). The problem of language production from this perspective is to determine the component systems and the constraints on their interaction. The best current hypothesis for such components is that they correspond to the set of rule systems required by the formal analysis of language: the components of a full grammatical theory.[1]

There are two caveats to be entered at this point. First, this is a hypothesis; there is no guarantee that whatever the human intellect can factor out of a complex process must, therefore, *be* an independent factor in that process.[2] The hypothesis is, nevertheless, powerfully indicated because the data to which it is responsive are *prima facie* determinants of the pronunciation and interpretation of sentences. For the hypothesis to fail would require that the real time exigencies of sentence analysis dictate significantly different informational interactions than do the reflective judgements of formal analysis.

The second caveat is simply a reminder that grammatical theory is not monolithic. It is, in its current incarnation, a relatively young science and there is not consensus to be had on hosts of structural issues. However, that is for present purposes not a pressing problem – the broad scale decomposition of the language faculty into phonological, morphological, syntactic, and semantic domains is not at issue, even though the boundaries and internal structure of those domains may be. Indeed, given initial support for the working hypothesis of a correspondence between processing types and rule types, the evolution of processing theories and grammatical theories may be more productively linked: the detailed organization of grammatical rule systems is a source of hypotheses about processing interaction, and conversely, evidence for or against processing interactions of a given type may provide an evaluation metric for grammatical analyses.

Consideration of the data bearing on language production processes suggests, to me, a provisional acceptance of the hypothesis that the computational decomposition of language processing does, indeed, reflect the grammatical decomposition of the language faculty. In succeeding sections, I will discuss some evidence from studies of normal and disordered language which indicates such a conclusion and which also suggests specific hypotheses about mental processes of lexical selection and phrasal construction.

B SOME GENERAL OBSERVATIONS ABOUT LANGUAGE PRODUCTION

There are a number of relatively non-controversial observations which one may invoke of human language production. They are useful because they suggest an outline of the process which more detailed examination reinforces and elaborates.

1 The successful attainment of the linguistic 'ideal' is relatively routine: speech is more often grammatical than not, and we may take it that the target of utterance is, in fact, grammatical speech.[3] Whether one considers mothers talking to their children (see, e.g. Newport, Gleitman and Gleitman, 1977), schizophrenic monologue (Rochester and Martin, 1979) or cocktail party chatter, the ubiquity of well-formed sentence structure is assured. Exceptions to that generalization are of two sorts – real and apparent. For the latter, I have in mind the frequently occurring fragmentary bits of sentences in conversational exchange, as: 'Well?', 'What for?', 'In a minute', etc. Such are not really an exception, of course, for they are well formed vis-à-vis the linguistic context of the discourse in which they occur. Sentence level structure is needed to explain why certain fragments consistently occur while innumerable others do not – a 'fragment grammar' requires sentence grammar, not the reverse.

The second exception – people *do* sometimes speak ungrammatically – requires a different sort of account, one that focusses not on the linguistic competence of speakers, but rather on the computational systems which instantiate it.

2 The computational systems for language production are not fool-proof. They fail in a variety of ways that are informative. In particular, there is a fairly frequent global failure to capture the precise intent of a speaker, and as a presumptive consequence, a change of plans for expression, often in mid-utterance, leaving behind the sometimes ungrammatical debris of the abortive attempt. If we label the speakers communicative intent his *message*, we may express this as a failed correspondence between message and sentence structure. If we accept this characterization of the circumstances, we may put the implication succinctly: the relation between message level representation and sentence level representation is not transparent.

Of course, one might claim that the phenomena in question are not veridical, and that one really has nothing particular in mind when one fails (or feels or asserts that one has failed) to attain ones putative communicative target. It is, however, hard to gainsay the common feeling of 'knowing something' while still struggling to express it. Not *too* much should rest upon this sensation – subjective conviction is far from infallible – but perhaps the minimal implication is not too much: there is a computationally significant distinction between what we have labelled the message level and sentence level representations.

There is another sort of failure of the sentence construction system, much rarer than the one we have just been discussing. These, which we will shortly make much of in spite of their relative rarity, may be described as a failure to execute the sentence level language expression correctly (where correct expression would satisfactorily match message level constraints). Here I have in mind the numerous types of speech errors (e.g. 'Spoonerisms') which involve word and sound substitutions or misplacements during normal spontaneous speech. So, for example, one may hear, '. . . but his fit shirts him' (for the intended '. . . shirt fits him'), or 'he uses "aye" as a fause pillar' (for '. . . pause filler') or 'he's got . . . another clutch firtch-down!' (for, '. . . clutch first-down'), or 'I don't know who sent him the damn menu', (for '. . . damn memo'). To say that such errors are 'rare', of course, is only to note their infrequency with respect to base rate of correct execution (by very rough estimate, a ratio of one in a thousand words).[4]

Such errors are, by current hypothesis, not message level errors at all, but are specific to sentence level constructive processes. As such, their generality across types (virtually all simple elements of sentence analysis appear in errors) and the detail of their contingencies (errors of different types are sharply constrained contextually) make them a particularly useful data base for inferences about real time sentence processes.

There are, of course, other failures of sentence composition than the two classes I have just mentioned. Occasionally we do talk ourselves into a syntactic corner,[5] and occasionally, in long rambling sentences with many a caveat and codicil, tense markers, or even whole copular verbs may fall between the NP cracks and never surface in utterance. These and similar cases are, at least in part, likely symptoms of the last general point I wish to raise, namely, that of time constraints on production processes.

3 The production system is time dependent in a variety of ways. Broadly cast, these are constraints imposed by the relation between rate of output speech and rate of planning processes. For example, at the slow end of the spectrum, we note that output rate must *exceed* the rate of decay for the representation of constraints imposed by the earlier uttered material; we would otherwise lose the thread of what we are saying, or speak ungrammatically. More stringent, for the fast end of the spectrum, the rate of accurate, fluent output can *not* exceed the rate at which decisions can be made about the effects of past and future commitments on the immediate utterance target position. The structure of what we have said and what we are planning to say must be rapidly brought to bear on what we are currently saying, or else we will be forced to pause, or perhaps find ourselves trying to say the syntactically unsayable.

So much is obvious, and the consequence – nonfluent speech – is constantly on display; that mundane fact is most important, however, for its implication is that we are, quite routinely, producing overt expressions at points when the construction of subsequent, partially dependent material is not yet fully determined. *A priori*, a break in the fluency of utterance may be regarded as an indication that the rate of speech output has overrun the rate of decision making either about what we will say or how we will say it. The study of such nonfluency – hesitation phenomena – thus, potentially, speaks to aspects of the language production process germane to the current discussion, as well as those (i.e. message level construction) we have set aside. We will later take up in more detail the question of sources for hesitations in spontaneous speech. Such data have, with good reason, long interested investigators of language production processes, for it is plausible, though of course not necessary, that the distribution of hesitation types would reveal basic organizational features of the production system.

4 In brief summary, the ubiquitous phenomena of spontaneous speech are these: grammaticality of the target constructions, coupled with imprecision of expression, changes of mind, nonfluency, and outright error. It is the fact that the target of utterance is well formed that permits the interpretation of these latter phenomena for their bearing on the real time constructive processes underlying language production. The analysis of such features of spontaneous speech provides a departure point for the formulation of production models.

To these 'naturally displayed' sources of evidence, we may add two others: patterns of language disorder, usually those associated with focal brain injury, and the results of direct experimental intervention in the production process. Brief comment on each of these is offered to indicate their role in the discussion to follow.

For investigators of language processes, particularly those interested in the relation between brain structure and behavioral function, language disorders have provided a rich source of data. Perhaps too rich, for a recurrent theme of criticism has been the heterogeneity of symptoms among individual patients and the consequent scope for an unfettered theoretical impulse. Much of the controversy, however, has centered around the attempt to relate particular injury sites to specific symptom complexes. When one abstracts from this issue, the situation is materially improved (though by no means rendered pellucid). There is a consensus that certain symptom complexes are commonly observed even if the neural antecedents of such are not so uniform as might be hoped. I will rely upon reports which reflect such consensus, interpreting the regularities reported against a background of theory derived from studies of normal performance.

In the last decade there have been increasing numbers of attempts to investigate language production processes by experimental means rather than through systematic observation of spontaneous speech. Such studies may use timed response or accuracy measures for sentence construction under constrained circumstances (e.g. the use of specific words, or the simultaneous performance of a perceptual or memory task). Indeed, the dependent measures in such studies are sometimes the very same phenomena of spontaneous speech discussed in 2 and 3 above. Thus, the distinction between 'observational' and 'experimental' studies is not so sharp as my expository devices might suggest, given that many experimental studies involve attempts to induce specific classes of speech errors or hesitations in laboratory settings. As with work on language disorders, I will not systematically review experimental studies, but will adduce experimental findings for the elaboration and evaluation of models based primarily upon analyses of hesitation and of speech errors.

C   ABSTRACTING A PRELIMINARY MODEL

The preceding discussion isolated three general components of the language production process: a message level, a sentence level, and an articulatory level. At this point, I will treat these as a working hypothesis about human language production, namely, that they label its minimal decomposition into autonomous subsystems.

Conceptually, the distinction among these components is hardly controversial – virtually every account of language production begins with the notion that there is 'something to be said' and that there is some process for determining what form it will take, including, ultimately, its precise physical specification in the motor system. But, though the distinctions are clear, their computational realization in human beings is not. Observation and experiment with normal and disordered language performance must provide the basis for particular claims about such computational processes. We need, therefore, a more specific statement of the presumed relations among these components and of the probable lines of their internal elaboration.

1 *The message level* may be viewed as a real time conceptual construct based upon the speaker's current perceptual and affective states and on his general knowledge of the world; message level representations must be compositional – i.e. there is a basic vocabulary of simple concepts (not, therefore, necessarily small in number, see below) and a syntax for constructing complex expressions.

Such representations are the proximal cause of sentence construction. On this view, sentence production is a development, under message level control, of representations sufficient to determine an appropriate control structure for articulation, where 'appropriateness' means yielding the original message as an interpretation of the utterance generated by the specified articulatory pattern. Thus, the empirical problem in the analysis of sentence production is to say what computational representations are required for sentence processing and how message level control is exercised for their construction.

Two further points about the message level should be made. The first is simply to caution against identifying it with the *semantic* level in various proposals for formal grammar (e.g. Katz and Fodor, 1963; Chomsky, 1965; Lakoff, 1971; Katz, 1972). This identification should be resisted for two reasons: one, because the message level is by hypothesis responsive to both linguistic and nonlinguistic information and, two, because there are, in any event, serious arguments against such a formal level of analysis in grammars (see, e.g. Fodor, Garrett, Walker and Parkes, 1980 and references therein). Note, this is certainly not to assert that the message level is not concerned with issues of meaning – quite the contrary is the case. The message level is, again by hypothesis, the locus of the myriad inferential processes which must necessarily be a part of structured discourse.

This brings us to the second point, which is a working hypothesis about the vocabulary which relates message level and sentence level representations to each other, i.e. the vocabulary which mediates the translation from nonlinguistic to linguistic levels of representation. The hypothesis that will be adopted here is the *surface* vocabulary of language is, to a first approximation, also the vocabulary of semantic processes. This hypothesis contrasts with the more usual view that the meaning of surface vocabulary items of a language is represented in terms of *definitions* stated in a vocabulary of primitive or atomic concepts, i.e. the thesis that the meaning of surface vocabulary elements is given by definitions at a semantic level of linguistic representation. On this latter view of word meaning, complexes of abstract semantic markers or features are assembled and ultimately replaced by representations in terms of surface vocabulary. In such systems, the vocabulary which mediates between linguistic and nonlinguistic expressions is one of abstract semantic primitives, and thus, insofar as aspects of sentence construction are dependent upon such nonlexical primitives, sentence construction may proceed independently of a determination of the identity of surface vocabulary elements. Another way to put this is to say that the specification of surface vocabulary may occur quite late in the process of sentence construction.

As noted, the preliminary model will not incorporate such a definitional construal of the meaning of lexical items; rather, it adopts what has been called a 'meaning postulate' approach; hence, the vocabulary which mediates the transfer from message level representation to sentence level representation is the morphologically simple surface vocabulary.[6] Grounds for this proposal derive in part from several experimental studies of definitional treatments of word meaning (Fodor et al., 1980; Fodor, Fodor and Garrett, 1975; Kintsch, 1974). In none of these were the predicted consequences of definitional structures found. To illustrate briefly, Fodor et al. (1975) contrasted processing effects of 'semantic negatives' (e.g. as the NEG in the putative definition of words like 'bachelor') with those of overt morphological negatives (like the 'un' in unmarried) and syntactic negatives (like the NEG in the analysis of 'doubt'); the latter two cases showed the characteristic processing decrements repeatedly found for negatives (e.g. Sherman, 1976) but the former did not. In similar vein, but using a different structural parameter, Fodor et al. (1980) found no reflection of the multiclausal structures in the definitions offered for causative verbs (e.g. 'kill' in 'NP$_1$ kill NP$_2$' analysed as [NP$_1$ CAUSE [NP$_2$ DIE]]). It should be stressed that the failure of such definitional structures to affect processing and judgment occurred in experimental circumstances shown to be sensitive to the same *types* of variables when based upon non-definitional criteria (i.e. deep syntactic structures or semantic relations between surface lexical items). Such results indicate that though the inferential relations expressed in the definitional structures are indubitably valid (i.e. it is true that, if John killed Mary then John caused Mary to die, and similarly, if John is a bachelor, then John is not married), they are not plausibly reconstructed by definitions. For reasons of these sorts of experimental findings, as well as a number of theoretical issues that cannot be presented here (see Fodor, 1975; Fodor et al., 1980), the hypothesis of choice for the vocabulary which connects message level and sentence level processes is, roughly, the simple surface vocabulary.

To place this in the context of the current terminology, each simple surface vocabulary element corresponds to a conceptually simple entity at the message level. This is not to say that the inventory of elementary *concepts* is exhausted by the inventory of simple surface vocabulary entries. It is to say that the compositional resources at the message level which may be recruited for the linguistic description of simple or complex concepts is exhausted by the surface vocabulary. Elementary constructs which are not associated with a simple surface vocabulary entry must be described in terms of those constructs which are. Lest one should suppose that this would work a descriptive hardship on the users of language, it should be remembered that the inventory of elementary vocabulary elements compatible with such constraints is of the order of tens of thousands.[7]

Beyond these matters, the hypothesis that the message level vocabulary includes the simple surface vocabulary permits whatever degree of lexical dependence may be required for sentence construction processes, specifically for syntactic processes; such may be effected at the earliest stages of the sentence production process. This assumption thus suggests early rather than late lexical specification.

2 *The sentence level* of processing may be viewed as the real time construction of such representations as are required for the logical and phonological specification of sentence form; roughly, that is for what might be called 'inferential packaging' on the one hand, and 'pronunciation packaging' on the other. We note that whether speaking of the logical force of a sentence or of the constraints imposed by its pronunciation in a given language, we must have recourse to descriptions in terms of the identity of the lexical elements in the string and in terms of their phrasal arrangement. The descriptions of the lexical elements will differ depending on whether the logical or phonological processes in which they are involved are at issue. In either case, sentence level processes require an accounting of lexical selection processes and phrasal construction processes. Thus, our analysis of observational and experimental evidence will be dominantly concerned with these processes, and one central expectations is that their structure will reflect an accommodation between the two principal sources of constraint on sentence form: those imposed by the requirement of accent free pronunciation, and those imposed by the requirement of communicatively appropriate interpretation.

3 *The articulatory level.* Here, we are concerned with the translation from sentence level structures to articulatory structures (including those responsible for respiration); to be precise, in this stage of the language production process, the distinctive feature matrix representing the phonetic level of sentence structure (including an associated super-segmental or prosodic structure specification) must be translated into instructions for control of the respiratory and articulatory system. This process must account for the relations holding between articulatory activity and the segmental values specified in the distinctive feature

matrix (e.g. the connection between distinctive feature values and such control parameters for the vocal tract as tongue movement, vocal cord tension, lip rounding, etc.).

Stevens and Perkell (1978) have talked of this relation in terms of articulatory goal states defined by sensory and motor conditions (i.e. those proprioceptive and tactile cues which are associated with an articulatory configuration with a characteristic acoustic consequence). They label such specifications of sensory and motor states 'orosensory patterns'. These provide for the translation from 'static' linguistic representations to articulatory movement. Matrices of orosensory patterns must be transformed into neural control signals which accommodate the dynamic influences of the context of utterance. Note that the translation from phonetic representations to such patterns of proprioceptive and tactile cues incorporates at least in part, the constraints imposed upon the realization of phonetic matrices by physical properties (including neurophysiology) of the articulatory apparatus. That is, such a discrete representation will confront the articulatory system only with possible configurational states. What remains is the integration of these into a continuous motor function (see Perkell, 1980).

It is a non-trivial question what the domain of these processes may be. There is evidence to indicate syllabic, lexical and even phrasal domains for the programming of such articulatory processes (see, e.g. Cooper and Paccia-Cooper, 1980). Given the latter possibility it becomes a question of theoretical significance *and* methodological difficulty to distinguish between those aspects of the language planning process which are responsive to phrasal structure and/or lexical structure because of its logical, syntactic and phonological consequences, and those language planning processes which are responsive to phrasal and lexical structures because of their articulatory role.

4   *The preliminary model* we have just sketched has three component sets of language planning activity of distinctively different type. For the subsequent discussion in this chapter, the focus will be on what we take to be evidence of sentence level processes. However, as the remarks above indicates, an examination of sentence level phenomena must also include an effort to distinguish such from those properly associated with either message level planning activity or articulatory level planning activity. We turn now to a consideration of some representative proposals which promote both objectives.

2   Some representative language production models

There are numerous examples of schema for language production at about the same level of specification as the preliminary model; one may find these in the literature discussing language disorders and hesitation phenomena, or in commentaries on language and thought. For example, the remarks of Wilhelm Wundt include a description of language production processes in which the first assumed event is a general impression of entities and the relations holding among them; based on this, specific entities are selected and a relational structure specific to sentential expression is determined; the processes which account for sound production and perception ensue (Blumenthal, 1970).

To take another example, this from the language disorders literature, Pick's view of sentence production (from Goodglass, 1976) is similarly organized. In Pick's account, the development of a sentence starts with a 'preverbal awareness of the general intent of the sentence', followed by a schematization of sentence form. The schema for sentence form includes 'a vague sense of the melody and word order, although the precise choice of words is not yet made'. Following this, there is a selection of the actual verbal content which is adapted to the sentence schema.

Wundt emphasizes the existence of structures which subsume the sentence as a whole, and it is these intentions which then resolve themselves into an analysis that guides the details of sentence production. This may be likened to the claim in our preliminary model that the message is, *vis-à-vis* the processes of sentential construction and articulatory specification, fully determined independent of the elaboration of the internal structure of the latter representations.[8] (The conviction that sentences possess an inner form and an outer form and that the former guides the construction of the latter is, in fact, a commonplace of discussion of language in the latter nineteenth and earlier twentieth century. The temporary abandonment of that essentially correct insight might be regarded as an abberation of early twentieth-century American psychology more than anything else.)

For our purposes, two more contemporary representatives of this general theoretical approach are the most useful. They are Goldman-Eisler (1968), whose analyses are based primarily upon observations of hesitation phenomena, and Fromkin (1971), whose analyses are based primarily upon observations of speech error phenomena. Their work represents emphases on two different aspects of the language production process: Goldman-Eisler on that which we have labeled message level construction, and Fromkin on that which we have labeled sentence level construction. It is instructive to examine the ways in which the processes of phrasal construction and lexical selection are accommodated in these two accounts of language production processes.

A   THE HESITATION MODEL: GOLDMAN-EISLER

We first consider Goldman-Eisler's proposals. She begins with the distinction, emphasized by Hughlings Jackson, between 'routine and therefore automatic verbal behavior' on the one hand and the creative or interpretive processes of thinking underlying language on the other hand. Her account of language production processes is an elaboration of this basic contrast. Observations of hesitations and rate phenomena in spontaneous speech by Goldman-Eisler and her co-workers lead her to associate processes in the planning of an utterance either with the creative, voluntary aspects or with the automatic, routinized aspects of language. Speaking roughly, the processes of detailed syntactic organization and articulatory function are related to the automatic stages of language production, while those of lexical selection and the determination of conceptual relations are related to the creative or voluntary stage of language formulation.

To be somewhat more specific, she isolates three classes of decisions which must be accomplished in the course of formulating speech (Goldman-Eisler, 1968, p. 32). The first is a content decision (which may include isolated lexical choices appropriate to a chosen semantic sphere – these perhaps provide anchor points for subsequent processes). Second, she notes that some decision must be made on 'the broad outlines of syntactic structure'. Third, she notes that word choice which is syntactically dictated and which is specific to the semantic plan must be accomplished. Note that these are meant to refer to the voluntary stages of language formulation; details of syntax and sound structure are part of the automatic speech routines. On this decision structure, she superimposes evidence for the temporal structure of spoken speech, that evidence being primarily in terms of measurements of rate and locus of hesitation. The presumption that is made is that decision is potentially associated with delay, i.e. that decisions at the voluntary level will be associated with variation in some temporal parameters measurable in the superficial aspects of utterances.

To illustrate the flavor of the analysis: Goldman-Eisler distinguishes two pause loci – those that are linguistically and semantically interpretable (those associated with grammatical juncture, i.e. with major phrasal structure) and those which are not so interpretable, i.e. those which are internal to linguistic units. To evidence the respective roles of these two types of breaks in the stream of speech, Goldman-Eisler contrasts pause location and duration during reading and/or highly practiced speech with that during spontaneous, creative speech. She notes that the pause loci of the former case are characteristically the linguistically and semantically defensible junctures, whereas the pause loci of the latter include the linguistic junctures but are also rife with interruptions as other points (p. 14). Thus, she argues that the latter class of pausal phenomena is characteristic of the creative stage of language formulation, whereas the former reflects the exercise of (automatic) skilled motor activities associated with speech.

Goldman-Eisler cites various experimental evidence for two specific determinants of pause: lexical uncertainty and conceptual complexity. In the former case, this means that pauses are more likely to precede words that are not easily predictable from their discourse context than words which are. Presumably, such variation in judged predictability indexes the relative accessibility of specific lexical targets for a speaker. In the latter case, that of conceptual complexity, it means that the frequency and duration of pausing increases as the difficulty of the encoding task increases. But, not only is more time spent in pauses under such circumstances, there is also a characteristic distribution of the increased pause time. Spontaneous speech, in moderately demanding circumstances (such as her experimental task of cartoon interpretation), has a macrostructure which consists of a series of alternations between hesitant and fluent phases of speech. There is first a phase of speech which is marked by the occurence of pauses at nonlinguistically defined loci and by increased duration of pauses; that phase of speech is followed by a relatively fluent stretch in which the duration and loci of pausing are more akin to that of reading or memorized speech. (Goldman-Eisler, 1968, p. 96.)

In terms of the preliminary model, hesitation phenomena are, for Goldman-Eisler, seen as associated with message level formulation and not with sentence level processes. Moreover, on this view, syntactic planning, insofar as it takes place, occurs during the same phase as that of message level planning. That is, the planning upon which the specific syntactic form of sentences depends is determined by processes at the hesitant phase of the alternation between hesitation and fluent phases. Given that fluent phases average about five clauses in length (Beattie, 1980), this amounts to a particularly strong claim about the extent of syntactic pre-planning during language production. We will return to a more detailed consideration of these issues.

In passing, we might note the relation between the sort of proposals made by Goldman-Eisler and some of those based on observations of language disorders. Goldman-Eisler relates her own construal of the language production processes to accounts by Jackson which arose from his observations of disordered language. Goldman-Eisler sees her analysis as quite compatible with the conclusions suggested by patterns of language disorder; in particular, of course, in the separation of the automatized and creative bases of behavior. There is in this a suggestion of a rationale for the correspondence between stable patterns of language breakdown and a particular partitioning of language processes: those processes which are automatic are those most likely to have specific neural tissue dedicated to their execution. Thus, one expects to see disturbances in which the conceptual resources of a speaker are preserved, while syntax and/or phonological structures are impaired, and vice versa. A good deal of interest *vis-à-vis* the relation between conceptual structures and language structures might, on this view, be made to turn on a determination of the precise character of the 'syntactic' and phonological structures which are so isolated – we will return to this general issue at a later point.

Finally, we note again that a dominant feature of the Goldman-Eisler account is the dissociation of lexical selections and the determination of surface syntactic form. Recall, however, that Goldman-Eisler includes the possibility of a specification of *some* of the lexical content of a sentence at the earliest stages of sentence formulation. Thus, though this and related construals of sentence production activity contain a rather definite separation of sentence form and lexical content as a part of their analysis, there is, nonetheless, some understandable equivocation on the question of the precise relation holding between the selection of lexical content items and the selection of syntactic frames. The flavor of the accounts is that the matter is idiosyntactic in its determination. In contrast to this, Fromkin's construal of sentence production processes, which we will consider next, contains rather specific claims about the relation between formulation of syntactic structures for sentences and the selection of particular lexical entries.

B   THE SPEECH ERROR MODEL: FROMKIN

Fromkin's account is based upon both the analysis of speech errors and upon observations about the formal linguistic structure of language. Her proposal for language production processes has the general structure of the preliminary model. Stage One in her outline provides for a specification of meaning. In the account she offers, that specification is in terms of nonlexical semantic primitives as opposed to representations that are identifiable with specific surface vocabulary items, and in this her account differs from the working hypothesis advanced in the preliminary model. However, the salient feature at this point is that one begins with the specification of a meaning representation which is then mapped by a series of subsequent processes into the ultimate utterance. The second stage in Fromkin's model accounts for the syntactic structuring of the meaning representation. At Stage Two, semantic features or constellations of semantic features are associated with syntactic roles in sentences. The output of this second stage process is a syntactic structure with semantic and syntactic features marked at lexical sites in the syntactic tree. At Stage Three, an intonation contour is assigned to this structure. This includes, of course, not only the syntactically dictated intonational features but also interpretively based features (e.g. contrastive and emphatic stress). At Stage Four of Fromkin's model, we encounter the first point for lexical lookup. This is based on the semantic and syntactic specifications at lexical sites in the tree. A meaning based lookup is followed by selection from an inventory of segmentally specified forms. Thus, Fromkin's account includes two aspects of lexical selection which are temporally ordered with respect to each other. The first is a semantically directed selection, the second determines the segmental specification of a semantically dictated element. Subsequent to this assignment of lexical forms to sites in the syntactic tree, the application of morpho-phonemic rules is assumed in order to spell out the phonetic shape of morphemes which are not fixed by the preceding processes. To this representation, phonological rules apply to yield a detailed phonetic specification which is then subject to interpretation for motor commands.

The primary observational base for these claims by Fromkin is speech errors of the sort briefly discussed in section 1. These errors, which involve either the mislocation of intended elements of an utterance or the deletion, addition or substitution of intended elements, show a variety of rather intricate regularities and interdependencies. So, for example, Fromkin observed, as had others, that the elements which are moved or substituted for are almost invariably susceptible of a linguistic description. That is, the vocabulary which one needs to describe the error structure is available in the constructs of formal linguistic analysis. By itself, of course, this is not a sufficient argument for the appropriateness of the linguistic labels in descriptions of the computational activity which underlies the speech errors. But, when one adds the observation that the intruding and displaced elements are of corresponding linguistic types, one has established a basis for the claim that the available linguistic descriptions are, in fact, functional in the error interaction. So, the fact that stems substitute for or exchange with stems and not with affixes, that verbs exchange or substitute for verbs and nouns for nouns, that consonants change with or substitute for consonants and not for vowels, etc. indicates that the description under which these elements are being manipulated, in each case, is one common to the intended element and to the intruding element. On such grounds, one may argue that virtually all the elementary structural types in linguistic descriptions are involved at one or another point in the process of sentence production.

Certain other features of the error patterns permit even stronger claims, namely, those for the ordering of certain of the constructive processes, as well as those for the independence of certain superficially similar types of representation. So, for the first case, we have instances in which the movement of error elements.

    (*a*) 'bloody students' → 'bloodent stewdies'
    (*b*) 'A current argument' → 'an arrent curgument'.

creates a new phonetic environment, e.g. as for example (*a*) and (*b*) (from Fromkin, 1971), for the plural marker and for the indefinite article. The phonetic form of those morphemes accommodates (i.e. /s/→/z/ and 'a'→ 'an') to the error induced phonetic environment. From this, Fromkin and others argued that the processes which give rise to these errors must precede the processes which endow such morphemes with their precise phonetic form. As we shall see, a good deal can be made to turn on the question of precisely which elements in error phenomena show such accommodatory processes.

The second claim involves the independence of stress assignment for words and phrases. So, for example, when two words or stems interchange in an error, phrasal stress is preserved – that is, the originally intended phrasal stress pattern appears in the error output. This indicates that the representation which is functional at the time of the error exchange does not identify the representation of stress with the segmental analysis of the particular lexical items assigned to a given phrasal site. For, if so, one would expect phrasal stress to move with the items which bear it; such is not the case. This is significant, for it not only indicates that the error processes which give rise to such cases must occur at points in which the analysis of the intended utterance distinguishes lexical and phrasal structure, but also provides evidence that the error mechanisms are responsive to processing stages prior to the actual motor programming of the intended utterance – i.e. the articulatory level in the preliminary model. This is so because at that level there would no longer be any evidence of the disparate sources of the relative levels of prominence of syllables in the structure of the utterance.

Though these observations on stress have been couched in terms of the independence of two types of processes, they might have been put in terms of ordering of processes, as were the accommodatory cases. In particular, one might state the claim as one concerning the order of decisions about assignment of lexical items to positions in a phrasal framework *vis-à-vis* the point at which the assignment of a phrasal stress contour is made. One could claim that the siting of the lexical items in the phrasal framework occurs prior to the point at which the stress contour is assigned. So, rather than talking about preservation of an already assigned stress contour, i.e. Fromkin's Stage Three, one might talk about the application of an algorithm to a syntactic structure for the assignment of phrasal stress at a point posterior to the assignment of words to their syntactic frames. We will return to this issue later.

C COMPARISON OF THE MODELS

We might first recall the basic contrast in these two treatments of the problem: Fromkin focusses her attention on the details of sentence level formulation and simply assumes the meaning representations required; Goldman-Eisler fixes on the case for a differentiation of conceptual processes and sentence level processes in the real-time control of speech. There is little detail in her treatment of either level, though the distinctions she finds support for are those in what we have called the message domain.

One possibility to be noted is that this contrast in treatment reflects not only the interests of the two investigators, but also the sensitivities of their chosen observational bases – perhaps speech errors are relatively opaque to message level influence while hesitations, as Goldman-Eisler argues, are exclusively of that province. We will shortly see that this, while not entirely wrong, cannot be fully sustained. In particular, there is strong indication that hesitations do reflect certain aspects of phrasal structure.

Aside from these matters, there is a quite different relation between lexical selection and phrasal construction in the two proposals. Fromkin's model places the process of lexical selection posterior to the formulation of a detailed syntactic structure; Goldman-Eisler's permits selection both prior to and posterior to detailed sentence level formulation, with the emphasis (based upon observations of hesitation) placed upon the occasions when lexical choice is delayed and this interferes with the fluent execution of the sentence.

Both accounts separate the processes of lexical selection and phrasal construction, though in somewhat different fashion. In Fromkin's model, when a constellation of semantic and syntactic features have been associated with a given phrasal site, the conditions for message based selection of a word have been met, and it remains to determine its segmental analysis. The syntactic formulation is a condition on the assembly of such feature constellations and hence, syntactic configurations must be available before lexical access proceeds. In Goldman-Eisler's account, the reason for that separation is, as earlier noted, because of the presumed voluntary control over lexical selection, as opposed to the automatic realization of syntactic and phonological organization. These two conceptions of the separation of lexical selection and syntactic construction are, therefore, necessarily distinguished because the former (Fromkin's) requires what the latter (Goldman-Eisler's) takes to be an automatic process (detailed syntactic commitments) as a condition on an independent and voluntary process (lexical selection). What one needs for some better understanding of this issue is more specific evidence bearing on the relation between the mechanisms for lexical retrieval and those for building syntactic and phonological structures. Though the matter is hardly overdetermined, there is some such evidence which we take up in a further discussion of speech error data and language disorders.

There is one further aspect of the two models which deserves separate comment. This concerns the role of the apparent cyclic macrostructure of alternating hesitant (planning) and fluent (execution) phases of spontaneous speech (hereafter referred to as the 'encoding cycle'). The chief distinguishing feature of the two phases is frequent pauses at *non-*junctural (phrase internal) locations – it is this that makes the hesitant phase hesitant, and the absence of such that makes the fluent phase fluent. In spite of this interrupted execution, the hesitant phase does not seem aprosodic. That is, the intonational and stress features are (perceptually) well formed. This prosodic structure will depend upon structure which extends beyond the hesitation locus – i.e. some detail of the entire phrasal geometry must already be fixed at many of these characteristic hesitation points.[9] In Fromkin's model, this can be dealt with by the assignment of prosodic contour to the (lexically un-interpreted) syntactic structures of her Stage Two. On these grounds, one may argue that some significant proportion of the hesitations charac-teristic of the nonfluent phase of the encoding cycle cannot be aimed at the determination of the phrase structure in their immediate vicinity (though they could represent some aspect of lexical selection). Goldman-Eisler, of course, does assume that the pauses in the hesitant phase are for lexical choice and for conceptual level relations (including broad scale syntactic planning) for both phases of the encoding cycle. The question of what role characteristic hesitations of the nonfluent phase play in specifically sentence level planning is an important one we will raise again (section 3A).

3   The hesitation model: extending the observational base

Goldman-Eisler was the first to make systematic objective observations of hesitation phenomena. Since then, a number of other investigators, some using her departure points, some not, have examined the problem. In several cases, Goldman-Eisler's observations have been confirmed and elaborated, and in others they have not. Briefly, the account we will consider runs as follows: the conclusion that hesitations in general do not show syntactic dependency is in error. However, the conclusion that the characteristic nonjunctural pauses in the hesitant phase of the encoding cycle are not caused by syntactic planning is likely to prove correct. It seems probable that there are, in fact, three classes of hesitation, lexical, syntactic and conceptual, and it is at least plausible that they stem from rather different underlying mechanisms. We will begin with a closer look at the encoding cycle.

A   THE ENCODING CYCLE

The initial experimental observation suggesting a temporal macrostruc-ture for spontaneous speech was, as noted, the alternation of stretches of speech in which quite different ratios of pause to phonation time obtained (Henderson, Goldman-Eisler and Skarbeck, 1966). It was argued that this succession of relatively hesitant and relatively fluent phases should be linked as a succession of planning/execution pairs; the compatibility of this with the general theoretical perspective of Goldman-Eisler is clear – voluntary planning precedes and enables automatic execution. Direct evidence for the linkage is of two sorts: a dependency in duration of the two phases, and a dependency in meaning. Henderson et al. (1966) reported a positive correlation between the duration of hesitant and fluent phases: longer fluent phases are associated with longer hesitant phases. Butterworth (1975) made similar observations and a significant further finding, namely, that of semantic dependence between the successive phases of an encoding cycle. Judges who were asked to segment transcripts of spontaneous speech samples into 'idea' groups tended to break the material into chunks which associated immediately successive hesitant and fluent phases – i.e. the boundaries of encoding cycles that were established on the basis of pause distribution correspond to a significant degree with intuitive semantic groupings. This fact, coupled with the relation between pause time in the first phase and phonation time in the second (fluent) phase provides reasonable grounds for accepting the encoding cycle as a provisional hypothesis, and, therefore, for seeking an account of its internal structure. However, in so doing, it should be borne in mind that though this seems a robust global feature of spontaneous speech, it is also quite variable in its realization, with substantial overall temporal range and internal variations. While the characteristic differences between the two phases of the cycle are quite striking, they are by no means absolute (e.g. nonjunctural pauses occur in both phases). Thus, ascriptions of a unitary function to the two phases should be viewed as approximations. That cautionary point having been made, I will proceed in what follows to speak in absolute terms.

There are a number of indicants of a qualitative difference in the hesitations of the two phases. The difference in their loci and duration have already been remarked. One difference we have not commented on is the most obvious one, namely the subjective sensations associated with the various pause loci. Certainly, one of the intuitively appealing aspects of Goldman-Eisler's construal of the phases of the encoding cycle is the correspondence between her characterization of the hesitant phase as one of voluntary intellectual effort and our own subjective experience of what transpires as we hesitate in the course of the spontaneous formulation of speech. It is certainly true that hesitations often 'feel' like decision-making minicrises – hence voluntary in some sense. But, it does not follow from that conscious feeling that the computations which precipitated the crisis are themselves in the domain of conscious decision. This is to say that accepting the significance of the subjective criterion for distinguishing pauses does not require accepting that the distinction arises from a contrast of voluntary and automatic processes. Thus, although more subjectively distinctive pauses may occur in the hesitant phase of the cycle (i.e. especially the nonjunctural pauses) it only provides some additional evidence for a difference in the pauses of the two phases of the cycle, not for the interpretation of that difference.

There are two other factors which also indicate differences in the character of the two phases in the cycle. These are their relations to gestural and gaze patterns during conversational exchanges. Beattie (1980) reports the results of several studies which seem to indicate dependencies between these variables and hesitation. Consider first some findings for speech relevant gestures.

Overall, speech related body motions are reported to be substantially more frequent during fluent than during hesitant phases, but more complex relations are revealed when specific gestural types are related to pause and phonation periods in the two phases. So, for example, when a distinction is drawn between iconic gestures and nonspecific movements for emphasis, the former were most frequent during the pauses of the fluent phase, while the latter were most frequent during the phonation periods of the hesitant phase (Butterworth and Beattie, 1978).[10]

The gaze patterns are described in terms of whether a speaker is looking at his conversational partner or not, and of the points at which there is a transition from partner directed gaze-to-gaze aversion. Again, there is a broad generalization concerning gaze contingency in the encoding cycle: gaze is more often averted during hesitant than fluent phases. This may not be simply a global feature of the first phase, for there is more specific evidence that gaze aversion occurs more often at clause internal hesitation points than at the fluent transitions within a clause. This contrasts with the lack of such a dependency for clause initial pause positions (Beattie, 1980).[11] That is, the loci of hesitation which are more typical of the initial phase of an encoding cycle are also more likely to be loci of gaze aversion, while those at junctural loci are not, thus reinforcing the view that there is a qualitative difference in these classes of hesitations.

There seem to be adequate grounds for considering the pausal phenomena of the two phases of the encoding cycle to differ in character. The question of what this means is more difficult. If we exclude lexically governed pauses for the moment, we may ask whether, for example, the pauses in the hesitant phase are the locus of planning for the syntactic and conceptual structures not only of the hesitant phase but of the fluent phase as well. Or, alternatively, are the characteristic pauses of the hesitant phase primarily determined by the elaboration of the conceptual structures underlying the whole cycle? In short, in terms of the preliminary model, does the encoding cycle reflect only message level planning, or that of the sentence level as well? Beattie (1980) and Butterworth (1980, p. 173) (albeit the latter somewhat hesitantly) opt for the stronger interpretation on a variety of grounds, the most central of which is the apparent lack of hesitation effects associated with detailed variation in syntactic structure, and particularly so for the second phase of the encoding cycle. So, for example, Goldman-Eisler (1968) as well as subsequent investigators,[12] found that a general measure of syntactic complexity (the 'subordination index' = proportion of subordinate clauses) was not linked to large differences in pause to phonation ratios. In Goldman-Eisler's experiments, both cartoon interpretation and personal interviews yielded speech with a high subordination index, but only the former was associated with markedly hesitant speech; the interviews showed pause times akin to structurally simpler speech.

There are several reasons for resisting this strongest of claims about the locus of the processing which determines syntactic structure. First is the availability of other evidence for the syntactic dependency of pauses. Second is that the very large domains over which syntactic preplanning would be required (five to eight clauses) do not comport with the domains indicated by speech errors (about two clauses). Third is simply the implausibility of the notion that overt pause is a necessary precondition to sentence planning, for it makes a mystery of the occasions on which we do speak spontaneously but fluently. We will turn to an examination of some further evidence concerning the connection between pauses and phrasal structure before returning to this issue.

B   SYNTACTIC EFFECTS ON HESITATIONS

We noted above that both Butterworth and Beattie report significantly greater concentrations of pause at the boundaries of surface structure clauses. A related previous observation was made by Boomer (1965). Boomer analyzed spontaneous speech samples into 'phonemic clauses' – a prosodically defined word sequence. It is a stretch of speech with a single phrasal stress center and a characteristic intonation contour terminating in one of the major phrasal junctures. He included in his analysis of hesitations only *non*junctural pauses. The distribution of such pauses showed only a single departure from chance expectation – that for the location immediately following the initial word of the phonemic clause. (The null hypothesis is a uniform distribution of pause across the available word boundary positions.) Boomer concluded that this finding indicated the planning of speech in units larger than a single word, and more particularly that the hesitation distribution was not perturbed by the predictability of individual lexical elements. This latter conclusion was based in part upon the correlation of word predictability and phrasal position – later positions are occupied by less predictable elements.[13]

Boomer's major conclusion – that a phrase length planning element is a major determinant of hesitation – seems secure, but there are reservations one may raise *vis-à-vis* the detail of his claim. First of all, we cannot say that it is specific to analysis of the unit as a phonemic clause. Several correlated phrasal descriptions might on grounds of statistical success be equally relevant – e.g. surface or deep syntactic clauses. In short, one can be fairly confident that some phrasal construct is relevant but not which one. We will turn momentarily to that question.

Another reservation one may have concerns Boomer's exclusion of junctural pauses. Though it is true they are syntactically conditioned, it is equally true that they may be the locus of hesitation on grounds of subjective experience. Barik (1968) argued for including pauses which occur at junctures but exceed 500 ms duration. He reports that when this criterion is adopted the modal position for pause in Boomer's analysis is, in fact, the juncture pause. Both that position and the one identified by

Boomer exceed chance expectation, and we find a convergence between this and results (e.g. Butterworth, 1980) noted earlier – namely, a clustering of hesitations at the beginnings of clauses. Finally, one might object to Boomer's apparent assumption that pauses distributed randomly in his analysis were not related to significant features of the sentence planning process. It is noted there are substantial numbers of clause internal pauses left unaccounted for on this assumption. That there is no position internal to the clause (barring the first ordered word boundary) which shows more than a chance level of occurrence does not mean that the pauses so occurring do not reflect some aspect of the constructive process; it only means that whatever that aspect is, it is not directly contingent upon clausal structure. (The processes of lexical selection and the conceptual level processes of the encoding cycle are, of course, candidates.) The implication of these observations is that specifically phrasal planning is associated with junctural loci or their immediate vicinity. There is direct evidence for this.

Ford (1978) in a recent series of experiments sought to do two things: first, to determine whether the clausal analyses relevant to speech planning is, as the preceding discussion suggests, that of surface clauses or whether it is the deep syntactic clause; and, second, to determine whether there are systematic differences in hesitation features as a function of specific clausal type. Ford used the same durational criteria as Butterworth and Beattie (200 ms) for her analysis of spontaneous speech samples. Her results indicate that when surface and deep clausal boundaries are unconfounded, the latter are as consistently associated with hesitation as the former. That is, for deep clause boundary positions which are not also surface clause boundaries, hesitation effects (with respect to both frequency and duration of pause) are as strong as those for surface clause boundaries. Since every surface clause boundary is also a deep clause boundary, the implication is that the functional structural unit is, in fact, the deep clause. Ford buttresses this interpretation by noting that there was no effect (on surface clause initial pauses) of the number of deep clauses contained in a surface clause. That is, if one accepted a specific role for the deep clause and sought a separate role for surface clauses (e.g. as the domain of integration for deep clauses), no evidence of such appeared in the pause durations – surface clauses with multiple deep clauses were not distinguishable; hence, her conclusion that only the first deep clause of a surface clause affects pauses at their beginnings.

Turning to the second issue of clausal type, Ford compared four types of structures: complement clauses (e.g. 'John knew *that Mary left*'.); adverbial clauses ('John left *when Mary came home*'.); relative clauses ('The body *who met Mary left*'.); conjoined clauses ('The boy met Mary *and left for home*'.). Though all these types showed significant pausing at their onset, there were several significant differences among them. So, for example, pausing was more frequent and protracted prior to conjunctions than prior to the other types, and complement clauses showed less frequent pausing than did adverb or relative clauses. Ford also reports differences in the pattern of pauses for these types when the position just following the clause introducing element was examined. In short, there are several indications of detailed syntactic influences on the hesitation pattern.

These results of Ford are complimented by those of a parallel experiment by Ford and Holmes (1978). The analysis of the spontaneous speech samples was precisely as that for the hesitation study of Ford reported above. The measure of structural effects, however, was reaction time (manual response) to a tone burst (1000 Hz) presented frequently and at random intervals while the speaker was talking on an assigned topic.[14] The outcome showed substantially the same pattern as the hesitation study. Speakers' reaction times differed at beginnings and ends of clauses; they showed faster responses at clause onset and elevated reaction times at ends of clauses, and again this pattern held for boundaries of deep clauses whether they were surface clause boundaries or not. Similarly, detailed differences were observed among the four types of embedded structures (complements, adverbials, relatives and conjunctions), though there was some difference from the patterning given by hesitation.

The conjoint evidence from Ford's study of hesitation and the experimental evidence from the Ford and Holmes reaction time study is persuasive: deep clause structure determines a significant phrasal planning domain. For these purposes, the notion 'deep clause' should be understood as a verb (usually overt, but sometimes implied) and its associated simple surface phrases. Usually these phrases are surface adjacent to the verb, though a few discontinuous cases were included in the hesitation study. The proposal is thus that the planning for sentence structure proceeds deep verb dominated group by deep verb dominated group in the order of their surface appearance in the sentence.[15]

These results are clearly compatible with the regularities previously reported for surface clauses (i.e. clustering at their onset), but place a different interpretation on those observations; such surface structure hesitation groups will initiate both surface and deep clause units, and Ford argues for the deep analysis as the causally effective one. Note further that the deep clause thesis will also encompass at least some pauses not previously given a syntactic interpretation – i.e. those deep clause boundaries internal to surface clauses. There are, however, some further aspects of the available pausing data which require additional structure.

Consider the following facts: in the hesitant phase of the encoding cycle, Beattie (1980) reports a relation between pause duration and surface clause length (counted in words); Cook, Smith and Lalljee (1974) report a similar result – longer clauses are preceded by longer pauses.

There is, moreover, a finding in Ford's results with the same flavor: when continuous and discontinuous clauses (e.g. center-embedded relatives) were compared, the onsets of the latter showed significantly longer pausing; such clauses would tend to subsume longer surface word sequences than would the continuous clauses. However, all these findings contrast with Ford's main finding on surface clause 'length', for when she directly tested for the effects of number of deep clauses in a surface clause, she found no significant variation due to length (here counted in number of deep clauses). Finally, we must add one further observation of Beattie's. He found no relation betwen pausing and surface clause length in the fluent phase of the encoding cycle; this in contrast to the positive relation between pausing and clause length he reported for the hesitant phase.

These facts taken together encourage the speculation that the major regularities in the results of Ford and of Ford and Holmes may be more typical of the relatively fluent phases of speech (i.e. phases in which sentence level phenomena dominate) than of the more hesitant phases. And that possibility, if we choose to identify the characteristic processes of the hesitant phase with message level activity, suggests that effects of surface clausal structure may depend on message level planning activity.

There is, in fact, yet another feature of pause distributions which may have a similar account. This is the finding (Goldman-Eisler, 1972; Ford, 1978) that full sentence boundaries show unusually high incidence and duration of pauses when compared with sentence internal clause boundaries. Here again is a candidate domain for the integration of multiclausal processes. Whether it should be regarded as a reflection of message level or sentence level activity is by no means evident. Moreover, since each full sentence will mark the onset of a surface clause, this could account for a significant proportion of the effects attributed to surface clauses.

At present, it is impossible to say how these several correlated findings of different investigators would emerge if a single uniform treatment of the structural domains were carried out. Ford's study comes closest to such a case, for she includes sentence boundaries, surface clause boundaries, and deep clause boundaries in her contrasts; however, she discounts the encoding cycle and does not include such a contrast in her analysis. If Beattie's results are representative, this may have obscured the effects of surface clausal structure. It seems that a reasonable summary at this time would not rule out the possibility that surface clausal structure is linked to hesitation distributions (whether because of message level or sentence level processes), but would reserve the possibility that the evidence for that role might be exhausted by assignment either to sentence boundary or deep clause boundary sources.

To recapitulate: Why are the 'junctural loci' to be deemed specific points for phrasal planning? There are two sets of observations, positive and negative, which indicate that conclusion. The positive evidence is the diverse observations showing that silent and filled pauses cluster at the onset of clauses (Boomer, 1965; Goldman-Eisler, 1972; Butterworth, 1980; Beattie, 1980; Ford, 1978). There is, moreover, sundry indication that clause type (e.g. relatives, complements, adverbials and conjunctions) and the local phrasal structure of different clause types have characteristic pause distributions (Goldman-Eisler, 1972; Rochester and Gill, 1973; Ford, 1978); this includes strong indications that the surface phrase boundaries of deep clauses are both pause loci and loci of increased decision latency (Ford, 1977; Ford and Holmes, 1978).

These findings are complemented by the 'negative' indications – i.e. indications that other pause positions internal to clauses are not likely to be loci for the determination of local phrasal structure. This includes Boomer's evidence that phrase internal pauses (barring those after the first word) are randomly distributed with respect to phrasal (phonemic clause) units. There is, in addition, the implication of prosodic structure planning requirements. On the assumption that hesitant speech is prosodically normal, [16] some detail of phrasal structure beyond the hesitation point is fixed. This conclusion is dictated not only by the theoretical requirement that prosodic contours be integrated over phrasal domains, but has also some experimental support from acoustic measurements of speech. Cooper and Sorenson (1977) compared values of fundamental frequency (f_0) at the onset of a given phrase when it initiated a lengthy construction, with f_0 values when it initiated a short construction; f_0 values were systematically higher for the onset of the longer constructions. Thus, we have some objective indication of what formal accounts of prosody would lead us to expect: the acoustic value of elements early in a phrasal sequence is set relative to the character of the upcoming phrase.

The final point on this issue is the need for some account of the fact that every putative planning unit is not marked by a pause that is, on grounds of subjective impression and/or duration, a hesitation pause. And, the first response to such a worry must, of course, be to question its assumption – that planning is invariably associated with overt, even conscious delay. Speech that is spontaneous but on topics with which we are familiar is sometimes produced with sustained fluency, and there is moreover, great individual variation in this capacity. It hardly seems likely that the basic processes of language manipulation vary from individual to individual in so gross a degree. Equally obvious, the second response to such a worry is to suggest a plausible, invariably available location for the necessary planning activity – one which comports readily with the pause data. Such a role may be suggested for junctural pauses even when they are not marked by prolonged silent interval or by subjective feelings of hesitancy. There is evidence to support such a view. For example, Martin (1971) reported that junctural points are perceived by listeners as the locus of pause even when objective measures show no, or extremely brief, cessation of phonation. In such cases, he reported significant lengthening of the final segment of the phrase terminating at the juncture point. Perceptually, these are points at which the local rate of speech is *correctly* judged to be reduced, but it is phenomenally identified with cessation of phonation even when that is objectively not the case. The salient point for our purposes is that there is a substantially invariant availability of a planning site at the termination of major phrase groups; both phrase final lengthening and (most usually) a silent interval provide it. There is, moreover, evidence other than that of the hesitation results to indicate a relation between these variables and upcoming sentence material. Cooper and Paccia-Cooper (1980) report results for a series of experiments which bear on this issue.

In the experiments they report, the duration of phrase final syllables and phrase final silent pauses are precisely measured and variation in those measures related to the detail of preceding and following phrasal structures. The relations they report are complex and multidetermined. However, it is clear from their experiments that the phenomena of phrase final lengthening is intricately linked to syntactic structures both preceding and following. For present purposes, the particular interest is their evidence that durations of phrase final elements are, indeed, related to the length and complexity of upcoming phrases.

What these observations show is that there is a uniformly available planning space that is linked to hesitation loci. One might speculate that pause time or perhaps duration of phrase final elements is lengthened to the subjective limen for consciously perceived hesitation on occasions when the processing of upcoming material is relatively more complex, *or* when the material just uttered is not intimately connected to the upcoming structure (i.e. and thus permits or requires conceptual level intervention). [17]

C   LEXICAL EFFECTS ON HESITATION

There is, in the argument relating hesitations to prosodic structures, a point that is complementary to the one just raised in the preceding section: some aspects of lexical selection are separable from immediate phrasal planning, for, by the assumption of normal prosody, the local phrasal structure has been fixed and, by argument from the hesitation locus (and other evidence noted below), lexical identity has not. Note that by the same arguments, one aspect of the lexical selection process that cannot be at issue is the grammatical category of the upcoming item.

As we noted earlier, Goldman-Eisler took lexical choice to be at issue for such hesitation points, and she supported this view by showing a relation between probability of hesitation and the predictability of the words in spontaneous speech samples. [18] Note: Goldman-Eisler found predictability from right context as well as that from left context to be relevant to hesitation. Though one cannot say just what the appropriate level of structural analysis may be, this too indicates an effect of structure beyond the immediate upcoming lexical site. Overall, the evidence suggests that upcoming phrase structure and meaning constraints are both relatively well developed at these points.

The more particular question concerns the nature of the lexical selection process at the problematic lexical site. Butterworth suggests that at least some such selections are form based, i.e. that the basis of retrieval is the segmental and supersegmental features of words. Recall that Butterworth and Beattie found speech relevant gestures to differ in fluent and hesitant phases of the encoding cycle, with iconic gestures typically occuring at pause sites just prior to lexical items in the fluent phase, and noniconic gestures of emphasis typically occuring during phonation in the hesitant phase. Butterworth suggests this indicates that a more precise (semantic) determination of lexical identity has been achieved at the immediately prelexical hesitation locus in the fluent phase. If one assumes a need for both meaning-based and form-based lexical retrieval processes, and if one accepts the semantic specificity of the gestural data, it might be reasonably argued that the lexical hesitations of the fluent phase reflect form-based access. This is Butterworth's interpretation. However, it may be that the conclusion should be drawn more generally – i.e. not restricted to the fluent phase of speech. There are some such indications in the analysis of speech errors to be discussed later. At this point, we will take up some other indications for the form based retrieval processes which may be related to the hesitation phenomena under discussion. The first such concerns anomic language disorders.

Word finding difficulties ('anomias') are common to several classes of language disorders. We wish to focus on those cases in which anomia is the principal notable dysfunction. The speech of anomic aphasics is, barring the lexical hesitations discussed momentarily, fluent and syntactically well formed. There is no impairment of comprehension processes, and in both these respects they contrast with Wernicke's asphasics, who though fluent, show comprehension deficits and certain syntactic, phonetic and semantic anomalies in their speech (see Saffran, Schwartz and Marin, 1980; Goodglass and Geshwind, 1977). Anomic aphasics provide a striking example of the failure to access word form in the presence of strong evidence that the meaning of the offending word is available. Buckingham's (1979) discussion of lexical retrieval (in posterior fluent aphasics) is instructive. For anomics, he notes the common occurrence of both definitional and pantomimic substitutions – e.g. when 'pen' is the target word, they may say 'it's for writing' and perhaps accompany this with a writing gesture. Buckingham goes on to note that their spontaneous speech is marked not only by circumlocutory and/or 'definitional' expressions offered in lieu of specific lexical targets, but also by very pronounced pauses which occur just prior to the troublesome lexical sites.

. These patients are very certain that they 'know' the word which they cannot utter and in this respect they might be compared to normal subjects in a tip-of-the-tongue (T.O.T.) state (Brown and McNeil, 1966). In such states normal subjects can provide some information about the target word – e.g. its initial sound. Goodglass, Kaplan, Weintraub and Ackerman (1976) compared anomics, Broca's, Wernicke's and conduction aphasics for their ability to produce the phonetic information normally available for T.O.T. words for items they failed to correctly label in a confrontation naming task; they found the anomics less able to provide such information than the others. As we shall see later, the normally available information in a T.O.T. state arguably includes some of the principal access parameters for retrieval from the mental inventory of word forms. Whatever one may be able to say of the specific detail of anomic disorders, their behavior at very least provides a very clear example of the dissociation of semantic descriptions and word form descriptions which is implicated in normal hesitation processes.

There is a further finding from studies of language disorder which may be clearly linked to hesitation. This is a study by Butterworth (1979) of a jargon aphasic. Such cases, typically, though not necessarily, observed among Wernicke's aphasics (Lecours, 1980), show fluent, prosodically normal sounding speech without notable articulatory deviations. Their speech displays most of the normal syntactic and morphological devices of the language though often in aberrant ways (e.g. inappropriate use of prepositions, violation of verb selection restrictions). The distinctive character of their language production is the presence of large numbers of nonsense forms – neologisms; on perceptual grounds, these are integrated into the apparent flow of speech with no more than the normal hesitancy. Butterworth showed for one such case that, in fact, the objectively measured pause preceding such forms is significantly greater than that preceding real word forms; Butterworth hypothesizes that the neologistic forms are generated by jargon aphasics in response to a word retrieval difficulty – rather than halt, the speaker generates a phonetically acceptable slot filler using the phonological and morphological structure building systems normally at one's disposal.[19] Lecours (1980) reports two other cases in which the frequency of interruptions associated with neologisms was compared with control words; he also notes a greater incidence of hesitations for the neologisms. On grounds of the interpretation we have entertained of normal hesitation, especially during fluent speech, one might associate this with failure of form based retrieval. However, since jargon aphasics evidence both form related and meaning related lexical difficulties, the issue is inclear. One cannot tell whether the neologisms should be regarded as arising exclusively from a failure of form based retrieval processes or of meaning based systems or both. We will return to this is our discussion of the normal retrieval mechanisms suggested by speech errors.

Two things seem abundantly clear: First, there is lexically mediated hesitation. Second, some aspects of lexical selection normally proceed independently of the elaboration of phrasal form – the normal hesitation data and the character of anomic and jargon aphasias indicate such a separation. Those processes seem to bear primarily on word form rather than on word meaning. That it *could* be otherwise is, of course, suggested by the typical failures of comprehension and production exhibited by Wernicke's aphasics; for such individuals, there is an apparent failure of both meaning and form constraints on lexical production with a substantial preservation of phrasal organization. Thus, one can imagine, and indeed, so it is asserted for the hesitant phase of normal speech (Goldman-Eisler, 1968), that lexical selection internal to the utterance of a phrase may invoke both meaning and form based decision parameters.

D   THE MECHANISMS OF HESITATION

Logically, there seem to be three types of circumstances which might produce hesitation pauses: (1) The output system halts because processing load is high, *not* in terms of calculation required for current output, but because long range (multilevel) planning momentarily requires all the organism's resources. This is a *limited capacity* account, and it is one in which there need be no direct relation between hesitation locus and the internal structure of the higher order processing. (2) The system normally computes its ouput (at some level) over a given structural domain, and the elements of that planning domain are not released until all elements are determined. This is a *planning unit* account, and it is clearly one in which some regular relation holds between the planning elements and hesitation locus – most naturally perhaps, at their surface initiation. (3) The system is multicomponential, and certain values of elements in a given planning domain are composed and supplied independently of it. This is a *coordination of components* account, and again there is a natural prediction about hesitation locus. Roughly summarized hesitation may reflect three modes: 'Don't bother me, I'm busy', 'Wait till the boat's loaded', and 'It's in the mail'.

The phenomena of hesitation we have discussed seem to be assimilable to these three types without strain. The hesitation pattern of the encoding cycle may be viewed primarily as a consequence of the first (the capacity limitation), junctural and phrasal hesitations of the second (planning units), and lexical hesitations of the third (coordination). This is not to argue that, for example, hesitations at junctural or prelexical loci are not also affected by the encoding cycle. Pauses at those loci are characteristically longer in the hesitant as opposed to the fluent phases of the cycle. What distinguishes this construal in some degree from that of Goldman-Eisler, and to a lesser extent from Butterworth's, is the overt identification of phrase boundary pauses with constructive syntactic activity which is not the consequence of long-term (i.e. multisentence) semantic commitments. We leave these issues for now and return in the context of a discussion of the 'speech error based' model.

4   The speech error model: extending the observational base

The evidence from studies of hesitation and related performances have given strong indications both of general features of the planning process for sentences, and more especially of the relation between message level processes and sentence level processes. Specific structural claims have been raised with respect to surface and deep clausal structure and of lexical selection processes relative to phrasal planning. We turn now to the other major evidential type under consideration, that of speech errors, for here there are further indications of the structure of the sentence processing level.

A   INTERNAL STRUCTURE OF THE SENTENCE PROCESSING LEVEL

On grounds of the speech error observations discussed by Fromkin, we already know that such data indicates significant internal details of the sentence construction process. We know, in particular, that we must distinguish between those processes which give rise to, e.g. sound movement errors and those which account for regular phonological variations – e.g. the sound processes which determine the phonetic shape of affixal elements like tense and number. Whatever aspects of sentence construction are implicated in such movement errors must be accomplished before the phonetic shape of the accommodating structures is fixed. One way to do this is to postulate the existence of sub-processing levels internal to the sentence construction level; for the case of accommodations, the target representation of such a processing level would specify the detailed phonetic shape of an utterance and would operate on (accept as input) representations whose properties will account for the constraints on such movement errors as may yield accommodations. We will consider several aspects of speech errors which elaborate this approach.

1   *Movement errors.* Speech errors come in variegated types. Among the most informative are those in which one or more of the intended elements are mislocated. I have argued previously (Garrett, 1975, 1976, 1980a) that the observed constraints on two types of movement errors, *exchanges* and *shifts,* converge on a system with at least two processing levels in addition to that which determines detailed phonetic form. I labelled these (on simple descriptive grounds *vis-à-vis* error regularities) the 'functional' and 'positional' levels. These were intended to account, respectively, for the lexical errors in which phrasal membership and role seem at computational issue, and for the sound and morpheme errors in which phrasal

location and lexical attachment seem at issue. The functional level is hypothesized to be the first ordered sentence level, and thus developed under message level control; correspondingly, the positional level is assumed to be developed from functional level structures. Under the strongest hypothesis, message level structures affect positional level structure *only* via functional level structure.

To illustrate briefly: if one first considers only (completed) exchange errors, involving whatever element type (e.g. (*a*)-(*c*), error elements in italics), several things are soon apparent. There are generally applicable

(*a*) 'Well you can cut *rain* in the *trees*'.
        'I think he *gave* and *came*. . .'. (a paper)
        'Why was that *horn* blowing its *train*?'

(*b*) 'That's why they sell the *cheaps drink*'. (drinks cheap)
        'But the *cleans twoer*'. (two's cleaner)
        'She *writes* her *slant*ing. . .'. (. . .slants her writing)

(*c*) 'No. . . it's. . . Bria*th* Kee*n*' (Brian Keith)
        '. . ./æbstrit/ and /kankrækt/'. (abstract and concrete)
        'And this is the *l*arietal *p*obe'. (parietal lobe)

constraints on error excursions – i.e. on the surface domain which error elements 'traverse'. One form of that constraint has been stated in terms of phonemic clauses. Boomer and Laver (1968) noted that the great majority of the error interactions which they had observed (these were mostly sound errors) involved two elements of the same phonemic clause. This converges with the conclusion drawn by Boomer from his analysis of hesitations. As we noted in our discussion of hesitations, however, the data suggesting this conclusion do not readily distinguish the merits of a characterization in terms of such prosodic units from one in terms of purely syntactic phrases. As we shall see, the matter is complex, for there are more detailed constraints than those of clause structure and they apply in different ways to different error types. Specifically, there seems to be a constraint of simple phrasal structure for both word exchanges (e.g. *a*) and sound exchanges (e.g. *c*). But, while the former are constrained to involve words of different phrases, the latter show the reverse property – they usually arise from two words in the same phrase. A further important feature of word exchanges is that the interacting words are of corresponding grammatical categories and play similar roles in their respective phrases; sound exchanges show no such respect for phrasal role even in those few cases which do involve elements of different phrases. To this we may add the observation that word exchanges typically traverse greater distances (measured in syllables or words) than do sound exchanges, and again, this holds even for the sound exchanges which cross phrase boundaries.

The facts adduced seem to require more than a single level of analysis in order to account for all exchange errors, to wit: the postulation, on the one hand, of a multiphrasal planning level in which the identity and phrasal role of lexical items is at issue (i.e. the functional level) and, on the other hand, a single-phrase planning level in which the serial position and lexically dependent aspect of the phonetic shape of lexical items is fixed (i.e. the positional level). In keeping with this, the evidence suggests various effects of the segmental analysis of words on sound exchanges (Fromkin, 1971, 1980 and references therein), but there is little indication of such influences on the items that appear in word exchanges (Garrett, 1980a). This latter point is further reinforced by a category of errors, so far not mentioned, in which a multiword string takes part in an exchange, either with another such or with a single word; in either case, the exchanged items have the properties of single word exchanges: they are of the same grammatical category in distinct phrases, and segmental similarity can scarcely be argued to play a role. Fromkin's case: 'I've got to get some *kids* for the *macadamia nuts*' is exemplary. What is at issue, in the word and phrase errors, is phrasal role of the exchanged elements, not their length or segmental structure.

2   *The exchange mechanism.* My working hypothesis has been that exchange errors arise as a consequence of the processes which relate planning levels to each other, and, in particular, those in which the ordering relations among the elements of the levels differ; thus, word exchanges are hypothesized to arise in the construction of the functional level from message level structures, and sound exchanges in the construction of the positional level from functional level structures. Some attention to another type of exchange error will make the presumed mechanisms more explicit.

Errors, like those of the example in (*b*) (called 'stranding errors' because the major portions of two words exchange leaving one or more segments behind), are predominantly within-phrase errors, and they are thus to be associated with planning of the positional level.[20] The elements stranded in such errors are by and large inflectional, though there is occasional involvement of some prefixes or suffixes of highly productive derivational types like adverbial *ly* and agentive *er*. It is clear that morphological structure is implicated since stranding exchanges which do not involve stems are rare. When these observations are combined with one further – namely that *all* exchanges, word, sound, and stranding, are almost entirely confined to major (lexical) categories (N, V, Adj, Prep) – a mechanism suggests itself; the development of positional level structures involves the assignment of segmentally specified major category items to sites in a surface phrasal planning frame which bears inflectional elements and minor category free forms. Sound exchanges are assumed to arise in the segmental interpretation of the lexical items as they are assigned to positions in the planning frame. If normal phrasal stress is assigned to such a frame (or, equivalently for these purposes, computed from its geometry), we may simultaneously account for the character of moved and stranded elements and for the preservation of phrasal stress (discussed in section 3). Indeed, it is principally the requirement of stress specification that justifies a claim for phrasal geometry at this point. Further, we may note that a 'negative' prediction which this account of exchanges commits one to is borne out: elements of the hypothesized planning frames do not themselves exchange (e.g. grammatical formatives whether bound or free). We will return to this hypothesized process in discussion of lexical selection processes indicated by word substitutions.

Shattuck-Hufnagel (1979) has argued for an exchange mechanism in which an independent framework of segmental slots is interpreted from the segmental information stored for each lexical item. On this view, a detailed segmental skeleton for each lexical site would be a part of the planning frame, and lexical retrieval would provide the detail of that structure. These suggestions irresistably call to mind the quite independently motivated formal proposals for phonological structures which separate segmental structures from stress and tonal features of language (see, e.g. Liberman and Prince, 1977; Halle and Vergnaud, 1980 and references therein). Such phonological structures consist of linked, but independent representations which accommodate the regularities of segmental and suprasegmental phenomena. We are not in a position to identify the planning structures under discussion with particular formal proposals, but as we shall see in a later discussion, there is indeed reason to seek such an identification.

One further class of errors may be readily assimilated to the account so far offered; these are errors, called 'shifts', in which a single element of the intended utterance is mislocated, and in the case of sound elements and bound morphemes, a certifiable 'hole' is left behind. The examples in (d) and (e) show typical word and morpheme shifts. The elements which predominate here

(d) 'Did you stay up * late *very* last night?'
  'You * have to *do* learn that. . .'.
  'Who * did I think *else* had left?'

(e) '. . .all those people mumble, mumble* behind*ing* the door'. (mumbling)
  'It probably get* out*s* a little'. (. . .gets out. . .)
  'I had forgot* about*en* that'. (. . .forgotten about. . .)

are just the ones so notable by their absence from exchanges. Given the assumption that these elements are represented in the planning frames, shift errors are understandable as a consequence of the processes which determine the siting of such elements in the (lexically interpreted) terminal string of the positional representation (see Garrett, 1980b).

As a final note, we should observe that shift errors also provide the only notable examples of stresses which move *with* their intended sites rather than remaining at whatever phrasal locus they would have appeared on in an error free utterance (Cutler, 1980). In short, phrasal stress (associated with sites of items that exchange) is preserved; the stress for items which shift (rather than exchange) moves with those items. This comports with the view that the stress of major category items is calculated from the phrasal geometry, while that associated with contrastive or emphatic stress is marked on the items bearing it.

The processes we have been discussing have a ready connection to the conclusions reached from examination of hesitation phenomena. We will explore that connection after discussing the implications of speech errors and certain language disorders for lexical retrieval mechanisms.

B   COMPUTATIONAL VOCABULARIES: OPEN AND CLOSED CLASSES

The distinction I have drawn between functional and positional levels incorporates a distinction between two classes of vocabulary elements; roughly, between 'content' and 'function' words or between major and minor grammatical categories. That distinction will be referred to as the contrast between *open* and *closed* class vocabularies to emphasize its computational reference. It is not clear precisely what the formal counterpart of the distinction may be for the speech error processes – though we will shortly consider some possibilities – nor precisely what relation holds among the similar distinctions that seem relevant to several performance domains other than speech errors: language development, language disorders, and various memory and comprehension processes. It is nevertheless clear that there is a very similar distinction at work in all these areas, and we will draw variously on observations made of them as we discuss the implications of word substitution errors.

The thesis that is indicated by the character of both the word substitution errors like those of (*f*) and (*g*), and by the properties of the movement errors we have just been discussing is that open and closed classes are recruited at quite different points in the sentence construction process. Moreover,

(*f*) 'If any of you cats are gonna be in Las Vegas in the *recent*. . . in the near future, and. . .'.
      'It's a far cry from the twenty-five *dollar* days'. (cent)
(*g*) 'You look all set for an *exhibition*'. (expedition)
      'He was carrying on about *optical* binary search'. (optimal)

the word substitution errors indicate two lexical retrieval steps for open class vocabulary. As suggested in our discussion of Fromkin's proposals, these are retrieval steps based, respectively, on word form and word meaning; (*f*) and (*g*) provide examples of the two types of error relations. We will first discuss the retrieval mechanisms for open class vocabulary and then consider their relation to the processing structures indicated by movement errors.

1   *Dissociation of meaning and form.* As the errors of (*f*) and (*g*) suggest, there are two quite clear types of relation which mediate word substitu-

tion errors in normal spontaneous speech. Errors of both these types are relatively common and we have. therefore, a relatively large sample upon which to base judgments of effective relations in such cases. Though there are certainly word substitution errors which do not fall easily into one of these two classes, they are a minority.[21] One of the most striking and, I believe, significant aspects of these two bases of error is their apparent independence of each other. It is the case that when a target/intrusion pair bear a strong similarity of form, there is rarely any discernable meaning relation, and the reverse is also true – if there is a clear meaning relation, similarity of form is not often observed. In short, if one were to propose a retrieval system for production in which words were simultaneously considered for their meaning and form – e.g. by the postulation of a system in which words were classified by their form internal to semantic categories, or by meaning internal to form categories, such systems would not survive the test of the error patterns. The indication is of two distinct systems for selecting lexical targets.

2   *Open class retrieval: the parameters of form.* If we examine the detail of similarities in form between target and intrusion words, we may expect to find some indications of the organizational principles of the form based word inventory. The first things to note are that the correspondence of form is most marked for word initial segments and that the grammatical categories of target and intrusion are almost invariably the same. In their analysis of such word substitution errors, Fay and Cutler (1977) use the meaning related errors in their corpus as a basis for evaluating the import of the apparent similarities of form for those substitutions which display no obvious meaning relation. Both meaning related and nonmeaning related substitution sets show the correspondence of grammatical category; however, the nonmeaning set displayed greater overall similarity of form, and this was most pronounced for word initial segments.[22] There is, as well, evidence for similar main stress placement and similar overall length. Again, these observations call to mind regularities of T.O.T. states. The similarities of form observed for word substitution errors are also found in lexical targets of T.O.T. reports: initial segmental analysis, number of syllables, and stress placement (see Browman, 1978, and references therein).

Fay and Cutler (1977) note the similarity of these descriptive parameters (particularly that of initial segments) to those effective in word recognition processes (see, e.g. Marslen-Wilson, 1980, for some recent experimental findings; see Browman, 1980, for some remarks connecting speech errors to lexical misperceptions). They argue that the speech error results may be accomodated by supposing that recognition and production processes employ the same inventory of word forms. If we accept this, and it is a plausible hypothesis, it suggests that the constraint of grammatical category observed for such errors may *not* have an account in terms of the retrieval code for lexical items. Such evidence as there is for a grammatical category effect on look up processes in word recognition is negative (see, e.g. Forster and Bednall, 1977; Swinney, 1980). This is not to say that such category constraints do not play a significant role in recognition processes or production process, but that such roles may best be considered an aspect of postaccess selection or decision processes rather than as determinants of primary contact with word forms.

To these observations of speech error regularities, we may add those concerning lexical errors in aphasics. Buckingham (1980) and Lecours (1980) observe that the two major classes of word substitution errors in normal speech, meaning based and form based, also occur in aphasic speech. Of particular interest is the apparent dissociability of the two error bases in different disorders – i.e. in some, the dominant error forms are semantic, with relatively few phonemic paraphasias occurring; in others (e.g. conduction aphasia), the reverse is true. The recovery sequence from neologistic jargon aphasia is relevant in this connection, for it appears (see, e.g. Buckingham and Kertesz, 1976 and references therein) that these error types are typically displayed with different time courses. Though these aspects of aphasic disorders comport with the independence of the two bases of lexical selection, the more detailed conclusions about the role of the serial position of sound segments and of stress pattern are less clear. Where word form does seem to connect a target/intrusion pair in aphasic speech, the correspondence of segments does not seem constrained in the same way as in normal form-based substitutions; e.g. segmental mismatches at word initial positions are not uncommon. I should stress that this 'conclusion' arises from no more than an inspection of published examples of form related substitutions (viz. those in references cited). Such observation is, however, quite compatible with a reservation about such word substitutions expressed by both Buckingham (1980) and Lecours (1980). Since phonemic para- phasias are common in these groups, it's quite possible that the 'word substitutions' are no more than sound substitutions which happen to yield a real word. Lecours reports a computer simulation of such errors in which random sound changes yield words in about the observed propor- tion (Lecours, Deloche and Lhermitte, 1973). If, however, it were to prove that sound based word substitutions did not occur in aphasia at all, it would be rather remarkable, and the more conservative view is simply that one cannot identify the 'real cases' with confidence. This seems a question worth careful consideration, however, for one must recall the Goodglass et al. (1976) finding that anomics (tested in a T.O.T. task) did not have access to just that information about word form which seems to mediate form-based substitutions.

3   *Open class retrieval: meaning relations.* Given the striking regularities of form based substitution errors, and the suggestion therein for specific

lexical access processes, one might reasonably undertake a similarly motivated investigation of meaning related substitutions. Matters are, however, rather less clear in the semantic arena.

There are two classes of meaning related word errors to consider – the word substitutions already noted and, in addition, word blends. These latter are cases in which elements from two words occupy the slot intended for only one, e.g. (*h*). With these we may also consider reports of meaning related errors in language disorders.

(*h*) 'Dinner is ret'. (ready/set)

    'They have more protein than meef'. (meat/beef)

    '. . .some burnt out cimber'. (cinder/ember)

In looking at such cases, one observes that substitutions and blends differ in the relations which (presumably) precipitate them: substitutions are usually between roughly antonymic pairs or between coordinate members of a class (viz, color terms, kinship terms, body part terms, etc.); there is a meaning relation, but it is not meaning preserving *vis à vis the intent of the speaker. The words of blends are, by contrast, virtually always 'synonomous'*[23] (N.B. that synonomy is situation specific, not context free; the words which blend have equivalent force in the intended construction, not in general). A further difference is that blends occasionally involve the combination of a subordinate and one of its superordinates (e.g. move/run combined to yield 'mrun', or meat/beef to yield 'meef'); this is rarely observed for substitution errors. (See Hotopf, 1980, for some discussion.) Thus, whether one considers substitutions and blends, or only the former, will determine how seriously one takes the restriction against interactions between subordinates and superordinates, and hence of whether one views the lexical selection process as one restricted by levels within a heirarchy of categories. Observations from language disorders are relevant to this particular question. Buckingham (1979) discusses meaning related word substitutions in aphasic speech (those for 'posterior fluent aphasia'), and he notes reports of substitutions which violate the level restriction noted for normal speech. He argues, however, that these might be more properly viewed as 'partial descriptions' intended to compensate for word finding difficulties rather than as errors. If so, then the true cases of error in the aphasic groups would comport with the regularities of word substitutions by normal speakers, and the claim for a level restriction might be maintained.

Buckingham treats this and other issues of meaning that he discusses within a definitional framework – as did Fromkin (see section 2B) in her construal of lexical selection processes. However, these observations, though they may, of course, be described in such ways, do not produce a substantive contrast between definitional treatments of word meaning and meaning postulate accounts (i.e. that adopted for the preliminary model, section 1C). Both normal speech errors and those of aphasics may be accommodated in a meaning postulate system since it does not have lesser descriptive power than a system of semantic features. What one would like of course, is some feature of error distributions (or of any other production phenomenon, for that matter) which is better accommodated on one or the other of these systems. The facts so far adduced do not provide a clear case, although if one presses the natural account of word substitutions in a definitional framework, the apparent levels restriction is somewhat at odds with it. That is, if one assumes that items with major featural overlap are candidates for substitution processes – witness the prominence of antonyms and coordinate class members in such, the seeming prohibition against intersubstitution of subordinates and super-ordinates is puzzling. All the features of a superordinate are shared by its subordinates, while the latter must differ from each other by at least one feature. So, one must observe that featural similarity is greatest for just the cases which do not (or only very rarely) produce substitutions. The existence of blend errors, which do cross levels, shows that the potential for such errors is there (in terms of the simultaneous activation of lexical candidates at different levels).[24]

Whatever the merits of such arguments, there are some other observations which provide reason to prefer a more unfettered inferential account than that provided by definitional structures. The clearly antonymic or co-category members do not exhaust the substitutions cases by any means, and many of the remainder display a context sensitivity reminiscent of the blends. Here we find substitutions which are not very compelling examples of feature overlap, but which are readily under-standable as inferences mediated by a parameter relevant to the speaker's communicative intention. Two examples will illustrate:

  (i) 'I just put it in the oven at a very low *speed*'. (temperature)
       (The idea to be communicated was that the ham was to cook slowly)
       'They've only been *awake* three weeks'. (open)
       (The idea to be communicated was that the establishment – a
       restaurant – was a just functioning, young operation; immature
       and deserving the benefit of the doubt.)

In sum, it is arguable that the retrieval process of meaning determined errors is more conceptual than lexical, and that this is so whether one considers only substitutions or includes blends as well. If such errors are assumed to originate during the process which maps from message to functional level, such a characterization would seem natural.

4   *Open class retrieval and phrasal planning mechanisms*. If we bring together the observations about word substitution errors with those about ex-change errors, some obvious coordinations suggest themselves. We note that word exchanges are identified with the process of constructing functional level representations, are constrained by grammatical cate-gory, confined to open class elements, and not influenced by word form. Just these observations may be made of meaning related word substitu-

tions, which we have construed in the previous section as inferential. Hence, the natural articulation of these observations associates such word substitutions with the processes which select lexical candidates for assignment to functional level structures. We may further reason that the lack of meaning relations between the items of word exchanges indicates that although lexical selection for this level is constrained both by the role of an item in functional level representations and by meaning relations, only the former determines assignment of a selected item to a functional level structure. This follows from the hypothesis that word exchange errors arise from the misassignment of items to functional level representations and from the observation that the items in exchanges do not show meaning relations of the same type as those holding between target and intrusion in word substitution errors (Garrett, 1976; MacKay, 1980). This is tantamount to the claim that sentence level processes, once set in train, are neither monitored for nor couched in terms of meaning parameters.

The connection of form based word substitutions to movement error mechanisms is similarly straightforward on the given hypotheses. Sound exchanges and stranding errors are uninfluenced by meaning, confined to open class vocabulary, and implicate various aspects of the segmental, morphological and stress descriptions of their source words. Just so, and in detail, for form based word substitution errors. We earlier commented on the similarities of word initial segments in form based word substitutions, so it is worth noting that the most common site of sound exchanges is at word initial positions. It is at least intriguing that the aspects of word form most clearly implicated in form based lexical retrieval are just the aspects of word form most likely to contribute to sound exchanges. Form based word substitutions, on this account, arise in the lexical selection process which, under the constraints of the functional level, retrieve items from an inventory of word forms for subsequent insertion into the phrasal planning frames of the positional level. These latter, it will be recalled, are assumed to represent those aspects of phrasal geometry which determine normal stress assignment, and to include the specification of closed class vocabulary, both bound and free.

Form related word substitutions are thus assumed to arise at a point in the process which sets the stage for sound exchange errors and most stranding errors. These latter, sound exchanges and stranding errors, are hypothesized to occur in the processes which associate segmental specifications of major category items with sites in the planning frame. It is unclear precisely how this process should be connected to lexical retrieval beyond the points already raised. Minimally, the mechanisms postulated for these processes must permit us to reconstruct the regularities of exchange and stranding errors; more ambitiously, we would like to assimilate regularities of language disorders like those of the

conduction aphasics, anomics and jargon aphasics who show impairments of lexical processing based on word form. Not much of detail can be
said of these matters on current evidence, though we will comment on
some possibilities in ensuing discussion.

Before raising such matters, we must first take note of some further
consequences of the preceding argument. These concern morphological
structure of words. First of all, note that forms at the functional level must
include derivational variants, both those involving prefixes and those
involving derivational suffixes. This follows not only from the fact that
such variations, unlike inflectional variants, frequently have meaning
consequences which are not derivable compositionally, but also from the
fact that suffixes change grammatical category. Since grammatical category is assumed to be determined at the functional level, we may not
assign such word formation processes to the mechanisms which map
from functional to positional representations. This is not to say, of course,
that the phonological consequences of such structures must be represented at that point. All that is required is that the derivational morphs be
associated with their lexical bearers. There are, in fact, some further
observations about lexical errors which suggest the conclusion that the
analysis of movement errors requires for derivational suffixes.

Cutler (1980) has argued for a morphological decomposition of words
in access processes for production on the basis of lexical stress errors. She
points out that the predominant stress error pattern is one in which
derivationally related forms are conflated. N.B.: this is not a case of
substitution of one derivational variant for another; rather, in these cases
the stress appropriate to one form (e.g. 'psychológical') appears in the
morphology of another (e.g. as when 'psychólogist' is pronounced
'psychológist'). Cutler argues that an interpretation of such errors as
misselections from an inventory organized by similarity of form is not
persuasive because many of the stress errors hold between words of
different surface phonetic form, length and, of course, stress locus. And,
as we have earlier noted, it is just these factors which strongly relate target
and intrusion for those word substitutions which do not involve meaning
relations. Stress errors, which *do* implicate meaning related word pairs,
are thus more like the errors of (*f*) than of (*g*), and Cutler accordingly
assigns them to, 'a fairly early level in the production process', (1980,
p. 71), i.e. to a point prior to form based selection in the model we are
discussing. As we have been describing the production process, derivationally related forms would be jointly represented at the point where
message level constraints determine lexical identity. Whatever the detail
of selection, the process which yields such stress errors must occur prior
to the point of word exchange errors, for grammatical category has been
fixed at that point.[25]

We have have just argued that derivational variants of form arising
from suffixation should not be assigned to processes which map from the

functional to the positional level, and we noted that because of the meaning consequences of prefixes, such must also be marked at the functional level. There is, however, a somewhat different aspect of the involvement of prefixes in the lexical retrieval processes which deserves comment. Recall that the most striking regularity for form based errors is correspondence of the word initial segments in target and intrusion. There are, in fact, occasional exceptions to this generalization, and when independently examined, they are informative. Fay (in press) reports on the regularities of such exceptions and finds that they are, by and large, understandable as the intersubstitution of stems and their prefixed forms, the inappropriate assignment of prefixes, or the substitution of phonetically similar stems (with different prefixes) for each other. In short, the indication is that the form inventory is stem organized, or minimally, includes stems as well as prefixed forms. On the assumption that the word form inventory for production is the same as that for comprehension, this interpretation of word substitution errors comports with independent evidence from word recognition studies. Several such studies indicate that 'prefix stripping' is a part of the access routine in word recognition (see, e.g. Taft and Forster 1976; Murrell and Morton, 1974).

Further relevant observations may be derived from studies of language disorders, particularly the jargon aphasias. It is clear that the essential features of derivational and inflectional morphology are preserved for such cases in spite of catastrophic impairment of control over base forms of lexical items. The neologistic jargon discussed by Buckingham (1980) and by Lecours (1980) presents forms which are properly inflected and which incorporate derivational affixes appropriate to their prosodic and lexical environment. Indeed, Lecours reports one case in which the neologistic productions were dominated by forms which combined real stems and real affixes but in improper combinations – i.e. particular affixes were attached to stems which did not normally bear them. All these observations indicate the possibility of dissociating the processes responsible for retrieval and segmental interpretation of stems from that responsible for the association of bound morphemes (whether inflectional or derivational) with their stems. And, the case described by Lecours quite clearly indicates that these word formation processes may themselves be impaired even when the segmental structure of the stems is correctly specified. That is, it is not because the segmental structure of the stems is impaired that the morphological processes are deranged. One natural account, as Lecours suggests, is that these departures are a consequence of the jargon aphasic's impaired semantic processes; this implicates the message to function level mapping – i.e. the locus of derivation which exchanges require.

We should take note at this point that such reports of language disorders do not on current analysis provide any support for the sharp distinction drawn in the speech error model between inflectional and derivational affixes – both seem to be preserved in neologistic jargon. It is likely that a careful examination of specific derivational and inflectional classes in jargon aphasia will be required to determine whether such data supports or disagrees with this feature of the speech error model.

Though we have not so far discussed it, the agrammatic symptoms of Broca's aphasia may be assimilated to the model we are discussing, for agrammatism seems in important respects to represent a preservation of what jargon aphasics have lost, with concomitant impairment of what jargon cases retain. We will take up this and related matters in the following sections.

5   *Closed class 'retrieval'*. In all the foregoing discussion, the separation of open and closed class mechanisms has been assumed; several reasons for that assumption have already been discussed. To recapitulate briefly; exchange and shift errors distinguish the two classes, for the former are dominantly movements of open class elements while the latter are dominantly movements of closed class elements, and this applies with equal force to bound and free forms. We have also noted that the major features of anterior and posterior types of language disorders distinguish the two vocabulary classes. In jargon aphasia, closed class vocabulary, bound or free, is relatively preserved in spite of grave difficulties with open class forms (Lecours, 1980; Buckingham, 1980). Lecours reports a systematic catalog of neologisms from samples of the speech of two such cases; the neologisms were entirely confined to nouns, verbs, adjectives and a few lexical adverbs, none occurred in any other category (including auxilliary verbs). Of some 697 neologistic forms, he was able to classify nearly all (undifferentiated cases were less than five percent).

In sharp contrast to the jargon of Wernicke's aphasia, the agrammatism of Broca's aphasia presents the complementary deficit. Saffran *et al.* (1980) comment specifically on this complementarity, describing agrammatics' characteristic failures with grammatical morphemes – what we are calling members of the closed class – as a problem specific chiefly to output systems. The other side of the coin, of course, is that agrammatic speakers' production and comprehension of open class forms is much better preserved than is that of the closed class. Note, however, that open class performance is by no means entirely spared – the range and type of open class items is substantially reduced in their production. In general, however, agrammatic aphasics are quite evidently in better possession than jargon aphasics of the lexical inventory as it is represented for inferential purposes (see also Zurif and Caramazza, 1976). What the agrammatics are notably deficient in is the language specific devices of phrasal integration. These latter are, for the speech error model, most obviously related to the mapping from functional to positional levels of representation, though it is by no means obvious that the deficit should be characterized solely in terms of the devices we have identified with that level. In particular, there is no overt expression of the role of verb structure in constraints on the positional level of the speech error model, though the natural place to express such would be at the functional level of representation in that model. In this regard, it is remarked that agrammatic speech is notably lacking in its use of verbs (Saffran *et al.*, 1980; Berndt and Caramazza, 1980). It is, however, not possible to make a definitive interpretation of this observation either with respect to the speech error model or with respect to features of agrammatism. In neither instance is there sufficiently detailed information upon which to base an analysis. We will have a subsequent occasion to return to the characterization of agrammatism. At this point, it is perhaps sufficient to note that the principal features of both agrammatism in Broca's aphasia and jargon in Wernicke's aphasia and conduction aphasia reinforce the conclusions reached on the basis of speech error analysis: closed and open class vocabularies play distinct computational roles in the sentence construction process.

The mechanism we have adopted for realizing this vocabulary distinction is one that associates specific error mechanisms (substitution, exchange and shift) with specific sentence building processes. So, for example, the processes which determine open class identity precede those which determine the segmental analysis of open class items, and both of these are distinct from the processes which determine the identity and form of closed class items. The former, open classes, are retrieved and elaborated to some significant degree independently of their phrasal environment, while the latter, closed classes, are *identified* with their phrasal configurations. The processes of their selection and segmental specification are thus sharply distinguished.

Given the argument that closed elements are features of positional frames, the notion 'closed class retrieval' is somewhat ill formed. Closed class identity is fixed by the (unknown) processes which select phrasal frames under the constraints imposed by functional level representation. We may, however, do as we did in discussion of open class retrieval and turn to studies of comprehension for some evidence. There we find, as before, evidence of a parallel distinction in recognition processes. A number of experimental results suggest qualitatively different recognition processes for open and closed class vocabulary (see Bradley and Garrett, 1980). In the absence of any clearly developed account of relations between comprehension and production systems at the level of phrasal construction and parsing, such a correspondence is, of course, merely suggestive. It is, however, of interest that agrammatics, who show such a striking production deficit for the closed class, also show anomalous recognition performance for such items (see Bradley, Garrett and Zurif, 1980).

Perhaps the minimal summary claim that is warranted on grounds of the speech error observations is that open and closed class selection procedures are distinct, and, based solely on the rarity of segmental errors involving the closed class items, one might further argue that, though their identity is fixed in positional frames, their segmental structure is not until a point following the lexical interpretation of the positional string – i.e. the point at which shift errors are assumed to occur. A version of such a claim is consequent upon an argument we will present in the following section, in which we consider a formal interpretation of the positional level.

C THE POSITIONAL LEVEL AS PHONOLOGICAL

The affinity of many of the observations we have made about positional level processes in speech errors with phonological processes in formal grammars is obvious. It should be borne in mind, however, that these observations of speech error processes, which indicate an isolation of computational processes along the same dimensions as those of formal accounts of language, are logically independent of the observational base of formal theories. Hence, the convergence, if such it is *in detail*, is of great interest. Though we cannot explore the matter at length here, it is well worth illustrating what sort of argument would support the identification of formal levels of linguistic analysis and the processing levels under discussion. We will consider two related sets of observations, one from speech errors and one from analysis of agrammatism.

The speech error case, as the agrammatic case, concerns prepositions. In the speech error data one observes an apparent anomaly: prepositions, which in ordinary parlance are classed with other 'function words', nonetheless appear in word exchange errors. Barring this case, one might properly say that only major category words (N, V, Adj) – the 'content words' – appear in word exchange errors typical of the functional level of processing (i.e. exchanges between phrases of words in corresponding roles). In fact, of course, the involvement of prepositions at this level is not anomalous, for they, like nouns, verbs, and adjectives, head a major phrasal class (prepositional phrases). It might therefore, be more apt to formulate the regularities of word exchanges in terms of phrasal heads. If one does so, however, the other horn of a hidden dilemma appears. For, the generalization about words which may themselves exchange holds also for words which may contribute to sound exchange errors – except for prepositions. In sound exchange errors, propositions behave like other minor category words. Thus, for example, while verbs and nouns in their NP arguments may exchange sound segments (or features), prepositions and words in *their* NP arguments do not seem to do so. Thus, prepositions, like inflectional morphemes, quantifiers, articles, conjunctions, etc. seem 'insulated' from sound exchange processes – i.e. they are closed class. How can an element be both closed (*vide* sound exchanges) and open (*vide* word exchanges) class? The answer, of course, lies in the already established separation of the functional and positional levels – at the functional level, prepositions are lexical, and at the positional level they are not. But the 'demotion' of prepositions to closed class estate as a consequence of that level shift is quite *ad hoc* if one construes both planning levels solely in syntactic terms. However, if one were to construe the shift from functional level to positional level as a shift from a specifically syntactic and/or logical level to the (systematic phonemic) phonological level, the prepositional shift in status would be required, for, phonologically, most prepositions behave with the minor classes.

This line of argument parallels one (of several) made by Kean (1977, 1980) for the formal characterization of the symptoms of agrammatism. Kean notes that a characterization of agrammatism as a specifically syntactic deficit runs afoul of this same problem. The sentence elements which agrammatics experience most difficulty with are a mixed bag syntactically – e.g. prepositions and determiners which are phrasally introduced are sorted together with other elements which are reflexes of their syntactic environment (e.g. genitive 'of', complementizers 'that', 'for', 'to'), plus inflectional devices only abstractly represented at the syntactic level. It is only at the phonological level of grammatical analysis that this heterogeneous set is rendered uniform. Thus, Kean's claim that agrammatism should be considered, formally, as a phonological deficit rather than as a syntactic one.

It should be stressed at this point that, for the positional level in speech errors or for the characterization of agrammatism, the identification of the descriptive type as phonological does *not* exclude syntactic categories from a role; the phonological level of representation includes the major features of surface syntactic phrasal organization. However, though the role of syntactic variables in speech processes at that level is entirely supportable on a phonological construal, our interpretation of error data must be affected in diverse ways if we adopt such a course. To cite one example only, the relevant sense of 'phrasal membership' is altered for errors deemed to occur in constructing the positional level – phonological phrasing rather than syntactic phrasing must be the domain of interaction for sound and stranding exchanges and for shifts. Very often, of course, this will not be decisive for our view of the data – phonological phrasing and syntactic phrasing are intimately connected, and the data will be susceptible of either description. This state of affairs recalls our earlier discussion of hesitation phenomena in which Boomer's analysis in terms of a prosodically defined unit (phonemic clauses) contends with surface and deep syntactic clauses. In that case, as in this one, though we cannot yet settle the matter definitively, there are preliminary grounds for choice So, for hesitations, it looks as though a syntactic account is preferred for results like those of Ford (1978) which show syntactically detailed hesitation dependencies for structures whose normal prosodic construal would not suggest boundary effects (e.g. as the left boundary of subject-less infinitives). Of course, without an attempt at systematic treatment of her cases in terms of a detailed prosodic theory, one cannot conclusively rule out such an account. Similarly, for speech errors, the matter will require careful inquiry not yet done; my initial examination of currently available error data does indicate that where sound exchanges might distinguish syntactic phrasing from the (inferred, normal) intonational phrasing, the latter is preferred. It must be borne in mind that, for this thesis, the sort of orthographic records on current error corpora permit only limited interpretation. Future data collection will require a more detailed record of stress and intonational features in order to deal satisfactorily with this class of questions.

At this point, it might seem that we have, *vis-à-vis* the speech errors, come full circle to the proposal originally offered by Boomer and Laver (1968), a proposal which bounded the speech error planning units as Boomer (1965) bounded the hesitations units – as phonemic clauses – a prosodically defined macrosegment.[26] There is, of course, some justice in such an observation. However, the 'round trip' even if such it proved to be, would not be in vain since we have picked up considerable useful baggage on the way which bears on the elaboration of such representations. That detail will help us in the process of evaluating the nature of phonological processes in sentence production – no trivial matter, since that theory domain is as stimulatingly lacking in detailed consensus as the rest of linguistics. There are, moreover, the structures implicated by word substitution and word exchanges which seem less readily dealt with in such terms. Indeed, there is at least some reason to look for a convergence between accounts of those error features and the hesitation distributions reported by Ford (1978), a possibility we will briefly consider in the next section.

One final note on the argument for phonological interpretation of the positional level. The examples given of the role of prepositions in speech errors and in agrammatism are, strictly speaking, independent arguments to a phonological interpretation of certain facts in each of these behavioral domains. Their proximity is not to suggest that they are, at this juncture, logically connected (other than by similarity of argument form). One needs, for something stronger, an argument which, on independent grounds, relates these domains to each other. Such is not in the offing. In the meantime we shall have to content ourselves with assembling detailed correspondences. And, there is, of course, more detail than the examples offered (see Kean, 1977, 1980; and Garrett and Kean, 1980 for some further discussion).

D   CONNECTIONS TO HESITATION PHENOMENA

There are a number of interesting points of contact between the analysis of production processes suggested by speech errors and that suggested by hesitations. These include both lexical selection and phrasal planning processes.

1   *The speech error model* requires that, in the normal course of events, prelexical hesitations be viewed as form based – i.e. the hesitation arises not out of a search for a lexical item which satisfies conceptual constraints, but rather out of the processes which retrieve items from the form based inventory. This follows from the earlier arguments that prelexical hesitations occur at a point for which surface phrasal geometry has been established; in the speech error model, that circumstance obtains *after* the functional level, and by the speech error hypothesis, lexical identity is already established at the functional level. Still, this is not to deny the possible existence of meaning based lexical hesitations – it is to place some constraint on their character. So, for example, one might look for a qualitative difference in the prosody for putatively meaning based lexical hesitations. They might precipitate some significant dysprosody, or, alternatively, they might be confined to lexical classes for which there is significantly lesser dependence of phrasal structure on lexical identity (e.g. many classes of nouns). It is certainly true that quite a substantial degree of phrasal structure may be sustained in the absence of lexical constraint – witness the ability of normal speakers to 'understand' and produce syntactically structured nonsense strings ('Jabberwocky'), and the phrasal organization of the speech of Wernicke's aphasics. One thing is clear: in this case as in most others in which the question arises, it will be no easy matter to distinguish meaning and form based determinants of behavior.

2   *Clausal limits.* In discussing the encoding cycle as a hesitation determinant, we noted suggestions (Beattie, 1980) that the domain of syntactic planning might span as much as an eight clause range. This, it will be recalled, was a consequence of the view that syntactic planning as well as semantic planning must be accomplished during the hesitant phase of the encoding cycle. That very strong conclusion is compromised in two respects. One we discussed in the hesitation section; that is the evidence that detailed syntactic planning may occur during the fluent phase of the cycle (minimally, at junctural loci). The second relevant observation is simply the maximum span of speech errors; that seems conservatively put at two surface clauses. It is, of course, quite possible to suppose that the nature of speech error processes excursions beyond that limit even though significant aspects of sentential structure are fixed for longer domains. Alternatively, one might argue that errors of larger scope do occur but that we don't recognize them as such – e.g. we take them for simple substitutions. There is no good response to such queries, but barring detailed argument or observation for or against such, I believe the two-clause limit should be taken as the best current working hypothesis. Indeed, in terms of frequency of errors and in terms of analysis of hesitations, one might opt for a smaller domain as the norm, that of two deep clauses at the functional level.

3   *Deep clause units and the functional level.* If we consider the hesitation
results of Ford (1977) and the reaction time findings of Ford and Holmes
(1978) in the context of the speech error model, there are several reasons
to place the sentence planning processes they have identified at the
functional level. First, recall that in our discussion of the phonological
interpretation of the positional level, we noted the likelihood that the
hesitation loci reported by Ford would not be well accounted for by
phonological units. Thus, if the hesitation units are to be assimilated to
the speech error model at all, it would be at the functional level. Beyond
this, of course, the positional level is deemed a single phrase level, while
the functional level is a multiphrase level (though the phrase types, as we
have argued, would be, respectively, phonological and syntactic). The
proposal of Ford and of Ford and Holmes is that planning proceeds by the
successive elaboration of deep verb dominated groups – the sentence is
planned in multiphrasal groups in the scope of a single verb. Again, that
is compatible with the properties of the functional level as indicated by
speech errors, with one emendation: the relatively frequent occurrence of
word exchanges between two verbs suggests that two deep clause groups
rather than one are often simultaneously under construction. To be more
specific, the hesitation and reaction time results suggest the functional
level processes might be as follows: (*a*) The set of lexical elements for the
simple phrases in the scope of a selected verb are identified and assigned
phrasal membership; in some cases, two such verb groups may be elaborated. The order of elaboration does not at this point correspond to
utterance order and the process might be considered functionally parallel
vis-à-vis the positional level. (*b*) The first verb set which is chosen for
elaboration is the set which will contain the first ordered phrase of the
utterance.

On these grounds, any difficulty encountered in the specification of
any of the elements of a verb set would appear as delay in the utterance of
the elements of the first uttered phrasal group. The question of where in
that group such delay could surface depends on detail of the control of
positional level processes by the functional level; detail of which we can
presently make no remark beyond the claims, already explored, for a
separation of the segmental interpretation of open and closed class
elements in terms of their identification with or insertion into the phrasal
planning frames of the positional level.

4   *In brief summary,* the implications of hesitations and of speech errors
seem similar in many respects. Both strongly indicate a significant separation in the processes of lexical selection and phrasal integration, and
both indicate that a single multiword planning domain is inadequate to
the description of sentence production processes – though they do pick
out somewhat different aspects of the planning domains. The speech
error data does not, by and large, seem to reflect regularities of message
level processes, barring the possible inferential account of some word

substitution processes. Hesitations, though also showing lexical and specifically syntactic effects, also seem to reflect the larger domains indicated by the full sentence effects and by the encoding cycle. Though motivated detail is still lamentably scarce in every indicated planning domain, the broad outlines indicated seem coherent.

5   The working model

A   SUMMARY SKETCH

We will briefly restate the claims for language production processes which seem supported by the several sorts of data reviewed.

1 Inferential processes applied to conceptual structures build a representation which is the real-time construct that determines sentence level construction.

MESSAGE LEVEL REPRESENTATION

2 Procedures applied to the Message level representation construct the first language specific level of representation. Three aspects of the process are distinguished: (*a*) determination of functional level structures, (*b*) meaning based lexical identification, and (*c*) assignment of lexical items to functional structures; representation is syntactic.

Lexical identification   Selection of functional structures

Assignment of lexical items to functional structure roles

3 Procedures applied to Functional level representations construct a representation which reflects utterance order directly. Four aspects of the process are distinguished: (*a*) determination of positional level phrasal frames specifying phrasal stress and closed class vocabulary, both bound and free, (*b*) retrieval of lexical forms, (*c*) assignment to phrasal sites, and (*d*) assignment of frame elements to positions in the terminal string of lexically interpreted phrasal frames; representation is phonological.

FUNCTIONAL LEVEL REPRESENTATION

Retrieval of lexical forms   Selection of positional structures

Assignment of lexical forms to phrasal sites

Assignment of frame elements to the terminal string

4 Procedures applied to Positional level representations construct a representation which specifies the phonetic detail consequent upon regular phonological processes.

POSITIONAL LEVEL REPRESENTATION

Regular phonological processes

5 Procedures applied to Phonetic level construct an articulatory representation.

PHONETIC LEVEL REPRESENTATION
Phonetic to articulatory coding
ARTICULATORY LEVEL REPRESENTATION

Two further observations should be recalled: First, for the Message level, the working hypothesis adopted is that the simple surface vocabulary is elementary at that level – i.e. lexical meanings are not expressed in terms of definitions given in a primitive (nonlexical) semantic vocabulary; rather, inference rules (e.g. meaning postulates) are associated with the simple surface vocabulary. Beyond that, no claim was made for message level format. Second, from hesitation studies, we take the implication that functional level processes are organized by verb dominated groups, and that functional level structure is developed by successive elaboration of a verb and its simple phrasal arguments.

B   SEMANTICS AND SENTENCE LEVEL STRUCTURES

Note that the domain of semantic processes is the message level and that we have not provided for possible feedback connections from lower to higher levels, nor, indeed, for any direct connection between non-adjacent levels. We thus deny the possibility of meaning based intervention in, e.g. positional level processes. The reasons we have offered for this are briefly noted, as well as some possible objections.

Throughout the examination of speech error, hesitation, and language disorder findings, we have called attention to the striking separation in processes sensitive to meaning and those sensitive to form. So, word substitution errors fall sharply into two such sets and the patterns of movement errors shows little evidence of such influences as associative or inferential connections between the words involved. Further, the patterns of language disorder support such a division. Though admittedly a broad abstraction, it does not seem improper to view in such light the preservation of lexically specific inferential processes in cases of Broca's aphasia in which productive control over most of the language specific devices of sentence construction is lost. Nor does it seem unreasonable to contrast that circumstance with the phrasally controlled but conceptually incoherent speech of Wernicke's aphasics. Such remarks do no justice to the intricate variety of symptoms in sundry disorders of language – but, it is not my impression that the detail when examined would prompt one to doubt the validity of the contrast invoked here.

Where are the worries then? They are in evidences that the sharp lines of demarcation between meaning based and form based processes may really be fuzzy lines. There are numerous fields of possible argument; I will give only two examples to show the cast of the problem.

Consider the sound exchange processes in the working model. They arise as a consequence of the segmental interpretation of lexical sites in phrasal planning frames; the segmental information involved is retrieved from an inventory of word forms, and though there is a connection between entries in that inventory and meaning representations, it is not relevant to the processes at hand. Against this, we set findings from experimentally induced sound segment exchanges. Baars, Motley and

MacKay (1975) and Motley and Baars (1976) report that such exchanges are affected by the lexical status and meaning of error products. In short-term memory tasks, they found that error products like 'barn door' (from 'darn bore') were more likely than products like 'bart doard' (from 'dart board'), and that, in addition, the meaning of the error products affected the likelihood of error (as when their interpretation was related to some situational features of the experiment). Spontaneous error distributions, by contrast, show no such tendencies so far as absolute levels of word and nonword error products are concerned. About 60% of error products are nonwords, and random sound exchange at normal exchange sites will yield real word products of roughly that order (Garrett, 1976). Though one might still argue for a statistical bias in favor of word status in error products, the effect must be small. But, given the experimental findings and some possible scope for their existence in spontaneous errors, where do they fit into the picture we have drawn in the working model? In strict terms, contact with the lexicon in that model is last accomplished at the point of retrieval of word form for a subsequent process of segmental interpretation of lexical sites in phrasal frames – in which process sound exchanges are presumed to arise. If the experimental findings are to be assimilated to the model, some plausible way to permit contact between error products and the form inventory must be found. One way would be to deny that the influence of lexical status or meaning bears on the primary error process, and to assign such influences to editorial processes which apply to the output of the segmental assignment process. Baars (1980) offers arguments and data in support of such a view; the question then becomes: what relation holds between such editorial processes and normal planning mechanisms? Should we introduce feedback loops into each part of the system to accommodate such possible editorial function or are editing functions confined to the 'end points' of the system? We cannot resolve the matter at present, but perhaps the discussion is sufficient to suggest the form of the problem that the working model sets in this area.

One other illustration of another class of questions will be useful. This concerns the issue of ordering of constituents for utterance. What is the point at which it is fixed, and what are the factors which determine it? In the working model, there are two relevant claims – one is that a verb group at the functional level is elaborated in parallel with respect to the positional level, and the other is that the positional level is the first level at which utterance order is directly expressed. Though I know of no currently incompatible experimental claims, there are classes of experimental effects which connect constituent order in utterances to such factors as semantic salience (Osgood and Bock, 1977) and egocentric value (Ertel, 1977). In the working model, such must have their influence at the message level. If such factors could be shown to operate at a point where constituent order has been fixed – e.g. the positional level – the lack of connections between message and positional levels would be compromised. To take a more specific example, consider recent experiments by Levelt and Maassan (1981). Using an experimental procedure in which subjects were required to produce syntactically determinated descriptions of simple visual arrays, they varied the availability (in terms of labelling latency) of the lexical labels for objects in the arrays and examined effects of that variation on the order of mention of the forms in the syntactic expressions. They reached two general conclusions: one, that ease of lexicalization did not seem to determine order of mention – though it did affect latency to utterance, and two, that ease of lexicalization did affect which of the two syntactic variants was chosen to realize a given order. From this, they inferred that the processes which determine order of mention proceed independently of the mechanisms which realize that decision, and that the effect of lexicalization on choice of syntactic frame indicated a feedback from positional to functional levels of representation. Evaluation of the latter point depends in part upon the sense in which one takes the term 'lexicalization' (viz. whether lexical identification or segmental interpretation is the appropriate focus of variation). Again, we can neither settle nor pursue further these interesting questions. They serve to illustrate the sorts of enquiry which may support or suggest changes in the working model.

C GRAMMARS AND PROCESSORS

If we return to the broad question with which we began this discussion, we may comment in the light of the working model. We asked, rhetorically, what might be the structure of the mental processes which determine language use in real time, and in particular, which of those processes are specific to the exercise of language. We assumed at the outset that the rule systems of formal grammars constituted the best hypothesis for the identity of such independent language processing types. The analysis and review of data from hesitations, language disorders, experimental enquiries of various sort, and of speech errors may be taken as an evaluation of that hypothesis.

If we look at the working model from this perspective, the processes isolated do not strike one as remarkable, in the sense that some unsuspected mode of processing activity must be postulated. On the contrary, the general lines are quite familiar; they differ only in detail from the outline in Fromkin (1971), and that in turn reflected the organization of formal grammatical accounts of language structure. What is striking and encouraging is that the correspondence we believe is antecedently reasonable to expect is one that detailed inspection of processing data requires us to maintain.

Given this conclusion, one might ask why one should preserve the labels in the model which are the residue of initial enquiry – open *vs* closed classes, functional and positional levels. Aren't they an unnecessary conceit? Perhaps. For now, I think not. One needs to be reminded that building real-time processing models and building theories of structure are closely related but distinct enterprises with diverse empirical constraint. They should be brought together self-consciously, not by accident of terminology.

Notes

1 N.B. This is *not* to say that internal structure of those rule systems, including the logical operations required for their function, must correspond directly to mental operations; rather, it is to say that the architecture of the processing system corresponds to that of the grammar: on this hypothesis, for each rule system there is a corresponding, autonomous subcomponent of the language processing system whose computational responsibility is to provide a representation equivalent to that of the grammatical rule system.

2 There are, for example, computational proposals for language comprehension which do not reflect in any compelling way the separation of syntactic variables (e.g. Schank, 1976; Winograd, 1972). There are also those which do (Kaplan, 1979; Marcus, 1978). Without a comparison of the computational adequacy of such proposals, it is difficult to assess their implication for this problem.

3 Evidently, in the normative, not the prescriptive sense.

4 We talk more than we think – though there is individual variation, to be sure. Even at such low occurrence rates, one may expect to hear several such 'speech errors' in the course of a few days; full exchange errors are rarer than those of copying or substitution, but even they crop up one or two a week.

5 As, for example, in: 'He's not the kind of man who you put on a backpack and go fishing with', in which the character of a locally determined conjunction conflicts with the scope of the stranded preposition.

6 The phrase 'morphologically simple surface vocabulary' should be given a limited interpretation; in this context, I would not wish to include morphological analyses which do not include a meaning criterion. I am also not confident about the place of derivational processes of word formation.

7 One consequence of adopting this view is the expectation that there are certain notions that are more readily available for surface expression than others. The actual empirical impact of this expectation is somewhat less than its statement might suggest, however, for it must be recalled that most of the moderately common vocabulary would be equivalently available on these constraints, for all such would be associated with elementary concepts. Only in cases for which there is an argument that an elementary concept is not associated with a single surface vocabulary realization will a prediction about the relative availability of sentential expressions for given semantic domains be possible.

8 Note that the independent elaboration of message level structure does *not* require that the entire message be formulated *prior* to the initiation of any activities at other levels of processing, even though those other levels are dependent upon message level input. The issue of temporal relations between the levels turns upon the conditions of inter-dependence among message level structures, for that will determine the possibility of effectively using partially elaborated message structures. The same holds for the relation between sentence level structures and articulatory activity.

9 At one point, Goldman-Eisler comments on her objective measures of speech flow as follows:

> Spontaneous speech was shown to be a highly fragmented and discontinuous activity. When even at its most fluent, two thirds of spoken language comes in chunks of less than six words, the attribute of flow and fluency in spontaneous speech must be judged an illusion.   (Goldman-Eisler, 1968, p. 31)

It seems quite plausible that the basis of this illusion is in the presence of higher order, integrative structures, one of whose most striking surface manifestations is the prosody of speech.

10 My remarks about both gestural and gaze patterning are meant to be illustrative and to advance the point under current discussion. Many more details of these features of communication are discussed in the references cited and they should be consulted for a more comprehensive picture of such phenomena.

11 One caution that should be borne in mind in interpreting this finding is the 200 ms pause criterion used in the study. Such a criterion will pick up 'normal' junctural breaks (i.e. those which may have no subjective experience of hesitancy associated). If the gaze variations are linked to those pauses which are subjectively hesitant, a longer pause criterion for junctures might yield a pattern similar to that for nonjunctural pauses of shorter duration.

12 See also Butterworth (1980), Beattie (1980) and references therein.

13 Beattie (1980) reports evidence which supports this claim about phrasal position and predictability. Using CLOZE procedure he found that the lower probability words in his spontaneous speech samples tended to occur towards the ends of clauses.

14 This procedure was first used by Valian (1971) for the study of online language production processes. Her results suggested both deep and surface clause effects.

15 Note, Ford did compare simple phrasal boundaries which were nonclausal with boundaries of deep clauses (that were not also surface clauses). The simple phrasal boundaries did not show significant pausing.

16 I know of no direct evidence on this point, beyond the perceptual impression derived from listening to hesitant speech. There is one suggestive finding by Danly, DeVilliers and Cooper (1979) which indicates that even the very hesitant production of Broca's asphasics shows evidence (from declination of f_o) of multiword planning domains.

17 Some indication of such a condition is suggested by Ford for the patterning at the boundaries of conjoined clauses – see Ford, 1977.

18 See also Butterworth (1980) and Beattie (1980) for reports of such dependency.

19 Any speaker can generate nonsense forms on request, and everyone on occasion produces nonce forms. Lecours, Travis and Osborne's (1980) investigations of voluntary glossolalia are convincing in the former regard; see Fromkin (1971) for examples of the latter.

20 In my initial treatment of such errors (Garrett, 1975), I associated such errors only with the processes which construct the positional level since most stranding errors that I had observed were phrase internal. Subsequent observation has revealed a fair number of such which involve elements of different phrases, and when this occurs, they, like the full word exchanges, show correspondence of grammatical categories. Thus, some stranding errors seem to be determined at the functional level.

21 One exception is what might be called 'environmental contaminants' (Garrett, 1980a); in such cases a word present in the speech environment (e.g. as one written on a billboard in the visual space of the speaker), but irrelevant to the conversation, intrudes into utterance. These are not interpretable as retrieval errors and where identifiable should be excluded from analyses aimed at discerning principles of organization of lexical storage systems.

22 The case for similarity of the ends of words is vexed by the limited variation in forms of derivational suffixes coupled with the correspondence of grammatical category. There is similarity; it's not clear what significance it may have.

23 The absence of synonyms from corpora of word substitution errors might be argued as an artifact of observation – i.e. synonymous substitutions preserve intended meaning and hence go unremarked. Hotopf (1980) argues against this on grounds of personal (subjective) observation; one 'knows' which word one meant to speak, and a substitution of even a synonym would be subjectively noted. Hotopf recalls no such personal observation for word substitutions and my own subjective experience is the same.

24 Fodor, Fodor and Garrett (1975) raise still further reservations against the definitional interpretation of meaning-related word substitution errors. They note that associative relations rather than semantic relations may underlie many such errors, and they note

that proper names, which are not semantically decomposable, are also often involved in such errors.

25 One possibility we have not considered is that stress errors arise in the way that word blends arise – i.e. they represent the combination of two alternative encoding lines that are simultaneously in progress. While some stress errors seem susceptible of such an account, there are others for which an alternative, communicatively equivalent expression using the intruding variant is hard to come up with.

26 See also Martin, Kolodziej and Genay (1971). They argued for assigning greater processing salience to phonological phrasing as compared with syntactic surface structure on grounds of its readier intuitive accessibility.

References

Arbib, M. and Caplan, D. (1980). Neurolinguistics must be computational. *Behavioural and Brain Sciences* **2**, 449–460

Baars, B. J. (1980). On eliciting predictable speech errors in the laboratory. *In* V. A. Fromkin (ed.), *Errors in Linguistic Performance*. New York: Academic Press

Baars, B. J., Motley, M. T. and MacKay, D. G. (1975). Output editing for lexical status in artificially elicited slips of the tongue. *Journal of Verbal Learning and Verbal Behaviour* **14**, 382–391

Barik, H. (1968). On defining juncture pauses: A note on Boomer's 'Hesitation and grammatical encoding'. *Language and Speech* **11**, 156–159

Beattie, G. (1980). The role of language production processes in the organization of behaviour in face to face interaction. *In* B. Butterworth (ed.), *Language Production*, Vol. 1, *Speech and Talk*. London: Academic Press

Berndt, R. and Caramazza, A. (1980). A redefinition of the syndrome of Broca's aphasia: Implications for a neuropsychological model of language. *Applied Psycholinguistics* **1**, 225–278.

Blumenthal, A. (1970). *Language and Psychology: Historical Aspects of Psycholinguistics*. New York: Wiley

Boomer, D. (1965). Hesitation and grammatical encoding. *Language and Speech* **8**, 148–158

Boomer, D. and Laver, J. (1968). Slips of the tongue. *British Journal of Disorders of Communication* **3**, 2–12

Bradley, D. C. and Garrett, M. F. (1980). Computational distinctions in vocabulary type. *Occasional Papers No. 12*, Center for Cognitive Science, MIT, Cambridge, Mass.

Bradley, D. C., Garrette, M. F. and Zurif, E. B. (1980). Syntactic deficits in Broca's aphasia. *In* D. Caplan (ed.), *Biological Studies of Mental Processes*. Cambridge, Mass.: MIT Press

Browman, C. (1978). Tip of the Tongue and Slip of the Ear: Implications for Language Processing. *UCLA Working Papers in Phonetics*, No. 42

Browman, C. (1980). Perceptual processing: Evidence from slips of the ear. *In* V. A. Fromkin (ed.), *Errors in Linguistic Performance*. New York: Academic Press

Brown, R. and McNeil, D. (1966). The tip of the tongue phenomenon. *Journal of Verbal Learning and Verbal Behaviour* **5**, 325–337

Buckingham, H. (1979). Linguistic aspects of lexical retrieval disturbances in the posterior fluent aphasias. *In* H. Whitaker and H. A. Whitaker (eds), *Studies in Neurolinguistics*, Vol. 4. New York: Academic Press

Buckingham, H. (1980). On correlating aphasic errors with slips of the tongue. *Applied Psycholinguistics* **1**, 199–220

Buckingham, H. and Kertesz, A. (1976). *Neologistic Jargon Aphasia: Neurolinguistics*, III. Amsterdam: Swets and Zeitlinger

Butterworth, B. (1975). Hesitation and semantic planning in speech. *Journal of Psycholinguistic Research* **4**, 74–87

Butterworth, B. (1979). Hesitation and the production of verbal paraphasias and neologisms in jargon aphasia. *Brain and Language* **8**, 133–61

Butterworth, B. (1980). Evidence from pauses. *In* B. Butterworth (ed.), *Language Production*, Vol. 1, *Speech and Talk*. London: Academic Press

Butterworth, B. and Beattie, G. (1978). Gesture and silence as indicators of planning in speech. *In* R. Campbell and P. T. Smith (eds), *Recent Advances in the Psychology of Language: Formal and Experimental Approaches*. New York: Plenum

Chomsky, N. (1965). *Aspects of the Theory of Syntax*. Cambridge, Mass.: MIT Press

Cook, M., Smith, J. and Lalljee, M. (1974). Filled pauses and syntactic complexity. *Language and Speech* **17**, 11–16

Cooper, W. and Paccia-Cooper, J. (1980). *Syntax and Speech*. Cambridge, Mass.: Harvard University Press

Cooper, W. and Sorenson, J. (1977). Fundamental frequency contours at syntactic boundaries. *Journal of the Acoustical Society of America* **62**, 682–692

Cutler, A. (1980). Errors of stress and intonation. *In* V. A. Fromkin (ed.), *Errors in Linguistic Performance*. New York: Academic Press

Cutler, A. and Isard, S. (1980). The production of prosody. *In* B. Butterworth (ed.), *Language Production*, Vol. 1, *Speech and Talk*. London: Academic Press

Danly, M., DeVilliers, J. G. and Cooper, W. (1979). Control of speech prosody in Broca's aphasia. *In* J. Wolf and D. Klatt (eds), *Speech Communication of the Acoustical Society of America*. New York: Acoustical Society of America

Ertel, S. (1977). Where do the subjects of sentences come from? *In* S. Rosenberg (ed.), *Sentence Production: Developments in Research and Theory*. Hillsdale, New Jersey: Erlbaum

Fay, D. (in press). The mental representation of prefixed words: evidence from prefix errors in spontaneous speech. *Journal of Verbal Learning and Verbal Behaviour*

Fay, D. and Cutler, A. (1977). Malapropisms and the structure of the mental lexicon. *Linguistic Inquiry* **8**, 505–520

Fodor, J. A. (1975). *The Language of Thought*. New York: Crowell

Fodor, J. D., Fodor, J. A. and Garrett, M. (1975). The psychological unreality of semantic representations. *Linguistic Inquiry* **4**, 515–533

Fodor, J. A., Garrett, M., Walker, E. and Parkes, C. (1980). Against definitions. *Cognition* **8**, 263–367

Ford, M. (1978). Planning Units and Syntax in Sentence Production. Unpublished Ph.D. Dissertation, University of Melbourne

Ford, M. and Holmes, V. (1978). Planning units and syntax in sentence production. *Cognition* **6**, 35–53

Forster, K. and Bednall, E. (1976). Terminating and exhaustive search in lexical access. *Memory and Cognition* **4**, 53–61

Fromkin, V. A. (1971). The non-anomalous nature of anomalous utterances. *Language* **47**, 27–52

Fromkin, V. A. (1980). Introduction. *In* V. A. Fromkin (ed.), *Errors in Linguistic Performance*. New York: Academic Press

Garrett, M. (1975). The analysis of sentence production. *In* G. Bower (ed.), *Psychology of Learning and Motivation*, Vol. 9. New York: Academic Press

Garrett, M. (1976). Syntactic processes in sentence production. *In* R. Wales and E. Walker (eds), *New Approaches to Language Mechanisms*. Amsterdam: North-Holland

Garrett, M. (1980a). Levels of processing in sentence production. *In* B. Butterworth (ed.), *Language Production*, Vol. 1, *Speech and Talk*. London: Academic Press

Garrett, M. (1980b). The limits of accommodation. *In* V. A. Fromkin (ed.), *Errors in Linguistic Performance*. New York: Academic Press

Garrett, M. and Kean, M-L. (1980). Levels of representation and the analysis of speech errors. *In* M. Aronoff and M-L. Kean (eds), *On Juncture*. San Francisco: AMNI LIBRI

Gazdar, G. (1980). Pragmatic contraints on linguistic production. *In* B. Butterworth (ed.), *Language Production*, Vol. 1, *Speech and Talk*. London: Academic Press

Goldman-Eisler, F. (1968). *Psycholinguistics*. London: Academic Press

Goldman-Eisler, F. (1972). Pauses, clauses, sentences. *Language and Speech* **15**, 103–113

Goodglass, H. (1976). Agrammatism. *In* H. Whitaker and H. A. Whitaker (eds), *Studies in Neurolinguistics*, Vol. 1. New York: Academic Press

Goodglass, H. and Geschwind, N. (1977). Language disorders (aphasia). *In* E. C. Carterette and M. Friedman (eds), *Handbook of Perception*, Vol. 7. New York: Academic Press

Goodglass, H., Kaplan, E., Weintraub, S. and Ackerman, N. (1976). The 'tip-of-the-tongue' phenomenon in aphasia. *Cortex* **12**, 145–153

Halle, M. and Vergnaud, J. R. (1980). Tiered phonology. Paper presented to the Conference of the CNRS, Abbé Royamount, June, 1980

Henderson, A., Goldman-Eisler, F. and Skarbeck, A. (1966). Sequential temporal patterns in spontaneous speech. *Language and Speech* **9**, 207–216

Hotopf, W. H. N. (1980). Semantic similarity as a factor in whole word slips of the tongue. *In* V. A. Fromkin (ed.), *Errors in Linguistic Performance*. New York: Academic Press

Kaplan, R. (1979). A general syntactic processor. *In* R. Rustin (ed.), *Natural Language Processing*. Eaglewood Cliffs, New Jersey: Prentice-Hall

Katz, J. (1972). *Semantic Theory*. New York: Harper and Row

Katz, J. and Fodor, J. A. (1963). The structure of semantic theory. *In* J. A. Fodor and J. J. Katz (eds), *The Structure of Language*. Eaglewood Cliffs, New Jersey: Prentice-Hall

Kean, M-L. (1977). The linguistic interpretation of aphasic syndromes: Agrammatism in Broca's aphasia, an example. *Cognition* **5**, 9–46

Kean, M-L. (1980). Grammatical representations and the description of language processing. *In* D. Caplan (ed.), *Biological Studies of Mental Processes*. Cambridge, Mass.: MIT Press

Kintsch, W. (1974). *The Representation of Meaning in Memory*. New York: Wiley

Lakoff, G. (1971). On generative semantics. *In* D. Steinberg and L. Jacobovits (eds), *Semantics*. Cambridge: Cambridge University Press

Lecours, A. R. (1980). On neologisms. Paper presented to the Conference of the CNRS, Abbé Royamount, June 1980

Lecours, A. R., Deloche, G. and Lhermitte, F. (1973). Paraphasies phonèmiques: description et simulation sur ordinateur. In *Colloques I.R.I.A. Informtique Medicale*, Vol. 1, 311–350

Lecours, A. R., Travis, L. and Osborne, E. (1980). Glossolalia as a manifestation of Wernicke's aphasia: A comparison to glossolalia in schizophasia and in possession. *In* M. Taylor-Sarno and O. Höök (eds), *Aphasia: Concepts of Analysis and Management*. Stockholm: Almquist and Wiksell

Levelt, W. J. M. and Maassan, B. (1981). Lexical search and order of mention in sentence production. *In* W. Klein and W. J. M. Levelt (eds), *Crossing the Boundaries in Linguistics: Studies Presented to Manfred Beirwisch*. Dortrecht: Reidel

Liberman, A. M. and Prince, A. (1977). On stress and linguistic rhythm. *Linguistic Inquiry* **8**, 249–336

MacKay, D. G. (1980). Speech errors: Retrospect and prospect. *In* V. A. Fromkin (ed.), *Errors in Linguistic Performance*. New York: Academic Press

Marcus, M. (1978). *A Theory of Syntactic Recognition for Natural Language*. Cambridge, Mass.: MIT Press

Marslen-Wilson, W. (1980). Speech understanding as a psychological process. *In* J. C. Simon (ed.), *Spoken Language Generation and Understanding*. Dortrecht: D. Reidel

Martin, J. G. (1971). On judging pauses in spontaneous speech. *Journal of Verbal Learning and Verbal Behaviour* **9**, 75–78

Martin, J. G., Kolodziej, B. and Genay, J. (1971). Segmentation of sentences into phonological phrases as a function of constituent length. *Journal of Verbal Learning and Verbal Behaviour* **10**, 226–233

Motley, M. T. and Baars, B. J. (1976). Semantic bias effects on the outcome of verbal slips. *Cognition* **24**, 177–188

Murrell, G. A. and Morton, J. (1974). Word recognition and morphemic structure. *Journal of Experimental Psychology* **102**, 963–968

Newport, E., Gleitman, L. and Gleitman, H. (1977). Mother, I'd rather do it myself: Some effects and non-effects of maternal speech style. *In* C. E. Snow and C. A. Ferguson (eds), *Talking to Children: Language Input and Acquisition*. Cambridge: Cambridge University Press

Osgood, C. E. and Bock, J. K. (1977). Salience and sentencing: some production principles. *In* S. Rosenberg (ed.), *Sentence Production: Developments in Research and Theory*. Hillsdale, New Jersey: Erlbaum

Perkell, J. (1980). Phonetic features and the physiology of speech production. *In* B. Butterworth (ed.), *Language Production*, Vol. 1, *Speech and Talk*. London: Academic Press

Rochester, S. R. and Martin, J. G. (1979). *Crazy Talk: A Study of the Discourse of Schizophrenic Speakers*. New York: Plenum Press

Rochester, S. R. and Gill, J. (1973). Production of complex sentences in monologs and dialogs. *Journal of Verbal Learning and Verbal Behaviour* **12**, 203–210

Saffran, E., Schwartz, M. and Marin, O. S. M. (1980). Evidence from aphasia: Isolating the components of a production model. *In* B. Butterworth (ed.), *Language Production*, Vol. 1, *Speech and Talk*. London: Academic Press

Schank, R. (1976). *Conceptual Information Processing*. Amsterdam: North-Holland

Shattuck-Hufnagel, S. (1979). Speech errors as evidence for a serial-ordering mechanism in sentence production. *In* W. E. Cooper and E. C. T. Walker (eds), *Sentence Processing: Psycholinguistic Studies Presented to Merrill Garrett*. Hillsdale, New Jersey: Erlbaum

Sherman, M. A. (1976). Adjectival negation and the comprehension of multiply negated sentences. *Journal of Verbal Learning and Verbal Behaviour* **15**, 143–157

Stevens, K. and Perkell, J. (1978). Speech physiology and phonetic features. *In* M. Sawashima and F. F. Cooper (eds), *Dynamic Aspects of Speech Production*. Tokyo: University of Tokyo Press

Swinney, D. (1980). The structure and time course of information interactions during speech comprehension: lexical segmentation access, and interpretation. Paper presented at the Conference of the CNRS, Abbé Royamount, June 1980

Taft, M. and Forster, K. I. (1976). Lexical storage and retrieval of polymorphemic and polysyllabic words. *Journal of Verbal Learning and Verbal Behaviour* **15**, 607–620

Valian, V. (1971). Talking, Listening and Linguistic Structure. Unpublished Ph.D. Dissertation, Northeastern University

Winograd, T. (1972). *Understanding Natural Language*. New York: Academic Press

Zurif, E. B. and Caramazza, A. (1976). Psycholinguistic structures in aphasia: Studies in syntax and semantics. *In* H. Whitaker and H. A. Whitaker (eds), *Studies in Neurolinguistics*, Vol. 1. New York: Academic Press

3

The Relation between Reading and Phonological Coding: Further Neuropsychological Observations

KARALYN E. PATTERSON
MRC Applied Psychology Unit, Cambridge, England

1 Introduction

It is obvious that a skilled reader of English can create a phonemic or phonological representation for a printed letter string. Never having seen this letter string before, you can readily pronounce *trelt*; your competence for translating graphemes into phonology is therefore not in doubt. But does such phonological recoding of a *familiar* word ever mediate between its printed form and its meaning? Despite numerous theoretical and empirical pronouncements upon this question, it remains something of an issue. Changes in the conception of the issue are however detectable. One extreme but often advocated position, that the printed word is always translated to a phonological code prior to comprehension, is now untenable on the basis of many sources of evidence (reviewed by Coltheart, 1980). The other extreme position, that comprehension of a printed word is never achieved by phonological coding, is surely also wrong: lexical access based on a phonological code may be a strategic option under certain conditions (Davelaar, Coltheart, Besner and Jonasson, 1978; Carr, Davidson and Hawkins, 1978). Presumably we should not be surprised when we fail to obtain straight answers to simple dichotomised questions. If comprehension of a written word *can* proceed from either a graphemic representation or a phonemic translation of the graphemic representation, perhaps the surprise would be if it always did so exclusively in one way or the other.

Being adaptable scientists, we psychologists then rephrase the question: no longer 'A or B?' but 'when A?' and 'what role B?', and so on. For the issue of concern here, such rephrasing might take the following form. It seems that comprehension of a familiar written word generally does not *require* phonological mediation.[1] Under what conditions then might phonological coding be called into service? One approach to this question, in fact the one which will be adopted here, is to investigate the ramifications of loss or impairment of phonological ability. If adequate phonological coding were not available to the adult reader, what difference would it make?

Before this question is examined, one critical distinction must be made. Psychologists have tended to use the term 'phonology' in a rather undisciplined way; with particular regard to reading, they have sometimes failed to distinguish between so-called *prelexical* and *postlexical* phonology (or, as I will chose to call them, *assembled* and *addressed* phonology). Some recent authors have however been at pains to dispel the confusion (e.g. Kleiman, 1975; Coltheart, 1978, 1980; Henderson, 1982), and I will merely attempt to summarise the distinction briefly.

In reading aloud, once a printed word has been recognised, its pronunciation can presumably be addressed or 'looked up' in a phonological lexicon, the same phonological lexicon which would subserve spontaneous speech. This is postlexical or *addressed* phonology; it may well play a role in text comprehension, but it is not the phonology of which many authors speak when they discuss the involvement of phonology in reading. Addressed phonology is retrieved *subsequent* to word recognition, whereas speculation regarding phonology in reading has primarily concerned the nature of the code which is used to *achieve* word recognition. As indicated in the first paragraph of this chapter, the question was whether identification and comprehension of a written word might be based on a phonological code. This latter code is prelexical or *assembled* phonology.

Conceptions about the process for assembling phonology from print, which have been changing dramatically in the last few years, will be considered later in the chapter. For the moment it will suffice to say that, however conceived or labelled, the distinction between the two varieties of phonology remains a critical one. Therefore, as Coltheart (1980) has noted, any question about the role of phonology in some task or process must query separately the potential involvement of addressed and assembled phonology. It is with the latter that this chapter is primarily concerned.

2   Evidence for a role of assembled phonology in reading

Coltheart (1980), in a recent comprehensive review, found a notable lack of evidence that assembled phonology plays any significant role in recognising and comprehending written words. Indeed, as many writers have noted (e.g. Underwood, 1979), one scarcely needs experimental data to discard a hypothesis of lexical access based solely on a phonological code, since we have no difficulty distinguishing between the written words *sees, seas* and *seize*. As Henderson and Chard (1980) have emphasised, however, the assumption is often made tacitly and sometimes explicitly (e.g. by Underwood, 1979) that phonological recoding implies loss of all graphemic information. This assumption is both unnecessary and unjustified, and thus in principle, lexical access could proceed on a largely phonological basis, backed up by a graphemic check (Rubenstein, Lewis and Rubenstein, 1971). The absence of difficulty with single written homophones is therefore not conclusive evidence against *any* reliance on phonology. There are, however, further sources of difficulty for the phonological hypothesis, even on reflection. For example, (1) the correct phonology for certain letter combinations can only be determined once the word has been identified, such as *ph* in *shepherd vs grapheme* and *ch* in *chase vs chasm*; and (2) the correct phonology for certain homographic words can only be determined once the word has been identified, such as *bass* (fish or voice) and *read* (present or past tense).

The experimental evidence most relevant to the issue of phonological recording classifies words as to whether they show a regular correspondence between spelling and pronunciation. Examples of regular and irregular words, respectively, are *spear* and *sword*. If word recognition and comprehension involved an assembled phonological code, then one might expect slower or less accurate responses to irregular words. Two main tasks have been used to assess this prediction. In lexical decision, the subject must decide whether a printed letter string is a legitimate word in the language. There has been some disparity in results from different investigators; but the most persuasive conclusion at present is that neither speed nor accuracy of lexical decisions on words is significantly influenced by regularity (Coltheart, Besner, Jonasson and Davelaar, 1979), at least under conditions of fast responding (Stanovich and Bauer, 1978). In semantic categorisation, the subject must decide whether a printed word belongs to a particular category. Experiments by Midgley-West (reported in Coltheart, 1980) indicate that categorisation judgements (whether 'yes' or 'no') are unaffected by regularity of spelling. In summary, the bulk of the evidence seems better handled by the hypothesis that lexical access can and normally does proceed without reference to an assembled phonological code.[2]

As Underwood (1979, p. 105) has noted, if we accept this conclusion, then the problem gets turned round: how are we to account for those phonological effects in reading which made us consider the phonological hypothesis in the first place? Underwood lists three such 'phonological effects': (1) acoustic confusions in immediate memory for visually presented strings of letters (Conrad, 1964); (2) higher error rates (misses) on silent *e*'s in a letter cancellation task while reading prose passages (Corcoran, 1966); (3) slower and less accurate 'no' responses in lexical decision when a nonword (e.g. *fraze*) is homophonic with a real word (Rubenstein *et al.*, 1971). The first effect can be dismissed because, while highly reliable, it probably reflects the characteristics of short-term auditory-verbal memory rather than anything specifically concerned with reading. The second effect can be dismissed because firstly, it is not at all clear that it would arise from assembled phonology, and, secondly, in any case it is apparently not a reliable effect. Smith and Groat (1979) have obtained a number of interesting phenomena in the letter cancellation task but have failed to replicate the 'silent *e*' effect. The third effect cannot be dismissed: it has been replicated (e.g. Coltheart, Davelaar, Jonasson and Besner, 1977); the effect does implicate assembled or prelexical phonology; and, while not exactly a reading task, lexical decision does at least require the subject to consult his internal lexicon. It must be emphasised, however, that the effect is restricted to nonwords. Coltheart (1978, 1980) concludes that phonological recoding may regularly occur in this task, but at a relatively slow rate. A word would tend to achieve lexical access on the basis of visual/graphemic information before an assembled phonological code could exert any influence. A nonword, on the other hand, would still be under consideration when its assembled phonology became available.

It would seem that we are left with precious little to explain: only one phenomenon suggests the influence of assembled phonology, and that phenomenon involves nonwords only. Despite this paucity of phonological phenomena, one could take the conservative position that the absence of an effect is never conclusive. On this basis, the aforementioned strategy would still be appropriate: instead of looking for putative effects of phonological recoding if it were occurring, let us look for changes in reading performance when phonological recoding cannot or does not occur.

Before 1978, this approach followed two main paths. Firstly, with normal readers as subjects, experimental psychologists have used a technique called articulatory suppression or concurrent articulation, in which the subject must read something silently while continuously articulating some other irrelevant utterance. The reader should consult Baddeley (1979) for some of the interesting results obtained with this technique and Coltheart (1980) for an analysis of problems with the technique. For current purposes, it is critical only to note that the technique fails to achieve what at least some investigators have assumed it to do. Concurrent articulation does not prevent the reader from assembling a phonological code for a written letter string. Neither Besner, Davies and Daniels (1981) nor Baddeley and Lewis (1981) have obtained a deleterious effect of concurrent articulation on speed of rhyme judgements or homophony judgements for written nonword pairs (e.g. *grake-traik* and *bew-bue*, respectively). Therefore, the strategy of examining reading in the absence of phonological coding cannot be accomplished with the technique of concurrent articulation.

The second pre-1978 focus for the study of reading without phonology comes from neuropsychology, in the form of case studies of adult neurological patients with a reading disorder known as 'deep' dyslexia (Marshall and Newcombe, 1973). In this syndrome, amongst a constellation of reading deficits (to be described presently) is a virtually total inability to assemble phonology for an unfamiliar written letter string (Shallice and Warrington, 1975; Patterson and Marcel, 1977; Saffran and Marin, 1977). Such patients can, however, read many words aloud correctly; and, even for words which they are unable to read aloud, they can often indicate recognition (e.g. in lexical decision tests) or comprehension (by matching the word to a picture or to another word with similar meaning). Reading in deep dyslexia has therefore been described as 'reading without phonology' (Saffran and Marin, 1977) and interpreted as evidence against the hypothesis that lexical access relies on a phonological code assembled from the graphemic information.

I have no quarrel with this interpretation: indeed, I have argued for it in the past (Patterson and Marcel, 1977) and I believe in it now. As evidence for the conclusion that reading can be accomplished without assembled phonology, however, patients with severe reading deficits leave something to be desired! As Beauvois and Dérouesné (1979a, b) were the first to point out, convincing neuropsychological evidence that reading does not require phonology would be a patient who cannot assemble phonology from print but who nonetheless shows competent reading performance. This syndrome, described for the first time by Beauvois and Dérouesné, a second time by Shallice and Warrington (1980), and for the third time in this chapter, is called phonological dyslexia.

3 Case report

A. M. (born 1915), formerly a supervisor in a printing firm, suffered a coronary thrombosis in August, 1977, followed several weeks later by cerebral embolism secondary to myocardial infarct. He was a *left*-handed man who wrote with his right hand (both before and after his neurological damage), having been instructed to do so at school. A CT brain scan in January 1980 revealed two low density areas in the right hemisphere, one frontal and one temporo-parietal, diagnosed as old infarcts in the territory of the right middle cerebral artery. Neurological examination in January 1980 revealed no major neurological signs apart from his language difficulties and a slight weakness of the left hand and arm.

For a period following his CVA, A.M.'s speech showed notable word-finding difficulty and occasional jargon. Within a year the jargon had completely resolved and the word-finding problem, while detectable, was fairly minor. His speech was somewhat hesitant, with a slight shortage of specific content words (which he tended to replace with more general words: for example, on one test occasion, he suddenly remembered the tape recorder and said, 'This isn't still doing, is it?'); but his speech was certainly grammatical, and its abnormalities were often not apparent unless one looked for them.

By reports of those who knew him, A.M. had apparently possessed superb command of both spoken and written language prior to his illness. That he retained considerable subtlety of expression after his CVA might be demonstrated by his response when I asked if he would mind my accompanying him for his brain scan: 'On the contrary,' he replied, 'I shall be strengthened by your presence'. His high level of cognitive competence might be indicated by his response when the neurologist asked him about his reading ability: A.M. said, 'Do you mean silent or aloud?' (Indeed, some psychological investigators fail to make this distinction when they talk about reading performance!). Finally, his sense of humour was ever-present and pleasant: having produced a test one day that he performed rapidly and without error, I commented that it had been easy for him. 'Well,' he replied, 'then we shan't be seeing *that* one again!'

I tested A.M. eight times between April 1978 and January 1980 to assess his language abilities, primarily reading and writing which were his major sources of difficulty. A.M. died in February 1980 following another coronary thrombosis.

A.M., left-handed and apparently with right-hemisphere language representation, was clearly not typical of the majority of the population; and it is always worth a note of caution when trying to draw general implications from such cases. We know considerably less about the organisation of language areas when the right hemisphere is dominant. This is not, however, a neurological study but a neuropsychological one. Left-handed people can read and, from the point of view of psychological processes, there is no indication that their reading skill differs from that of right handers. Also, the pattern of reading performance shown by A.M. has also been observed in right-handed patients (Beauvois and Dérouesné, 1979a). As Oatley (1978) has so succinctly put it, the most valuable contribution of lesion studies is in identifying the components of behaviour, not in localising them.

A   STANDARD TEST RESULTS

1   *General*. A.M.'s nominal abilities were reasonably well preserved: on the naming tests described by Coughlan and Warrington (1978), although his responses were rather slow, he was error-free (15/15) in naming objects when confronted with them and he was able to name most objects (12/15) from a verbal description. His auditory comprehension of single lexical items, even low-frequency ones, was excellent: on the four-alternative picture-word matching test devised by Shallice and McGill (personal communication), A.M. was 100% correct on the concrete words, 97% correct on the abstract words (for example, the picture to match the word 'forethought' is a person fastening a seat belt) and 80%

correct on the emotional words. His auditory comprehension of grammatical distinctions was also good. Bishop (1980) has designed a four-alternative picture-sentence matching test to evaluate understanding of syntactic features such as singular/plural, gender, negation, word order, etc. A.M. was correct on 37/40 or 93% of these items, making errors on two reversible sentences and on one singular/plural distinction.

Despite his satisfactory performance on relatively straightforward grammatical distinctions, A.M. could not do the Coughlan and Warrington (1978) form of the Token Test (De Renzi and Vignolo, 1962) consisting of rather long and syntactically complex instructions. This failure is no doubt related to his impaired short-term auditory-verbal memory (digit span = 4 forwards, 2 backwards), an interpretation supported by the fact that his performance on these instructions was very much better (12/15 correct) with visual instead of auditory presentation. Reading comprehension, while probably more tolerant of a short-term memory deficit than is auditory comprehension, still relies on short-term memory to some extent (Levy, 1977; Coltheart, 1980). It is thus reasonable that visual presentation should reduce but not eliminate A.M.'s difficulty with the complex Token Test instructions.

A.M.'s articulation was good and he could repeat multisyllabic words like 'miscellaneous' and 'procrastinate'. He also repeated sentences well, although he occasionally paraphrased (e.g. 'He had no means of defending himself' → 'He had no means to defend himself') or omitted a few words, which is not surprising in view of his short-term memory impairment.

2 *Reading.* Given lists of single content words, A.M. read with reasonable accuracy. On the Schonell (1942) graded word reading test he read 83/100 words correctly, and a number of his misreadings were inflectional or derivational errors indicative of knowledge of the word (e.g. *scintillate* → 'scintillating'). On Nelson's Adult Reading Test (Nelson and O'Connell, 1978) of extremely difficult irregular words (e.g. *gauche, drachm, puerperal*) he read 31/50 correctly, yielding a verbal IQ estimate of 112, i.e. normal. The kinds of reading errors he made, and investigations of various facets of reading performance, are the substance of this report and will be presented shortly. For the moment, it is sufficient to note that, in terms of oral reading of single content words, A.M.'s accuracy was virtually normal. Furthermore, his performance was robust, showing relative insensitivity to manipulations such as reduced exposure duration or unusual visual format. Ninety nouns, all of which A.M. had previously read correctly when presented in normal lower-case print 'over the desk' (i.e. with unlimited exposure duration), were divided into three sets: (1) one set of words was presented in a tachistoscope at 200 ms per word, and A.M. correctly reported 29/30 words; (2) one set was presented (over the desk) in mixed case, e.g. *bLoOd*, and A.M. correctly read 28/30; (3) the

final set was given with asterisks separating the letters, e.g. *t*r*u*t*h*, and he again read 28/30 correctly. (See Saffran, 1980 and Saffran and Marin, 1977 for use of these latter two manipulations with deep dyslexic patients; see Warrington and Shallice, 1980 and Patterson, 1981 for discussions of effects of all three manipulations in various syndromes of acquired dyslexia).

3 *Writing and spelling.* A.M.'s ability to write (to dictation) was clearly impaired and more so than his reading. On the Schonell graded word spelling test, (*a*) he found the test very effortful and begged to be allowed to stop after 66 (out of 100) words; (*b*) he wrote 41/66 = 62% of the words correctly. His 25 errors were of four types: omissions (e.g. 'ground', 'lowest'); derivationally related word errors (e.g. 'sat' → *seat*, 'hoped' → *hopes*); visually or phonologically related word errors (e.g. 'doll' → *dog*, 'amount' → *among*); and misspellings, or what Ellis (chapter 4, this volume) calls errors of partial lexical knowledge (e.g. 'daughter' → *dougher*, 'description' → *dispection*). Unlike R.G., the phonological dyslexic patient described by Beauvois and Dérouesné (1979a, b), A.M. *never* produced a spelling which was orthographically incorrect but phonologically acceptable (e.g. 'fight' → *fite*). Indeed, in terms of patterns of performance on writing and spelling, A.M. and R.G. could scarcely have been more different. R.G., although he could not read phonologically, could and did spell in this manner; thus in spelling to dictation, he wrote nonwords quite competently, and he made many phonologically plausible errors on words (e.g. 'bateau' → *bato*). R.G. was also perfect at oral spelling of orthographically regular words and nonwords. He showed some characteristics of classical 'alexia without agraphia', however, and for example was very poor at copying nonwords. A.M., by contrast, was (*a*) much more seriously dysgraphic than R.G.; (*b*) could copy both words and nonwords perfectly, even from script to print; (*c*) could not spell a single nonword in writing to dictation; (*d*) could not do oral spelling even of very simple words (e.g. 'net' → 'e, not e; h, not h; n . . . h, no, no I can't').

B EXPERIMENTAL INVESTIGATIONS

When I first saw A.M. in April 1978, I had never heard of phonological dyslexia,[3] and I judged him to be a very mild deep dyslexic; but it gradually became apparent that his reading performance lacked a number of the symptoms of deep dyslexia. Table I lists what are generally considered to be the distinguishing features of deep dyslexia (see various chapters in Coltheart, Patterson and Marshall, 1980), and indicates which ones were characteristic of A.M.'s reading. I shall first present the evidence upon which the 'no' assignments in Table I have been based, and then proceed to evidence regarding A.M.'s reading impairments.

Table I   A list of the major phenomena in oral reading by deep dyslexic patients, with an assessment of whether A.M.'s reading performance showed each of these characteristics

Deep dyslexia	A.M.
Deficit in assembling phonology from print (e.g. reading nonwords)	yes
Deficit in reading abstract words (relative to imageable/concrete words)	no
Deficit (relative to nouns) in reading:	
Adjectives	no
Verbs	no
Function words	yes
Occurrence, in reading, of:	
Semantic paralexias	no
Visual paralexias	no (?)
Derivational paralexias	yes
Omissions	no (?)

1   *Abstract words.* It is already evident from A.M.'s good performance on the Schonell and Nelson reading tests, both of which contain many abstract words, that he had no major deficit in reading this word class. For a specific evaluation of this variable, A.M. was given the list devised by Coltheart (personal communication) consisting of 28 high and 28 low imageability nouns matched for frequency and word length. A.M. read 54 of these 56 words correctly; his two errors occurred on imageable rather than abstract words.

For a different kind of assessment of A.M.'s performance on abstract words, he was given a lexical decision test consisting of 150 low-frequency abstract words (like *oblivious* and *degraded*) intermixed with 150 nonwords formed by changing one letter in each of the words (e.g. *oblavious, defraded*). He correctly responded 'yes' to 145/150 words; his 5 misses on this test can be compared to a mean of 6.4 misses by a control group of normal subjects performing the same test (Patterson, 1979). A.M. correctly responded 'no' to 141/150 nonwords; his rate of 9 false positives is essentially identical to the mean of the control group of 8.6. A.M.'s lexical decision performance on this abstract word test is thus unequivocally normal.

Finally, since neither oral reading nor lexical decision evaluates comprehension, A.M. was given several comprehension tests of written abstract words on which at least some deep dyslexic patients are impaired (Shallice and Coughlan, 1980; Patterson, 1981). As already mentioned in the earlier section on standard test results, A.M. showed no discrepancy between concrete and abstract words (probability correct = 1.0 and .97, respectively) in Shallice and McGill's (unpublished) word-picture matching test. Indeed, A.M.'s performance on the abstract items was better than a control group of 20 normal subjects (mean probability correct = 0.86; Shallice, personal communication). Secondly, on a test (unpublished) devised by Coltheart where printed pairs of words are to be judged for synonymity, A.M.'s probabilities of correct judgement were 0.94 on the imageable/concrete words and 1.0 on the abstract pairs. The dimension of abstractness is simply irrelevant to A.M.'s oral reading and reading comprehension.

2   *Adjectives.* No specific test was performed to evaluate A.M.'s reading of adjectives; but if the Schonell words are classified for part of speech, A.M. correctly read 0.86 of the nouns and 0.83 of the adjectives.

3   *Verbs.* Since deep dyslexic patients show considerable difficulty in reading verbs, it seemed worthwhile to test A.M. rather extensively on this part of speech. On Klee and Legge's (1976) list of verbs, he correctly read 188/200 = 0.94. (Most of his errors were derivational paralexias, like *frustrate* → 'frustration', which will be discussed later.) At an absolute level, this is not quite normal reading performance: nine members of the subject panel at the Applied Psychology Unit were given this same list of 200 verbs to read aloud; one subject made two errors (*bathe* → 'bath', *condone* → 'condún'), two subjects made one error each (*despise* → 'disprise'; *forestall* → 'for-est-all') and the remaining six subjects made no errors (although there were some initial error responses which were immediately corrected, e.g. prove → 'prōve, prove'). Unlike deep dyslexic patients, however, A.M.'s reading of verbs showed (*a*) a slight rather than a severe deficit relative to normal subjects, and (*b*) no deficit relative to his own reading of nouns and adjectives.

4   *Semantic paralexias.* All of A.M.'s 17 reading errors on the Schonell list and his 12 errors on the Klee and Legge verb list appear in Table II, classified according to the criteria used for paralexic errors in deep dyslexic patients (see, e.g. Marshall and Newcombe, 1973; Shallice and Warrington, 1975). A.M. never, in reading single words aloud, produced a purely semantic error of the sort which occurs with deep dyslexic patients (e.g. *anxiety* → 'nervous'). One of his reading errors (but only one) might be classified as visual and/or semantic: *satirical* → 'sarcastic'.

5   *Visual paralexias.* The judgement in Table I is that this type of error was not a major characteristic of A.M.'s reading; but this judgement carries a query, for three reasons. Firstly, the other phonological dyslexic patients described in the literature (see Beauvois and Dérouesné, 1979a, b; Shallice and Warrington, 1980) made visual errors in reading. Secondly, some of the paralexic errors in Table II have been classified as visual, and therefore even for A.M. one could not say of visual paralexias (as I have just said of semantic paralexias) that they simply did not occur. On the other hand, such errors occurred very rarely (five or six responses in reading 300

Table II A.M.'s reading errors on the 100 words of the Schonell (1942) reading test and on the 200 words of Klee and Legge's (1976) verb list

	Schonell		Klee and Legge	
Paralexic errors				
Derivational	book	→ 'books'	*amputate*	→ 'amputation'
	think	→ 'thinking'	*fail*	→ 'failure'
	applaud	→ 'applause'	*frustrate*	→ 'frustration'
	disposal	→ 'dispose'	*initiate*	→ 'initiative'
	diseased	→ 'disease'	*offend*	→ 'offense'
	situated	→ 'situate'	*provide*	→ 'provided'
	fascinate	→ 'fascinating'	*revise*	→ 'revised'
	recent	→ 'recently'	*solve*	→ 'absolve'
	scintillate	→ 'scintillating'	*write*	→ 'writing'
	ineradicable	→ 'eradicate'		
	judicature	→ 'judiciary'		
Visual	metamorphosis	→ 'metaphorical'	*contemplate*	→ 'compensate'
	bibliography	→ 'biography'	*sip*	→ 'sup'
			violate	→ 'velocity'
Vis and/or *sem*	satirical	→ 'sarcastic'		
Nonword	idiosyncracy	→ 'idiocratic' (idiosyncratic?)		
Omissions	homonym			
	somnambulist			

words) and, with one exception, on rather long and difficult words. Thirdly, one might wonder whether some of the errors classified as derivational could not just as sensibly be considered visual. This same question has been raised with regard to derivational and visual errors by deep dyslexic patients, and some arguments for maintaining separate categories for these errors in that syndrome have been given elsewhere (Patterson, 1978, 1980). I have no definitive justification for classifying A.M.'s error *initiate* → 'initiative' as derivational rather than visual. My reasons for so doing are that (1) so few of his errors are visual but clearly not derivational; (2) on a *purely* visual basis, *initiate* for example is probably more similar to *imitate* than to *initiative*; (3) A.M.'s reading performance constitutes a more coherent and more theoretically interesting pattern if we can conclude that only one type of paralexic error, derivational, occurred often enough to require an account.

6 *Omissions.* As with visual paralexias, the data in Table II make it inaccurate to say that there were never omissions in A.M.'s oral reading. Failure to respond to two uncommon words in the reading of 300 words does however seem negligible.

The aspects of reading impairment which A.M. did share with deep dyslexic patients will now be discussed, commencing with the most prominent one.

C   PHONOLOGICAL READING

Like the other phonological dyslexic patients who have been described
(Beauvois and Dérouesné, 1979a, b; Dérouesné and Beauvois, 1979;
Shallice and Warrington, 1980), A.M. was impaired on any task which
required him to assemble a phonological code for an unfamiliar word or
letter string. Before these tests are presented, A.M.'s ability to name and
sound individual letters should be mentioned. I do not have complete
data here, partly because A.M. was initially very impaired on these skills,
and he would get upset and ask to stop. Because he was troubled by his
difficulty in letter naming, his speech therapist worked on this with him
extensively, and he gradually improved (though he was never error-
free). Unfortunately, I did not see him with sufficient regularity to chart
this improvement. When I first tested A.M., he managed to name 3/10
randomly presented lower-case letters, making no response to the other
seven, and then asked to stop. He was unable to sound individual letters
at this time, responding to several with a whole word (e.g. m → 'mother')
but mostly unwilling to try. On a subsequent occasion, he correctly
named 5/12 upper-case letters before stopping; most of his failures here,
rather than omissions, were production of a word beginning with the
appropriate letter (e.g. G → 'George', Q → 'queen'). He reliably named a
few letters which he had learned to associate with phonologically equivalent words, such as J (jay, the bird) and M (em, a printer's measurement).
This deficit in sounding and naming letters was clearly at a phonological
level. A.M.'s ability to recognise or identify individual letters was intact,
as demonstrated informally by responses like G → 'George' and more
formally by his perfect performance at matching upper- and lower-case
versions of letters.

Four different tests were used which require assembly of a phonological code from a printed letter string, and one in which performance
would be affected by such coding if it were occurring.

1   *Reading nonwords.* A.M. was tested five times between April 1978 and
July 1979 on reading aloud lists of nonwords. All of the nonwords were
orthographically regular (thus easily pronounceable by a normal reader)
and most were single syllable items of 3–6 letters in length. On two
occasions there was a manipulation of homophony (lists 3 and 4) where
approximately half of the nonwords were phonologically equivalent to a
real word (e.g. *ile, rair*) while the others were not (e.g. *soof, dode*). On one
occasion the nonwords were randomly inter-mixed with an equal number of real words (list 5). Proportions of correct reading responses for
nonwords on the five tests are shown in Table III. For the reader who is
interested in more detail, each of the nonwords from list 4 and A.M.'s
response to it are presented in Appendix 1.

Table III   A.M.'s performance in oral reading of nonwords

List	Date	No. of nonwords	Special characteristics	Proportion read correctly
1	April 1978	24	—	0.00
2	July 1978	24	—	0.08
3	Oct. 1978	36	homophonic	0.47
			nonhomophonic	0.26
4	July 1979	40	homophonic	0.35
			nonhomophonic	0.10
5	July 1979	26	intermixed with words	0.19
Homophonic nonwords from lists 3 + 4		37	high visual similarity	0.58
			low visual similarity	0.32

The following points summarise A.M.'s performance in reading nonwords.

(a) On the first occasion A.M. would not really attempt the task beyond the first item, saying that he could not do it.[4] On each subsequent test, he tried to read every item. Although there were a few omissions in response to nonwords on lists 2–5, most of A.M.'s incorrect responses were visually similar real words (e.g. *soof* → 'soot') and often a series thereof (*klack* → 'slack; black; flock'). His *first* response to a nonword was in fact usually a real word, which might then be followed by other real words (as in the example just given) or by some incorrect nonwords (e.g. *prab* → 'pram, pranch, prad') or eventually by the correct response (e.g. *warse* → 'worse, war, warse'). I have counted an item as correct if he gave a correct response at any point in a series of attempts. If only *first* responses were scored, then his proportion correct on list 5, for example, would be 0.08 rather than 0.19.

(b) There seems to have been an improvement in his phonological skills between occasions 2 and 3, though no further increase thereafter. The nonwords in list 3, though not specifically designed for this purpose, were somewhat simpler in structure (e.g. *hin, beed*) than those in other lists; this may account for his rather good performance on this occasion. It is important to note that the improvement in phonological skill was not accompanied by any change in his reading performance on real words. Indeed, on the same date that he managed to read only 0.08 (list 2) of nonwords, he correctly read 0.95 of a list of content words varying in imageability and concreteness (from Marcel and Patterson, 1978) which includes fairly uncommon words like *decree* and *phase*.

(c) Like some of Dérouesné and Beauvois' (1979) patients, A.M.'s reading of nonwords was clearly facilitated when the nonwords were homophonic with real words. There is some uncertainty about an account for this effect. In my view, it is attributable to A.M.'s use, at least in part, of a particular strategy for reading nonwords. This same strategy is used by deep dyslexic patients: find and pronounce a visually similar real word. (Indeed this appears to be the *only* strategy available to some deep dyslexic patients, a restriction which does not apply to A.M.; this contrast will be discussed further at the end of this section.) With this strategy, there is one and only one type of nonword which might be read 'correctly': a nonword which is both homophonic with a real word and visually similar to it, e.g. *toun*. 'Correctly' is in inverted commas because, as was noted in Patterson and Marcel (1977), such a response is, in a way, spuriously correct. If the response to *toun* is achieved by locating *town* in one's lexical system (by means of an approximate visual or graphemic specification) and then retrieving its pronunciation, the process involved is no different from responding to *hin* by finding *him* and retrieving its pronunciation. The experimenter however labels *toun* → 'town' correct and *hin* → 'him' wrong.

By this analysis, the finding that A.M. was better at reading nonwords when they were homophonic with real words is reasonable, but incomplete: the degree of visual similarity between the nonword and its word homophone should also matter. *Phude* may be homophonic with a real word, but a graphemic code is rather unlikely to provide access to that word. I did not deliberately manipulate visual similarity, but a *post hoc* analysis is possible. The homophonic nonwords in lists 3 and 4 can be classified as having high or low visual similarity with their word counterparts.[5] There are, unfortunately, not a large number of observations; but there is at least a suggestive difference in favour of the hypothesis, as shown at the bottom of Table III.

The reason for the alleged uncertainty of this account is that Beauvois and Dérouesné (1979b), while obtaining a significant superiority of homophonic to nonhomophonic nonwords, did not find a difference in their patient's reading of homophonic nonwords as a function of visual similarity to the word counterparts. This discrepancy between their results and mine remains to be resolved. It may arise at least in part from a difference in instructions: R.G. (Beauvois and Dérouesné, 1979b) was told which nonwords were homophonic with words whereas A.M. was not.

(*d*) There does not appear to be any major difference between A.M.'s reading of nonwords when in homogeneous lists and when intermixed with familiar words.

(*e*) It is worth noting that A.M. was utterly unconfident about his responses to nonwords; his intonation, for example, virtually always ended on a rising pitch, i.e. with a question mark. This was of course sensible for many responses (which were wrong), but it was also characteristic of his occasional correct nonword readings. As already mentioned, he often made a sequence of attempts at an item; the fact that a correct response tended to terminate a sequence does not indicate that he was finally satisfied, but rather that I was and told him so. When he could not achieve a pronunciation for a nonword, I or the speech therapist would often say it for him. He would then repeat it, but with a definite sense of 'I'll take your word for it' (literally) rather than 'yes, I recognise that as correct'.

(f) Finally, as implied by the last sentence, A.M.'s difficulty in reading nonwords cannot be attributed to an output problem because he was reasonably good at repeating nonwords. On the same date that A.M. read 0.08 of a list of 24 nonwords, he correctly repeated 0.83 of a list of 30 nonwords. Almost all of his few repetition errors involved substitution of a similar real word (e.g. 'rabe' → 'rave', 'nime' → 'nine').

2 *Judging homophony.* Coltheart (personal communication) has developed a test in which the subject or patient is presented with printed pairs of letter-strings and judges whether the two members of each pair would sound identical if pronounced. The test has three separate parts, each consisting of 50 pairs, 25 of which are homophonic and 25 of which are not. In part 1, all letter strings are regularly spelled words; examples of pairs which should receive 'yes' and 'no' responses, respectively, are *pause-paws* and *pause-pads*. In part 2, all letter strings are words but many are irregularly spelled words (which require addressed rather than assembled phonology to attain correct pronunciation); examples for 'yes' and 'no' are *berry-bury* and *ferry-fury*. In part 3, all letter strings are nonwords (which require assembled phonology); 'yes' and 'no' instances are *feks-phex* and *nime-nume*. When first confronted with part (3), A.M. said that he could not do it and gave up after a few pairs; several months later however he completed the entire test.

A.M.'s performance, in terms of hit rate, false positive rate and d' (a measure of discriminability between pairs which are homophonic and those which are not) appears in Table IV. His scores on parts (1) and (2), though not quite perfect, were competent and did not differ for irregular and regular words. He was very much worse on nonwords, but above

Table IV   A.M.'s performance in judging homophony of word and nonword pairs

		Hit rate	FP rate	d'
1	Regular words	0.84	0.01	3.31
2	Irregular words	0.92	0.04	3.15
3	Nonwords	0.64	0.12	1.54
	Nonword pairs begin with same letter?			
	yes (N = 32)	0.75	0.19	
	no (N = 18)	0.45	0.00	

chance; he was quite surprised when I indicated that he had judged some correctly, since he claimed merely to be guessing. He described his strategy as follows: 'In general, if the two began with different letters, I said no'. In the test, of course, pairs beginning with the same letter are equally likely to be homophonic (e.g. *eaf-eeph*) or nonhomophonic (*erf-eeps*), and the same is true for pairs which do not share first letter (*caum-kawm vs cade-rald*). Thus his strategy does not 'help' him; but his use of it is certainly evident when performance is calculated separately for pairs which do and do not share first letter (see Table IV).

3   *Auditory-visual matching of nonwords.* A.M. was given a single printed nonword on a card; the experimenter read aloud three nonwords, and A.M.'s task was to indicate which of the three spoken items was the auditory equivalent of the printed nonword. (This test was devised for deep dyslexic patients D.E. and P.W.; Patterson, 1978.) In one version of the test, the three nonword alternatives were phonologically quite distinct from each other (e.g. 'fleb, trean, mide') while in the other version they were phonologically similar (e.g. 'pabe, pame, pake' or 'quob, queb, quib'). A.M.'s proportions of correct choices on these two sets respectively were 0.79 and 0.60. This performance is (*a*) significantly better than chance (0.33); (*b*) not surprisingly, worse on the second, more difficult version; (*c*) interesting when compared with performance by the deep dyslexic patients for whom the test was originally intended. On the phonologically distinct set, scores for D.E. and P.W., respectively, were 0.80 and 0.75; on the confusable set, these patients managed only 0.44 and 0.36 (Patterson, 1978). In other words, A.M.'s score was significantly above the deep dyslexic patients on the confusable set, but there was no difference between the two types of patients on the distinct set.

4   *Reading names* (or 'Ben Murdock but *not* Endel Tulving'). I gave A.M. the 1974 staff list from the Psychology Department at the University of Toronto and asked him to read the names aloud.[6] A quantitative summary of his performance would be relatively meaningless without the stimulus list; but a reasonably accurate qualitative summary is that he could read both first names and surnames which were in his 'vocabulary', but he was unable to produce unfamiliar names. Thus he read *Ben Murdock* but not *Endel Tulving*. In general, and not surprisingly, he managed more first names than surnames; but unusual first names yielded his typical reading behaviour with nonwords (e.g. *Rona* → 'Ron, Ran, Rons'). Other examples where he managed to find and produce a visually similar name are *Berlyne* → 'Beryl', *Efran* → 'Fran', *Fergus* → 'Ferguson'. For some names he produced whatever bits he could extract (*Biederman* → 'it begins with the letter B and ends with man'), while for others he simply gave up in despair (Moscovitch and Mrosovsky)!

5   *Lexical decision with homophonic nonwords.* It is well established that

normal subjects are slower and less accurate in their lexical decisions to nonwords if these are homophonic with real words (Rubenstein *et al.*, 1971; Coltheart *et al.*, 1977). Deep dyslexic patients do not show this effect (Patterson and Marcel, 1977), presumably because they do not perform the phonological coding of nonwords to which the effect is attributed. A.M. was given four lexical decision lists, each consisting of 34 items, 17 words and 17 nonwords. The nonwords in two of the lists were homophonic with real words (e.g. *korse*) and in the remaining two were not (e.g. *hort*) (see Patterson and Marcel, 1977, for details). He made only one error in the entire set of four lists, a 'miss' error on a word in one of the nonhomophonic lists; thus the accuracy of his performance clearly showed no influence of the homophony of nonwords. This absence of errors may have been achieved at a cost in speed: although he was asked to do the test as quickly as possible, A.M. performed this test (and most others) rather slowly and deliberately, more slowly than either normal or deep dyslexic subjects. His rate of processing was however virtually identical on the two different sorts of lists. Mean times to complete the lexical decision lists were 59 s for the lists containing homophonic nonwords and 58.5 s for lists with nonhomophonic nonwords.

6 *Summary of phonological reading.* A.M. showed poor performance on all of the tests requiring assembled phonology for printed letter strings, and he failed to show the normal effect of phonological coding on nonwords in lexical decision.[7] I would not try to argue that he utterly lacked the ability to assemble phonology from print; his performance on some of the tests was certainly better than the particular deep dyslexic patients whom I have tested. The important points about A.M.'s phonological deficit, however, are these:

(*a*) He was impaired on what was arguably the easiest test, auditory-visual matching of phonologically distinct nonwords. Even the most minimal ability to assemble a phonological code from graphemes should enable one to judge that *treap* matches 'treap' rather than 'foach' or 'bem'. A.M.'s score of 0.79 on this test, though clearly much better than chance, is also much less than perfect; furthermore it is virtually identical to the scores obtained on this test by deep dyslexic patients D.E. and P.W.

(*b*) There is almost certainly a range of phonological ability even within the set of reported deep dyslexic patients, all of whom show a severe deficit in this regard. It is possible to conclude (as far as the parallels can be drawn, given differences in testing procedures and stimulus materials) that A.M., while at the high end of this range, was not actually outside it. Some deep dyslexic patients manage to read a few nonsense syllables. V.S., a deep dyslexic patient studied by Saffran and Marin (1977), scored 0.70 on auditory-visual matching of 3-letter nonwords with highly similar distractors; indeed she was perfect on those where the various alternatives differed only on initial letter, whereas A.M. made errors on comparable items (choosing, for example, 'nask' to match *dask*).

(c) Perhaps both A.M. and a few deep dyslexic patients either retained or regained a minimal degree of ability to assemble phonology for written letter strings. Thus one might not want to argue for these patients, as I did for D.E. and P.W. (Patterson, 1978), that all correct responses on a task like auditory-visual matching of nonwords were actually accomplished not via assembled phonology but rather via *addressed* phonology for real words visually similar to the nonwords. That is, A.M. may have tried to assemble phonology when the task demanded it because he had a very slight ability to do so; certain deep dyslexic patients like D.E. and P.W., having no such ability, would simply apply a different strategy. Obviously, however, nonwords which demand assembled phonology occur as stimuli only for analytic purposes; and the important question both practically and theoretically is what the patients do when faced with words. I would argue that A.M.'s ability to assemble a phonological code was so minimal, so slow, so hesitant and so error-prone that it is exceedingly unlikely to have played any role in his confident and accurate reading of real words. This argument is supported by the fact that A.M. improved in ability and/or willingness to do nonword tasks from the first few test sessions to subsequent ones, while his performance on real content words did not change at all over the same period, either in accuracy or speed. This absence of improvement could be due to a ceiling effect: his reading and comprehension of content words in early test sessions were excellent. That, however, merely makes the same point in a different way: someone who cannot or at least does not assemble phonology for letter strings can still show competent comprehension and oral reading of single content words.

By this line of reasoning, a deficit in assembling phonology *might* cause or at least contribute to those facets of reading performance which are impaired in both deep and phonological dyslexia, but it cannot be used to account for symptoms which occur in deep but not phonological dyslexia. To take a specific example, a number of investigators studying deep dyslexia have considered the possibility that semantic paralexias might be attributable to the failure of assembled phonology. The most recent and explicit statement of this hypothesis is to be found in Newcombe and Marshall (1980). The notion is that semantic specifications accessed from written words are, by themselves and even in the normal reader, imprecise; identification of the exactly correct word from amongst semantically similar alternatives is assisted by additional information from an assembled phonological code, which thus prevents semantic paralexias in reading. By the present line of argument, however, this description seems problematic. I have argued that, in the early stages, A.M. could not (or at least would not) assemble phonology from print, and that, even in later stages, he did not attempt to do so unless the presentation of nonwords absolutely required it; yet at no time did he make semantic paralexias in reading single words aloud. Furthermore, as already noted, some deep dyslexic patients have apparently retained or regained a minimal skill for assembling phonology (not much, but arguably as much as A.M.). Yet the deep dyslexic patients can continue to make frequent semantic paralexias like *protein* → 'carbohydrate', where it would seem that even the most minimal phonological recoding would, *if* it functioned in this way, block the error. A reasonable conclusion would therefore seem that semantic paralexias are not attributable to the loss of assembled phonology. Consonant with this position is the occurrence of semantic paralexias when Japanese deep dyslexic patients read single words written in kanji, the Japanese logographic script derived from Chinese. Assembled phonology is irrelevant to kanji which carries no nonlexical phonological information. How then could the impairment of assembled phonology (revealed in Japanese deep dyslexics by severe deficits in reading kana, the syllabic phonological script) disrupt the reading of kanji to produce semantic errors?

I have indulged in this rather extended discussion of semantic paralexias in deep dyslexia because it is a good specific example of this general point: if A.M., a phonological dyslexic patient, had no greater functional use of assembled phonology than (at least some) deep dyslexic patients, then symptoms present in deep but not phonological dyslexia are unlikely to be attributable to the phonological deficit. It remains a possibility, however, that a deficit in assembling phonology from print is implicated in those symptoms shared by the two syndromes. Notable features which A.M. shared with deep dyslexic patients were derivational paralexias and difficulty in reading function words.

D DERIVATIONAL ERRORS

In fact I did not test A.M.'s reading of single content words all that extensively because, right from the start, he made few errors unless the words were extremely rare and difficult. From the data I do have, however, it is clear that A.M.'s most probable type of reading error was a derivational paralexia. Eleven of his 17 reading errors on the 100 Schonell words (1942) and nine of his 12 reading errors on Klee and Legge's (1976) list of 200 verbs were derivational paralexias (see Table II). Although derivational errors obviously occurred on single-morpheme words (all of the 200 verbs, for example, were uninflected), the rate of such errors was higher on inflected or derived words. A.M. read a set of 96 abstract words (from various lexical decision tests; Patterson, 1979, 1980) consisting of 44 single-morpheme words (such as *reason, enough, deceit*) and 52 inflected or derived words (such as *guessed, meant, productive*, etc.). He only made $1/44 = 0.02$ derivational errors on the single morpheme words in this set, but $11/52 = 0.21$ derivational errors on the affixed words. His errors were not always restricted to the bound morpheme portion of the target word: for example, in *inanimate* → 'animated', he has not only dropped the prefix but has added a gratuitous suffix. The fact that his error rate was an order of magnitude higher on the affixed words does however suggest that these bound morphemes provided a specific source of difficulty. The same phenomenon has been observed with deep dyslexic patients (Patterson, 1980).

A.M.'s difficulty with derivational forms was perhaps most prominent in reading aloud, but it was also detectable in other tasks. Firstly, given a lexical decision test where all 35 words were suffixed (e.g. *costly*, *nearest*) and all 35 nonwords were composed of a real base morpheme with a real but illegitimate suffix (e.g. *passly*, *fearest*), A.M.'s hit rate was 0.86 and his false positive rate was 0.09 (d' = 2.42). While this does not amount to a major deficit, it is clearly lower than his typical ability to make lexical decisions: a lexical decision test with low frequency abstract words and minimally distinguishable nonwords, for example, yielded a d' of 3.43. Secondly, in an auditory-visual matching test where he was given a single printed word (e.g. *angry*) and asked to identify it amongst three spoken derivational alternatives ('angrily, angry, anger'), he scored 19/24 = 0.79 correct. Once again, while this is moderately good performance (and considerably better than that of deep dyslexic patients on the same test; Patterson, 1980), it is not at a normal level. Finally, A.M. made a few errors on a test of selecting the correct derivational form of a word to fit in a written sentence. For example, in *The plants have really (growing/grown) this week*, he chose the first alternative. His performance on this task was 22/26 = 0.85 correct, far better than deep dyslexic patients D.E. and P.W., but once again measurably lower than a normal reader would obtain.

E FUNCTION WORDS

On the rather loosely defined class of words known as function words (which includes prepositions, conjunctions, pronouns, articles, auxillary verbs, and certain adverbs and adjectives), A.M. showed a reading deficit. This was not, as it is for most deep dyslexic patients, a deficit of huge proportions; but it is worthy of attention because it was (*a*) consistent; (*b*) specific to reading (that is, A.M.'s spontaneous speech showed normal use of function words); and (*c*) his only word-class deficit.

A.M.'s performance on several different tests involving written function words is presented in Table V. Firstly, he was quite normal and unimpaired in his lexical decision performance on a test where function words were to be discriminated from nonwords obtained by changing one letter in a function word (e.g. *thore* from those, *whare* from where, etc.). This almost perfect score is scarcely surprising given his generally good lexical decision performance and given unimpaired lexical decision for function words by deep dyslexic patients; but it seemed worth confirming. Secondly, his oral reading performance on lists of function words was in the range 0.70–0.78. His errors included some omissions, very occasionally a content word response (e.g. *an* → 'can'),[8] and primarily substitution of a different function word. Most of these had a

Table V   Lexical decision and oral reading tests on function words

---

Lexical decision
   60 function words   (e.g. *which, our*) hit rate = 0. 98
   60 nonwords   (e.g. *thise, weth*) FP rate = 0.00

Reading lists of function words
   June 1978   28/40 correct   = 0.70
   March 1979   98/126   = 0.78

Content – Function comparison
   4 lists of each type, N = 15 words for each list

	Content	Function
Mean proportion correct per list	0.92	0.72
Range of proportions correct over 4 lists	1.0–0.87	0.87–0.53
Mean time per list (seconds)	34.25	50.0
Range of times over 4 lists (s)	28–42	42–68

---

strong element of visual similarity (e.g. *if* → 'it', *with* → 'which', *they* → 'there'), but a few were visually dissimilar (e.g. *that* → 'which'). A corpus of function word errors appears in Appendix 2.

A comparison was made of A.M.'s accuracy and speed of reading on content and function words. Eight 15-word lists were used, comprised of four lists of each word class and, within word class, two lists each of one-syllable and two-syllable words. He was asked to read each list straight through, in the sense that if he could not get a word, he was to go on to the next one rather than persevere on the difficult one. Time required to read each 15-item list was recorded to the nearest second; content and function word lists were tested in alternation. The results are shown in Table V. The exact numbers are of course fortuitous; I would scarcely conclude that A.M.'s performances on content and function words form non-overlapping distributions. On this test, though, as it happened, the highest proportion correct on a function-word list just equalled the lowest proportion correct on a content-word list, and the fastest time on a function-word list just equalled the slowest time on a content-word list. Syllabic length, by the way, made no difference; the lists of two-syllable words were, if anything, read more quickly. These tests demonstrate that A.M., with no syntactic deficit in speech production and no (or only the most minor) syntactic deficit in auditory comprehension, was consistently slower and less accurate in oral reading of function words than of content words.

What about his comprehension of written function words? I do not have fully adequate data on this question; but the available data suggest a conclusion similar to those of (*a*) Morton and Patterson (1980), regarding comprehension of written function words by a deep dyslexic patient; (*b*) Beauvois and Dérouesné (1979b), regarding oral reading of function words by a phonological dyslexic patient; and (c) Schwartz, Saffran and Marin (1980), regarding comprehension of spoken function words in agrammatic aphasic patients. The operative variable is in the words themselves: some function words have significant semantic content, for example pronouns (like *she*), spatial prepositions (like *under*) and time-related prepositions (like *before*); other function words serve an almost purely syntactic or grammatical role, the best example of which may be case-marking prepositions like *of* and *at*. Furthermore, the same function word may have both semantic and syntactic dimensions: *he* and *him* for example are roughly the same semantically but different syntactically. All of the reports mentioned above conclude that aphasic or dyslexic patients can be relatively competent at producing and/or comprehending seman-tically rich function words but impaired on the purely syntactic words or features of words. This conclusion provides a reasonably good descrip-tion of A.M.'s comprehension of function words. He easily ordered written quantity words (*none, one, few, some, several, many, all*) and fre-quency words (*never, once, seldom, sometimes, often, usually, always*). He usually managed to follow written instructions involving spatial pre-positions, correctly performing for example 15/18 instructions like *Put the cup below the saucer*. With written sentences, he made no errors on those items of a sentence-picture matching test (designed by Bishop, 1980) that evaluate comprehension of pronouns and spatial prepositions.[9]

A.M. was tested on parts of the function word triad test devised by Morton and Patterson (1980), examples of which appear in Table VI along with an indication of A.M.'s performance. It is difficult to know, for this test, what instruction to give apart from 'Which one of these first two words "goes with" this third word?' together with some easy examples. P.W., the deep dyslexic patient for whom these tests were designed, needed no further instruction: although his judgements were adequate only on some types of triads, in all cases P.W. appeared to understand what was required of him and proceeded to complete the test. A.M., on the other hand, while managing reasonable performance on some types of triad, simply gave up on other types of judgement, saying not only that he could not do it but that he did not understand what he was supposed to do. It is for this reason that some of the judgement types in Table VI carry no score. With a few exceptions, the varieties of judgement on which he was successful are consonant both with P.W.'s performance and with the rough summary 'semantic, but not syntactic'. Time, space and gender specifications are all strongly semantic, and logical conjunc-tion words could be so considered. Person and especially case of pronouns seem largely syntactic. Demonstrative number is less easy to classify, but P.W.'s good performance on this type (Morton and Patterson, 1980) makes A.M.'s difficulty slightly surprising. Most surprising of all was A.M.'s failure on the interrogatives, which seem intuitively to have a strong semantic component. In summary, although these triad tests did

Table VI   A.M.'s performance on triad tests for assessing comprehension of written function words

Successful triad tests

Type	Examples				Probability correct
Time	now then	later	before after	since	1.00
Space	over under	up	ahead behind	back	0.90
Gender	she he	hers	her him	he	0.80
Logical conjunctions	therefore however	because	but and	however	0.80

Unsuccessful triad tests

Pronouns (person)	us them	we	me he	his	—
Pronouns (case)	he him	her	my me	our	—
Demonstratives (number)	this these	that	that those	many	—
Interrogatives	why who	person	which where	thing	0.20

not 'work' well with A.M., they suggest that his difficulty in oral reading of written function words is accompanied by at least some (probably syntactic) deficit in comprehension.

4   Discussion

A.M.'s accuracy in comprehension and oral reading of individual words departed from normal only with respect to function words and derivational or inflectional morphemes. The question which must now be addressed is whether these effects might plausibly be related to his severe deficit in assembling phonology from graphemic information. It is worth noting that, while Coltheart (1980) failed to find any influence of assembled phonology in normal adult reading, the stimulus materials in the studies which provided this conclusion were (I believe without exception) uninflected content words. Coltheart's conclusion does not, therefore, logically deny the possibility that assembled phonology might be germane to the reading of grammatical words and morphemes. Is there, however, any reason to suppose such a relationship? A consideration of this question will require some discussion of the processes involved in assembling phonology.

While it has always been clear that the *procedures* for translating graphemes to phonology would have to be complex in a language like English, psychologists did not until recently attempt to model these procedures. It was simply assumed that the reader had acquired a set of 'grapheme-phoneme' rules; these were described as nonlexical because, while presumably derived at least in part from lexical knowledge, the rules were to be applied without reference to the lexical system at the time of trying to assemble phonology for a letter string. Difficulties were noted, in particular the fact that such a procedure would create erroneous phonology for all the irregular words in English; but in any case no one believed that lexical access would be *always* and *exclusively* based on a phonological code. Alternatives were noted, in particular the possibility of assembling phonology for a nonword or new word by analogy with known words (Baron, 1977); but no detailed process model was proffered for pronunciation by analogy, either.

This situation has changed dramatically within the last few years. Firstly, Coltheart (1978) has presented a detailed account of how a nonlexical grapheme-phoneme procedure might work. Secondly, several authors have begun to question the assumption that the system for assembling phonology from print is 'nonlexical' (Glushko, 1979; Marcel, 1980; Shallice and Warrington, 1980; Henderson, 1982). In one sense these new accounts represent an attempt to specify the process of pronunciation by analogy. The notion is that, for words and nonwords alike, phonology is assembled by dividing the letter string into graphemic segments and determining how each segment is pronounced in known words. The critical question is no longer whether the letter string generates a *regular* pronunciation, but whether, when the various lexical analogies are consulted, it generates a *consistent* pronunciation. Graphemic segments like *ave* have an inconsistent pronunciation in words (*wave vs have*), and Glushko (1979) has demonstrated that both nonwords (e.g. *tave*) and words (e.g. *cave*) containing inconsistent segments are slower to be read aloud than those with segments pronounced in only one way in familiar words. Furthermore, both Glushko (1979) and Kay and Marcel (1981) have shown that the actual pronunciation given to nonwords, instead of being determined simply by regular grapheme-phoneme rules, is influenced by lexical factors. Thus the nonword *tave* is sometimes pronounced to rhyme with the word *have* (Glushko, 1979), especially if *have* has recently been read aloud (Kay and Marcel, 1981).

What has all this to do with grammatical morphemes? One particular version of this class of new models for assembled phonology (Shallice and

Warrington, 1980) proposes a sort of lexicon of graphemic segments with phonological counterparts. Phonological alternatives for a given segment (e.g. *ea* as in *bead vs head*) are represented, and the frequency with which a particular pronunciation occurs in known words exerts a significant influence. Assembled phonology can be obtained for any word or letter string by segmenting it into sufficiently small units (down to individual letters if necessary) to be found in this phonological system. *Short frequent words* and *subword sized segments which occur very frequently* are however represented as whole units.[10] What are the most likely instantiations of these two classes, respectively, if not function words and bound morphemes (affixes)?

Another feature of Shallice and Warrington's (1980) model is critical here: it specifies that there are only two procedures for pronouncing a written word. One involves orthographically based identification of the word, which provides access to the word's semantic representation, which in turn addresses phonology in an output lexicon of known words. The other is the phonological system just described, in which a process of graphemic segmentation and phonological assembly will be required for most words but in which phonology for a short frequent word or segment will be available as a whole. Suppose that the process involving the semantic system and addressed phonology is not especially well suited to reading function words and bound morphemes which serve a largely syntactic role. The only alternative or at least supplementary procedure for dealing with these elements will be the phonological system; and this system, moreover, *is* particularly well equipped to provide a phonological code for these items, a code which would support oral reading and might even assist comprehension. By this account, any patient with a deficient phonological assembly system should have difficulty reading function words (especially the more purely syntactic ones) and should make derivational errors in reading.

Unfortunately, no flood of evidence can be called forth to support the conjectured relationship between assembled phonology and grammatical morphemes; but the following points seem relevant.

Firstly, although arguments by association in neuropsychology are notoriously risky (since tomorrow a new patient may present the critical dissociation), to date I know of no reported patient with a serious impairment in assembling phonology from print who has not also had difficulty in reading grammatical morphemes. All deep dyslexics show this association, and all reported phonological dyslexics do as well (though the two patients described by Shallice and Warrington (1980) apparently read function words well, only displaying a notable difficulty with affixes). A.R., a patient described by Warrington and Shallice (1979) who was unable to read by assembling a phonological code did not show a *special* difficulty with grammatical morphemes. His oral reading ability was however poor for any sort of word, function words included. The disconfirming case would be a patient who cannot assemble phonology from print but who competently reads all sorts of grammatical morphemes, including affixes.

Secondly, it is possibly worth recalling that in Japanese, function words and affixes are written in the syllabic script kana. In kana and other phonologically shallow scripts (e.g. Serbo-Croatian: Lukatela, Popadić, Ognjenović and Turvey, 1980), it appears that lexical access may involve a phonological code (Sasanuma, 1980). Allport (1979) has noted as worthy of consideration the possibility that in alphabetic scripts, '. . .content words may be interpreted semantically without any phonological mediation, whereas syntactic morphemes (like kana), if they are to be explicitly understood, depend on phonological coding' (p. 232).

Thirdly, in one of the very few investigations of normal readers' performance on function words, Bradley (1978) has studied reaction time in lexical decision as a function of frequency of occurrence of the words. Latency of decision for content words is characterised by a strong inverse relationship with frequency, but there is no hint of such a relationship for function words. Over the (admittedly somewhat restricted) range of frequencies, the curve for function words is flat. Bradley's interpretation is that recognition for the two classes of words proceeds via different retrieval mechanisms. There is nothing in this result, of course, which specifically implicates the phonological system in retrieval of function words; but the result does lend support to a more general hypothesis that function words require special treatment in our process models.

Finally, it has been observed in rapid oral reading of text by normal readers that the highest rate of errors is on function words and bound morphemes (Morton, 1964). At first glance this fact might seem to cause difficulty for the hypothesis that the phonological system has a special affinity for grammatical morphemes. The process of reading text, however, even aloud, appears to be largely guided by the semantic system (Kolers, 1966); and if grammatical morphemes are inadequately handled by the semantic system, then one would expect them to suffer. There is evidence that they do suffer in silent reading: grammatical morphemes engender a significantly high miss rate in letter and word detection tasks (Drewnowski and Healy, 1977; 1980). Oral reading of text plausibly involves much the same processes as silent reading (with, obviously, some additional ones). As the high error rate in detecting the word *the* in silent reading disappears when the words are presented as lists rather than text (Drewnowski, 1978), one might predict that the errors on grammatical morphemes in oral reading (by normal subjects) should largely disappear given word lists rather than text.

One reaction to the proposed relationship between assembled phonology and grammatical morphemes, given that it appears both *post hoc* and somewhat contorted, might be to dismiss it. The two deficits in phonological dyslexia would then be viewed as two independent deficits.

This is certainly possible; but note that it still requires an account of the difficulty in reading function words and affixes. One apparently simple proposal might be that for the normal reader, grammatical morphemes are comprehended and pronounced just like other words or word components; the deficit for these elements in phonological dyslexia might then arise in the semantic/syntactic systems, or in the connection from these to the output lexicon, or even in the output lexicon itself. Such a proposal however encounters the problem that the spontaneous speech of patients like A.M. is normal – or at least is certainly grammatical. The locus of the deficit would thus have to be pushed to an earlier stage, prior to the point at which, in most models, oral reading and speech are presumed to share common mechanisms. In other words, one could locate the problem either in the visual input lexicon (visual input logogen system in Morton's (1979) model, visual word-form system in Warrington and Shallice's (1980) model) or in its connection to the semantic system. A.M.'s perfect performance in lexical decision on function words however would seem to rule out the former and might even cause difficulties for the latter, given evidence for involvement of the semantic system in the lexical decision task (James, 1975; Warrington, 1975). The point to be made is simply this: while the account considered above may have its problems, alternative accounts are not necessarily straightforward either.

Thus far, it has been convenient to group function words and bound morphemes into a single class of 'grammatical morphemes'. Given their important syntactic role, it is plausible that the two should be related; but there are also reasons, both logical and empirical, why function words and affixes may require separate accounts.

Firstly, in at least one task, namely lexical decision, A.M. was differentially affected by function words and affixes. He was essentially perfect (certainly normal) on the function word test, as he was in almost all lexical decision tests; but he showed a lower hit rate and a higher false positive rate in lexical decision with words like *nearest* and nonwords like *fearest*. Thus he appeared to know which affixes are acceptable in English but to be somewhat uncertain whether a particular bound morpheme was legitimate in a particular context.

Secondly, while function words are free morphemes, affixes are bound morphemes. Any suggestion of separate treatment assigned to the root and bound morphemes composing a single word entails a sophisticated segmentation process: *warmer* must be decomposed into two morphemes while *bitter* must not. Such a procedure, though complex, is apparently feasible (Thorne, Bratley and Dewar, 1968); and several theories of word recognition propose that different derivational forms of the same base word (at least those with regular inflections) have either one common recognition unit or, if multiple units, then non-independent ones (e.g. Murrell and Morton, 1974; Stanners, Neiser, Hernon and Hall, 1979; Taft, 1979). One interesting possibility in the present context is that the same graphemic segmentation process required by the phonological assembly system also precedes visual word recognition. Space limitations here preclude further comment on the possible involvement of segmentation in word recognition (see Taft, 1979, for a good discussion). It is worth noting, however, that graphemic segmentation may well be differentially involved in or required by elements of the different sorts under consideration here (Marcel, 1980). Thus the reading of nonwords would absolutely depend upon segmentation in order to achieve chunks or graphemes whose pronunciation can be obtained; the correct reading of affixes would probably require a less complex segmentation, between root and bound morphemes; function words (or indeed any short frequent words) would require minimal graphemic segmentation. It is perhaps not so surprising, on this analysis, that a function word deficit should be a variable feature of phonological dyslexia. R.G. (Beauvois and Dérouesné, 1979b) and A.M. both displayed this deficit but G.R.N. and B.T.T. (Shallice and Warrington, 1980 and personal communication) did not. All four patients however were impaired on affixes and severely impaired at reading nonwords. What one ought not to observe, for example, is a patient with a function word deficit who perfectly reads affixes.

To summarise, it is suggested that the system for assembling phonology from print might play a role in normal reading specifically with regard to grammatical morphemes (function words and bound morphemes). There is scarcely any evidence for this hypothesis from studies of normal word processing; but very few such studies have employed grammatical morphemes as materials. There is not even much evidence from studies of language deficits, apart from the fact that the hypothesised co-occurrence appears in both deep and phonological dyslexia. The prediction here is that as further cases of acquired dyslexia are studied, (1) patients with a deficit in assembling phonology from print (deep and phonological dyslexia) will invariably show selective difficulty in reading grammatical morphemes; (2) patients with an impairment in reading via the semantic system who are therefore likely to rely on the phonological system for reading (surface or semantic dyslexia) should never show selective difficulties on grammatical morphemes.

5   Concluding remarks

The preceding discussion has centred on the possibility of a specific involvement of phonological coding in reading; but the more critical message from the syndrome of phonological dyslexia is the very limited scope of this possible involvement. A.M.'s oral reading and comprehension of single words, apart from a difficulty with grammatical morphemes (which itself was not especially severe), was simply normal. Thus the evidence from this neurological syndrome is entirely consonant with studies of normal subjects: both lines of research suggest that, in general, recognition of the printed word does not require and indeed typically does not involve a phonological code assembled from the graphemic information.

The most common assumption about the apparent puzzle of a system which has such a skill but makes no vital use of it is that *learning* to read requires or is facilitated by phonological assembly. There is indeed some evidence for reliance on phonological recoding in word comprehension by young readers, which diminishes as children grow older (Doctor and Coltheart, 1980). Though the skilled reader can recognise words largely without reference to phonology, he may continue to assemble phonology (1) *even* if it is mostly superfluous, simply out of habit, and (2) because sometimes it is presumably *not* superfluous, e.g. for pronouncing unfamiliar words or names. As we have seen, A.M. had grave difficulty reading unfamiliar names. It may seem odd to propose that the same system should deal with those graphemic items which the reader has encountered least often or indeed never (new words) and those which he has encountered most often (grammatical morphemes). What these two classes of items have in common, however, is a deficiency of semantic information. You would probably have almost as much difficulty defining *of* as you would do *groak*. A code obtained from your phonological system would enable you to pronounce both of these items, and might help you to 'comprehend' the former in the sense in which it contributes to the meaning of the sentence in which it occurs.

One final note regarding phonology of the other sort, postlexical or addressed phonology: there is evidence that the process of comprehending text (or written sentences) involves some speech-like code. This code may be phonological (as suggested by Kleiman, 1975; Coltheart, 1980; and others) or it may be articulatory (as suggested by Baddeley and Lewis, 1981). In either case the notion is that one needs some temporary memory storage when interpreting sentences rather than single words, and that a speech-like representation is particularly suited to this task. As each word in the sentence is recognised and understood, its phonological and/or articulatory code can be addressed and placed in temporary memory while subsequent words are processed to obtain comprehension of the whole message. This topic has been ignored here not only because of space limitations but because phonological dyslexia may not provide any special source of information regarding the role of *addressed* phonology in reading. A.M. did in fact have some difficulty in interpreting syntactically complex written sentences. He also had a general short-term memory deficit, however; and his problem in sentence comprehension probably concerns the memory system itself rather than the process of obtaining addressed phonology as input to that memory system.

APPENDIX 1

This appendix lists 40 nonwords presented to A.M. for reading in July 1979 (list 4 in Table III) and his responses to them. The nonwords were taken from the set published in Coltheart *et al.* (1970). Half of the 40 nonwords were homophonic with real words and the other 20 were not.

Homophonic nonwords   *Nonhomophonic nonwords*

Correct responses

wun → ✓	*murld* → ✓
leke → ✓	*barl* → bowel, ✓
waid → ✓	
ahms → ✓	
braik → ✓	
soal → ✓	
peese → 'peace, bees, ✓'	

Incorrect nonword responses

boaled → 'bulled'	*hefe* → 'haw'
fraze → 'frade'	*brait* → 'brack'
horl → 'hoil'	
hoal → 'hoid'	
woar → 'wode'	
floo → 'flude'	

Omissions

chuze	*kie*

*Incorrect word responses**

ile → 'eel'	*rild* → 'rind'
brooze → 'booze'	*gaks* → 'gates'
taks → 'takes'	*porce* → 'porch'
throan → 'through, throw, throwed'	*dode* → 'doze'
stawk → 'stag, stagged'	*flure* → 'fluid'
bair → 'bed, bode, baled'	*bol* → 'bow'
	dake → 'dale'
	korp → 'corpse'
	ploo → 'flow'
	trude → 'treasure, tread'
	brone → 'bronze, bonze'
	mobe → 'mode, made'
	phroo → 'pro, prose'
	wute → 'won, wunt'
	dort → 'dote, dode'

---

*Or, in the case of multiple attempts, some combinations of incorrect word and nonword responses

APPENDIX 2

This appendix presents a corpus of A.M.'s errors in reading function words, divided into three main groupings: (1) Omissions, self-evidently, are cases where he made no response. (2) 'Unrejected' single-word paralexics are cases where he produced a single incorrect word; this is not meant to imply that he believed these responses to be correct, but only that he did not overtly reject them. (3) 'Rejected' paralexias are cases where he knew his response was wrong and so indicated by following it with 'no', but was still unable to provide the correct response. (Sometimes these cases consisted of a single response and sometimes more.) Some investigators might treat group (3) as paralexic errors not to be differentiated from the 'unrejected' ones, while others might consider them as omissions. Since I do not know how to treat them, I present them separately.

Omissions			*'Unrejected' single-word paralexias*		
though	*does*	→ 'do'	*yet*	→	'that'
did	*which*	→ 'what'	*your*	→	'yours'
how	*with*	→ 'which'	*is*	→	'his'
the	*this*	→ 'these'	*they*	→	'there'*
on	*its*	→ 'it'	*the*	→	'when'
us	*were*	→ 'where'	*then*	→	'them'
with	*their*	→ 'they'	*in*	→	'is'
if	*therefore*	→ 'before'	*in*	→	'an'
like	*those*	→ 'these'	*or*	→	'of'
without	*neither*	→ 'either'			
yourself					
beneath					
after					

'Rejected' paralexias

he	→ 'his, no'		*has*	→	'here, no; have, no'
was	→ 'other, no'		*that*	→	'which, no; there, no'
our	→ 'on, no'		*of*	→	'off, no; over, no'
as	→ 'our, no'		*they*	→	'there*, no; the, no'
at	→ 'and, no'		*him*	→	'he, no; his, no'
if	→ 'it, no'		*here*	→	'there, no; hair, no'
have	→ 'when, no'		*an*	→	'in, no; can, no'
with	→ 'when, no'				
those	→ 'you, no'				
from	→ 'before, no'				
out	→ 'on, no'				
that	→ 'but, no'				
it	→ 'of, no'				
had	→ 'add, no'				

*or 'their'

Notes

1 Neither this nor any other statement in this chapter is meant to apply to children, but only to adults who have already learned to read.

2 It should however be noted that this conclusion is based on certain definitions of spelling regularity and on certain conceptions of procedures for assembling phonology. As discussed subsequently in the chapter, such conceptions and definitions are presently in a volatile state. As they evolve, the present conclusion may need reassessment.

3 I first heard of Beauvois and Dérouesné's investigations at the meeting of the European Brain and Behaviour Society in London in July 1978.

4 His comment, when asked to read nonwords this first time, is in fact worth recording: 'No, I can't; that's what I haven't got; if I had that, everything else would be all right'. A patient's theory of reading?

5 Obviously this similarity is a continumm rather than a dichotomy, but for simplicity I have treated it as the latter. My criterion for high similarity was either (1) just one letter different, as in *bern (burn)* or (2) a position reversal of two letters, as in *cride (cried)*. All other items were considered low similarity, e.g. *chuze (choose)*, *sute (suit)*, etc.

6 I am grateful to the members of that department for allowing these rather unusual references to their names!

7 The importance of the lexical decision result is perhaps vitiated by A.M.'s rather slow rate of responding.

8 He had developed strategies for reading certain function words: for example, given *at*, A.M. first would say 'hat' and then, with visible effort, delete the /h/ and say 'at'. Like some deep dyslexic patients who use very similar procedures (see, e.g. Morton and Patterson, 1980), A.M.'s strategies were often but not invariably successful. *An* → 'can' may be an instance where the deletion part of the strategy failed.

9 He did make a few errors on other types of sentence in this test: most difficult for him were reversible passive sentences like *the horse is chased by the girl*, where he was just as likely to select the picture of a horse chasing a girl.

10 Ironically, as the reader will no doubt have noted, this account in one sense turns assembled phonology into addressed phonology, for these frequent words and segments. The distinction however is to be maintained because the phonological assembly system is dealing with orthographic strings which have not yet been understood as familiar words. 'Prelexical' phonology is not the right label since 'lexical' information is being used in the assignment of phonology; yet this term had something of the right flavour in that phonology is being assigned independently of the functions usually associated with the notion of 'lexical access', namely specific word identification and comprehension. Assembled phonology still seems a preferable label since most words will require graphemic segmentation and phonological assembly.

Acknowledgements

I am grateful to Dr M.F.T. Yealland (Department of Neurological Surgery and Neurology, Addenbrooke's Hospital, Cambridge) for permission to publish neurological and psychological details of patient A.M. I also wish to express my appreciation to Mrs Jean Dockerty (Department of Speech Therapy, Clarkson Hospital, Wisbech) for her considerable assistance in my study of A.M. Finally, I thank a number of my colleagues for helpful discussions of the issues and/or comments on the manuscript: Marie-France Beauvois, Max Coltheart, Jacqueline Dérouesné, Andrew Ellis, Tony Marcel, John Morton and Tim Shallice.

References

Allport, D. A. (1979). Word recognition in reading. *In* P. A. Kolers, M. E. Wrolstad and H. Bouma (eds), *Processing of Visible Language*, Vol. 1. New York: Plenum Press

Baddeley, A. D. (1979). Working memory and reading. *In* P. A. Kolers, M. E. Wrolstad and H. Bouma (eds), *Processing of Visible Language*, Vol. 1. New York: Plenum Press

Baddeley, A. and Lewis, V. (1981). Inner active processes in reading: the inner voice, the inner ear and the inner eye. *In* A. M. Lesgold and C. Perfetti (eds), *Interactive Processes in Reading*. Hillsdale, New Jersey: Erlbaum

Baron, J. (1977). Mechanisms for pronouncing printed words: Use and acquisition. *In* D. LaBerge and S. Samuels (eds), *Basic Processes in Reading: Perception and Comprehension*. Hillsdale, New Jersey: Erlbaum

Beauvois, M. F. and Dérouesné, J. (1979a). Phonological alexia: Three dissociations. *Journal of Neurology, Neurosurgery and Psychiatry* **42**, 1115–1124

Beauvois, M. F. and Dérouesné, J. (1979b). Reading without phonology: data from phonological alexia without expressive or receptive aphasia. Paper presented to the International Neuropsychology Society, Holland, June 1979

Besner, D., Davies, J. and Daniels, S. (1981). Phonological processes in reading: the effects of concurrent articulation. *Quarterly Journal of Experimental Psychology* **33**, in press

Bishop, D. V. M. (1980). Comprehension of complex sentences by language disordered children. Paper presented to the Experimental Psychology Society, Cambridge, July 1980

Bradley, D. C. (1978). Computational distinctions of vocabulary type. Unpublished Ph.D. thesis, MIT, Cambridge, Massachusetts

Carr, T. H., Davidson, B. J. and Hawkins, H. L. (1978). Perceptual flexibility in word recognition: strategies affect orthographic computation but not lexical access. *Journal of Experimental Psychology: Human Perception and Performance* **4**, 674–690

Coltheart, M. (1978). Lexical access in simple reading tasks. *In* G. Underwood (ed.), *Strategies of Information Processing*. London: Academic Press

Coltheart, M. (1980). Reading, phonological recoding, and deep dyslexia. *In* M. Coltheart, K. Patterson and J. C. Marshall (eds), *Deep Dyslexia*. London: Routledge and Kegan Paul

Coltheart, M., Besner, D., Jonasson, J. T. and Davelaar, E. (1979). Phonological encoding in the lexical decision task: *Quarterly Journal of Experimental Psychology* **31**, 489–507

Coltheart, M., Davelaar, E., Jonasson, J. T. and Besner, D. (1977). Access to the internal lexicon. *In* S. Dornic (ed.), *Attention and Performance*, VI. New York: Academic Press

Coltheart, M., Patterson, K. and Marshall, J. C. (1980). *Deep Dyslexia*. London: Routledge and Kegan Paul

Conrad, R. (1964). Acoustic confusion in immediate memory. *British Journal of Psychology* **55**, 75–84

Corcoran, D. W. J. (1966). An acoustic factor in letter cancellation. *Nature* **210**, 658

Coughlan, A. K. and Warrington, E. K. (1978). Word-comprehension and word-retrieval in patients with localized cerebral lesions. *Brain* **101**, 163–185

Davelaar, E., Coltheart, M., Besner, D. and Jonasson, J. T. (1978). Phonological recoding and lexical access. *Memory and Cognition* **6**, 391–402

De Renzi, E. and Vignolo, L. A. (1962). The token test: a sensitive test to detect receptive disturbances in aphasics. *Brain* **85**, 665–678

Dérouesné, J. and Beauvois, M. F. (1979). Phonological processing in reading: Data from alexia. *Journal of Neurology, Neurosurgery, and Psychiatry* **42**, 1125–1132

Doctor, E. A. and Coltheart, M. (1980). Children's use of phonological encoding when reading for meaning. *Memory and Cognition* **8**, 195–209

Drewnowski, A. (1978). Detection errors on the word *the*: evidence for the acquisition of reading levels. *Memory and Cognition* **6**, 403–409

Drewnowski, A. and Healy, A. F. (1977). Detection errors on *the* and *and*: evidence for reading units larger than the word. *Memory and Cognition* **5**, 636–647

Drewnowski, A. and Healy, A. F. (1980). Missing *-ing* in reading: Letter detection errors on word endings. *Journal of Verbal Learning and Verbal Behavior* **19**, 247–262

Glushko, R. J. (1979). The organization and activation of orthographic knowledge in reading aloud. *Journal of Experimental Psychology: Human Perception and Performance* **6**, 674–691

Henderson, L. (1982). *Orthography and Word Recognition in Reading*. London: Academic Press

Henderson, L. and Chard, J. (1980). The reader's implicit knowledge of orthographic structure. *In* U. Frith (ed.), *Cognitive Processes in Spelling*. London: Academic Press

James, C. T. (1975). The role of semantic information in lexical decisions. *Journal of Experimental Psychology: Human Perception and Performance* **104**, 130–136

Kay, J. and Marcel, T. (1981). One process, not two, in reading aloud: lexical analogies do the work of nonlexical rules. *Quarterly Journal of Experimental Psychology* **33**, in press

Klee, H. and Legge, D. (1976). Estimates of concreteness and other indices for 200 transitive verbs. *Journal of Experimental Psychology: Human Learning and Memory* **2**, 497–507

Kleiman, G. M. (1975). Speech recoding in reading. *Journal of Verbal Learning and Verbal Behavior* **14**, 323–339

Kolers, P. A. (1966). Reading and talking bilingually. *American Journal of Psychology* **79**, 357–376

Levy, B. A. (1977). Reading: speech and meaning processes. *Journal of Verbal Learning and Verbal Behavior* **16**, 623–638

Lukatela, G., Popadić, D., Ognjenović, P. and Turvey, M. T. (1980). Lexical decision in a phonologically shallow orthography. *Memory and Cognition* **8**, 124–132

Marcel, T. (1980). Surface dyslexia and beginning reading: A revised hypothesis of the pronunciation of print and its impairments. *In* M. Coltheart, K. Patterson and J. C. Marshall (eds), *Deep Dyslexia*. London: Routledge and Kegan Paul

Marcel, A. J. and Patterson, K. E. (1978). Word recognition and production: reciprocity in clinical and normal research. *In* J. Requin (ed.), *Attention and Performance*, VII. Hillsdale, New Jersey: Erlbaum

Marshall, J. C. and Newcombe, F. (1973). Patterns of paralexia: A psycholinguistic approach. *Journal of Psycholinguistic Research* **2**, 175–199

Morton, J. (1964). A preliminary functional model for language behaviour. *Audiology* **3**, 216–225

Morton, J. (1979). Facilitation in word recognition: experiments causing change in the logogen model. *In* P. A. Kolers, M. E. Wrolstad and H. Bouma (eds), *Processing of Visible Language*, Vol. 1. New York: Plenum Press

Morton, J. and Patterson, K. (1980). 'Little words – No!'. *In* M. Coltheart, K. Patterson and J. C. Marshall (eds.), *Deep Dyslexia*. London: Routledge and Kegan Paul

Murrell, G. A. and Morton, J. (1974). Word recognition and morphemic structure. *Journal of Experimental Psychology* **102**, 963–968

Nelson, H. E. and O'Connell, A. (1978). Dementia: the estimation of premorbid intelligence levels using the new Adult Reading Test. *Cortex* **14**, 234–244

Newcombe, F. and Marshall, J. C. (1980). Transcoding and lexical stabilization in deep dyslexia. *In* M. Coltheart, K. Patterson and J. C. Marshall (eds), *Deep Dyslexia*. London: Routledge and Kegan Paul

Oatley, K. (1978). *Perceptions and Representations: The Theoretical Bases of Brain Research and Psychology*. London: Methuen

Patterson, K. E. (1978). Phonemic dyslexia: Errors of meaning and the meaning of errors. *Quarterly Journal of Experimental Psychology* **30**, 587–607

Patterson, K. E. (1979). What is right with 'deep' dyslexic patients? *Brain and Language* **8**, 111–129

Patterson, K. (1980). Derivational errors. *In* M. Coltheart, K. Patterson and J. C. Marshall (eds), *Deep Dyslexia*. London: Routledge and Kegan Paul

Patterson, K. E. (1981). Neuropsychological approaches to the study of reading. *British Journal of Psychology* **72**, 151–174

Patterson, K. E. and Marcel, A. J. (1977). Aphasia, dyslexia and the phonological coding of written words. *Quarterly Journal of Experimental Psychology* **29**, 307–318

Rubenstein, H., Lewis, S. S. and Rubenstein, M. A. (1971). Evidence for phonemic recoding in visual word recognition. *Journal of Verbal Learning and Verbal Behavior* **10**, 645–657

Saffran, E. M. (1980). Reading in deep dyslexia is not ideographic. *Neuropsychologia* **18**, 219–223

Saffran, E. M. and Marin, O. S. M. (1977). Reading without phonology: Evidence from aphasia. *Quarterly Journal of Experimental Psychology* **29**, 515–525

Sasanuma, S. (1980). Acquired dyslexia in Japanese: clinical features and underlying mechanisms. *In* M. Coltheart, K. Patterson and J. C. Marshall (eds), *Deep Dyslexia*. London: Routledge and Kegan Paul

Schonell, F. J. (1942). *Backwardness in the Basic Subjects*. Edinburgh and London: Oliver and Boyd

Schwartz, M. F., Saffran, E. M. and Marin, O. S. M. (1980). The word order problem in agrammatism. 1. Comprehension. *Brain and Language* **10**, 249–262

Shallice, T. and Coughlan, A. K. (1980). Modality specific word comprehension deficits in deep dyslexia. *Journal of Neurology, Neurosurgery, and Psychiatry* **43**, 866–872

Shallice, T. and Warrington, E. K. (1975). Word recognition in a phonemic dyslexic patient. *Quarterly Journal of Experimental Psychology* **27**, 187–199

Shallice, T. and Warrington, E. K. (1980). Single and multiple component central dyslexic syndromes. *In* M. Coltheart, K. Patterson and J. C. Marshall (eds), *Deep Dyslexia*. London: Routledge and Kegan Paul

Smith, P. T. and Groat, A. (1979). Spelling patterns, letter cancellation and the processing of text. *In* P. A. Kolers, M. E. Wrolstad and H. Bouma (eds), *Processing of Visible Language*, Vol. 1. New York: Plenum Press

Stanners, R. F., Neiser, J. J., Hernon, W. P. and Hall, R. (1979). Memory representation for morphologically related words. *Journal of Verbal Learning and Verbal Behavior* **18**, 399–412

Stanovich, K. E. and Bauer, D. W. (1978). Experiments on the spelling-to-sound regularity effect in word recognition. *Memory and Cognition* **6**, 410–415

Taft, M. (1979). Lexical access via an orthographic code: The basic orthographic syllable structure (BOSS). *Journal of Verbal Learning and Verbal Behavior* **18**, 21–39

Thorne, J., Bratley, P. and Dewar, H. (1968). The syntactic analysis of English by machine. *In* D. Michie (ed.), *Machine Intelligence*, 3. New York: American Elsevier

Underwood, G. (1979). Memory systems and the reading processes. *In* M. M. Gruneberg and P. E. Morris (eds), *Applied Problems in Memory*. London: Academic Press

Warrington, E. K. (1975). The selective impairment of semantic memory. *Quarterly Journal of Experimental Psychology* **27**, 635–658

Warrington, E. K. and Shallice, T. (1979). Semantic access dyslexia. *Brain* **102**, 43–63

Warrington, E. K. and Shallice, T. (1980). Word-form dyslexia. *Brain* **103**, 99–112

4

Spelling and Writing
(and Reading and Speaking)

ANDREW W. ELLIS
Department of Psychology, University of Lancaster, Lancaster, England

1 Introduction

According to one Chinese fable, writing was invented by the four-eyed dragon-god T'sang (Fromkin and Rodman, 1974). More prosaic, but probably more accurate accounts suggest that the major writing systems of the world developed between about 3000 and 1000 B.C. and sprang out of earlier 'picture writing' systems (Gelb, 1963). As a means of transmitting information, writing proper should be distinguished from picture writing, symbolic marks in prehistoric caves (Marshack, 1972) and such modern means of visual communication as motorway signs and company 'logos'; the difference being that the units of writing proper correspond to units of spoken language, and only indirectly to objects or ideas. Bolinger (1968) and Fromkin and Rodman (1974) provide good introductions to writing systems; fuller treatments can be found in Gelb (1963; 1974), Trager (1974) and Haas (1976).

It is conventional to divide the world's writing systems into three types. The first is *logographic writing* where each symbol represents a different word of spoken language (e.g. Chinese script and Japanese Kanji); second are *syllabic systems* where there is one symbol for each syllable of the language (e.g. Japanese Kana), and third, *alphabetic systems* where there is (ideally) one symbol representing each distinctive sound or *phoneme* in the language (an ideal which is approximated most closely in Finnish and less closely in English, French and German). This tripartite division is, however, only a rough one, and can be misleading. As Abercrombie (1965, p. 87) observes, '*All* systems of writing known to us give their symbols to words; the differences between them lie in the way these symbols are constructed'. Abercrombie's point is that in English writing, as in all other forms, the primary unit is the word, but linguistic units both larger and smaller than the word may also be represented (in Allbrow's (1972) term, English orthography is 'polysystemic'). The lowest level of correspondence between units in English speech and script is that between phonemes (i.e. distinctive speech sounds used to distinguish between words) and letters or groups of letters (p,b,a,oo,sh,th, etc.).

Syllabic representation only occurs in such oddities as *Bar-B-Q* and *I.O.U.* Morphemic representation, on the other hand, is important (morphemes being the smallest meaningful units of language: the word *unhappiness* contains three morphemes – *un, happi,* and *ness*). In English, the past tense morpheme is spelled *ed* in *kissed* where it is pronounced /t/, in *plagued* where it is pronounced /d/, and in *faded* where it is pronounced /ed/. Similarly, the plural morpheme is spelled *s* in cats, dogs, and horses where it is pronounced /s/,/z/, and /ɪz/ respectively. In experiments described by Baker (1980), subjects were required either to act as linguists and respell words in such a way that the spelling reflected the sound of the word as closely as possible, or to act as spelling reformers and respell words in what they considered to be the most rational way. Subjects would write DOGZ and CATS when being linguists, but DOGS and CATS when being spelling reformers, preferring in the latter task to preserve morphemic identity rather than phonemic accuracy. Morphemic representation may be adaptive in that there is evidence to suggest that morphemes within words may be segmented and recognized independently in reading (Morton, 1979).

Spelling may also preserve morphemic identity in the case of groups of related words which share common morphemes, even at the expense of phonemic accuracy (Chomsky and Halle, 1968; Weir and Venezky, 1968; Halle, 1969). This process can be seen in sets of words like bom*b*/bom*b*ardment, medical/medicine, damn/damnation, and sig*n*/sig*n*ature, although Tauli (1977) notes the existence of counter-examples like prof*ou*nd/prof*u*ndity and delu*d*e/delu*s*ion.

Lexical (word-level) representation in script is most obviously displayed in the fact that it is words, not morphemes or phrases, which dictate spacing between letters. An additional lexical influence noted by Bradley (1906) and Bolinger (1946) is the tendency of English script to differentiate wherever possible between homophones (i.e. words having the same sound but different meanings) even at the expense of spelling regularity – compare *rain/reign, no/know, I/eye, one/won, right/rite/write/ wright* (as in wheelwright), and *Gladly the cross I'd bear vs Gladly, the cross-eyed bear*.

Going above the word level, punctuation may be used to mark phrases or clauses and make distinctions such as that between restrictive relatives ('Students who are industrious. . .') and non-restrictive relatives ('Students, who are industrious, . . .'). Beyond phrases and clauses are sentences which are, of course, delimited by full stops and capitals, and beyond the sentence are paragraphs which signify (one would like to think) coherent semantic or discourse units larger than the sentence.

Even this catalogue does not exhaust the range of information encoded in writing; other elements include the grammatical and other uses of question and exclamation marks, the enclosure of speech within quotation marks, the stylistic use of other means of representing emphasis, and so on. The skilled writer has all this and more as it were at his fingertips, and the ultimate psychological model of writing must account for the integration of this knowledge. This chapter will, however, pursue a more modest goal, which is the development of a model sufficient to account for the production of single written words in English. As we shall see, that is a difficult enough task in itself.

2 Developing a model for spelling

Suppose that a child is asked to 'Write down the names of as many things you can think of in which people travel across water'. After writing down 'ship' and 'boat', the child may think of the word 'catamaran' but be uncertain as to its spelling. The child knows what a catamaran *is* (in the terminology of cognitive psychology, he possesses a semantic representation of 'catamaran') and he knows its spoken name. We must credit him, therefore, with a device for converting semantic representations into phonemic forms. Following the model developed by John Morton (e.g. Morton, 1980) the semantic representation will be held to originate in the *cognitive system*, be converted by a word-store termed the *speech output logogen system* into a phonemic form which is then held in a short-term memory which I shall call the *phonemic buffer* (equivalent to the response buffer in the logogen model – cf. Ellis, 1979a).

Returning to our child attempting to spell 'catamaran' – if he is of normal intelligence and has been reading and writing for a few years, he will be reasonably adept at generating plausible spellings for new words (Marsh, Friedman, Welch and Desberg, 1980). We can say, then, that the child has acquired procedures for converting sounds (phonemes) into letters (graphemes). These procedures may be applied to the phonemic form of 'catamaran' held in the phonemic buffer to generate a candidate spelling which will, in turn, require a short-term holding store (the *graphemic buffer*). The model which arises out of these considerations can be expressed diagrammatically as in Fig. 1.

The question then arises: Is Fig. 1 acceptable as a model not only of the production of candidate spellings of unfamiliar words, but also of the processes underlying the spelling of familiar words by normal skilled spellers? Luria (1970, pp. 323–4) appears to advocate a model of this sort when he writes: 'Psychologically, the writing process involves several steps. The flow of speech is broken down into individual sounds. The phonemic significance of these sounds is identified and the phonemes represented by letters. Finally, the individual letters are integrated to produce the written word'.

There are, however, strong arguments for rejecting Fig. 1 as a complete model of skilled spelling. Imagine our child had thought of a single rather than a double-hulled sailing vessel. Phoneme-grapheme conversion procedures might have generated YOT or YOTT as candidate spellings, but never YACHT. Such irregular spellings must be retrieved on a whole-word basis. This could, in principle, be done by means of a lexicon (as opposed to a set of correspondence rules) which would accept whole-word phonemic forms as input and give whole-word spellings as output. Such a proposal would, however, run aground against the problem of the number of homophones in English. For example, given the phonemic form /rid/ such a lexicon might proffer REED and READ as candidate spellings (though not REDE, WREDE or WREAD), but it has no means of knowing which spelling is correct on which occasion.

What is needed, then, is for the spellings of familiar words to be held in a *graphemic output logogen system* from which they may be retrieved in response to one or more access codes which specify each word uniquely and which discriminate between homophones. An obvious suggestion is that words may be accessed by the same semantic code which is used to retrieve the phonemic form of words from the speech output logogen

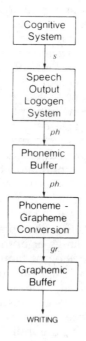

Fig. 1   A model for phonologically-mediated spelling (*gr.* = graphemic code; *ph.* = code; *s.* = semantic code)

system in speech production. If words are accessed by a semantic code, then misselection errors might be expected to result in a word being inadvertently produced which is related in meaning to the intended word. Semantic errors in writing to dictation (e.g. writing *moon* in response to the spoken word 'star') have been observed in some brain-injured patients classed as 'deep dyslexics' (see Newcombe and Marshall, 1980). Semantic writing errors also occur as normal slips-of-the-pen (Ellis, 1979b; Hotopf, 1980), but they are less common that phono-logically-based writing errors such as 'scene' for *seen*, 'there' for *their*, 'sought' for *sort* or 'surge' for *search* (Hotopf, 1980).

The influence of phonological similarity on word-level writing errors has been used by theorists such as Frith (1979) and Hotopf (1980) as support for models of spelling based on phonological mediation. In his extension of the logogen model to the production of writing, Morton (1980) suggests that spellings may be accessed from the graphemic output logogen system by a combination of *two* codes, semantic and phono-logical. The word selected will normally be the one whose description matches both input specifications, but mistakes may be based on either of the two input codes, resulting in both semantic and phonological errors. The resulting model (Fig. 2) is based on Morton (1980) though it also has affinities with the earlier proposals of Personke and Yee (1966) and Simon and Simon (1973).

To summarise, Fig. 2 affords two 'routes' by which a word's spelling may be produced. Firstly, words whose spelling is familiar have entries in the graphemic output logogen system. Each individual logogen unit within that system makes available its grapheme string in response to a unique combination of semantic and phonemic specifications. The semantic code originates in the cognitive system where it simultaneously activates the appropriate logogen unit in the speech output logogen

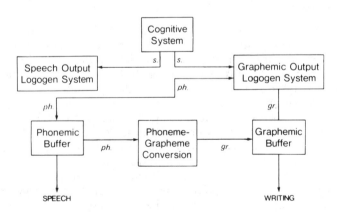

Fig. 2   A 'dual-route' model for spelling (abbreviations as for Fig. 1)

system, releasing the phonological form. (Leslie Henderson in a personal communication has suggested that the phonemic code that accompanies writing serves a 'sequencing and keeping-track' function. This accords well with my own introspections of the role of the phonemic code, which I conceive of as being recycled as 'inner speech' (Ellis, 1979a). I would add that, for me, inner speech also serves a 'monitoring and evaluating' function: to paraphrase the little girl slightly, 'How can I know what I think 'til I hear what I write.').

In addition to being recycled as inner speech, the phonemic code combines with the semantic code to release the graphemic code from the graphemic output logogen system. This code is stored in the graphemic buffer from whence it may be outputted as writing. This mode of spelling will be referred to as the 'lexical route'.

Where a word is unfamiliar, and hence lacks an entry in the graphemic output logogen system, an alternative 'nonlexical mode' of spelling may be used. On this route phoneme-grapheme conversion procedures operate upon the contents of the phonemic buffer to derive a plausible, but not necessarily correct rendering such as YOT for *yacht*. In fact, although I shall use the term 'nonlexical' to refer to this route for spelling unfamiliar words or nonwords, I would like to remain agnostic over the issue of whether it exploits individual sound-to-letter mappings (the converse of the grapheme-phoneme correspondences (GPCs) discussed by Coltheart, 1978), or whether it exploits larger, multiletter conversion procedures, based perhaps on real word analogies (cf. Glushko, 1979). What matters – as we shall see in sections 3, 4 and 5 – is that the lexical (whole-word) and the nonlexical (subword) routes should be separable and dissociable.

3   The lexical route

Clear supporting evidence for two spelling modes or routes would be provided if one could find patients who, as a result of brain damage, were obliged to spell either entirely by the lexical route, or entirely by the nonlexical route. The former condition (reliance solely on the lexical route) has been described by Shallice (1981) under the heading of 'phonological agraphia' while the latter condition (reliance solely on the nonlexical route) is approximated in a patient described by Beauvois and Dérouesné (1981) whose syndrome they term 'lexical agraphia'.

The case of phonological agraphia described by Shallice (1981) is of a 57-year-old computer salesman (P.R.) who suffered an extensive left internal carotid artery thrombosis. At the time of testing P.R. was scoring above average on Verbal and Performance IQ tests and average or better on tests of long-term memory, face and word recognition, object naming, etc. Spontaneous speech is described as fluent with good word choice, though limited in grammatical construction and poor in control of tense. On the Schonell reading test he scored at 90/100, equivalent to an IQ of 108. He made only 2 errors in reading a list of 337 low frequency (uncommon) words and only one error on a list of 39 irregular words.

When tested on spelling to dictation, both his written and oral spelling of words was shown to be comparatively well preserved whereas his spelling of nonwords was extremely poor (on about one-third of trials he was unable to produce any response at all). P.R. spelled 91.3 percent of a list of 622 words correctly, being 100% correct on the more common words. (He did make errors on function words which involved substituting one function word for another, e.g. 'or' for *of*. This deficit appears related to a problem with the comprehension, though not the repetition, of certain function words, and may be an associated deficit, rather than an integral or necessary part of phonological dysgraphia.

With the exception, then, of a certain difficulty with function words, P.R.'s spelling of real words was reasonably good. In marked contrast stands his performance on the spelling (both written and oral) of nonwords. For example, P.R. could correctly repeat a set of ten 4-letter spoken nonwords, read aloud eight of them, but spell only two. Thus his deficit was not perceptual (since he could repeat the nonwords correctly), and he did not suffer from a general phonological deficit (since his reading of nonwords was far better than his spelling – those errors on reading which did occur were close approximations to the 'correct' response). It is hard to see how a model such as that in Fig. 1, where all spelling is done by phoneme-grapheme conversion, could account for this patient's ability to spell correctly many real words but very few regular nonwords.

If P.R.'s were the only case report available, it would be possible to argue that spelling nonwords does not rely on different processes from spelling familiar words but is merely more sensitive to deficit than the tests of real word spelling. Fortunately these potential criticisms have been circumvented by the report of Beauvois and Dérouesné (1981) of a 'lexical agraphic' patient who shows the converse pattern to P.R.; that is, he is markedly better at spelling nonwords than real but irregular words – a classic 'double dissociation'.

Beauvois and Dérouesné's patient R.G. was an agricultural machinery sales manager before he was obliged to undergo a brain operation at the age of fifty-two. His post-operative IQ remained normal, as did his speech comprehension and production (with the exception of difficulties naming objects from touch – Beauvois, Saillant, Meininger and Lhermitte, 1978). R.G. would produce plausible spellings for virtually any nonword (both oral and written spelling) but managed to spell correctly only 38 percent of dictated irregular words. His performance on real words was worst for totally irregular words, better (but not good) on phonographically ambiguous words which can be given more than one 'regular' spelling, and best on unambiguous words which permit only one regular spelling. That is, the likelihood of R.G. being able to spell a word depends to a considerable extent on the predictability of the word's spelling from nonlexical phoneme-grapheme conversion procedures.

However, although R.G. appeared to spell predominantly by phoneme-grapheme conversion, some preservation of lexical spelling (of irregular words) is reported. In particular, his spelling of high frequency words is better than low frequency. Similar preservation of the spelling of high frequency words has been documented by Hier and Mohr (1977) and Ulatowska, Baker and Stern (1979) in two patients diagnosed as Wernicke's aphasics. In one test, Hier and Mohr's (1977) patient was required either to say or to write the names of pictures of objects. For objects with high frequency names he could produce the correct spelling on 52 percent of trials but could only produce the correct spoken name on 4 percent of trials. For objects with low frequency names his performance fell to 24 percent correct on written naming and none correct on spoken naming. Marshall (1977) has argued that a satisfactory account of many of the symptoms of the speech of Wernicke's aphasics may be possible in terms of the selective loss of all but high frequency words. It would appear from the above evidence that such selective loss is also possible for written words.

When Hier and Mohr's (1977) patient misspelled a word the errors tended not to be phonographic approximations, but rather letter deletions, additions, substitutions or misplacements (e.g. 'onarge' for *orange*; 'steetr' for *street*). These errors may be characterised as displaying *partial lexical knowledge* in that the patient either knew some but not all of the letters, or all the letters but not the correct order. Similar errors were noted by Seymour and Porpodas (1980) in two adult developmental dyslexics they studied. These dyslexics would typically produce phonetic misspellings of words they were unable to spell correctly; however, irregular words – particularly high frequency ones – would sometimes elicit errors such as 'sowrd' (*sword*), 'tounge' (*tongue*) or 'mucle' (*muscle*).

Evidence for partial lexical knowledge may also be found in studies of the spelling errors of normals. For example, the undergraduate students studied by Baron, Treiman, Wilf and Kellman (1980) produced errors such as 'colormel' and 'colnel' for *colonel*, 'rhythem' and rhythum' for *rhythm*, and 'pnewmonia' and 'pnemonia' for *pneumonia*, and Barron (1980, personal communication) notes that 'most of the phonetically inaccurate errors [made by children who were good readers – see Barron (1980)] appeared to be reasonable approximations to the correct spellings. For example, subjects seems to know that BUSINESS had an I, a U and two Ss somewhere in the word, but their placement of these letters was incorrect, and not phonetically motivated'. [Note that partial lexical knowledge of order information can result in grapheme reversals (e.g. 'sowrd' for *sword*). Reversals also occur as involuntary slips of the pen but it will be argued below that these occur at a lower, motoric level; an example of the potentiality for the same type of error existing at more than one locus in the system].

The presence of the unpredictable *l* in 'colnel', *h* in 'rhythum' or *p* in 'pnewmonia' oblige us to propose that a state can exist where the entry for a particular word in the graphemic output logogen system can contain some but not all of the letters of a target word (a graphemic 'tip-of-the-tongue' state?). This partial entry would need to be fleshed out by supplementary use of the nonlexical route.

A pathological form of partial lexical knowledge may have arisen in the case of a young woman patient documented briefly by Morton (1980). When asked to generate words from a specified category (e.g. countries or animals) she was often unable to say anything until she had written down one or more of the letters of the sought-for word. Sometimes – particularly, Morton states, when searching for a rarer word – she wrote more than one letter, but (1) these were not always contiguous letters though they were spaced out appropriately (e.g. Tur   y for *Turkey*; C   na for *China*), and (2) 'she did not write them fluently but rather had to search for every one' (Morton, 1980, p. 128). Thus she had access to partial graphemic information pertaining to positionally-coded letters; information which was sufficient to 'deblock' the spoken name which she was then able to produce (see Morton, 1980 for a discussion of possible mechanisms).

Two further points may be made at this stage. The first is that the patients of Hier and Mohr (1977) and Morton (1980) both showed evidence of being able to access words for spelling which they could not access for speech. Also, Lhermitte and Dérouesné (1974) and Basso, Taborelli and Vignolo (1978) report patients whose spelling remains intact while their speech is subject to gross phonological distortions. Such observations create problems for theories which require a word's spelling to be derived from its phonemic form. Figure 2, in contrast, can accommodate these findings (as it can permit the complementary syndrome of intact speech with jargonised spelling – Basso *et al.*, 1978; Rosati and Bastiani, 1979).

The second point concerns the suggestions that the graphemic output logogen system only contains irregular words or, alternatively, that it contains only the irregular *portions* of irregular words (e.g. Weigl, 1975; Dodd, 1980; Frith, 1980). Both of these suggestions would appear to fall foul of the patient P.R. who spelled lexically but who had access to the complete spellings of both regular and irregular words (Shallice, 1981). Given the general readiness to accept the notion of a visual lexicon used in reading to identify *all* familiar letter strings as particular words and make available the appropriate semantic code, it is hard to see why a graphemic lexicon mediating the reverse translation should not be equally acceptable.

4   The nonlexical route

The notion of two spelling modes, lexical and nonlexical is reminiscent of
the so-called 'dual-route' models of reading (e.g. Coltheart, 1978) which
propose that letter strings may be identified as known words either
'directly', as familiar visual letter sequences (the lexical route) or
'indirectly' by applying grapheme-phoneme conversion procedures with
the word being recognised on the basis of its derived phonemic form (the
nonlexical route). No sooner were dual-route models achieving broad
acceptance than they were criticised by Glushko (1979) and Marcel
(1980a) who advocated single-route models in which nonwords are read
by analogy with real words.

As with reading, so with spelling, the existence of two classes of patient
(lexical dysgraphic and phonological dysgraphic) creates difficulties for
all one-route models whether of the phonological mediation or analogic
type. A 'pure' lexical dysgraphic would rely entirely on the nonlexical
route and would thus be prone to phonographically-acceptable spelling
errors which are the hallmark of the nonlexical route (Beauvois and
Dérouesné, 1981). Examples of such phonographically-acceptable errors
from Beauvois and Dérouesné's patient R.G. include 'habil' and 'abile' for
habile, and 'fauteui' and 'fhoteuil' for fauteuil.

In skilled spellers, the nonlexical route is seen as a back-up mode to be
used when a word lacks an entry in the graphemic output logogen system (or
to supplement an incomplete entry). For illustration, consider Sloboda's
(1980) report that of 55 errors produced by university students and staff,
50 were phonographically plausible (e.g. 'pummice' for pumice, 'reble' for
rebel and 'dirth' for dearth – N.B. the remainder showed evidence of partial
lexical knowledge).

However, amongst the examples listed in studies of spelling errors, one
finds cases like 'tacksaytion' for taxation, 'thevefish' for thievish, and
'freakwently' for frequently. As Orton (1931), from whom these examples
are taken, observes, these show evidence of spelling based on analogy
with real words. It is also of interest to note that on the few occasions
when Shallice's (1981) phonological dysgraphic patient P.R. succeeded in generating a plausible spelling for a nonword it was usually
through the mediation of a similar sounding real word, as when he
spelled sim as 'sym' (via symbol) and spelled jund via junta and junk. This
strategy led to errors such as 'ault' for sult (via assault) and 'gn' for na (via
gnat). This observation suggests that spelling by analogy is a different
process from spelling by phoneme-grapheme conversion; that the two
processes are clinically dissociable; and that spelling by analogy is functionally associated with lexical rather than nonlexical spelling.

What, then, does nonlexical phoneme-grapheme conversion involve?
Fortunately, limitations of space restrict me to a few relatively straightforward observations. The first is that phoneme-grapheme conversion,

analogic or otherwise, only has a hope of success if the phonemic input to the conversion processes is correct. Orton (1931) gives examples of errors arising from nonstandard (Boston) pronunciations (e.g. 'invertation' for *invitation*; 'dangerss' for *dangerous*; 'garrowscope' for *gyroscope*; 'specalatin' for *speculating*), illustrating the point that even regular words are only regular with reference to a particular dialect. (This point is discussed with reference to Black American English by Desberg, Eliott and Marsh, 1980.) For speakers of 'nonstandard' dialects even more words become irregular and can only be spelled correctly if represented in the graphemic output logogen system.

Two stages in nonlexical conversion can be identified, namely (1) *Segmentation* of the spoken word into its component phonemes and/or syllables, and (2) *Conversion* of phoneme strings into grapheme strings. It is clear from tests administered by Shallice (1981) that the phonological dysgraphic patient P.R. was deficient in both these stages. As evidence of poor segmentation, he was both slow and error-prone on a task which involved deciding whether underlined letters sound the same in two words (e.g. stage, fig). P.R. even had difficulty producing the constituent sounds of a word clearly and separately (*cat* → '/k/ . . . /ae/ . . . /t/'). Regarding phoneme-grapheme conversion, P.R. could write letters in response to their spoken names ('bee, jay, aitch'), but not in response to their sounds ('buh, juh, huh') and, of course, he was very poor at spelling dictated nonwords which he could repeat perfectly well.

Segmentation clearly does not come easily even to normal children or adults. Experiments summarised by I. Liberman, A.M. Liberman, Mattingly and Shankweiler (1980) have shown that whereas identifying the number of syllables in a word is relatively easy for young children, the further division into phonemes is considerably more difficult. A study carried out in Portugal by Morais, Cary, Alegria and Bertelson (1979) found that phonemic segmentation was much harder for adult illiterates than for a group of literate adults. This suggests that learning to read (or spell) may actually teach segmentation rather than segmentation being a necessary pre-condition to learning to read (see Marcel, 1978).

Marcel (1980b) has observed certain very particular spelling errors which occur in young children, in adult illiterates and in some aphasic patients and which are apparently tied to problems of segmentation. The errors in question are errors like 'tay' for *tray*, 'boold' for *blood*, or 'med' for *mend* in individuals whose production and perception in speech of the target words is normal and good. Marcel (1980b) shows that these errors [technically, the omission or misplacement of liquids (*l* and *r*) when preceded in initial consonant clusters by a stop (as in *plan* or *scrap*), and liquids and nasals (*m* and *n*) when followed by a stop or fricative in terminal consonant clusters (as in *milk, bent* or *suns*)] must be described as primarily phoneme rather than grapheme omissions and are remarkably similar to (1) phoneme omissions in the speech of young children (e.g.

'tee' for *tree*; 'hep' for *help*) and (2) the spellings 'invented' by a group of preschool children studied by Read (1975). Marcel suggests a distinction between automatic processing of phoneme units in spontaneous speech and the availability of a conscious representation of those phonemes which can be considered, manipulated, segmented and used as input to phoneme-grapheme conversion, and he argues that the imperfect availability of this conscious representation in some way lies at the root of the problems of his subjects.

Conversion from phonemes to graphemes is, at present, no less mysterious a process than phonemic segmentation. Two points may, however, be made. The first is that phoneme-grapheme conversion is not simply grapheme-phoneme conversion operating in reverse (Haas, 1970; Henderson and Chard, 1980). For instance, although the 'regular' (i.e. commonest) sounding of the letter *k* is the phoneme /k/, the reverse is not true since the 'regular' spelling of /k/ is *c*. The second point is that the conversion procedures are sensitive to more than just phonemic information. In experiments reviewed by Smith (1980), subjects were asked to spell nonwords presented in sentence contexts. Results showed that subjects were sensitive not only to the phonemic form but also to the stress pattern of a nonword, whether it was presented as a noun or a verb, and whether it was perceived as belonging to the Latin/Greek/French group of English words, the Germanic group or the group of words of more exotic origins.

5   Individual and group differences in spelling mode

A   SKILLED READER-SPELLERS

The potential of dual-route models for predicting and explaining individual differences in preferred reading and spelling mode among skilled reader-spellers has been exploited in a series of studies by Baron and his co-workers. In the first such study, Baron and Strawson (1976) gave their student subjects tests designed to assess their efficiency in lexical and nonlexical reading. The tests of lexical reading involved first reading and spelling 'difficult' words and, second, selecting the correct spelling from pairs like INSISTENT-INSISTANT and GUIDANCE-GUIDEANCE where the correct spelling can be chosen only on appearance, not pronunciation. The test of nonlexical reading involved deciding whether nonwords, when pronounced, would sound like real words (e.g. CAWS, KNOE, SAWCE) or not (e.g. TAKKEN, HOUGHT, NAL). From a large pool of students, Baron and Strawson (1976) were able to isolate some subjects whom they called *Chinese* readers who were better at the lexical tasks than nonlexical tasks and a second and opposite group whom they called *Phoenician* readers (because the Phoenicians invented the alphabet) who were better at nonlexical than lexical tasks. Note that the majority of students tested were good or mediocre on both sorts of task. Baron and Strawson (1976) went on to show that Phoenician (nonlexical) readers pronounced regular words aloud more rapidly than irregular words whereas Chinese readers were faster on the (more common) irregular words.

More recently, Baron et al. (1980) have looked at the Chinese-Phoenician dimension as applied to spelling. Unlike the Baron and Strawson (1976) study, Baron et al.'s (1980) students were screened only on nonlexical skills. Specifically, they were required first to generate as many acceptable respellings as possible for eight given words and, second, to select from a number of nonwords those which, when pronounced, would sound the same as a given word (e.g. given *roof*, underline *rufe, wroof, rhoof* and *rooph* but not *ruf* or *roogh*). These two tests assess nonlexical spelling and reading respectively. 'Phoenicians' were defined as those scoring better than 90 percent on both tests, and 'Chinese' as those who scored less than 65 percent on both tests. The two groups were then tested on spelling a set of 32 commonly misspelled words (19 regular and 13 irregular). The groups did not differ on the total number of errors made, but the 'Phoenicians' produced a higher proportion of phonographically-acceptable misspellings (due entirely to their tendency to 'regularise' the spelling of irregular words). In another test, 'Phoenicians' were shown to be better than 'Chinese' at spelling nonwords which contain illegal sequences of phonemes (e.g. 'tlee' or 'zdree').

A problem with Baron et al.'s (1980) study is that supposedly 'Chinese' and 'Phoencian' reader-spellers were only discriminated on nonlexical tests. Thus, we know that the 'Chinese' subjects were poor and that the 'Phoencians' were good at nonlexical reading and spelling. What we do *not* know is that the 'Chinese' were necessarily good and the 'Phoenicians' necessarily bad at lexical reading and spelling (unlike the Baron and Strawson, 1976 study, in which subjects were screened on both lexical and nonlexical tasks). Some of Baron et al.'s (1980) 'Chinese' may have been comparatively poor at both nonlexical and lexical reading and spelling, though given that all the subjects used were university students this is perhaps less likely than the alternative possibility that some (or most) of their 'Phoenicians' were good at both nonlexical and lexical functions (not good at *only* nonlexical functions as were Baron and Strawson's Phoenicians). That is, Baron et al.'s (1980) 'Chinese' were probably a mixture of pure Chinese (lexical) reader-spellers and all-round poor reader-spellers, while their 'Phoenicians' were a mixture of pure Phoenician (nonlexical) reader-spellers and all-round good reader-spellers (i.e. good at both lexical and nonlexical functions). This flaw in the selection procedure may be responsible for the failure of Baron et al. (1980) to find any more general strategies or aptitudes which distinguished 'Chinese' from 'Phoenicians'.

B   GOOD VERSUS POOR READER-SPELLERS

Several studies have looked at the errors of children described as being good or poor readers. The errors have either been elicited by asking the children to spell lists of dictated words (e.g. Spache, 1940; Holmes and Peper, 1977; Barron, 1980; Frith, 1980) or extracted from samples of free writing (e.g. Williams, 1974). The investigator then looks at the proportion of the misspellings of each child which are phonographically acceptable approximations to the target word (e.g. 'koff' for *cough*). These studies have produced mixed findings. Spache (1940), Williams (1974), and Frith (1980b) found a higher proportion of the misspellings of good readers were 'phonetically' accurate than was the case for poor readers, suggesting a better knowledge of phonographic conversion rules among good readers than poor readers, though Holmes and Peper (1977) report no difference. Barron (1980) reports a higher proportion of 'phonetic' misspellings of regular words from good-for-IQ readers than for poor-for-IQ readers (though this difference was not found with misspellings of irregular words).

The discrepancies between these studies could arise from a number of sources. The criteria for distinguishing good from poor readers differ widely, as do the ages of the children studied. There are also problems inherent in this type of study. As Frith (1980b) and Nelson (1980) point out, the good readers may be misspelling a quite different set of words from the poor readers, and different words may lend themselves to different types of error. Given these problems, it is unlikely that analysing spelling errors from free writing or unselected lists will yield any unequivocal information about spelling strategies. Another reason for believing that simple comparisons between good and poor readers will prove unfruitful is the evidence, which will now be discussed, for individual differences in spelling mode among both poor readers (or developmental dyslexics) and good readers.

C   INDIVIDUAL DIFFERENCES AMONG DEVELOPMENTAL (AND ACQUIRED) DYSLEXICS

We have already seen how spelling can be exclusively (or predominantly) lexical in acquired phonological dysgraphia and in normal 'Chinese' spellers. Boder (1973) has claimed to identify a subgroup of developmental dyslexic children who likewise spell lexically. These children, whom Boder terms 'dysphonetic dyslexics' spell familiar words well, but their attempts at unfamiliar words are phonographically bizarre (e.g. 'sleber' for *scrambled*; 'coetere' for *character*).

In acquired lexical dysgraphia spelling is predominantly via the non-lexical, phoneme-grapheme route, as it is in normal 'Phoenician' spellers. The same is true, apparently, of a subgroup of developmental dyslexics whom Boder (1973) terms 'dyseidetic dyslexics' whose attempts at spelling are replete with such phonographically-correct errors as 'laf' for *laugh*, 'hows' for *house* and 'onkl' for *uncle*.

The possible existence of another variety of spelling dysgraphia is suggested by studies of acquired reading disorders which have identified a variety known as 'surface dyslexia' (Marshall and Newcombe, 1973). In surface dyslexia the patient has lost the ability to read lexically, attempts to read nonlexically, but has only imperfect mastery of English grapheme-phoneme correspondences. It should be possible to identify the graphic analogue of surface dyslexia, i.e. surface dysgraphia. One would be looking here for a patient who was obliged to attempt to spell phonographically but who failed to obey certain standard spelling rules; for example misspelling *kite* as 'kit' through non-application of the vowel-lengthening final *e*-rule. Marshall and Newcombe (1973) suggest that a multilingual patient described by Luria (1960) may be amenable to a retrospective diagnosis of surface dysgraphia. The patient in question was much more successful at spelling Russian (which has a comparatively regular spelling system) than the relatively irregular French language, even though he was more familiar with French than with Russian, and his errors may be phonographic in nature, but the case report is unfortunately too brief for us to be sure.

Finally, Bastian (1869, p. 232) describes the case of a man who had only slight difficulties with spoken language, but whose spelling of words was entirely random, though he knew the shapes of letters and could reproduce them well. Bastian (1869) coined the term 'amnestic dysgraphia' for this syndrome of abolished spelling with preserved writing abilities. Klein (1951) describes a similar case with no demonstrable aphasia. In terms of the model, this syndrome represents the dual and total impairment of both lexical and nonlexical spelling routes. The developmental variant of this syndrome may be manifested in Boder's (1973) group of 'mixed dysphonetic-dyseidetic dyslexics' whose attempts at spelling include such undisciplined efforts as 'Je' for *to* and 'ge' for *play*.

6   From graphemes to movements

The discussion thus far has been concerned with spelling more than with writing. When the graphemic form of a word is deposited in the graphemic buffer, by whichever route, the representation involved must still be of an abstract nature, capable of being realised as cursive handwriting, lower-case script, or capital letters, as finger movements in typing, or as oral spelling. Even if we restrict ourselves to writing, the question arises as to how that abstract graphemic code is converted ultimately into movements of the pen.

In an experiment by Seymour and Porpodas (1978), subjects heard the instruction 'Backward' or 'Forward', then heard a 5-letter word spoken, then saw a single letter displayed on a card. The task was to name as fast as possible the letter in the word which occurs either before (Backward) or after (Forward) the single visually-presented letter (e.g. given 'Forward', 'drink', r, the answer is 'i'). For eleven-year-old competent readers, Forward instructions produced faster responses than Backward instructions, particularly for the third, fourth and fifth letters. Seymour and Porpodas (1978, 1980) interpret this as indicating a *directional polarisation* of the (graphemic) code, though I would suggest that an alternative interpretation is that the graphemic code has no intrinsic left-to-right or first-to-last polarisation, but that the natural direction of scanning or read-out of the contents of the graphemic buffer is left-to-right (cf. Hampson and Morris, 1978).

One line of research which promises to provide insights into writing processes is the analysis of those involuntary slips of the pen which result in the unintentional misplacement, omission or substitution of letters. It is important to appreciate that the errors under discussion in this section are errors of performance not errors of knowledge (spelling errors); that is, these are errors which occur even though the writer is fully aware of the correct spelling of a word.

In a recent paper (Ellis, 1979b) I presented an analysis of 766 of my own writing errors, collected over a period of approximately eighteen months. I endeavoured to record all of my own errors whether noticed at the time of writing or when rereading. Each error was transcribed as accurately as possible onto cards, together with a note of the intended words. Here, I shall attempt to examine the implications which some of the categories of error discussed in Ellis (1979b) have for models of the processes intervening between graphemes and movements.

All graphemes can be realised in at least two different forms – upper-case (capitals) and lower-case (script). However, many writers use two or more different forms for certain upper- or lower-case letters. Following such linguists as Pulgram (1951), McIntosh (1956) and Hamp (1959) I shall refer to these letter forms as *allographs*. Even the same allograph will be written in perceptibly different ways on different occasions – the term *graph* will be used to refer to the concrete realisation of an allograph on paper. Figure 3 illustrates these distinctions as applied to the grapheme f in my own handwriting.

The first stage which must be postulated after the graphemic buffer is an *allographic long-term store* from which appropriate allographs must be chosen. Information used to select allographs must include (1) upper- *vs* lower-case (e.g. Is the letter beginning a sentence, the first letter of a name or proper noun, or part of a sequence of words being written in upper-case?), (2) within-word position and/or information concerning the form of the preceding allographic context (e.g. using a script s in word-initial positions but a cursive in word-final – see Wing, 1979), and (3) formality – as in the tendency toward script forms in material for general consumption and cursive forms in private jottings. An error at this stage will result in the confusion of upper- and lower-case forms, for example:

(1) to English → to eng
(2) CONTROL and R.C. LISTS → CONTROL AND R.C.
(3) UNIVERSITY → UNi
(4) FREUD → fr

(N.B. In these and all subsequent examples of slips of the pen, the intended form is given to the left of the arrow and the actually produced [error] form to the right of the arrow.)

Other errors which appear to be graphemic in nature are *letter antici-pations* and *perservations*. The evidence for this assertion comes from errors such as (5)-(8):

(5) J. Neurol. Neurosurg. → J. Seuro
(6) Cognitive → Go
(7) If not → N
(8) Pye Cambridge → Pyce

In example (7), for instance, the letter *n* which would have been lower case in the intended version, has transposed into a position where the intended letter would have been upper-case. The result is the accommo-dation of the *n* to the new context so that it becomes capitalised. This accommodation was also noted by Wells (1906, pp. 90–91) in an excellent paper on linguistic lapses. The simplest way to account for this process is to propose (Ellis, 1979b) that letter anticipations and perservations occur at a *graphemic level* before the allographic forms have been selected, or in the act of transcribing from the graphemic buffer to an *allographic buffer*, via the allographic long-term store.

The allographic code must still be relatively abstract since a given letter form can be executed by wrist and finger movements in normal right-

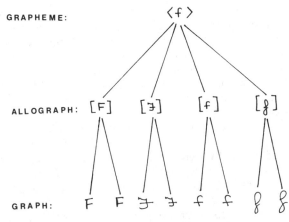

Fig. 3   Forms of the grapheme *f* in the author's own writing

handed writing, by large arm and shoulder movements when writing on a blackboard, or for that matter by a foot or the nose. The allographic code is probably best conceived of as a *spatial code* in Lashley's (1951) sense; that is, as a code which specifies letter shapes without specifying either the absolute size of the letter or the muscle system to be involved in its execution.

In Ellis (1979b), I suggested that certain types of letter error may be allographic rather than graphemic. One of these is the type of error which MacKay (1969) termed *letter masking* and which involves the omission of one of a pair of repeated letters, for example:

(9) satisfactory → satifa
(10) than when → than wen
(11) listening → listeing
(12) SHORT-TERM → SHOR-TERM

The justification for proposing that letter masking may be an allographic phenomenon is that all the examples in my corpus involve the omission of one of two identical allographic forms (see Ellis, 1979b where examples of these and other types of error are reproduced in their hand-written form).

Another type of error which appears to be allographic is what Ellis (1979b) called *haplologies*, but for which the term *haplographies* (Hotopf, 1980) might be more appropriate. Haplographies involve the omission of one of two repeated letters plus the letters intervening between the repeated pair, for example:

(13) dependence → depence
(14) initial → inial
(15) Appropriate → Appriate
(16) storage and → storan
(17) began as → begas

As with the letter masking errors, the haplographies in my corpus all occur between identical letter forms. The argument from identical letter forms is admittedly an inductive one, and a letter masking error like Memory → Meory or a haplography like Perception → Ption may crop up tomorrow and cause a reconsideration of the processing level to which either category is assigned. However, there is probably sufficient justification on purely computational grounds for postulating an allographic code and associated buffer store.

Having derived an allographic spatial representation of a word, how is that converted into co-ordinated muscle movements, and what sorts of error are associated with these final stages? There are other types of error which appear to occur below the allographic stage. The first of these is the *letter reversal* where two letters undergo a mutual exchange of positions. Now, in the domains of speech errors and short-term memory errors it seems reasonable to treat cases of reversals as the combination of an anticipatory error and a complementary perseverative error (Ellis, 1979a;

Shattuck-Hufnagel, 1979); the same, however, would not appear to be true of writing errors. Whereas anticipations and perseverations will occur between words and span several letters, all the 23 reversals in my own corpus occur within words, and all involve adjacent letters (e.g. *Chris* → 'Chirs'; *vulgar* → 'vulag'), although other studies give examples of one-apart reversals (e.g. 'silibants' for *sibilants* and 'padoga' for *pagoda* from Douse, 1900). Further, reversals tend to involve allographically similar forms such as *u* and *n*, *a* and *g*, and *i* and *l*, a tendency which does not appear to characterise anticipations and perseverations (though this has yet to be proved statistically).

Allographic similarity also seems to be implicated in *letter substitution errors* in which a letter form is replaced by another form not in the surrounding context, for example:

(18) Ambiguous → Amp
(19) within → mi
(20) from → tr
(21) MALE → MAT
(22) and → ang
(23) Touch → Touck

In an attempt to account for these errors, I should like to propose that the spatial code of the allographic buffer does not specify the actual ordered sequence of movements or strokes necessary to create a letter form; instead, the spatial description is used to select from a store the appropriate *graphic motor pattern* (Van Galen, 1980) whose execution will realise the desired allograph. Misselections (substitutions) or misorderings (reversals) may then arise as a consequences of similarity between the spatial code and the motor pattern. Following Van Galen (1980) the motor pattern is thought of as specifying the sequence, direction and relative size of strokes without specifying the absolute size (or duration) of strokes or the particular effector muscles to be employed. The independence of shape (motor pattern) from scale (absolute size) can be seen in Fig. 4 (errors 24–26) which I term 'scale errors'.

The analysis of slips of the pen suggests, therefore, that Fig. 2 should be expanded along the lines indicated in Fig. 5 to include an allographic store, allographic buffer, a store of the graphic motor patterns, and a

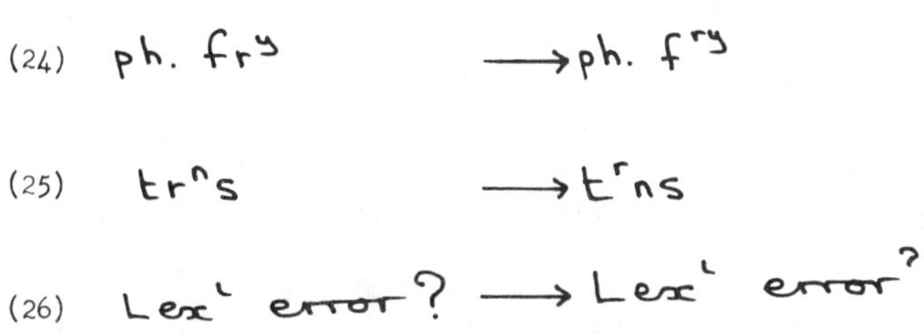

Fig. 4   Scale errors in the author's own slips of the pen

component – as yet unanalysed – for the execution of those motor patterns. Having sketched the rudimentary outlines of the steps by which a graphic code is translated into movements, we shall now look at how those steps can be disrupted in pathology.

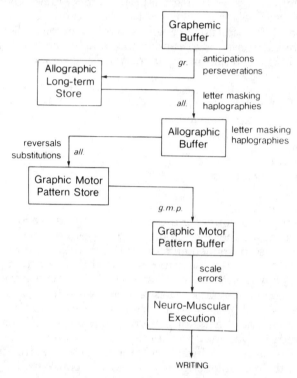

Fig. 5   A model for the processes intervening between the graphemic buffer and writing movements showing the proposed locus of different types of slips of the pen (*all.* = allographic code; *g.m.p.* = graphic pattern code; *gr.* = graphemic code)

7   Pathology from graphemes to movements

A   DEVELOPMENTAL DYSGRAPHIA

Lecours (1966) analysed the many errors to be found in the diary of Lee Harvey Oswald, who Lecours (1966) diagnosed as a 'developmental dysgraphic'. It is very clear from Lecours's classification that these errors are indistinguishable, except for their frequency, from normal slips of the pen. For example, Lecours's Type II deletion errors involve letter masking, and Lecours' Type II–III are haplographies. Lee Harvey Oswald's spelling difficulty would seem to be attributable to 'a difficulty with the reproduction of the conventional serial order of letters in the words' (Lecours, 1966, p. 233). That is, Oswald presented in developmental form a pathology marked only by a heightened proneness to the same errors that skilled writers make.

A similar interpretation can be given to developmental dysgraphia of a different sort discussed by writers such as Orton (1931), Hermann and Voldby (1946) and Hermann (1949). In the cases discussed by these writers, the errors would appear to occur at a lower level than those of Oswald. The errors include:

1 *Reversals* – e.g. 'gosd' for *gods*, which Orton (1931) terms 'kinetic reversals'.

2 *Orientation errors* – e.g. 'bogs' for *dogs* which Orton (1931) terms 'static reversals', but which may be better conceptualised as a subset of the substitutions of similars discussed by Hermann and Voldby (1946) which includes other letter pairs such as n–m, a–o, r–v and h–k. These are reminiscent of the substitutions which occur as slips of the pen.

3 *Contaminations* – the fusion of two adjacent letters (Hermann and Voldby, 1946, p. 358 and fig. 6) apparently identical to those slips of the pen which in Ellis (1979b) I called *switches*; indeed, Hermann and Voldby (1946, p. 358) remark that 'this phenomenon is rather frequently seen with adults practiced in writing, when they write quickly and slovenly'.

B CONFUSIONAL STATES

Chedru and Geschwind (1972) studied the writing of 34 acutely confused patients. They report that most of the patients' letter errors were analysable into the same categories as used by Lecours (1966); that when not in a confused state the patients made no more errors than a group of normal control subjects; and that the confused state was associated with increases in some types of error (e.g. omissions, substitutions and whole word errors) though not in other types, notably inversions (i.e. reversals). This last observation furnishes further evidence that reversals occur at a different stage from omissions (e.g. masking and haplographies).

C SPATIAL DYSGRAPHIA

Another pathological state which results in frequent writing errors arises as a consequence of damage to the parietal lobe of the right hemisphere of previously normal adults (Critchley, 1953) and has been termed *spatial dysgraphia* (Hécaen, 1967; Hécaen and Marcie, 1974) or *afferent dysgraphia* (Lebrun and Rubio, 1972; Lebrun, 1976). The condition is characterised by a spatial-perceptual disorder shown by slanting or undulating lines of script and enlarged left-hand margins (this aspect of spatial dysgraphia shows an impairment of an aspect of writing which I have not discussed – namely the ability to orient the letters and the lines correctly with respect to the page). More pertinent to the present concerns are the letter errors made by spatial dysgraphics which are predominantly reduplications of strokes, most commonly the vertical strokes in the letters *m*, *n*, and *u*. The difficulty may be conceptualised as one of updating the motor pattern during its execution, a conclusion supported by Lebrun's (1976) report of a case of spatial dysgraphia where the patient made numerous errors in writing, but none in oral spelling. Lebrun (1976) has observed the same phenomenon in normal subjects writing with eyes closed and D. Lauer (personal communication) has obtained errors of this sort when subjects are writing without view of their hand whilst playing a keyboard exercise simultaneously with their left hand. Lebrun (1976) notes similar errors in studies which have experimentally delayed the visual feedback subjects get from seeing their pen movements (van Bergeijk and David, 1959; Kalmus, Fry and Denes, 1960; Smith, 1962).

This suggests that, in normals, visual feedback serves to update the motor programme for writing. The situation must, however, be slightly more complex; spatial dysgraphics continue to make errors when writing with the eyes closed, and normal subjects under the same circumstances still manage to execute the majority of letters normally. A compromise suggestion is that visual feedback supplements another form of feedback (possibly, but not necessarily, kinaesthetic feedback from wrist and finger movements). The right parietal lobe damage causing spatial dysgraphia would appear to compromise the interpretation of utilisation of both visual and kinaesthetic feedback.

8   The comparison of written and oral spelling

Oral spelling of words ('Dee, Oh, Gee = Dog') presumably shares certain processes in common with written spelling while diverging from writing at some point at or beyond the graphemic buffer. Hence one would expect those agraphias which impair spelling *per se* (lexical, phonological, and surface) to compromise oral spelling too. This is certainly true of Beauvois and Dérouesné's (1981) agraphic patient and of the phonological dysgraphic patient P.R. (Shallice, 1981). Agraphias which affect the actual writing process, however, might be expected (at least in some cases) to leave oral spelling intact. This is true of spatial dysgraphia, where oral spelling may be unaffected (Lebrun, 1976). Also Lange (1930) reports the case of a female patient who showed letter reversals in writing but not in oral spelling, supporting the view that (some) letter reversals may arise at a low, graphic level. Matters are complicated slightly, however, by Hermann's (1949) mention of an eleven-year-old girl patient suffering from an early acquired dysgraphia which resolved in a matter of months who showed letter reversals in writing, oral spelling and spelling with block letters. Conceivably these latter reversals were true spelling reversals rather than the motoric reversals found in slips of the pen.

Kinsbourne and Warrington (1965) and Kinsbourne and Rosenfield

(1974) report two patients who appear to provide a 'double dissociation' between oral and written spelling. Kinsbourne and Warrington's (1965) patient scored near average on test of written spelling but was very poor at oral spelling, though he correctly named all but two letters of the alphabet (interchanging x and z) and pointed correctly to named letters. In addition to his oral spelling deficit, the patient was poor at identifying words spelled orally by an examiner but was very much better if the component letters of words were presented visually one-at-a-time.

In direct contrast, Kinsbourne and Rosenfield's (1974) patient was substantially worse at written spelling (where the errors tended to be letter intrusions) than at oral spelling (where the majority of those errors which occurred were of letter order). Examples of the patient's writing errors are 'irrestiable' for *irresistable*, 'exazarate' for *exaggerate* and 'opetunity' for *opportunity* (N.B. these words would probably be correct if spelled orally).

Marcel (1980b) reports briefly an experiment in which normal adult spellers were asked to spell aloud bisyllabic words such as *petrol, crimson,* or *igloo.* Pauses were apparently placed predominantly between the two consonants constituting the internal cluster (i.e. P, E, T . . . R, O, L; C, R, I, M, . . . S, O, N etc.) which Marcel interprets as division at syllable boundaries. If true, it creates something of a problem for Model 3. If familiar words like *petrol* are accessed via a *graphemic* lexicon and represented in a *graphemic* code, why should oral spelling show evidence of *syllabic* division – the syllable being a phonological, not a graphemic unit? Perhaps it will be necessary to admit syllabic division in the graphemic buffer, in which case graphemic slips of the pen might be expected to show evidence of syllabic constraints. Like so much of our hypothesising concerning oral spelling this must remain tentative at present.

Clearly, oral spelling must diverge from the pathway of written spelling at some stage. Valenstein and Heilman (1979) describe a patient with no disturbance of speech comprehension or production (apart from a mild dysarthria), and with intact reading. The patient could spell words orally and understand oral spelling. He could also type with his left hand (he was naturally left-handed), but his attempts at writing 'produced large, poorly formed letters, only a few of which were identifiable'. This description suggests the loss, or disconnection, of the allographic long-term store. Furthermore, the preservation of oral spelling would seem to indicate that oral spelling is based on a graphemic code, and that the divergence of the pathway for oral spelling (and typewriting) occurs after the graphemic output logogen system and before the allographic long-term store.

Oral spelling is an enigma: most adults rarely if ever do it, yet when called upon they experience little difficulty. In our present state of knowledge further speculation is unlikely to be fruitful.

9   Writing and reading

A   THE INDEPENDENCE OF WRITING AND READING

Reading proceeds from marks on paper to meanings and sounds whilst writing proceeds from meanings and sounds to marks on paper. It might seem reasonable, therefore, to conceive of writing as engaging the same psychological processes operating in the opposite direction to that employed in reading (see, for example, Seymour's, 1976, model). There is, however, evidence showing this view to be misguided; rather it would appear that writing and reading (like speaking and hearing) are quite separate and separable processes.

One very telling piece of evidence comes from analyses of the reading of Beauvois and Dérouesné's (1979, 1981) lexical agraphic patient R.G. It will be recalled that R.G. spelled nonlexically; that is, he spelled each word as if it were a nonword by the application of phoneme-to-grapheme conversion procedures resulting in frequent phonologically-acceptable misspellings. Now, the surprising thing about this patient is that his reading showed quite the opposite pattern – he *read lexically* and was very poor at reading nonlexically. Thus, he read forty 5- to 9-letter nouns entirely correctly, but could pronounce only 10 percent of 4- or 5-letter nonwords although he could repeat aurally-presented nonwords faultlessly (Beauvois and Dérouesné, 1979). Interestingly, he pronounced twenty 4-letter nonwords correctly and thirteen of twenty 5-letter nonwords correctly when the nonwords were spelled aloud by the experimenter. This suggests that the nonlexical reading impairment results from a *disconnection* of visual graphemic input from grapheme-phoneme conversion procedures rather than loss of the rules *per se*, since the rules can be accessed and applied when the input is aural.

A similar pattern of lexical reading and nonlexical spelling has been studied by Frith (1978a, b, 1979, 1980b) in a group of 11- to 13-year-old children who were of at least average verbal intelligence, whose reading was normal for their age, but whose spelling was poor. However, although these children were poor at producing the conventional spellings of words, they were nevertheless comparable to good spellers when required to generate spellings of nonwords. Also, their misspellings tended to be phonographically-acceptable (cf. also Nelson, 1974). In contrast to their good spelling of dictated nonwords they were poor at reading (pronouncing) written nonwords, thus paralleling R.G. remarkably closely.

Evidence from normal children pointing to the same conclusion comes from the work of Bryant and Bradley (1980). They gave young children words to read on one occasion, and found that children would sometimes be able to read a word correctly but not spell it, or conversely spell it correctly but not read it. Of 30 words presented to 6- to 7-year-old children for reading and spelling, the four words which were most commonly read but not spelled were SCHOOL, LIGHT, TRAIN and

EGG, whilst the words most commonly spelled but not read were BUN, MAT, LEG and PAT. The obvious conclusion is that children can read common irregular words but not spell them, and can spell short regular words which they hear dictated but cannot always read them. That is to say, young children (or, at least, the children in Bryant and Bradley's sample) read by a lexical ('Chinese') strategy but spelled by a nonlexical ('Phoenician') strategy. That the lexical reading is a preferred rather than an obligatory strategy is shown by Bryant and Bradley's (1980) demonstration that the same children succeeded in reading BUN, MAT, LEG, PAT, etc. when those words were presented in a list of regular nonwords such as WEG and BIP. These nonwords force a switch to a nonlexical grapheme-phoneme strategy for reading and enabled the previously illegible BUN, MAT, LEG and PAT to be read (one assumes that these words would not have been read correctly if simply re-presented in the original list of real words). If this assumption is correct, then the fact that children can sometimes read but not spell a common irregular word such as *light* itself suggests that the unit in the reading lexicon which recognises *light* cannot be used generatively to help spell that word.

A quite separate line of evidence suggesting that reading and writing are independent processes comes from studies in which subjects have learned to read and write different material at the same time. The first such study was carried out by Leon M. Solomons and Gertrude Stein at the Harvard Psychological Laboratory (Solomons and Stein, 1896 – see also Downey and Anderson, 1915; Spelke, Hirst and Neisser, 1976; and Hirst, Spelke, Reaves, Caharack and Neisser, 1980). The ability of subjects to read stories silently with comprehension whilst at the same time writing down dictated words is more readily accommodated by models which posit separate input and output channels for heard, read, spoken and written words than by models which hold writing (and/or reading) to be parasitic upon internal speech.

B THE VISUAL CHECK

Although it seems accurate to say that 'spelling isn't reading backwards' (Gould, 1976), nevertheless reading is often assigned a major role in spelling in its capacity to provide a *visual check* on spellings produced (e.g. Simon and Simon, 1973). Tenney (1980) has provided experimental evidence that subjects benefit from being able to write down and see two alternative spellings of a word (one correct spelling and one common misspelling) before choosing between them, though the effect was not a large one.

If we accept the notion of a visual check, however, we then face something of a dilemma as regards the performance of Beauvois and Dérouesné's patient R.G., Frith's good readers/poor spellers, and Bryant and Bradley's young children. If these individuals spell nonlexically but read lexically, why can they not use the lexical reading as a visual check upon the candidate spellings generated by rule? The answer which Frith

(1980b) suggests is that good readers/poor spellers may rely on only some of the letters in a word in order to recognise it, hence misspellings which preserve some of a word's letter structure (e.g. 'frezze' for *freeze*) may pass undetected. The same might conceivably be true for the phonological dyslexic/lexical dysgraphic R.G.

I would suggest, however, an alternative possibility. It is a commonplace observation that we do not need all the letters of a word before we are able to recognise it (for example, given elxphxxt few people fail to 'recognise' *elephant*). Rayner and Posnansky (1978) and Posnansky and Rayner (1977) have shown that if a picture of an object is accompanied at presentation by a written nonword which shares some letters in common with the object name (e.g. hcnre for *horse*), then picture naming speed is increased. We also know that skilled readers are prone not to spot errors introduced into words in recognition (Pillsbury, 1897; Cohen, 1980) or proof reading (Downey, 1918) tasks. Many misspellings, including those used in Tenney's (1980) experiments will bear a sufficiently close affinity to the correct spelling to activate the word's entry in the visual input logogen system used to identify written words (Morton, 1980), which means that the lexical route for reading is likely to be inefficient as a means of detecting those errors which are visually similar to the target word. However, the lexical check is not the only form of visual check; one can also apply a nonlexical check by applying grapheme-phoneme correspondences to the candidate spelling to see if it *sounds* right. Many errors which are visually similar to the target will be detected this way; those which escape both lexical and nonlexical visual checks will be those pernicious and common errors which both look like and sound like the correct spelling (e.g. seize/sieze, rarefied/rarified, harass/harrass, omitted/ommitted). Note also that Beauvois and Dérouesné's patient R.G. and Frith's good readers/poor spellers have only the lexical visual check available to them which, I have argued, may be an inefficient means of error detection.

C COPYING

A final aspect of the relation between reading and writing concerns the ability to copy written text. Several authors note that copying may be preserved or intact both in developmental dyslexia (e.g. Critchley, 1968) and in acquired dyslexia with or without accompanying aphasia (Bastian, 1869; Elder, 1900; Weigl and Fradis, 1977). Unfortunately, the nature of the preserved copying has usually only been superficially analysed. One can postulate at least three types of copying (cf. Critchley, 1970):

1 *Pictorial copying* as one might use when copying an inscription in an unknown script or forging a signature; that is, reproducing the physical appearance of the sample of writing as accurately as possible.

2 *Graphemic copying*. Patients have been reported who are unable to write spontaneously, but who can recode a capital letter into script or

script into cursive handwriting (Weigl and Fradis, 1977). This is more than mere pictorial copying; it implies the ability to identify abstract graphemes and select allographs which are variants of that grapheme. In terms of the model, it implies a link between the visual analysis system and the graphemic buffer for a transfer of graphemic information which bypasses the reading and writing lexicons.

3 *Lexical copying.* This is probably the dominant form where words are recognised lexically and written lexically through the intervention of a semantic code (or, possibly, via a direct link between the entries in the reading and writing lexicons – see Morton, 1980).

There are close similarities here with the discussion of copy drawing provided by Gardner (chapter 10, this volume) and, if the preceding analysis is correct, it should be possible to find patients with selective impairments of pictorial, graphemic and lexical copying.

10   Summary and conclusions

At this point it is perhaps worth drawing together the various claims scattered throughout this chapter. It is proposed that a normal skilled speller can derive a word's spelling by one of two routes, a *lexical route* and a *nonlexical route*. On the former route, a lexical memory (the *graphemic output logogen system*) stores the spellings of familiar words, both regular and irregular, and makes them available in response to a specification from the cognitive system of the meaning of the required word (combined possibly with a phonological specification from the speech production component). The graphemic output logogen system is separate and distinct from the visual input logogen system involved in direct visual-semantic word recognition in reading, and distinct also from the speech output logogen system and auditory input logogen system involved in the production and perception (respectively) of spoken words. Ease of retrieval of words from the graphemic output logogen system is thought to be a function of the word's frequency of usage in spelling. Retrieval is not all-or-nothing: only some of the letters of an infrequently-used word may be retrievable from the graphemic output logogen system in which case this partial lexical specification may be supplemented by the second, nonlexical route.

On the nonlexical route phoneme-grapheme conversion procedures are applied to the phonological form of a word in an attempt to derive a plausible candidate spelling. These conversion procedures may be phoneme-grapheme correspondences, multiphoneme-multigrapheme correspondences, or may be based on whole word analogies (in which case the term 'nonlexical' may be something of a misnomer); this issue is at present an open one. What *is* argued here is that these procedures are distinct from those involved in nonlexical grapheme-phoneme reading.

These two routes may be differentially impaired (and hence differen-

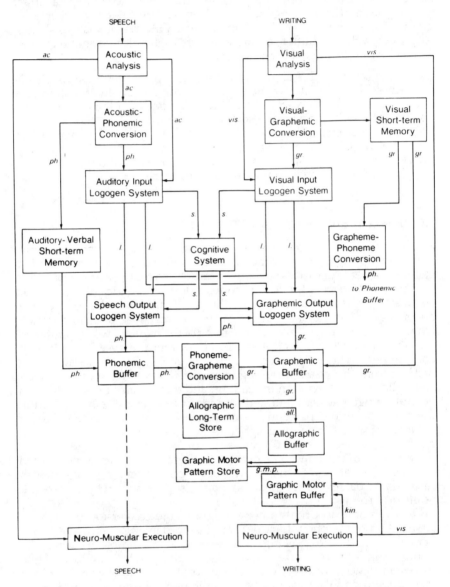

Fig. 6 A model for spelling and writing (and reading and speaking and hearing). *ac.* = acoustic code; *all.* = alographic code; *g.m.p.* = graphic motor pattern code; *gr.* = graphemic code; *kin.* = kinaesthetic code; *l.* = lexical code; *ph.* = phonemic code; *s.* = semantic code; *vis.* = visual code

tially relied upon) in various acquired and developmental dysgraphic conditions and also in individuals within the 'normal' population. Acquired lexical and developmental dyseidetic dysgraphics are impaired in use of the lexical route and consequently rely more or less exclusively on the nonlexical route, as do normal 'Phoenician' spellers. Acquired phonological and developmental dysphonetic dysgraphics are impaired in use of the nonlexical route and perforce rely more or less exclusively on the lexical route, as do normal 'Chinese' spellers. Both routes are impaired in acquired amnestic and developmental dyseidetic-dysphonetic dysgraphics whose spellings are therefore virtually random.

Whichever route is employed by a given speller on a particular occasion, the spelling obtained is represented in a graphemic code stored in the *graphemic buffer* upon which the two routes converge. The graphemic code does not specify the desired form of a given letter; this is decided subsequently in the retrieval of a spatial description from an *allographic long-term memory*. This description is spatial but does not specify the sequence, direction or relative size of strokes; this latter information being contained in *graphic motor patterns* which serve as input to the neuro-muscular execution component. It is possible to assign various types of slip of the pen occurring in normal writers to different stages in the translation from graphemes to movements. It is also possible, using the proposed sequence of stages, to give an account of various acquired and developmental dysgraphic syndromes in which the primary impairment is one of writing rather than spelling.

I close with a model (Fig. 6) which embodies, but goes beyond, the foregoing considerations. It draws heavily and unrepentently on the work of Morton (e.g. 1979, 1980; Morton and Patterson, 1980), and also from Klatt (1979), Seymour (1979) and Marshall and Newcombe (1980). The model only attempts to sketch the basic architecture of the system, indicating the functional components and their interconnections. As such it is meant to supplement, not substitute for, a detailed analysis of the mode of operation of each of the subsystems. This analysis is only just beginning.

Acknowledgements

I should like to thank Leslie Henderson, Norman Hotopf, Mary Smyth and Andrew Young for comments on an earlier draft of this chapter. I only regret not being able to answer satisfactorily each and every one of the points they raised.

References

Abercrombie, D. (1965). *Studies in Phonetics and Linguistics*. London: Oxford University Press
Allbrow, K. H. (1972). *The English Writing System: Notes Toward a Description*. (Schools

Council Programme in Linguistics and English Teaching, Series II, Vol. 2). London: Longmans

Baker, R. G. (1980). Orthographic awareness. *In* U. Frith (1980a)

Baron, J. and Strawson, C. (1976). Use of orthographic and word-specific knowledge in reading words aloud. *Journal of Experimental Psychology: Human Perception and Performance* **2**, 386–393

Baron, J., Treiman, R., Wilf, J. F. and Kellman, P. (1980). Spelling and reading by rules. *In* U. Frith (1980a)

Barron, R. W. (1980). Visual and phonological strategies in reading and spelling. *In* U. Frith (1980a)

Basso, A., Taborelli, A. and Vignolo, L. A. (1978). Dissociated disorders of speaking and writing in aphasia. *Journal of Neurology, Neurosurgery and Psychiatry* **41**, 556–563

Bastian, H. C. (1869). On the various forms of loss of speech in cerebral disease. *British and Foreign Medico-Chirurgical Review* **43**, 209–236; 470–492

Beauvois, M.–F. and Dérouesné, J. (1979). Phonological alexia: three dissociations. *Journal of Neurology, Neurosurgery and Psychiatry* **42**, 1115–1124

Beauvois, M.–F. and Dérouesné, J. (1981). Lexical or orthographic dysgraphia. *Brain* **104**, 21–50

Beauvois, M.–F., Saillant, B., Meininger, V. and Lhermitte, F. (1978). Bilateral tactile aphasia: A tacto-verbal dysfunction. *Brain* **101**, 381–401

Boder, E. (1973). Developmental dyslexia: a diagnostic approach based on three atypical reading-spelling patterns. *Developmental Medicine and Child Neurology* **15**, 663–687

Bolinger, D. L. (1946). Visual morphemes. *Language* **22**, 333–340

Bolinger, D. L. (1968). *Aspects of Language*. New York: Harcourt, Brace and World

Bradley, H. (1906). On the relations between spoken and written language with special reference to English. *Proceedings of the British Academy* **6**, 1–22

Bryant, P.E. and Bradley, L. (1980). Why children sometimes write words which they do not read. *In* U. Frith (1980a)

Chedru, F. and Geschwind, N. (1972). Writing disturbance in acute confusional states. *Neuropsychologia* **10**, 343–353

Chomsky, N. and Halle, M. (1968). *The Sound Pattern of English*. New York: Harper and Row

Cohen, G. (1980). Reading and searching for spelling errors. *In* U. Frith (1980)

Coltheart, M. (1978). Lexical access in simple reading tasks. *In* G. Underwood, (ed.), *Strategies in Information Processing*. London: Academic Press

Critchley, M. (1953). *The Parietal Lobes*. London: Edward Arnold

Critchley, M. (1968). Dysgraphia and other anomalies of written speech. *Pediatric Clinics of North America* **15**, 639–650

Critchley, M. (1970). *Aphasiology and Other Aspects of Language*. London: Edward Arnold

Desberg, P., Elliott, D. E. and Marsh, G. (1980). American Black English and spelling. *In* U. Frith (1980a)

Dodd, B. (1980). The spelling abilities of profoundly pre-lingually deaf children. *In* U. Frith (1980a)

Douse, T. le M. (1900). A study of misspellings and related mistakes. *Mind* **9**, 85–93

Downey, J. E. (1918). The proof-reader's illusion and general intelligence. *Journal of Philosophy, Psychology and Scientific Methods* **15**, 44–47

Downey, J. E. and Anderson, J. E. (1915). Automatic writing. *American Journal of Psychology* **26**, 161–195

Elder, W. (1900). The clinical varieties of visual aphasia. *Edinburgh Medical Journal* **49**, 433–454

Ellis, A. W. (1979a). *Speech production and short-term memory*. *In* J. Morton and J. C. Marshall (eds), *Psycholinguistics Series*, Vol. 2, *Structures and Processes*. London: Elek

Ellis, A. W. (1979b). Slips of the pen. *Visible Language* **13**, 265–282

Frith, U. (1978a). Spelling difficulties. *Journal of Child Psychology and Psychiatry* **19**, 279–285

Frith, U. (1978b). From print to meaning and from print to sound or how to read without knowing how to spell. *Visible Language* **12**, 43–54

Frith, U. (1979). Reading by eye and writing by ear. *In* P. A. Kolers, M. Wrolstad and H. Bouma (eds), *Processing of Visible Language*. New York: Plenum Press

Frith, U. (1980a, ed.). *Cognitive Processes in Spelling*. London: Academic Press

Frith, U. (1980b). Unexpected spelling problems. *In* U. Frith (1980a)

Fromkin, V. and Rodman, R. (1974). *An Introduction to Language*. New York: Holt, Rinehart and Winston

Gelb, I. J. (1963). *A Study of Writing*. Chicago: University of Chicago Press

Gelb, I. J. (1974). Writing, Forms of. *Encyclopaedia Brittanica*, 15th edn, *Macropaedia*, Vol. 19, 1033–1045

Glushko, R. J. (1979). The organization and activation of orthographic knowledge in reading aloud. *Journal of Experimental Psychology: Human Perception and Performance* **5**, 674–691

Gould, S. M. (1976). Spelling isn't reading backwards. *Journal of Reading* **20**, 220–225

Haas, W. (1976, ed.), *Writing Without Letters*. Manchester: Manchester University Press

Halle, M. (1969). Some thoughts on spelling. *In* K. S. Goodman and J. T. Fleming (eds), *Psycholinguistics and the Teaching of Reading*. Newark, Del.: International Reading Association

Hamp, E. (1959). Graphemics and paragraphemics. University of Buffalo, Department of Anthropology and Linguistics, *Studies in Linguistics* **14**, 1–6

Hampson, P. J. and Morris, P. E. (1978). Some properties of the visual imagery system investigated through backward spelling. *Quarterly Journal of Experimental Psychology* **30**, 655–664

Hécaen, H. (1967). Brain mechanisms suggested by studies of parietal lobes. *In* C. H. Millikan and F. L. Darley (eds), *Brain Mechanisms Underlying Speech and Language*. New York: Grune and Stratton

Hécaen, H. and Marcie, P. (1974). Disorders of written language following right hemisphere lesions. *In* S. J. Dimond and J. G. Beaumont (eds), *Hemisphere Function in the Human Brain*. London: Elek

Henderson, L. and Chard, J. (1980). The reader's implicit knowledge of orthographic structure. *In* U. Frith (1980a)

Hermann, K. (1949). Alexia-agraphia: a case report. *Acta Psychiatrica et Neurologia* **25**, 449–455

Hermann, K. and Voldby, H. (1946). The morphology of handwriting in congenital word-blindness. *Acta Psychiatrica et Neurologica* **21**, 349–363

Hier, D. B. and Mohr, J. P. (1977). Incongruous oral and written naming: evidence for a subdivision of the syndrome of Wernicke's aphasia. *Brain and Language* **4**, 115–126

Hirst, W., Spelke, E. S., Reaves, C. C., Caharack, G. and Neisser, U. (1980). Dividing attention without alternation and automaticity. *Journal of Experimental Psychology: General* **6**, 98–117

Holmes, D. L. and Peper, R. J. (1977). An evaluation of the use of spelling error analysis in the diagnosis of reading disabilities. *Child Development* **48**, 1708–1711

Hotopf, N. (1980). Slips of the pen. *In* U. Frith (1980a)

Kalmus, H., Fry, D. and Denes, P. (1960). Effects of delayed visual control on writing, drawing and tracing. *Language and Speech* **3**, 96–108

Kinsbourne, M. and Rosenfield, D. B. (1974). Agraphia selective for written spelling: an experimental case study. *Brain and Language* **1**, 215–225

Kinsbourne, M. and Warrington, E. K. (1965). A case showing selectively impaired oral spelling. *Journal of Neurology, Neurosurgery and Psychiatry* **28**, 563–566

Klatt, D. H. (1979). Speech perception: a model of acoustic-phonetic analysis and lexical access. *Journal of Phonetics* **7**, 279–312

Klein, R. (1951). Loss of written language due to dissolution of the phonetic structure of the word in brain abscess. *Journal of Mental Science* **97**, 328–339

Lange, J. (1930). Fingeragnosie und Agraphie. *Mschr. f. Psych.* **76**, 129 (cited in Hermann, 1949)

Lashley, K. S. (1951). The problem of serial order in behaviour. *In* L. A. Jeffress (ed.), *Cerebral Mechanisms in Behaviour*. New York: J. Wiley

Lebrun, Y. (1976). Neurolinguistic models of language and speech. *In* H. Whitaker and H. A. Whitaker (eds), *Studies in Neurolinguistics*, Vol. 1. New York: Academic Press

Lebrun, Y. and Rubio, S. (1972). Reduplications et omissions graphiques chez des patients attients d'une lésion hémisphérique droite. *Neuropsychologia* **10**, 249–251

Lecours, A. R. (1966). Serial order in writing – a study of misspelled words in 'developmental dysgraphia'. *Neuropsychologia* **4**, 221–241

Lhermitte, F. and Dérouesné, J. (1974). Paraphasies et jargonaphasie dans le langage oral avec conservation du langage écrit. *Revue Neurologique* **130**, 21–38

Liberman, I., Liberman, A. M., Mattingly, I. and Shankweiler, D. (1980). Orthography and the beginning reader. *In* J. F. Kavanagh and R. L. Venezky (eds), *Orthography, Reading and Dyslexia*. Baltimore: University Park Press

Luria, A. R. (1960). Differences between disturbance of speech and writing and Russian and in French. *International Journal of Slavic Linguistics and Poetics* **3**, 13–22

Luria, A. R. (1970). *Traumatic Aphasia*. The Hague: Mouton

MacKay, D. G. (1969). The repeated letter effect in the misspellings of dysgraphics and normals. *Perception and Psychophysics* **5**, 102–106

Marcel, A. J. (1978). Prerequisites for a more applicable psychology of reading. *In* M. M. Gruneberg, P. E. Morris and R. N. Sykes (eds), *Practical Aspects of Memory*. London: Academic Press

Marcel, A. J. (1980a). Surface dyslexia and beginning reading – a revised hypothesis of the pronunciation of print and its impairments. *In* M. Coltheart, K. E. Patterson and J. C. Marshall (eds), *Deep Dyslexia*. London: Routledge and Kegan Paul

Marcel, A. J. (1980b). Phonological awareness and phonological representation. *In* U. Frith (1980a)

Marsh, G., Friedman, M., Welch, V. and Desberg, P. (1980). The development of strategies in spelling. *In* U. Frith (1980a)

Marshack, A. (1972). Upper paleolithic notation and symbol. *Science* **178**, 817–828

Marshall, J. C. (1977). Disorders in the expression of language. *In* J. Morton and J. C. Marshall (eds), *Psycholinguistics Series*, Vol. 1. London: Elek Science

Marshall, J. C. and Newcombe, F. (1973). Patterns of paralexia: a psycholinguistic approach. *Journal of Psycholinguistic Research* **2**, 175–199

McIntosh, A. (1956). The analysis of written Middle English. *Transactions of the Philological Society* (1956), 26–55

Morais, J., Cary, L., Alegria, J. and Bertelson, P. (1979). Does awareness of speech as a sequence of phones arise spontaneously? *Cognition* **7**, 323–331

Morton, J. (1979). Word recognition. *In* J. Morton and J. C. Marshall (eds), *Psycholinguistics Series*, Vol. 2. London: Elek

Morton, J. (1980). The logogen model and orthographic structure. *In* U. Frith (1980a)

Morton, J. and Patterson, K. E. (1980). A new attempt at an interpretation, or, an attempt at a new interpretation. *In* M. Coltheart, K. E. Patterson and J. C. Marshall (eds), *Deep Dyslexia*. London: Routledge and Kegan Paul

Nelson, H. E. (1974). The aetiology of specific spelling disabilities – a neuropsychologist's approach. *In* B. Wade and K. Wedell (eds), *Spelling: task and learner*. University of Birmingham: Educational Review, Occasional Publications, No. 5

Nelson, H. E. (1980). Analysis of spelling errors in normal and dyslexic children. *In* U. Frith (1980a)

Newcombe, F. and Marshall, J. C. (1980). Transcoding and lexical stabilization in deep dyslexia. *In* M. Coltheart, K. E. Patterson and J. C. Marshall (eds), *Deep Dyslexia*. London: Routledge and Kegan Paul

Orton, S. T. (1931). Special disability in spelling. *Bulletin of the Neurological Clinic* **1**, 159–192

Personke, C. and Yee, A. H. (1966). A model for the analysis of spelling behaviour. *Elementary English* **43**, 278–284

Pillsbury, W. B. (1897). A study in apperception. *American Journal of Psychology* **8**, 315–393

Posnansky, C. and Rayner, K. (1977). Visual-feature and response components in a picture-word interference task with beginning and skilled readers. *Journal of Experimental Child Psychology* **24**, 440–460

Pulgram, E. (1951). Phoneme and grapheme: a parallel. *Word* **7**, 15–20

Rayner, K. and Posnansky, C. (1978). Stages of processing in word identification. *Journal of Experimental Psychology: General* **107**, 64–80

Read, C. (1975). Lessons to be learned from the preschool orthographer. *In* E. H. Lenneberg and E. Lenneberg (eds), *Foundations of Language Development*, Vol. 2. New York: Academic Press

Rosati, G. and Bastiani, P. de (1979). Pure agraphia: a discrete form of aphasia. *Journal of Neurology, Neurosurgery, and Psychiatry* **42**, 266–269

Seymour, P. (1976). Retrieval and comparison operations in permanent memory. *In* V. Hamilton and M. D. Vernon (eds), *The Developmental Cognitive Processes*. London: Academic Press

Seymour, P. (1979). *Human Visual Cognition*. West Drayton, Mddx: Collier-Macmillan

Seymour, P. and Porpodas, C. (1978). Coding of spelling by normal and dyslexic readers. *In* M. M. Gruneberg, P. E. Morris and R. N. Sykes (eds), *Practical Aspects of Memory*. London: Academic Press

Seymour, P. and Porpodas, C. (1980). Lexical and nonlexical processing of spelling in developmental dyslexia. *In* U. Frith (1980a)

Shallice, T. (1981). Phonological agraphia and the lexical route in writing. *Brain* **104**, 413–429

Shattuck-Hufnagel, S. (1979). Speech errors as evidence for a serial-ordering mechanism in sentence production. *In* W. Cooper and E. C. T. Walker (eds), *Sentence Processing*. Hillsdale, New Jersey: Erlbaum

Simon, D. P. and Simon, H. A. (1973). Alternative uses of phonemic information in spelling. *Review of Educational Research* **43**, 115–137

Sloboda, J. A. (1980). Visual imagery and individual differences in spelling. *In* U. Frith (1980a)

Smith, K. U. (1962). *Delayed Sensory Feedback and Behaviour*. Philadelphia: Saunders

Smith, P. T. (1980). Linguistic information in spelling. *In* U. Frith (1980a)

Solomons, L. M. and Stein, G. (1896). Normal motor automatisms. *Psychological Review* **3**, 492–512

Spache, G. (1940). Characteristic errors of good and poor spellers. *Journal of Educational Research* **34**, 182–189

Spelke, E., Hirst, W. and Neisser, U. (1976). Skills of divided attention. *Cognition* **4**, 215–230

Tauli, V. (1977). Speech and spelling. *In* J. A. Fishman (ed.), *Advances in the Creation and Revision of Writing Systems*. The Hague: Mouton

Tenney, Y. T. (1980). Visual factors in spelling. *In* Frith, U. (1980a)

Trager, G. L. (1974). Writing and writing systems. *In* T. Sebeock (ed.), *Current Trends in Linguistics*, Vol. 12. The Hague: Mouton

Ulatowska, H. K., Baker, T. and Stern, R. F. (1979). Disruption of written language in aphasia. *In* H. Whitaker and H. A. Whitaker (eds), *Studies in Neurolinguistics*, Vol. 4. New York: Academic Press

Valenstein, E. and Heilman, K. M. (1979). Apraxic agraphia with neglect-induced paragraphia. *Archives of Neurology* **36**, 506–508

van Bergeijk, A. and David, E. (1959). Delayed handwriting. *Perceptual and Motor Skills* **9**, 347–357

van Galen, G. P. (1980). Handwriting and drawing: a two-stage model of complex motor behaviour. *In* G. E. Stelmach and J. Requin (eds), *Tutorials in Motor Behaviour*. Amsterdam: North-Holland

Weigl, E. (1975). On written language: its acquisition and its alexic-agraphic disturbances. *In* E. H. Lenneberg and E. Lenneberg (eds), *Foundations of Language Development*, Vol. 2. New York: Academic Press

Weigl, E. and Fradis, A. (1977). The transcoding process in patients with agraphia to dictation. *Brain and Language* **4**, 11–22

Weir, R. H. and Venezky, R. L. (1968). Spelling-to-sound patterns. *In* K. S. Goodman (ed.), *The Psycholinguistic Nature of the Reading Process.* Detroit: Wayne State University Press

Wells, F. L. (1906). Linguistic lapses. *In* J. McK. Cattell and F. J. E. Woodbridge (eds), *Archives of Philosophy, Psychology and Scientific Methods,* No. 6. New York: The Science Press

Williams, A. (1974). A study of spelling errors. *In* B. Wade and K. Wedell (eds), *Spelling: Task and Learner.* University of Birmingham: Educational Review, Occasional Publications, No. 5

Wing, A. M. (1979). Variability of handwritten characters. *Visible Language* **13**, 283–298

5

Object Recognition: Some Deductions from the Clinical Evidence

GRAHAM RATCLIFF* and FREDA NEWCOMBE

Department of Psychology, University of Reading, England and Neuropsychology Unit, The Radcliffe Infirmary, Oxford, England

Our current interest in the recognition of objects was stimulated by our encounters with patients who had lost the ability to recognise them following damage to the brain. Our views on object recognition were developed while working with these patients, and represent the conceptual framework which we find most helpful in attempting to understand and document their deficits rather than a model which we have attempted to test by examining them. This clinical bias has influenced our approach to this chapter in which we focus on the disorders of object recognition known in the clinical literature as 'agnosia'.

1 The concept of agnosia

Agnosia is traditionally defined as a disorder of recognition which is not secondary to generalised intellectual deterioration, sensory dysfunction, or language deficit. Visual recognition has been more extensively studied than recognition in other modalities, and when the term 'agnosia' is used in isolation it can be assumed that the disorder includes the failure to recognise visually presented objects. However, the general term is sometimes qualified according to the type of stimulus which is not recognised and the modality that is affected. Thus auditory agnosia (Vignolo, 1969; Oppenheimer and Newcombe, 1978), colour agnosia (Geschwind and Fusillo, 1966; Oxbury, Oxbury and Humphrey, 1969), prosopagnosia (Meadows, 1974) are distinguished from visual object agnosia, although the majority of patients with visual object agnosia are impaired in the

* Present address: Western Psychiatric Institute, University of Pittsburgh, Pennsylvania, USA.

recognition of colours and faces, and many of them are also unable to recognise objects by touch. The recognition of environmental sounds, on the other hand, may be preserved in patients who are unable to recognise the sources of the sound through other modalities.

This traditional view of agnosia as a specific disorder of recognition has been subjected to two main types of criticism. One school of thought, exemplified by the work of Bay (1953) and recently re-emphasised by Bender and Feldman (1972) claims that all alleged visual agnosias can be explained by subtle alterations in perceptual function, or the combined effects of perceptual dysfunction and generalised intellectual deterioration. This view is logically irrefutable; it is always possible that the examination of a patient's perceptual status has been incomplete, that a further test might reveal an unexpected deficit, and that the integrity of the untested perceptual process might be necessary for object recognition. Bay's work has been useful in drawing attention to this possibility and stimulating more thorough examination of visual perception but, in practice, it seems clear that visual agnosia can exist in patients in whom exhaustive examination of visual perception has revealed no deficit (e.g. Newcombe and Ratcliff, 1975, Case 1), in patients whose perceptual deficits are no more severe than those of nonagnosic patients (Ettlinger, 1956; Ettlinger and Wyke, 1961) and in patients whose ability to make easily recognisable copies of drawings that they do not recognise suggests that inadequate perception of the stimulus is not the reason for their failure to recognise it (Rubens and Benson, 1971; Taylor and Warrington, 1971; Newcombe and Ratcliff, 1975).

The other objection to the concept of agnosia is that it implies the existence of recognition as a psychological process separate from perception on the one hand and language on the other (Geschwind, 1965; Teuber, 1965). This criticism (and to some extent Bay's point) is a question of semantics – an argument about the scope of the terms 'perception' and 'language'. One could, for example, take the view that we normally perceive a world inhabited by recognisable objects and people rather than an array of contours and colours. In this view the failure to recognise an object would constitute a perceptual deficit in itself, making the concept of agnosia redundant.

We regard this kind of argument about the validity of the term 'agnosia' as less important than the independent question of whether the disorders to which the term is commonly applied actually exist as distinctive neuropsychological syndromes and, if so, what are the characteristic features of the condition. It is now quite clear that they do exist (although they are very rare) and that they can be distinguished from other disorders which are conventionally described as disorders of language and perception. Rather than offering an arbitrary definition of perception or language and excluding disorders in which these processes are disturbed from the class of agnosias, we prefer to point out the differences between the disorders usually grouped under each heading and, by doing so, to isolate the cognitive processes impaired in each group of patients.

The ability to name an object or to give an account of how it would be used, either verbally or by mime, is generally accepted as evidence that the object has been recognised. A better term might be 'identified' because recognition in the sense of recognition memory (i.e. recognising that a stimulus is identical with one which has previously been presented) is not acceptable evidence of recognition in this context (viz. Warrington's, 1975, patient who was shown a photograph of a table tennis bat which he did not recognise and when subsequently shown another photograph of the same bat taken from a different angle remarked that he had already said that he did not know what it was).

2 Disorders of object naming

A NOMINAL DYSPHASIA

The inability to name objects is often the first formal indication that a patient does not recognise them because object naming is usually a part of the neurologist's mental status examination and is included in all aphasia test batteries. But by far the commonest reason for failing to name objects is nominal dysphasia. Most aphasic patients have an object naming deficit which is independent of the modality in which the stimulus is presented (Goodglass, Barton and Kaplan, 1968) and unaffected by degradation of the stimulus (Corlew and Nation, 1975; Hatfield, Howard, Barber, Jones and Morton, 1977). Their errors, when they are not outright failures or perseverations, typically consist of responses which bear some semantic or phonological similarity to the stimulus (see Table I) and naming is facilitated by the provision of linguistic or phonological cues

Table I   Examples of object naming errors made by aphasic patients

Stimulus picture	Response
anchor	um . . . ankle . . . congle . . . angle
anvil	forge
dice	what do you call them . . . play ludo
gyroscope	beings with a 'g' . . . dryascope
key	lock, like a lock
metronome	something to do with music – a timebeater
microscope	a thing you look through . . . a stereoscope
octopus	opipus
pencil	pen . . . pent . . . penshal
xylophone	sinophone

such as a linguistic context ('she bought a new saddle for her. . .'.) or the sound of the initial consonant and vowel of the target ('ho. . .') (Pease and Goodglass, 1978). These patients are usually able to mime the function of an object which they cannot name, thus demonstrating that they recognise it, and it is this aspect of their performance which distinguishes them from agnosic patients.

The dissociation between recognition and naming in aphasia is essentially a dissociation between the retrieval of object names and the retrieval of other stored information about the object in question (particularly its function) and it requires a model of object recognition which allows the possibility of access to function information without access to names. Figure 1 shows a very simple schema which satisfies this requirement and in which the term 'semantic system' is used to refer to a store which we assume, for the moment, contains all information about objects, concepts, and word meanings except their names.

The characteristics of nominal dysphasia outlined above are consistent with the view that the naming deficit in these cases is purely a word-finding difficulty – that is to say that the patients in question are able to retrieve information about the object from an intact semantic system but are not able to retrieve its name. However there is some evidence to suggest that the semantic system itself may not be entirely normal in some aphasic patients (Zurif, Caramazza, Meyerson and Galvin, 1974; Caramazza and Berndt, 1978; Whitehouse, Caramazza and Zurif, 1978; Goodglass, 1980) and two other studies conflict with those mentioned earlier in showing that real objects are better named by aphasic patients than line-drawings (Bisiach, 1966; Benton, Smith and Lang, 1972). This suggests that their disorder is not entirely post-perceptual but there are two reasons for qualifying this interpretation. First, the poorer performance with line drawings may simply reflect the additional difficulty for all subjects of this kind of material which might be obscured by a ceiling effect in normal subjects or aggravated by some nonaphasic perceptual disorder in brain damaged patients. Second, one of these

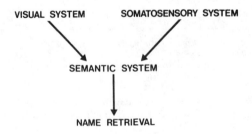

Fig. 1 A simple provisional model of the processes involved in object naming which is consistent with the data on nominal dysphasia so far presented

studies (Bisiach, 1966) included patients with 'optic aphasia' who form a special and problematical subgroup.

B OPTIC APHASIA

Optic aphasia is a visual modality specific disorder which affects the ability to *name* pictorial stimuli or real objects (Freund, 1889). Recognition is said to be preserved in these patients because they can indicate the use of objects and point to named objects. The latter test needs to be interpreted with caution as superior performance in pointing to named objects over free-naming may be a consequence of the restricted number of alternatives from which the patient has to choose, and scores in such object-recognition tasks can be altered by manipulating the similarity between the target and distractors. It is also possible that the apparent superiority of miming over naming may be partially attributable to the comparative imprecision of mime. Consider the hypothetical case of a patient who has been shown a picture of a shoe. A mime consisting of fitting an imaginary object over a foot might be considered a correct response but the name 'sock' or 'boot' would not, though both would be compatible with the mime. Unless carefully matched stimuli are used, the evidence for preservation of tactile naming may also be questionable as there is a tendency to use relatively common, readily available and easily manipulable stimuli in tactile naming tasks while picture naming tasks frequently include pictures of unusual objects which are not drawn to scale. For example, the Oldfield-Wingfield object naming test used in our laboratory includes drawings of a xylophone and an anvil but we have never asked any subject to identify these objects by touch.

Nevertheless, a *prima facie* case has been made for the existence of a naming disorder which is specific to the visual modality and not accompanied by a recognition deficit. The nonperseverative errors of such patients resemble those of patients with nominal dysphasia in being predominantly semantic rather than visual confusions. But the preservation of tactile naming precludes an explanation on the basis of failure to retrieve the names for items which have been correctly addressed in an intact supramodal semantic system. Yet preservation of the ability to indicate the use of objects suggests that their semantic representations have been correctly addressed.

It is clear that any model of object recognition which takes account of these data must allow for modality specific processing at a later stage than envisaged in Fig. 1 as well as separating the stage which permits recognition from that which permits naming. There seem to be two possible ways of satisfying this requirement. One might postulate independent semantic systems for each modality which feed separately into name retrieval systems which might or might not be modality specific. We are reluctant to take this approach because the duplication of semantic systems seems unnecessarily redundant.

Alternatively one might construct a model analogous to that envisaged in some accounts of word recognition which allows for a nonsemantic route to naming (see Fig. 2). Suppose that for each sensory modality there is a system used in object recognition whose function is similar to that of input logogens in word recognition (Morton, 1979). The term 'pictogen' has been suggested for these units in the visual modality (Morton, 1979) and, for the moment, we will regard them simply as picture or object recognisers whose activation does not by itself provide information about the function of the object in question but is a necessary step towards accessing information in the semantic system. Suppose further that, for each sensory modality, the pictogens or their equivalents are connected to the name retrieval system (output logogens in this analogy) by two routes: one passing through the common, supramodal semantic system and a nonsemantic route which bypasses it. If this were the case optic aphasia could be caused by disruption of the nonsemantic route in much the same way as deep dyslexia is associated with loss of nonsemantic routes for reading (Marshall and Newcombe, 1973). One patient with optic aphasia (Lhermitte and Beauvois, 1973) is reported to have been able to write the names of objects which he could not name orally. Presumably in this case a route to written output was preserved.

This hypothesis has the merit that it avoids the necessity for postulating the existence of multiple modality-specific semantic systems and that the semantic and nonsemantic routes suggested here may well have parallels in the word-recognition system. Schwartz, Saffran and Marin (1980) have described a patient who was able to name irregular words (e.g. leopard) without apparently being able to access their meaning. It is difficult to see how this could have been achieved by the operation of grapheme-phoneme conversion rules, but it could plausibly be explained by a direct input logogen-output connection. We are suggesting that an equivalent

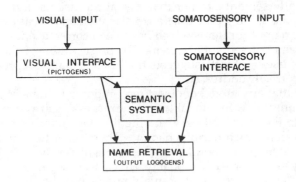

Fig. 2 Modification of the model shown in Fig. 1 to take account of 'optic aphasia' and the tactile modality specific naming deficit described by Beauvois *et al.* (1978)

route in a pictogen system may be dysfunctioning in optic aphasia. This would account for the modality-specificity and, if one allows for some fuzziness in the mapping of the semantic system onto output logogens, it would also be consistent with the occurrence of semantic errors in naming with preservation of recognition measured by the ability to mime.

One consequence of this interpretation of optic aphasia is that it allows the possibility that object recognition could be disturbed in the same way as word recognition was disturbed in Schwartz, Saffran and Marin's patient if only the nonsemantic route were functioning. Such a disorder of object recognition would consist in preservation of the ability to name objects without the ability to give any other evidence of recognition because of loss of access to the semantic system. This state of affairs has not to our knowledge been described but patients are rarely asked to mime or describe the function of objects if they have named them correctly, so it is conceivable that it may exist but have remained unnoticed.

The dual routes to naming, which we propose, provide a possible explanation for a puzzling aspect of the experiment by Bisiach (1966) mentioned earlier. He found that stimulus degradation affected his patients' naming without affecting their recognition and a similar result was obtained by North (1971, cited by Goodglass, 1980). Thus the performance of aphasic patients under conditions of stimulus degradation resembles that of patients with optic aphasia when shown undegraded stimuli: they recognise but cannot name. This would be consistent with the existence of a nonsemantic route to naming which requires a more redundant specification of the stimulus (and is thus more susceptible to stimulus degradation) than the route into the semantic system which remains functional even when the stimulus is degraded.

In summary then, the object naming deficit in most cases of aphasia can be explained by a defect in retrieving the name associated with the concept which is intact, or nearly intact, although in some cases there may be some disturbance of the semantic system itself. In the special case of optic aphasia it becomes necessary to postulate either separate semantic systems for each sensory modality or disturbance of a route to naming which is modality-specific and does not involve accessing the semantic system. We repeat, however, that the evidence for preserved object recognition in optic aphasia, which distinguishes it from visual agnosia, can be questioned and we note that individual patients may fluctuate between the conditions (Rubens, 1979). Given the uncertainty about the evidence we cannot regard the dual pathway hypothesis we have proposed as anything more than a tentative suggestion.

3 The agnosias

Agnosic patients, who by definition do not recognise stimuli, must in our terms either be deprived of input from pictorial stimuli to the semantic system, or have suffered damage to the semantic system itself. In practice, if the above account of optic aphasia is correct, they must also have lost direct access to the name retrieval system as correct naming is regarded clinically as evidence of recognition. Three broad categories of visual agnosia can be distinguished on clinical grounds and each of these seems to be attributable to a disorder at a different stage of processing.

A   APPERCEPTIVE VISUAL AGNOSIA

Disorders of object recognition which seem to reflect the failure of a very early stage of processing are known in the neurological literature as 'apperceptive' visual agnosia. The term derives from Lissauer (1890) who distinguished between 'apperception' (the act of conscious perception of a stimulus) and 'association' (the act of associating the contents of perception with other ideas). Patients with apperceptive visual agnosia are unable to copy or match to sample drawings which they cannot recognise, and the recognition and matching of all other stimuli which demand shape or pattern perception is similarly affected (Rubens, 1979). Colour discrimination may be preserved and the recognition of coloured (Rubens, 1979) or moving (Botez, 1975) stimuli may be less severely affected.

As Rubens (1979) has pointed out in an excellent review of the subject, some patients who are described as apperceptive visual agnosics (e.g. Adler, 1944) appear to be similar to those who are considered to be suffering from Balint's syndrome (Balint, 1909; Tyler, 1968), or simultanagnosia (Wolpert, 1924; Luria, 1959; Luria, Pravdina-Vinarskaya and Yarbus, 1963). These disorders involve a disturbance of visual attention which Rubens (1979) has described as bilateral visual neglect with macular sparing and which results in a constriction of the effective visual field although the field may appear full on perimetric examination. This is associated with a disorder of visual scanning, and patients are able to report only one part of a scene or a stimulus at a time. It is in cases like these that the claim that the alleged agnosia is attributable to complex perceptual defect has most force and we will not consider them further.

We are, however, aware of two patients with a disorder that might be described as apperceptive agnosia, who merit further discussion. One of these (Benson and Greenberg, 1969) was thought to be blind for several months following carbon monoxide poisoning until he was seen successfully navigating his wheelchair along a corridor. Subsequent testing showed that his visual fields were full to a 3 mm stimulus, that he could reach accurately for fine threads on a piece of white paper, detect small differences in size, luminance and wavelength, and that he was aware of small movements of visual stimuli. However, he was unable to recognise objects, letters or numbers and unable to discriminate between any visual stimuli which differed only in shape.

The other patient is being studied by Barbara Wilson (unpublished data) at Rivermead Rehabilitation Centre in Oxford. A year after a closed head injury this patient (H.S.) is able to recognise almost all solid objects but still has a moderate difficulty in recognising line drawings. When asked to select the drawing of an object named by the examiner from an array of drawings, her errors consisted exclusively of pointing to an object which was visually similar to the target. She can recognise faces and read; and she is able to access semantic information by a verbal route. A quadriplegia has prevented adequate testing of tactile recognition or her ability to copy drawings but the data thus far would be consistent with the diagnosis of apperceptive visual agnosia. However, her ability to match random shapes and the orientation of lines is grossly defective.

The disorder in these two cases therefore could be described as a pattern or shape recognition deficit rather than a selective defect of object recognition.[1] We would prefer to classify this as a perceptual disorder, ascribing it to an earlier stage of processing than the pictogens of Fig. 2. We will suggest later that there is indeed a form of agnosia which is attributable to failure of a process similar to that described by Lissauer as 'apperception', but the clinical literature has not yet produced a convincing account of apperceptive agnosia as a distinct neuropsychological syndrome.

B   ASSOCIATIVE VISUAL AGNOSIA

Associative visual agnosia, on the other hand, undoubtedly exists and two forms of the disorder can be distinguished on clinical grounds. One form is specific to the visual modality and can plausibly be explained on the basis of a visual-verbal disconnection, while the other affects both visual and tactile object recognition and does not fit the disconnection hypothesis so comfortably. Both types differ from apperceptive agnosia in that the patient can make recognisable copies of drawings which he does not himself recognise and successfully perform matching tasks (Rubens and Benson, 1971; Taylor and Warrington, 1971; Newcombe and Ratcliff, 1975). They differ from nominal dysphasics in that the naming of three-dimensional objects, especially if they are moved or rotated in the patient's visual field (Levine, 1978) is superior to naming of line drawings. Naming of an object from a verbal description of its function ('What do you wear on your wrist and use to tell the time?') may be much better than naming of the visually presented object itself (Newcombe and Ratcliff, 1975) which suggests that the deficit is not simply a difficulty in retrieving names.

1   *The disconnection hypothesis.* The disconnection explanation for visual agnosia is similar to that given for dyslexia without dysgraphia and colour agnosia (Geschwind, 1965). An intact left hemisphere language area is presumed to be disconnected from visual input, usually by extensive destruction of the posterior part of the left hemisphere including damage

to the optic radiation or striate cortex and interruption of the forceps major which carries information from the right occipital lobe to the left hemisphere via the splenium of the corpus callosum. The patients for whom this explanation seems most appropriate are those who have a right homonymous hemianopia, dyslexia and colour agnosia as well as an object recognition deficit; their tactile object recognition, which would be unaffected by these lesions, should be unimpaired.

The absence of hemianopia does not preclude a disconnection explanation as the disconnection could be caused by damage to forward projections from an intact left occipital lobe. This anatomical picture has been found at postmortem examination of the brain of a pure dyslexic patient (Greenblatt, 1973), suggesting that the occasional preservation of the ability to read in visual agnosic patients (Newcombe and Ratcliff, 1975, Cases 1 and 2; Albert, Reches and Silverberg, 1975; Mack and Boller, 1977) is not sufficient reason for discounting visual-verbal disconnection as an explanation. Only the inferior projections from the left occipital lobe were damaged in the patient studied by Greenblatt who suggested that more superior fibres might be mediating her object recognition and colour naming. Although, as he points out, the case only demonstrates that the inferior pathway was necessary for word recognition and not that it was sufficient, it raised the possibility that anatomically separate pathways may subserve word, object and colour recognition and that any of these pathways may be separately disconnected. This explanation was offered by Mack and Boller (1977) for the preservation of reading in a patient with visual object and colour agnosia and by Holmes (1950) in his study of a patient with pure word blindness who could recognise objects.

Positive evidence for the importance of interhemispheric disconnection comes from two patients with incomplete right sided visual field defects who were nevertheless much better at naming visual stimuli presented to the defective right half field than those shown in the intact left half field (Albert *et al.*, 1975; Oxbury, personal communication). Other evidence, however, casts doubt on the adequacy of disconnection as a general explanation for all cases of associative agnosia. First, it should be noted that if one accepts that object recognition (as opposed to naming) is mediated by the semantic system, then the disconnection must be a visual-semantic one and not merely visual-verbal. But patients whose cerebral commissures have been surgically sectioned are able to extract meaning from words and pictures when visual input is restricted to the right hemisphere (Sperry, 1974; Zaidel, 1978). This makes it seem unlikely that disconnection of an intact right hemisphere would be sufficient to cause agnosia unless one discounts the split brain evidence on the grounds that these patients' brains exhibit an unusual functional organisation, or explains it on the grounds that, unlike patients with partial damage to the commissures, their right hemispheres have been released from the inhibition normally exerted by the dominant left hemisphere.

Second, there are patients who exhibit tactile as well as visual recognition difficulties that cannot be explained simply by disconnection of visual input from later stages of processing (Taylor and Warrington, 1971; Newcombe and Ratcliff, 1975, Cases 1 and 2; Warrington, 1975). Further, all but one of these patients had full visual fields and all were able to read although word naming was better than word comprehension, particularly in Warrington's patients. Although none of these things by themselves exclude the possibility of a disconnection explanation, the constellation of preserved abilities suggest that they constitute a clinically distinct type of agnosia; and the superiority of word naming over word comprehension is particularly difficult to reconcile with disconnection of the left hemisphere from visual input.

2 *The semantic memory hypothesis.* Warrington's (1975) study of three patients in whom associative visual agnosia was identified on initial clinical examination introduced the notion that the disorder was attributable to a disturbance of the semantic system itself, although other authors have also suggested that a specific categorisation defect for visual stimuli plays a part in the genesis of agnosia (Albert *et al.*, 1975; Hécaen, Goldblum, Masure and Ramier, 1974).

All three of her patients had diffuse atrophic cerebral disease. In all three visual acuity was normal, fields were full to confrontation and performance on a variety of visual and perceptual tests, including matching of pictures of objects taken from different angles, was within normal limits although one patient (C.R. who also had some generalised intellectual deterioration) was mildly impaired on a face matching test. Picture naming was quite severely impaired in all three patients and although details are not given in Warrington's report she states that errors of both recognition and naming were recorded. Recognition of tactually presented objects is not reported but two patients (A.B. and C.R.) were severely impaired in the recognition of environmental sounds and all three were impaired at naming objects from a description of their functions.

The spontaneous speech of all three patients showed an impoverished vocabulary and on formal testing there was evidence of impaired word and sentence comprehension as well as mildly impaired word reading (in the sense of word naming) and spelling although only one of them (E.M.) showed overt dysphasia at the conversational level. All three had significant memory impairments, as do most agnosic patients but patients with global amnesia do not typically exhibit visual agnosia so this is not by itself sufficient to account for object recognition difficulty.

The clinical picture, then, was of associative visual agnosia (worse in A.B. than E.M. or C.R.) in the presence of memory impairment and word finding difficulty but with only mild intellectual deficit as measured by intelligence tests (at least in A.B. and E.M.) and without evidence of

obvious perceptual deficit. Warrington investigated her patients' ability
to access knowledge about visually presented objects and visually and
auditorily presented words by asking them to point to the picture (in an
array of three) which had a particular property (e.g. 'Which is largest?'
'Which is an animal?') and to answer questions about pictures and words
which demanded knowledge of the object named or depicted ('Is it an
animal?' 'Is it bigger than a cat?'). She also asked them to define words.
All three patients were impaired on these tasks, two being worse when
the stimulus was a picture (A.B. and C.R.) and one exhibiting the reverse
pattern (E.M.). Knowledge of superordinate category (e.g. animal/not
animal) seemed to be better preserved than knowledge of the attributes
and associates of objects (English/not English, bigger/smaller than a cat)
and in the most severely agnosic patient knowledge about size and
weight (heavier/lighter than a telephone directory) was most severely
affected. This patient, unlike the other two, also exhibited a puzzling
superiority in the definition of abstract over concrete nouns.

Warrington concluded that inability to access semantic information
was the cause of her patients' difficulties with object and word recognition. She regarded preservation of the ability to make same/different
judgements with respect to photographs of objects taken from different
angles as evidence of preserved 'perceptual classification' and suggested
that analysis at this level corresponded to the achievement of a word form
without meaning or semantic attributes. This corresponds approximately
to our notion of the function of a pictogen. Because of the evidence for
some hierarchical organisation of the patients' preserved semantic knowledge, specifically the relative preservation of superordinate categories,
she located the disturbance in the semantic system itself rather than in
access to it. The partial dissociation between picture and word recognition deficits led her to propose that there may be two 'partially distinct
modality specific meaning systems . . . the one primarily visual and the
other primarily verbal'.

This proposal requires comment because it is not clear what is meant by
'modality-specific' and it is not certain that the deficit must be in the
semantic system itself rather than a failure of adequate access to it. The
dissociation described by Warrington was between types of stimulus
material rather than *modality* of presentation – i.e. there was no difference
between visual and auditory word recognition but visual word recognition and visual object recognition were not well correlated. A division of
the semantic system into 'separate' components (one for pictorial
material, the other for verbal material) might account for this difference
but the term '*material*-specific' seems more appropriate to this distinction
than 'modality-specific', cf. material specific memory loss following
temporal lobectomy (Milner, 1970), and there is good evidence for independence of pictorial and verbal recognition systems at earlier stages of
processing (Seymour, 1979). However, as Seymour points out, the avail-

able data suggest that these systems, which he calls the Pictorial and Lexical Memories, converge on a common 'central semantic system which is accessible from the (independent) interface structures of the Lexical and Pictorial Memories'.

According to Seymour's model, therefore, a dissociation between the recognition of pictorial and verbal material would have to be attributed to differential access to the central semantic system from verbal and pictorial routes rather than to damage to distinct material specific components of the semantic system itself. We see no reason to reject this explanation for Warrington's data although admittedly the functional locus of the damage would have to be close to the central semantic system to allow for her patients' normal performance on the 'unusual-views' test of perceptual classification, and would have to affect both lexical and pictorial access to some degree. Her main grounds for supposing that the semantic system itself was damaged, the preservation of access to superordinate category information, could presumably be explained on the basis of partial access to an inadequately addressed item in the semantic store. Another finding which at first sight is difficult to accommodate within a semantic access account of Warrington's data is the difficulty her patients experienced in retrieving the name of an object given a verbal description of that object. However, since access could have been disturbed from verbal as well as pictorial stimuli it is possible that the terms used in the description may themselves have failed to access the semantic system. Of course, the possibility of accounting for Warrington's data by a semantic access deficit does not imply that her own hypothesis of impaired semantic memory is necessarily incorrect.

We can conceive of one other sense in which the semantic system might be said to be divided into material specific components. Suppose that one component contains information about the physical attributes of objects (size, shape etc.), possibly including physical attributes which are not necessarily evident on visual inspection (e.g. weight, texture etc.) while the other stores information about semantic category (e.g. animal, furniture, etc.), non-structural attributes (e.g. English/not English) and possibly function (e.g. used for telling the time). This information bears some similarity to Paivio's (1975) dual coding hypothesis but we do not claim that physical attribute information is more directly accessible to the imagery system (Pictorial Memory in Seymour's terms) than to the verbal (Lexical) system. Paivio suggested that perceptual attributes were more accessible to the imagery system because performance in tasks requiring the mental comparison of objects with respect to a perceptual attribute (size) was faster when the stimuli were pictures than when they were names (Moyer, 1973; Paivio, 1975). However, it has since been shown that this pictorial superiority effect also occurs for judgements about presumably non-perceptual attributes such as intelligence, pleasantness and monetary value (Paivio, 1977; Banks and Flora, 1977). Accordingly we follow Seymour (1979) in assuming that both components of the semantic system are equally accessible via pictorial and verbal routes.

Given the assumption of equal access, we cannot explain Warrington's (1975) data on the basis of damage to the physical information component of semantic memory. Pictorial and verbal stimuli should be equally affected by such damage though it might affect judgements about the appearance of objects more than judgements about their function, irrespective of the form in which stimuli were presented. There is just a suggestion of this effect in A.B., the most severely agnosic of Warrington's three patients, whose judgements about the size, weight and colour of objects and animals were on the whole slightly less accurate than judgements about whether they were English, dangerous, or normally used indoors. Stronger, though not conclusive, evidence comes from a patient (M.S.) whose case we have been following for 10 years. Some of our findings have been reported elsewhere (Newcombe and Ratcliff, 1975) and we summarise these below before pointing out the similarities and differences between his case and those described by Warrington.

Case report

M.S. was a 23-year-old left-handed police cadet who contracted a febrile illness in January 1970 with frontal headache and vomiting. Two weeks after onset, he became photo-phobic, drowsy and uncooperative. Lumbar puncture produced xanthochromic CSF at 200 mm with 30 000 red cells and protein 100 mg percent. Carotid and vertebral angiograms were normal, but an EEG showed severe bilateral disturbance with the main abnormality over the right occipital area. Brain scan (9 March) revealed an area of abnormal uptake over the right parieto-occipital area; but an air-encephalogram (11 March) showed only slight generalised ventricular dilatation. A CT scan carried out in March 1980 showed extensive bilateral infarction of the posterior part of the brain, mainly occipital but extending forward into the parietal and temporal lobes, particularly in the right hemisphere where the lesion was most extensive. The presumptive diagnosis was initially herpes encephalitis although this has never been confirmed by viral antibody studies, and examination of the recent CT scan suggests a vascular origin.

In the acute phase his mental state was described as extremely disturbed; he was thought to be deluded and probably hallucinated. By September 1971 he was described as 'cooperative' with no physical problems other than a left homonymous hemianopia with some macular sparing. He was oriented in time and place although he had a marked topographical disorientation, global amnesia, visual and tactile agnosia, a central disturbance of colour vision (Mollon et al., 1980) and was unable to recognise his parents by sight. His verbal IQ was 101 though performance IQ was grossly reduced. His condition has remained essentially unchanged since then although he is now able to work in the sheltered setting of a Remploy factory and, by dint of a great deal of practice and with the aid of maps and verbal mnemonics, he has learned his way to work and over some other routes near his home. During the last two or three years the content of his spontaneous conversation has increased and includes reference to current affairs but this apparent amelioration of his amnesia has not been reflected in formal memory tests.

His agnosia has not resolved. He recognises only 8 out of 36 line drawings of objects but is able to name 20 out of 36 from a verbal description of their function. On the occasions when he has offered an incorrect name it tends to be the name of an object bearing a physical resemblance to the stimulus (e.g. anchor → umbrella, anvil → bed → 'the only thing I can think of . . . a settee') but his copies of drawings which he cannot name are remarkably accurate although they appear to be achieved by a line by line copying strategy (see Fig. 3). By contrast his free drawing of objects named by the examiner (for example his responses to the request 'draw an anchor' shown in Fig. 4) are poor and generally unrecognisable. His naming of objects placed in his hands (6 out of 10 in the left hand, 5 out of 10 in the right hand) is marginally better than his naming of the same objects on visual presentation (4 out of 10) which, in turn, is better than his naming of photographs or line drawings of these objects (1 out of 10 in each case). Matching of identical objects is virtually perfect, both intramodally and across modalities. Recognition of environmental sounds is within normal limits. When he is asked to point to the picture of an object whose name is spoken by the examiner his performance is very poor and most, but not all, of his errors consist in pointing to objects which bear a physical resemblance to the target. Performance on visual recognition tasks using random shapes is within normal limits and his visual acuity has repeatedly been found to be normal (6/5 for distance; N5 for near) although there is a dramatic depression of the modulation transfer function at high spatial frequencies which we are unable to explain.

Reading, in the sense of word naming, is normal. His performance is within normal limits (46 out of 50) at making true/false judgements about absurd sentences (e.g. 'psychiatrists are used in cooking'), his age scale score on the WAIS vocabulary is 9 and he is able to define some words that he cannot produce in confrontation naming tasks (e.g. anchor → 'a brake for ships') but he has more difficulty in saying what the object in question would look like. However, in all these tasks there is occasional evidence of failure to access semantic information by a verbal route – he is, for example, unable to define 'a nightingale'.

These results indicate that M.S. is not an apperceptive agnosic in the conventional sense, because of his good performance on copying and matching tasks. Moreover, disconnection is an implausible, though not impossible, explanation for his disorder, chiefly because of the preservation of reading and the impairment of tactile naming. In these respects, he is similar to Warrington's patient A.B. although the dissociation between word and object recognition is greater in the case of M.S.

In our original account of this case (Newcombe and Ratcliff, 1975) we proposed that object identification was achieved by the extraction of visual features of the stimulus (e.g. its size, distinctive contour, shininess, etc.) and a subsequent search through a 'form of lexicon for objects' for items which had these attributes. We concluded that the 'lexicon for objects' was damaged in M.S. However, we were not clear whether the damaged structure was to be regarded as the 'physical information' component of the semantic system or as something more like the pictogens of Fig. 2 and the perceptual categorisation system described by Warrington (1975; Warrington and Taylor, 1973; 1978). Either of these possibilities would be consistent with the occurrence of errors in object naming that reflected confusion between objects of similar appearance. A pictogen deficit however would only explain the selective deficit in picture recognition. A deficit at the semantic level would account for his difficulty in retrieving information about the *appearance* of named objects but would not explain his particular difficulty with pictorial stimuli.

Fig. 3   Copy by M.S. of a drawing of an anchor. The model is shown on the left

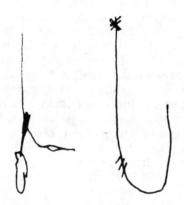

Fig. 4   Two attempts by M.S. to respond to the request 'Draw an anchor'

We explored the relative contributions of these two putative deficits by adapting a task devised by Wilkins and Moscovitch (1978). M.S. was presented, in separate blocks of trials, with two kinds of stimuli, pictures of objects and the typewritten names of these objects. On separate occasions he was asked, for each picture and for each name, to say whether the object represented was larger or smaller than a chair (a physical attribute) and whether it was living or man-made (a judgement which is less directly dependent on knowledge of the physical structure of the stimulus). He was also asked to name all the pictures and words and we ensured that he understood the terms larger and smaller and could use them appropriately. The results are shown in Table 2. It is clear that performance on both kinds of judgement is much worse with pictorial stimuli than with words, and this has been true for all the tasks in which we have compared the two kinds of stimulus. We conclude that M.S. has a specific difficulty in accessing semantic information from a pictorial route and that his agnosia is not totally explained by disturbance of the semantic system itself.

Table II   M.S. Performance on a modified version of the semantic memory task devised by Wilkins and Moscovitch (1978)

	Errors (Maximum = 32)	
	Pictures	Words
Size judgements	13	3
Living/man-made judgements	4	0
Naming	28	0

It will also be noted that M.S.'s performance was worse on size judgements than living/man-made judgements for both classes of stimuli. This would be consistent with selective disturbance of the 'physical attribute' component of the semantic system (or of selective inaccessibility of physical attribute information) but we are unwilling to take it as conclusive proof of the separation of semantic memory into material specific components. Many of the stimuli in this task were animals: it seems that these may represent a special case for M.S., as a class of stimulus about which he can generally access superordinate category information (namely that the stimulus is an animal) but little else, even when given the name of the animal in question. For no other class of stimulus that we have investigated (furniture, methods of transport, household articles, foodstuffs) is this true and knowledge of the superordinate category 'animal' is sufficient to determine that the stimulus is living but not sufficient to determine its size. All his errors on size judgements with verbal stimuli occurred when the stimulus was the name of an animal and most of his living/man-made errors with pictorial stimuli in this and other tests were responses to pictures of non-prototypical animals (e.g. snake, bee, snail, whale, penguin, caterpillar) which do not have a body and four legs and thus might not be considered good examplars of the perceptual category to which most animals belong (Rosch, Mervis, Gray, Johnson and Boyes-Braem, 1976). However he cannot *name* even prototypical examples (e.g. pig, lion and mouse).

Whatever may be the state of M.S.' semantic system, it is clear that his main difficulty is accessing it from a pictorial stimulus and his perform-ance on Warrington's 'unusual-views' test, which she kindly loaned us, throws some light on the nature of this deficit. This task requires the patient to make same/different judgements with respect to pairs of photographs of objects.

One member of each pair shows a conventional or canonical repre-sentation while the other, which might or might not be the same object, shows a non-canonical view. It will be recalled that Warrington's (1975) patients performed normally on this task, even though they did not recognise the objects depicted, but M.S.' performance was near chance. This suggests that he suffers from a disorder of 'perceptual classification' in Warrington's terms (Warrington and Taylor, 1973; 1978) or a deficit at the level of the pictogens in terms of the provisional model shown in Fig. 2.

However, we now wish to offer a more elaborate account of this stage of processing. So far we have been content to treat pictogens as pre-semantic picture recognisers but we have not distinguished between the possible role of pictogens themselves as an interface between appropriate visual input and the semantic system (the function of the 'Pictorial Interface' in Seymour's 1979 model) and the representation of the visual input in a form suitable for activation of the appropriate pictogen (the 'Pictorial Encoding' function in Seymour's terms). We now make this distinction because it is the pictorial encoding function which we think is impaired in M.S. and we have found Marr's computational theory of vision (Marr and Nishihara, 1978a, b; Marr, 1980) helpful in our attempts to specify the nature of the impairment.

3 *The '3-D model representation' hypothesis*   Marr specifies three levels of visual representation. The first of these – the 'primal sketch' – makes explicit the intensity changes and geometry of the retinal image. The second – the '2½-D sketch' – takes account of the depth, orientation and discontinuities of the visible surfaces. These two representations are viewer centred but, in Marr's opinion, object recognition requires the construction of a third and more elaborate representation – '3-D model representation' – which provides an object-centred description of the

three-dimensional structure whose two-dimensional image falls on the retina. Recognition also requires the existence of an appropriately organised store of such descriptions and a way of relating a newly derived description to those held in store. Marr and Nishihara (1978a, b) give an account of how these requirements might be achieved, at least for certain classes of shape, relying chiefly on the identification of the principal axes of the stimulus and its component parts, and their relationship to each other. Access to the store is provided via several indices which allow the derived 3-D model representation to be related to stored items on the basis of its general shape but also allow the match to be constrained by the structure of specific components. They regard the final match as the result of a gradual process 'that overlaps with, guides and constrains the derivation of a description from the image'. The end product of this process is a description of the three-dimensional structure of an object which is orientation free allowing the viewer to know how it would appear from different viewpoints, assuming that there are no marked and unpredictable irregularities on the hidden surfaces.

The inability to derive such a description would account for M.S.' poor performance on the 'unusual-views' test and it fits well with some other aspects of his performance. M.S. is better at naming real objects than line drawings as are other patients with agnosia (Newcombe and Ratcliff, 1975; Mack and Boller, 1977: Kertesz, 1979; Rubens, 1979) and his errors in naming and pointing tasks consist chiefly of responses which indicate objects that bear some physical similarity to the target item. These facts can be explained at least as well by the failure to derive an adequate 3-D model representation (which could be improved with more information about the stimulus) as by the lack of an interface between an adequate pictorial code and the semantic system.

Warrington and Taylor (1973, 1978) have shown that difficulty in recognising photographs of objects taken from certain non-canonical views, which presumably makes it difficult for the observer to form an appropriate 3-D model representation (Marr and Nishihara, 1978a, b), is associated with right parietal lesions; and there is other evidence implicating right hemisphere damage in failure to recognise pictures that have been degraded in other ways (De Renzi and Spinnler, 1966; Warrington and James, 1967; Lansdell, 1968; Newcombe and Russell, 1969). M.S. has extensive damage to the posterior part of his right hemisphere and the recognition difficulty associated with unilateral right hemisphere lesions may be a milder form of his deficit.

M.S. also had difficulty in drawing and describing the appearance of objects from memory. This would be consistent with loss or inaccessibility of information about the appearance of objects in the central semantic system and we accept that M.S. may have such a deficit though we do not think it is a major factor in the genesis of his agnosia.[2] An alternative explanation is suggested by Seymour's schematic representation of the Pictorial Memory (Seymour, 1979 Fig. xiii, 2.1). He assumes that pictorial descriptions of standard examplars of object classes, which he calls prototypes, are held in a presemantic 'pictorial data store'. We take this store to be similar to the store of 3-D model representations envisaged by Marr and Nishihara (1978a, b) and Seymour's model allows the pictorial data store to be consulted via the pictorial interface in setting up a pictorial code. This serves two purposes in his model: it provides a mechanism whereby permanently stored knowledge of the appearance of objects may facilitate their recognition and, together with the pictorial interface, it underlies 'the phenomena of imagery and visualisation' (Seymour, 1979). An inadequate pictorial data store, then, might account for M.S.' apparent difficulty in visualising objects and contribute to his object recognition deficit. Indeed it might totally account for his object recognition deficit if consultation of the pictorial data store plays a large enough part in setting up the pictorial code. We also note that, if we interpret Seymour's diagram correctly, the pictorial data store is the *only* point at which damage to the system could interfere with object recognition without disturbing the ability to copy drawings unless copying can be achieved by some route not included in his pictorial memory system.

It is very likely that such a route does exist. The 'primal sketch' provides all the stimulus information necessary to make an accurate copy of a line drawing and M.S.' copying strategy, a slavish line-by-line approach, suggested that he was indeed reading out just such information. Accordingly we have included in Fig. 5 a route to constructional output which is nonpictorial in the sense in which reading by the application of grapheme-phoneme conversion rules could be said to be nonlexical. We also speculate, though with less confidence, that he is able to represent visual information adequately at the intermediate level of the '2½-D sketch'. Marr (1980) and Marr and Nishihara (1978b) point out that this level is sufficient to describe a shape for later reproduction by milling of a block of metal as the milling process depends explicitly on information about local depth and orientation. It should also provide sufficient information for a visual stimulus to be matched with one palpated by the hands, an ability which M.S. possesses and which is otherwise difficult to explain.

4   Conclusions

We conclude that the schematic representation of the processes involved in object recognition shown in Fig. 5 is sufficient to account for the clinical data and, as far as we are aware, it does not conflict with data derived from experiments on normal subjects. We do not imply that the stages or levels of processing envisaged in this schema cannot be further subdivided (the construction of the 3-D model representation, for example,

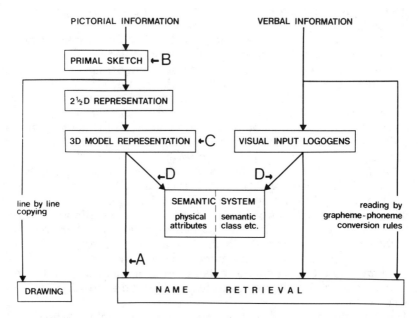

Fig. 5 Schematic representation of the processes involved in object recognition. See text for explanation

probably involves several components of Seymour's Pictorial Memory system) or that there cannot be other components or connections we have not shown. We have included an outline representation of the more familiar lexical system to point the similarity between object and word recognition.

The functional locus of damage in 'optic aphasia', if it exists, is indicated by the letter A. 'Apperceptive agnosia', as described in the clinical literature, would result from damage at or before B, but the functional locus of the disorder which we see as the major causal factor in M.S.' agnosia (indicated by the letter C) could equally well be described as a deficit in 'apperception'. The disorder in Warrington's patients must have been occurring at D, or beyond and we think it likely that all cases of associative agnosia which are not susceptible to an explanation in terms of visual-verbal disconnection are attributable to dysfunction at sites C or D or both. We do not wish to locate any of these processes precisely in any part of the brain, or even in a particular hemisphere, but it would be reasonable to suppose that the right hemisphere is more intimately involved with pictorial encoding functions than the left. It cannot be exclusively responsible for the construction of 3-D model representations, however, as lesions restricted to the right hemisphere do not cause object recognition deficits that approach in severity the disorder we have described in M.S.

This formulation takes no account of M.S.' difficulty with tactile object recognition. We have not studied this in any detail and can only suggest that it may be either the reflection of a similar kind of disorder in a tactile recognition system (which may or may not be organised in a similar way) or the product of a mild impairment of the semantic system. Nor do we offer any explanation for the apparent preservation of environmental sound recognition in M.S. other than to say that it is further evidence of the preservation of some semantic knowledge in his case and a difference between him and Warrington's patient A.B.

More generally, it is our contention that the examination of patients like M.S. and A.B. whose perceptual and/or cognitive functions have been impaired by cerebral lesions can provide valuable evidence about the nature of the processes involved in normal human cognition. This has been amply demonstrated in connection with word recognition (Coltheart, Patterson and Marshall, 1980) and our experience suggests that it also applies to object recognition. Equally, we are convinced that the attempt to interpret clinical data in terms of cognitive and computational models will facilitate our understanding of the disorders we see in the clinic.

We share the caution of the nineteenth-century neurologist and model-maker (Lichtheim, 1885) who, while 'well aware of the restricted foundations on which we may safely build, and what a space theoretical reasoning has still to occupy in the discussion' went on to justify his approach in words that we cannot improve upon:

if I have, nevertheless, not kept my views myself, it was on the principle, that we must not recoil from the consequences deducible from our hypotheses. In proportion as we draw these conclusions, we shall obtain the necessary data whereby to correct, or if need be, abandon them. Again, no simple observer can collect material enough to accomplish this task, which requires the cooperation of many; and under these conditions even erroneous assumptions may prove of advantage in the search for truth.

Notes

1 More recent data cast some doubt on this interpretation of the deficits in Wilson's patient. She appears to be able to learn the names for line drawings of objects which she cannot recognise, and can retain them for long periods. This suggests that her visual perception is adequate for object recognition. As yet we have no satisfactory explanation for these apparently conflicting results.

2 Note that patients who report a subjective loss of the capacity for mental imagery and whose description of absent objects are severely impaired may still be capable of recognising and responding adequately to objects when they are actually encountered (Brain, 1954; Basso, Bisiach and Luzzatti, 1980).

Acknowledgements

We thank Drs Alan Baddeley, Dorothy Bishop, Morris Moscovitch, Elizabeth Warrington and Arnold Wilkins for the loan of some of the test materials which we used with M.S. Drs Moscovitch and Wilkins also discussed his case with us.

References

Adler, A. (1944). Disintegration and restoration of optic recognition in visual agnosia. *Archives of Neurology and Psychiatry* **51**, 243–259

Albert, M. L., Reches, A. and Silverberg, R. (1975). Associative visual agnosia without alexia. *Neurology* **25**, 322–326

Balint, R. (1909). Die Seelenlähmung des Schauens, optische Ataxie räumliche Störung der Aufmerksamkeit. *Monatsschrift für Psychiatrie und Neurologie* **25**, 51–81

Banks, W. P. and Flora, J. (1977). Semantic and perceptual processes in symbolic comparisons. *Journal of Experimental Psychology: Human Perception and Performance* **3**, 278–290

Basso, A., Bisiach, E. and Luzzatti, C. (1980). Loss of mental imagery: a case study. *Neuropsychologia* **18**, 435–442

Bay, E. (1953). Disturbances of visual perception and their examination. *Brain* **76**, 515–550

Beauvois, M. F., Saillant, B., Meininger and Lhermitte, F. (1978). Bilateral tactile aphasia: a tacto-verbal dysfunction. *Brain* **101**, 381–401

Bender, M. B. and Feldman, M. (1972). The so-called 'visual agnosias'. *Brain* **95**, 173–186

Benson, D. F. and Greenberg, J. (1969). Visual form agnosia. *Archives of Neurology* **20**, 82–89

Benton, A. L., Smith, K. C. and Lang, M. (1972). Stimulus characteristics and object naming in aphasic patients. *Journal of Communication Disorders* **5**, 19–24

Bisiach, E. (1966). Perceptual factors in the pathogenesis of anomia. *Cortex* **2**, 90–95

Botez, M. I. (1975). Two visual systems in clinical neurology: readaptive role of the primitive system in visual agnosic patients. *European Neurology* **13**, 101–122

Brain, W. R. (1954). Loss of visualization. *Proceedings of the Royal Society of Medicine* **47**, 288–290

Caramazza, A. and Berndt, R. S. (1978). Semantic and syntactic processes in aphasia: A review of the literature. *Psychological Bulletin* **85**, 898–918

Coltheart, M., Patterson, K. and Marshall, J. C. (1980). *Deep Dyslexia*. London: Routledge and Kegan Paul

Corlew, M. M. and Nation, J. E. (1975). Characteristics of visual stimuli and naming performance in aphasic adults. *Cortex* **11**, 186–191

de Renzi, E. and Spinnler, H. (1966). Visual recognition in patients with unilateral cerebral disease. *Journal of Nervous and Mental Diseases* **142**, 515–525

Ettlinger, G. (1956). Sensory deficits in visual agnosia. *Journal of Neurology, Neurosurgery and Psychiatry* **19**, 297–307

Ettlinger, G. and Wyke, M. (1961). Defects in identifying objects visually in a patient with cerebrovascular disease. *Journal of Neurology, Neurosurgery and Psychiatry* **24**, 254–259

Freund, D. C. (1889). Über optische Aphasie und Seelenblindheit. *Archiv für Psychiatrie und Nervenkrankheiten, vereinigt mit Zeitschrift für die gesamte Neurologie und Psychiatrie* **20**, 276–297; 371–416

Geschwind, N. (1965). Disconnexion syndromes in animals and man. *Brain* **88**, 237–294 and 585–644

Geschwind, N. and Fusillo, M. (1966). Color-naming defects in association with alexia. *Archives of Neurology* **15**, 137–146

Goodglass, H. (1980). Disorders of naming following brain injury. *American Scientist* **68**, 647–655

Goodglass, H., Barton, M. and Kaplan, E. (1968). Sensory modality and object naming in aphasia. *Journal of Speech and Hearing Research* 11, 488–496

Greenblatt, S. H. (1973). Alexia without agraphia or hemianopsia. *Brain* 96, 307–316

Hatfield, F. M., Howard, D., Barber, J., Jones, C. and Morton, J. (1977). Object naming in aphasics – the lack of effect of context or realism. *Neuropsychologia* 15, 717–727

Hécaen, H., Goldblum, M. C., Masure, M. C. and Ramier, A. M. (1974). Une nouvelle observation d'agnosie d'objet. Deficit de l'association ou de la categorisation, specifique de la modalité visuelle? *Neuropsychologia* 12, 447–464

Holmes, G. (1950). Pure word blindness. *Folia psychiatrica, neurologica et neurochirurgica Neerlandica* (Amsterdam, Nederland), 53, 279–288

Kertesz, A. (1979). Visual agnosia: the dual deficit of perception and recognition. *Cortex* 15, 403–419

Lansdell, H. (1968). Effect of extent of temporal lobe ablations on two lateralized deficits. *Physiology and Behavior* 3, 271–273

Levine, D. N. (1978). Prosopagnosia and visual object agnosia: A behavioral study. *Brain and Language* 5, 341–365

Lhermitte, F. and Beauvois, M. F. (1973). A visual-speech disconnexion syndrome. *Brain* 96, 695–714

Lichtheim, L. (1885). On aphasia. *Brain* 7, 433–484

Lissauer, H. (1890). Ein Fall von Seelenblindheit nebst einem Beitrage zur Theorie derselben. *Archiv für Psychiatrie und Nervenkrankheiten, vereinigt mit Zeitschrift für die gesamte Neurologie und Psychiatrie* 21, 222–270

Luria, A. R. (1959). Disorders of 'simultaneous perception' in a case of bilateral occipitoparietal brain injury. *Brain* 82, 437–449

Luria, A. R., Pravdina-Vinarskaya, E. N. and Yarbus, A. L. (1963). Disorders of ocular movement in a case of simultanagnosia. *Brain* 86, 219–228

Mack, J. L. and Boller, F. (1977). Associative visual agnosia and its related deficits: the role of the minor hemisphere in assigning meaning to visual perceptions. *Neuropsychologia* 15, 345–349

Marr, D. (1980). Visual information processing: the structure and creation of visual representations. *Philosophical Transactions of the Royal Society of London*, Series B, 290, 199–218

Marr, D. and Nishihara, H. K. (1978a). Representation and recognition of the spatial organisation of three-dimensional shapes. *Proceedings of the Royal Society of London*, Series B, 200, 269–294

Marr, D. and Nishihara, H. K. (1978b). Visual information processing: Artificial intelligence and the sensorium of sight. *Technology Review* 81, 2–23

Marshall, J. C. and Newcombe, F. (1973). Patterns of paralexia: a psycholinguistic approach. *Journal of Psycholinguistic Research* 2, 175–199

Meadows, J. C. (1974). The anatomical basis of prosopagnosia. *Journal of Neurology, Neurosurgery and Psychiatry* 37, 489–501

Milner, B. (1970). Memory and the medial temporal regions of the brain. In K. Pribram and D. E. Broadbent (eds), *Biology of Memory*. New York: Academic Press

Mollon, J. D., Newcombe, F., Polden, P. G. and Ratcliff, G. (1980). On the presence of three cone mechanisms in a case of total achromatopsia. In G. Veriest (ed.), *Colour Vision Deficiencies* V. Bristol: Hilger

Morton, J. (1979). Facilitation in word recognition: Experiments causing change in the logogen model. In P. A. Kolers, M. Wrolstad and H. Bouma (eds), *Processing of Visible Language*. Plenum: New York

Moyer, R. S. (1973). Comparing objects in memory: Evidence suggesting an internal psychophysics. *Perception and Psychophysics* 13, 180–184

Newcombe, F. and Ratcliff, G. (1975). Agnosia: a disorder of object recognition. In F. Michel and B. Schott (eds), *Les Syndromes de Disconnexion calleuse chez l'Homme*. (Colloque International de Lyon, 1974). Hôpital neurologique de Lyon, Lyon

Newcombe, F. and Russell, W. R. (1969). Dissociated visual perceptual and spatial deficits in focal lesions of the right hemisphere. *Journal of Neurology, Neurosurgery and Psychiatry* **32**, 73–81

North, E. (1971). Effects of stimulus redundancy on naming disorders in aphasia. Boston University Ph.D. dissertation. Cited by H. Goodglass (1980)

Oppenheimer, D. O. and Newcombe, F. (1978). Clinical and anatomic findings in a case of auditory agnosia. *Archives of Neurology* **35**, 712–719

Oxbury, J. M., Oxbury, S. M. and Humphrey, N. K. (1969). Varieties of colour anomia. *Brain* **92**, 847–860

Paivio, A. (1975). Perceptual comparisons through the mind's eye. *Memory and Cognition* **3**, 635–647

Paivio, A. (1977). Mental comparisons involving abstract attitudes. Unpublished paper cited by P. H. K. Seymour (1979)

Pease, D. M. and Goodglass, H. (1978). The effects of cuing on picture naming in aphasia. *Cortex* **14**, 178–189

Rosch, E., Mervis, C. B., Gray, W. D., Johnson, D. M. and Boyes-Braem, P. (1976). Basic objects in natural categories. *Cognitive Psychology* **8**, 382–439

Rubens, A. B. (1979). Agnosia. *In* K. M. Heilman and E. Valenstein (eds), *Clinical Neuropsychology*. New York: Oxford University Press

Rubens, A. B. and Benson, D. F. (1971). Associative visual agnosia. *Archives of Neurology* **24**, 305–316

Schwartz, M. F., Saffran, E. M. and Marin, O. S. (1980). Fractionating the reading process in dementia: evidence for specific print-to-sound associations. *In* M. Coltheart, K. Patterson and J. C. Marshall (eds), *Deep Dyslexia*. London: Routledge and Kegan Paul

Seymour, P. H. K. (1979). *Human Visual Cognition*. London: Collier-Macmillan

Sperry, R. W. (1974). Lateral specialization in the surgically separated hemispheres. *In* F. O. Schmidt and F. G. Worden (eds), *The Neurosciences: Third Study Program*. Cambridge, Mass.: MIT Press

Taylor, A. and Warrington, E. K. (1971). Visual agnosia: a single case report. *Cortex* **7**, 152–161

Teuber, H.-L. (1965). Post script: some needed revisions of the classical views of agnosia. *Neuropsychologia* **3**, 371–378

Tyler, H. R. (1968). Abnormalities of perception with defective eye movements (Balints syndrome). *Cortex* **4**, 154–171

Vignolo, L. A. (1969). Auditory agnosia: a review and report of recent evidence. *In* A. L. Benton (ed.), *Clinical Contributions to Neuropsychology*. Chicago: Aldine

Warrington, E. K. (1975). The selective impairment of semantic memory. *Quarterly Journal of Experimental Psychology* **27**, 635–658

Warrington, E. K. and James, M. (1967). Disorders of visual perception in patients with unilateral cerebral lesions. *Neuropsychologia* **5**, 253–266

Warrington, E. K. and Taylor, A. M. (1973). The contribution of the right parietal lobe to object recognition. *Cortex* **7**, 152–164

Warrington, E. K. and Taylor, A. M. (1978). Two categorical stages of object recognition. *Perception* **7**, 695–705

Whitehouse, P., Caramazza, A. and Zurif, E. (1978). Naming in aphasia: Interacting effects of form and function. *Brain and Language* **6**, 63–74

Wilkins, A. and Moscovitch, M. (1978). Selective impairment of semantic memory after temporal lobectomy. *Neuropsychologia* **16**, 73–79

Wolpert, I. (1924). Die Simultanagnosie: Störung der Gesamtauffassung. *Zeitschrift für die gesamte Neurologie und Psychiatrie* **93**, 397–415

Zaidel, E. (1978). Auditory language comprehension in the right hemisphere following cerebral commissurotomy and hemispherectomy: a comparison with child language and aphasia. *In* A. Caramazza and E. Zurif (eds), *Acquisition and Breakdown of Language, Parallels and Divergences*. Baltimore: The Johns Hopkins Press

Zurif, E., Caramazza, A., Meyerson, R. and Galvin, J. (1974). Semantic feature representations for normal and aphasic language. *Brain and Language* **1**, 167–187

6

The Human Face

DENNIS C. HAY AND ANDREW W. YOUNG
Department of Psychology, University of Lancaster, Lancaster, England

1 Introduction

Every day most of us encounter a myriad of human faces, each composed of a few essential elements and yet each unique. From these we are able to identify with remarkable accuracy the faces of people we know, despite the fact that any one face will seldom, if ever, form exactly the same visual pattern on two different occasions (though it will do so in a photograph). In addition, information concerning a person's race, age and sex can often be accurately derived from inspection of his or her face, as can moods and feelings.

In this chapter, we will examine some of the evidence concerning the ways in which faces are seen and recognised, and outline a model which is intended to help to account both for the normal processes involved in the recognition of familiar and relatively unfamiliar faces, and for some of the disorders found in people who, because of cerebral injuries, experience difficulties in seeing and recognising faces. This model will not be very precisely formulated, because there are so many obvious gaps in our knowledge of face recognition, but it is hoped that it will none the less help to provide a useful framework within which to view the available evidence. No attempt at a comprehensive review of this evidence will be made, since reviews already exist (Ellis, 1975; Davies, Ellis and Shepherd, 1981) and many studies have been addressed to question that, whilst interesting in themselves, are not of central importance to the model proposed. We will, however, try to relate our proposals concerning the processing of faces to known properties of other perceptual and cognitive systems in order to ascertain the extent to which a special face processing system may be involved.

As already stated, we will concentrate on the ways in which familiar and unfamiliar faces are recognised, and will only attend to other questions concerning the interpretation of physical characteristics and feelings of people from their faces when these are of importance to the question as to how faces are recognised. The production of facial movements and expressions will not be considered. The model proposed is intended as a functional model, and precise localisation of functions to cerebral structures will not be attempted or necessarily regarded as valid. We will, however, discuss certain gross aspects of localisation, and particularly cerebral hemisphere differences, in so far as they affect our model.

There are a number of potential sources of information for the construction and testing of models of face recognition. These can be divided into lines of evidence deriving from normal and clinical subject populations. As they will be drawn on quite freely throughout the chapter they will be briefly introduced here.

The most obvious source of information is the numerous experimental studies of face recognition using normal subjects. These studies are sometimes intended to examine directly the properties of some hypothesised component of the face recognition system, though there are also a number of studies that are concerned with problems whose theoretical significance is indirect, such as the construction of effective Photofit and Identikit systems. Although useful information has been provided by results of several of these studies, it is unfortunate that others have often proved inconclusive and contentious for reasons that will gradually become clear.

Another line of evidence derives from studies of normal subjects in which brief lateral presentations of faces have been used in order to project stimulus information to the left or right cerebral hemispheres. Such studies depend on the fact that information concerning stimuli falling to the left of the point at which a person is looking (in the left visual hemifield, or LVF) is projected to the right cerebral hemisphere, whilst information concerning stimuli falling to the right of the point at which a person is looking (in the right visual hemifield, or RVF) is projected to the left cerebral hemisphere (Cohen, 1977; Young, 1982). Thus, provided stimuli are presented for less than the time needed to make an eye movement which would bring them into central vision, it is possible to know to which of the cerebral hemispheres they were initially projected. The abilities of the left and right hemispheres can then be compared. It must be stressed that such comparisons are at present relatively gross, since we only know to which of the cerebral hemispheres stimuli were initially projected, and it is not understood how information is then coordinated and integrated by means of the cerebral commissures (Young, 1982). None the less, interesting findings have emerged from studies using this general procedure, and we hope it will become clear why we are regarding them as of importance to functional as well as localisational models.

A third line of evidence, which is seldom used, derives from peoples' reports (in this case from the authors and a few colleagues) as to when, how and why they sometimes fail to recognise faces correctly. These are especially important to the present chapter as we are seeking to make comparisons of normal and disordered face recognition systems. Of course such reports are introspective in nature. We do not seek to enter into debate as to their consequent philosophic status, but merely maintain that as common experiences they require explanation. Fortunately, the few experimental studies that have deliberately examined failures of recognition of known faces substantially confirm these introspections.

Turning to the evidence from clinical subject populations, two lines can be distinguished. The first involves studies of patients with unilateral cerebral injuries (i.e. injuries affecting only one cerebral hemisphere). Unilateral injuries often impair patients' ability to recognise faces, and studies of the types of impairment resulting from lesions in different locations in the left and right cerebral hemispheres have been carried out. In common with other chapters in this book we will take the view that an adequate functional model of face recognition should be able to account for these different types of impairment.

The second line of evidence from clinical subject populations involves case reports of prosopagnosic patients. Although prosopagnosia should strictly be considered as a loss of the ability to recognise *known* faces, we will use the term in the fashion used by many clinicians, to apply to any severe and relatively specific disorders of face processing.

Although the case reports of prosopagnosic patients are of great importance, it is unfortunate for present purposes that they are often (though not always) analysed and presented with regard to the question of whether prosopagnosia can be identified as a discrete and dissociable defect. As a result, questions regarding the precise nature of the difficulties experienced by particular patients have not always been addressed. For this reason we are often forced to rely on hints and anecdotes provided in the various reports instead of on systematic, quantitative data.

The chapter is sectioned for convenience, being primarily centred around a proposed model of face recognition which is introduced in the next section. Following this, the three main components of the model are examined in turn. Attention is then focussed on two questions; whether there is more than one route to face recognition and whether or not a special face processing system exists. The final section provides a summary of the conclusions reached and the implications of the proposed model for future studies.

2   A model of face recognition

Having outlined the types of evidence to be used, and having explained that these will be drawn on quite freely, it is necessary to make certain distinctions which will be seen as essential to the proposed model of the processing of facial information.

First, we will distinguish *face recognition* from *person recognition*. The point of this distinction is that face recognition is only one of the many ways in which a person may be recognised. Person recognition can also often be based on such cues as voice, gait, posture, and clothing. In addition, face recognition is here regarded as distinct from person recognition because people sometimes recognise a person's face (in the sense of identifying it as a face known to them) without being able to identify in any other respect the person to whom it belongs. We will thus regard person recognition as involving the accessing of information from memory about a known person. Although the principal concern of this chapter is with the recognition of people by means of their faces it will obviously be necessary to consider both how face recognition is itself achieved and how it relates to person recognition (in the sense of the accessing of other information concerning the owner of the recognised face).

Second, we will distinguish *representational processing* of stimulus faces from *visual processing*. Representational processes are taken to be those processes involved in furnishing an adequate representation of the stimulus face for the purposes of recognition and subsequent visual processing. Visual processes can operate on the representations provided by representational processes. This might, for example, be done in order to make inferences concerning a person's age, sex, race or mood, in order to encode the characteristics of unfamiliar faces in various ways to effect recognition over short periods of time, in order to render unfamiliar faces familiar, or in order to access information about a known person by means of salient visual features, both facial and non-facial. Although it is convenient for present purposes to make this distinction of representational and visual processing, it should be noted that it does not correspond to the everyday use of the terms 'representation' and 'vision'. Nor does our use of 'representation' necessarily correspond to all the various other ways it is used within psychology and neuropsychology.

A third distinction that we wish to introduce concerns face recognition and what we will term *stimulus recognition*. This distinction is probably of little importance to the normal, everyday processing of faces, but it may be crucial in interpreting some of the studies that have been carried out on patients and on normal subjects under laboratory conditions. Such studies have often used photographs as stimuli. We do not regard this as intrinsically unacceptable, but it does eliminate the more 'dynamic' aspects of face processing, and it also raises problems when tasks are so arranged that recognition is regarded as having occurred when the *same* photograph of the *same* face is to be recognised. This we will consider to be stimulus recognition, since face recognition is not necessarily involved. Face recognition proper can only be said with certainty to occur when *different* photographs of the *same* face are to be treated as equivalent. When a task involves stimulus recognition it is usually open to subjects to adopt strategies based on face recognition or to adopt strategies not based on treating the stimuli as faces, such as looking for prominent flaws in the picture surface, patterns of light and shade, and so on. We will thus adopt the conservative position of regarding studies involving stimulus recognition tasks as of little relevance to models of face recognition unless there is independent reason to believe that subjects in the studies concerned were in fact using strategies based on face recognition.

A fourth, and final, distinction concerns familiar and unfamiliar faces. There are at least two different senses in which a face used as a stimulus in a study might be said to be familiar. It may be familiar because it is the face of someone known to the subjects, or it may become familiar during the course of the study because the same photograph of a face that was initially unfamiliar is shown many times. Applying the distinction of face and stimulus recognition made previously it is clear that the use of faces of people known to the subjects involves face recognition, whereas when a single photograph of a given face is repeated until familiar it may only involve strategies of stimulus recognition. For this reason we will distinguish the use of known or familiar faces from the use of known or familiar stimuli. If it is desired that an initially unknown or unfamiliar face is to become a familiar *face* (as opposed to a familiar stimulus) during the course of a study it is clearly essential either that a number of different photographs of that face are used or that independent evidence that face (as opposed to stimulus) recognition processes operated is adduced.

The model of face processing and recognition that we propose is shown in Fig. 1.

The aim of this model is to highlight the functional organisation of the various processes involved in face and person recognition, and especially hypothesised face recognition units. For this reason, the hypothesised components are not always precisely specified, and those components drawn in circles in the diagram are not intended to be considered as discrete processes, but as functional components that themselves involve sets of interrelated processes. Similarly, the interaction of the components of the face recognition system with other cognitive processes is only loosely specified at the points at which such interactions may occur.

In outline form, the model proposes that representational processes operate upon stimulus faces in order in provide an internal representation. This representation may then be acted upon in one of two fundamentally different ways. First of all, what we have called 'visual processes' may be applied to determine such factors as age, sex, and race, to compare faces, and to effect temporary storage of the internal representation. Visual processes do not depend on recognising the particular face presented, and are conceived of as being flexible and under the control of other cognitive processes. They are particularly important in the case of unfamiliar faces, and are also used to make unfamiliar faces familiar by creating new face recognition units.

The second use of the internal visual representation is to provide input to face recognition units. The idea is that each face with which a person is familiar will be represented by a different face recognition unit which responds selectively when the particular familiar individual's face is seen. Face recognition units provide the means of access to other information about the individual (occupation, personality characteristics etc.). As a convenient shorthand we shall refer to face recognition mediated by recognition units as 'semantic processing'.

In the following sections of this chapter we will explore some of the components and features of this model, and their application to the results of existing studies.

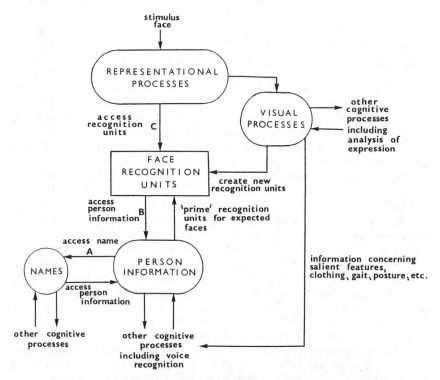

Fig. 1   Model of the functional components involved in face recognition

3   Representational processes

The processes involved in furnishing a facial representation suitable for further semantic and visual analyses have not been clearly established, with the result that deficits in representational processes may not be identified with any degree of precision. At least three deficits at this level of analysis can be tentatively differentiated on the basis of information derived from studies of prosopagnosic and metamorphopsic patients. Because of the difficulties involved in making inferences solely on the basis of the symptoms of brain injured patients, and the current lack of corroborative evidence deriving from other sources, we do not at present wish to attempt to specify in detail the underlying processes associated with these deficits.

The first of the deficits involves the extraction of feature information from the face. A prosopagnosic disorder in extracting feature information has been described, which may be restricted to the eye region of faces (De Renzi, Faglioni and Spinnler, 1968; Gloning and Quatember, 1966). This observation neatly complements other evidence also indicating differential feature saliency and indicating the importance of this facial area; for example, work on the development of infant abilities in discriminating faces from other visual stimuli (Haith, Bergman and Moore, 1977; Maurer and Salapatek, 1976) and on the perception and memory of faces in normal adults (e.g. Shepherd, Ellis and Davies, 1977). Such a perceptual deficit, however, is not always observed in prosopagnosic patients, as is indicated by the case investigated by Gloning, Gloning, Jellinger and Quatember (1970), who failed to observe any deficit in the matching and recognition of eye regions in a severely prosopagnosic patient.

Although feature extraction is important, it is clear that faces are not merely the sum of their structural components. The clinical literature has many documented cases of prosopagnosia in which the patients are described as being able to identify and recognise all of the individual features but unable to 'put them together', or in which the parts of the face do not 'add up' (Beyn and Knyazeva, 1962; Cole and Perez-Cruet, 1964; Pallis, 1955). This aspect of representational processes – the second to be identified – involves the synthesis of facial gestalts. Deficits of this synthesis will prevent further semantic or visual processing that cannot be accomplished by examining features in isolation. For example, although the patient observed by Cole and Perez-Cruet (1964) could distinguish faces from animal portraits it is probable that sufficient feature cues were available to enable discrimination. A more suitable task for investigating facial synthesis was used by Hay (1981) in an investigation of the facial processing abilities of the cerebral hemispheres. This task required subjects merely to decide whether a laterally presented stimulus was or was not a face. The non-faces comprised facial stimuli in which the internal features had been systematically rearranged. As all the stimuli, both faces and non-faces, contained two eyes, a nose, and a mouth, the decision as to whether or not a stimulus was a face depended upon the configuration. The results of this study indicated a LVF latency advantage with right-handed normal subjects, suggestive of a right hemisphere superiority for facial synthesis.

The third and last aspect of representational processes to be highlighted is one for which testing procedures employing photographs of faces may be inappropriate, as this aspect seems to involve three-dimensional information. In addition to prosopagnosia in the sense of impaired memory for faces there are reports of a 'metamorphopsia' restricted to faces (Hécaen and Albert, 1978). This condition distorts the percepts of faces, but in such a way that some of the relationships between the features may be unaffected. For example, the third patient described by Bodamer (1947) suffered from a facial metamorphopsia in which faces appeared flat. This patient could in fact recognise faces, but precisely how this was done was not reported. Whiteley and Warrington (1977) report a case in which a patient, who had great difficulty in recognising faces, saw them as being ugly and distorted, like fish heads. This patient may have suffered from a metamorphopsia of such severity as to prevent faces being encoded in a fashion suitable for recognition. Whether the patient would later have become able to discriminate and recognise 'fish heads' could not be determined since after irradiation of a right parieto-occipital tumour the symptoms 'had largely resolved'.

It seems, then, that in cases of facial metamorphopsia the relationships of the features may be preserved but distorted in three-dimensional visual space. In one case of permanent metamorphopsia (Hécaen and Albert, 1978) the distortion of faces occurred only with real faces, not with pictures of faces. This patient, however, attributed her ability to deal with pictures to the immobility of the facial features. The nature of the relationship between feature information extraction and the synthesis of a three-dimensional representation of a face can only be answered by additional investigation. This case, however, casts doubt on an assumption implicit in the majority of studies employing photographic stimuli, namely that similar processes underlie the early stages of analysis of photographs and real faces.

4 Face recognition units

One of the favourite questions asked by investigators interested in face recognition concerns the nature and specification of the perceptual analysis and features used to achieve recognition. How is it possible for a system to function so effectively despite considerable transformations in angle of view and expression, and despite changes in age, hairstyle and so on?

Although some clarification of the processes responsible for recognition has been made, at least to the extent that it is evident that the internal features of familiar faces, and especially the eyes and mouth, are of considerable importance (Ellis, 1975; Ellis, Shepherd and Davies, 1979), research has not really been very successful in tackling such questions. In this respect it does not differ from research on other aspects of visual recognition, such as word recognition or object recognition, where the perceptual processes involved in achieving recognition are equally mysterious (Seymour, 1979).

In other respects, however, research on word and object recognition has made advances that do not find parallels in research on face recognition. These advances have often been stimulated by Morton's logogen model, and its subsequent modifications (Morton, 1969, 1979; Seymour, 1973, 1979).

The interesting feature of logogen models of word and object recognition, for present purposes, is that they avoid questions as to the perceptual processes by which recognition is achieved. Instead they assume that for each word or object that can be recognised some kind of recognition unit exists, and then focus attention onto the properties of the recognition units themselves. We wish to suggest that a similar tactic may be of use to research on face recognition, though the model we propose is not really a model of the logogen type. A similar suggestion is made by Ellis (1981).

We will assume, then, that for every face that a person can recognise there exists a face recognition unit. Face recognition occurs when the results of representational analysis of a stimulus face are such as to activate one of the recognition units. Recognition does not occur when the results of representational analysis of a stimulus face do not activate a recognition unit. Learning to recognise a new face can be seen as involving the creation of a new face recognition unit, a process which will be discussed in the next section. The recognition units are considered to function in such a fashion that activation can depend on a variety of factors such as the frequency with which particular faces are encountered and the contexts in which encounters occur. We do not at present wish to commit ourselves to any view on the question of how this is achieved. Possible mechanisms might include increasing levels of activation, so that less information is needed to activate recognition units for expected faces, or lowering thresholds for activation.

It now becomes possible to ask how the face recognition units are organised in relation to other aspects of information about people. In attempting to answer this question it is instructive to consider the ways in which the recognition of people by means of their faces can be defective under everyday conditions. Our introspections, and those of other people we have asked, indicate to us that two types of failure can be quite common.

(a) A person's face is recognised as familiar, and information can be given concerning where that person is usually encountered, his or her occupation, and other personal characteristics, but the person's name cannot be recalled.

(b) A face is recognised as familiar, but no information can be given concerning the person to whom it belongs.

Thus in case (*a*) the appropriate face recognition unit is activated and semantic information concerning the seen person has been retrieved (i.e. person recognition has also taken place), but the name remains inaccessible. We will refer to this as a naming difficulty. In case (*b*) only the face recognition unit is activated, and neither person recognition nor name retrieval have occurred. We will refer to this as a difficulty of person recognition. Paralleling these difficulties of naming and person recognition are misidentifications in which the person is correctly recognised but incorrectly named, or incorrectly recognised and incorrectly named.

A simple way of trying to account for such phenomena is to point to the traditional distinction of recognition and recall. Identifying a face as one that has been seen before is a recognition task, whereas accessing the name involves recall, and it is known that recognition is nearly always an easier task than recall. There is certainly something in this argument in the sense that if a task of recognising instead of recalling the name were involved, performance would probably be much improved. However, it is not fully satisfactory as an explanation because the accessing of person information is also in a sense a recall task (even though for convenience we refer to it here as person recognition). Yet, as the existence of naming difficulties and errors in the presence of intact person recognition shows, recall of other personal characteristics can be easier than recall of the name. Moreover, recall of person information not only *can* be easier than name recall, but it nearly always *is* easier, since at the time of writing we have been unable to find anyone who admits to having experienced in everyday life the hypothetical case in which they recognised a face as familiar and knew the owner's name, but were unaware of any of his or her other personal characteristics.

The model shown in Fig. 1 can encompass these phenomena. Of course this is by no means the only possible model, but it has certain points in its favour that endear it to us.

The model hypothesises that representational processing of a stimulus face activates face recognition units, and that these are in turn responsible for establishing person recognition. Names are only accessed once the *person* has been recognised, so that it is not possible that a face and its name will both be known in the absence of person recognition. Failure of the system at point A in Fig. 1 will lead to naming difficulties or errors (case *a*) and failure at point B will lead to difficulties and errors of person recognition (case *b*). A third potential point of failure, marked C in Fig. 1, might result in our failing to recognise the face of a known person as being at all familiar, which will be referred to as failures in accessing recognition units (case *c*). Strictly speaking, these are the true failures of face recognition, but we are here also using face recognition as a generic term to include face recognition and naming. How often failures in accessing recognition units of the type just described occur is not open to introspection, as we are only made aware of them if someone points out to us that we are failing to recognise that we know them. Such instances may be rare in comparison to the total number of failures that occasion no comment. None the less, most people have had such experiences, so that failures in accessing face recognition units clearly do occur from time to time. Other possible sources of error at this level could arise when a face accesses the wrong recognition unit, or an unfamiliar face accesses one of the recognition units.

One of the most common circumstances in which people report difficulties and errors of person recognition is when a person is met outside the context in which he or she is usually seen. For reasons of this type our model is intended to allow the face recognition units to be 'primed' by expectation and context. It is also necessary to postulate that other cognitive processes have access to both name and person information, as it is possible to ask someone to go to the station to meet his acquaintance Mr Smith, or even to go to the station to meet a newsreader from the BBC. Priming face recognition units by means of the person's name is seen as only occurring indirectly via the system of semantic information involved in person recognition.

This simple model has been designed in order to cope with both the introspective reports already discussed and with evidence deriving from more systematic studies of normal and clinical subject populations. This evidence will now be reviewed, and suggestions made as to implications of our model that remain unexplored.

By presenting photographs of famous people and asking subjects to name them Yarmey (1973) was able to study several cases in which subjects were unable to recall the name, but felt it to be on the 'tip of the tongue'. When in this state they were often able to describe the target person's profession, the place he or she was most often seen, and how recently. Of these different kinds of information most detail could be given concerning profession, less concerning place, and least concerning recency. In some cases subjects could also give phonemic information as to the first letter of the desired name, the number of syllables, and similar sounding names.

In addition to providing interesting findings concerning the tip of the tongue phenomenon, Yarmey's (1973) study substantially supports the introspective reports introduced here. Curiously, however, of the 623 instances of the tip of the tongue state studied by Yarmey, in only 364 did the target person's name turn out to be the name that the subject felt that he or she was seeking. This high rate of what would appear to be misidentifications is in itself interesting, though it may arise only when stimulus faces are those of people known only slightly, and only through the mass media.

Bruce (1979) has provided the most extensive published study of normal subjects that is of relevance to the properties of our general model of the face recognition system. Her tasks involved searching for familiar faces in arrays of familiar and unfamiliar faces, and were arranged to prevent what we have termed stimulus recognition by using different pictures of the target faces. In her first experiment she demonstrated a visual search rate that was slowed by an increase in the number of targets in the range 1–8 targets. This relationship held both when subjects were searching for faces and when they were searching for printed names. A second experiment showed that when subjects were searching for four target faces their search rates were slowed by the presence of visually similar distractor faces in the search set, but were not affected by familiarity or unfamiliarity of the distractor faces. There was also, however, an effect of the semantic category (politicians *vs* actors) to which faces belonged, with faster rejection of nontarget faces down from a different semantic category to target faces. Bruce (1979) suggests that in visual search tasks visual and semantic analyses can proceed in parallel, with both providing information that can be employed in making a decision. Which type of analysis subjects choose to rely on will then depend on individual preferences and the demands made by given tasks.

Bruce's (1979) findings can be readily assimilated to the model presented here, which also distinguishes the visual processing of faces from semantic processing (via face recognition units). Her experiments are also important to the present discussion in that they demonstrate the flexibility of the face processing mechanisms at subjects' disposal, and in that visual search effects for faces were not found to be different in nature to search effects known to exist for words. Unfortunately, her results do not confirm the existence of face recognition units, as no effect of familiarity of the distractor faces was found in her experiments 2 and 3. In neither of these experiments, however, would familiarity have provided a sufficient basis to distinguish target and nontarget faces, so the possibility remains open that face recognition units would be utilised more directly in search tasks for which they would be more helpful.

The mechanism by which the semantic category to which a face belongs might affect rejection latencies is not specified by Bruce (1979). One possibility is that recognition units for faces belonging to a particular category are 'primed' to be more readily activated. Priming of face recognition units is also suggested by Young and Bion (1981) as a possible factor implicated in the findings of studies that have used lateral presentations of known faces to investigate the right hemisphere superiority for face recognition. Young and Bion (1981) demonstrated that when known faces were drawn from an unpredictable set LVF and RVF performance levels did not differ. LVF superiorities for processing known faces were only obtained when known faces were drawn from a set that was predictable to subjects, in which case the observed LVF superiority was due to an improvement in LVF but not RVF performance. Since studies of prosopagnosic patients indicate that a complete inability to recognise faces is nearly always accompanied by bilateral cerebral lesions (Meadows, 1974a), Young and Bion (1981) proposed that both cerebral hemispheres possess face recognition units but that those of the right hemisphere may be more readily primed on the basis of expectation or past experience.

A study by Warrington and James (1967) of patients with unilateral cerebral injuries is of considerable interest to the present discussion. Warrington and James (1967) asked patients to identify and name photographs of the faces of well-known people (Winston Churchill, Marilyn Monroe, etc.). They noted two types of error; *naming errors*, in which the face was recognised and such personal details as its bearer's occupation given, but he or she could not be named, and what Warrington and James termed *recognition errors*, in which the person was misrecognised or apparently not recognised at all.

Warrington and James' (1967) results indicated that naming errors were more often associated with left than right hemisphere lesions, whereas recognition errors were more common with lesions of the right than with lesions of the left hemisphere. The study thus demonstrated difficulties and errors paralleling those described here from introspections of normal subjects, and showed that naming and recognition errors were associated with different cerebral lesions. Unfortunately, Warrington and James' (1967) category of recognition errors is too broad to be of further use here, as it does not distinguish difficulties and errors attributable to what we have here regarded as failures of person recognition (case *b*) and difficulties and errors attributable to failures to activate appropriate recognition units (case *c*). It would have been useful to know whether patients felt that faces they could not identify were familiar or unfamiliar to them.

A number of reported observations of the difficulties experienced by prosopagnosic patients are also of interest to any discussion of face recognition units, but the nature of these difficulties has often been inadequately specified. Although a class of prosopagnosic deficits involving face memory clearly exists (Meadows, 1974a) many studies have not distinguished between the different potential types of deficit that would be predicted by the model proposed here. Although it is often evident from published reports that person information remains intact (as it can be accessed by means other than face recognition) it is seldom clear whether the difficulty with faces is one of accessing and activating face recognition units, or whether recognition units are activated but cannot themselves access person information.

A useful discussion of several prosopagnosic cases is given by Hécaen and Angelergues (1962). They do refer to some cases in which faces looked 'face-like', and expressions were understood correctly, but patients were not able to identify the person or the context in which he or she had previously been seen, despite being aware of having seen that person before. These certainly appear to be examples in which recognition units have been activated but person recognition has none the less not been achieved. In one case, however, a patient could not identify the face of Adolf Hitler and was not aware of ever having seen it before. The same patient, who was interested in bicycle racing, could not identify the faces of well-known cyclists, but *was* aware that they were cyclists. This suggests that the patient could only access certain readily available recognition units, and that even then the recognition units did not access person information. Such an interpretation might have been confirmed if he could have recognised Hitler as familiar when the appropriate recognition unit was primed. For instance, he might have been able to pick out Hitler's face from a collection of unfamiliar faces, on the basis of its familiarity, if instructed to search for Hitler.

Another important observation from clinical reports is that the metamorphopsic form of prosopagnosia, in which faces look distorted, is not always felt by clinicians to be accompanied by serious disturbances of face memory (Hécaen and Angelergues, 1962; Benton and Van Allen, 1972). For this reason, some authors do not consider metamorphopsia to be a 'true' prosopagnosia, but it is convenient to regard it as such here. In the metamorphopsic form of prosopagnosia (which we have suggested is caused by interference with representational processes), then, face recognition may be relatively effective. This raises the interesting question as to whether recognition is possible because the distorted information provided by the metamorphopsic's representational analysis remains sufficient to access recognition units in existence before the injury that caused the matamorphopsia, or whether new recognition units are created that can accept this distorted information. In the latter case it would be expected that the metamorphopsic patient would recover the ability to recognise faces rather gradually following the injury, and would be unable to recognise the faces of people who were known before the injury occurred but not seen since. However, we are not aware of any case report that provides observations of sufficient detail to answer this question.

5   Visual processes

Considered in this section are those processes which may be applied to faces irrespective of whether they are familiar or novel. For convenience these are termed visual processes and are seen as including;

   (*a*) Processes for the extraction of information concerning the age, race and sex of the individual.

   (*b*) Processes for comparing two representations of a face.

   (*c*) Processes for the short-term storage and maintenance of face information, and

   (*d*) Processes necessary for constructing new face recognition units.

Although much research has been conducted that is of relevance to understanding how these processes handle novel faces, it will be seen that few unambiguous results are available. Much of the evidence has to be drawn from studies addressed to purposes quite different from the investigation of what we have here termed visual processes. In many of the clinical studies, for instance, the principal aim has been to develop measures that are sensitive to general difficulties in processing faces. Studies of normal subjects have often used novel faces or schematic faces simply as convenient stimuli, without any interest in the visual processes applied to faces *per se*. Studies that have presented faces in the LVF or RVF have usually been concerned to demonstrate the existence of right hemisphere superiority for some aspect of face processing, and have only comparatively recently begun to address the question of which components of face processing the right hemisphere is superior for.

Because of the variety of purposes contained in these studies, many of the tasks chosen by investigators have simultaneously involved more than one of our list of visual processes, and there are inconsistences between studies in the choice of stimuli and experimental procedures, making it impossible either to draw definite conclusions concerning visual processes or to compare results across different studies too directly.

Little is known about how information is extracted from faces, but evidence does exist indicating that some prosopagnosic patients experience difficulty in determining race (Cole and Perez-Cruet, 1964), sex (Beyn and Knyazeva, 1962) and age (Beyn and Knyazeva, 1962; Gloning *et al.*, 1970); Whiteley and Warrington, 1977). It is difficult to judge the degree of these difficulties because of the absence of quantitative testing. In almost every case information was derived from patients' verbalisations. Even when testing has been attempted, as for example by Benton and Van Allen (1972) who asked one patient to estimate the ages of four medical staff, the methods employed tend to be sufficiently sensitive to detect only the most gross deficits. What can be concluded, however, is that the patients reported as having such disorders are also those already classified as having representational deficits of the type which interfere with the construction of facial gestalts. Thus, it is at present impossible to state whether these patients suffer from an additional deficit in the processes required to extract age, sex and race information or whether these processes are intact, but fail to operate due to the distorted input from disordered representational processes. Our model predicts that a deficit in judging age, race and sex could occur even in patients with intact representational processes, but in the absence of suitable information no definite judgement as to the dissociability of the defects can be made.

The bulk of the normal experimental literature concerning visual processes is formed of studies investigating the comparison of novel stimulus and test faces. Since such tasks are relatively easy to construct, and require only the simplest of responses from subjects these have also been adopted by clinicians in investigating brain injured and prosopagnosic patients. It should be appreciated, however, that a number of variants of this paradigm exist, usually necessitating the employment of different sets of visual processes, and that the saliency of particular visual processes differ within variants. As a result, the following discussion has been structured around the types of tasks employed, and an attempt is made to indicate which processes are the most important for each particular variant. This is made difficult, however, by the procedure commonly adopted in the clinical literature of producing composite scores from a number of different matching tasks in order to arrive at a measure of overall performance (Benton and Van Allen, 1968; De Renzi *et al.*, 1968; De Renzi, Scotti and Spinnler, 1969; Whiteley and Warrington, 1977). As a result, it is at present impossible to determine the precise nature and number of deficits of visual processes associated with right hemisphere brain injuries or with prosopagnosia.

Many studies of the comparison processes used by normal subjects have involved tasks that require subjects to match schematic faces (e.g. Bradshaw and Wallace, 1971; Matthews, 1978; Patterson and Bradshaw, 1975; Smith and Nielsen, 1970). Although this allows the easy manipulation of feature sets, the tasks have to be arranged in such a way that subjects regard the schematic faces as the same only when they possess the same sets of features in the same arrangement. As explained previously, this is a stimulus (as opposed to face) matching paradigm, and the conclusion emanating from such research (e.g. Anderson and Paulson, 1978) that faces are stored as sets of feature descriptions may not hold for real faces. In addition, the controversy as to whether such sets are compared in a serial or parallel fashion may, in fact, be a result of the use of schematic faces in tasks requiring stimulus recognition. A similar point is made by Ellis (1981).

It is thus essential for present purposes that studies of the comparison processes involved in matching faces use reasonably realistic stimuli. An interesting study in this respect is that of Bertelson, Vanhaelen and Morais (1979), who asked right-handed normal subjects to match photographs of faces presented in the LVF or in the RVF. The initially presented face was always photographed in ¾ pose while the test face was either ¾ pose (so that the task required *stimulus* matching) or full face (so that the task required *face* matching). A right hemisphere reaction time advantage was observed only in the face matching condition. Taken together, these results and those from studies described by Moscovitch, Scullion and Christie (1976) and Moscovitch (1979), which also failed to reveal LVF superiorities for early stages of face processing, suggest that right hemisphere superiorities in normal subjects are most readily found when some operation is to be performed on the information coming from the representational processes, though this is not to deny that a sufficiently sensitive task would also reveal hemisphere superiorities for representational processes, as Hay's (1981) results indicate. In the absence of unambiguous data from clinical studies, however, the idea that a selective deficit may exist in the processes necessary for handling changes in pose remains only a possibility.

Matching tasks have also been employed to investigate the comparison of centrally presented faces. Among the most interesting studies are those of Carey and Diamond (1977) and Diamond and Carey (1977), which are discussed later.

Perhaps the most frequent use of matching tasks is when attempting to investigate the short-term storage of unfamiliar faces. This is usually accomplished by varying the interstimulus interval (ISI), that is the time between the presentation of the face that is to be remembered and the test face or faces. Clinicians examing the performances of patients with unilateral injuries have often used such procedures, finding that right hemisphere damage leads to poorer matching even when the delay is minimal (De Renzi and Spinnler, 1966; De Renzi et al., 1968; Milner, 1968; Warrington and James, 1967). In all cases, however, no firm evidence of a differential effect of delay has been found. Although the results of Milner's (1968) study have been interpreted (though not by Milner herself) as indicative of poorer performance with delayed recognition than with immediate recognition, the conclusion is hardly justified, as the performance of the subject group with right hemisphere injuries was equivalent in both conditions of her study.

Complementing these clinical studies are these from the normal experimental literature which have also failed to find performance varying with ISI (e.g. Hilliard, 1973; Laughery, Fessler, Lenorovitz and Yoblick, 1974). Such findings lend support to the simple conclusion that patients suffering from right cerebral injuries are likely to experience difficulty in matching two faces presented at different times, but that memory interval alone does not seem to be an important factor.

One of the most important uses of visual processes is in the creation of new recognition units for the face memory system. This has received little attention, except in the work of Ellis and his colleagues. Ellis et al. (1979) presented evidence which suggests that the internal representations of known faces differ from those used for unfamiliar faces. This is consistent with the idea advanced here that only familiar faces can access separate semantic processing via face recognition units. It has also been shown that the longer the inspection of an unfamiliar face, and hence the greater the time allowed to construct a recognition unit, the better recognition becomes (Ellis, Davies and Shepherd, 1977).

It can be seen, then, that whilst the available evidence concerning visual processes is consistent with the suggested list of processes offered here, much remains to be discovered. This is because it is comparatively rare to find studies using tasks that do not simultaneously involve different visual processes to unspecified and unpredictable extents. This is particularly noticeable in studies of visual hemifield differences for face processing, which have often relied on the use of faces of people not known to subjects as stimuli. Although relevant to understanding visual processes, most of these studies have not been discussed here because of the complex and ambiguous nature of the findings for present purposes. To end the section, however, a few comments will be made as to how tasks might be constructed that could identify more precisely which aspects of visual processes are better performed by the right cerebral hemisphere.

Supporting the clinical observations of right hemisphere superiority for at least some of the visual processes are the findings of an advantage for the processing of stimulus faces presented to normal subjects in the left (as opposed to right) visual hemifield (Geffen, Bradshaw and Wallace, 1971; Rizzolatti, Umilta and Berlucchi, 1971). These studies have generally taken one of two approaches. The first involves the use of a small number of target faces, or even a single face, shown before presentation of a block of individual test faces, with inspection time being in terms of minutes (e.g. Moscovitch, Scullion and Christie, 1976, Expt. 2; Patterson and Bradshaw, 1975, Expts. 2 and 3, Rizzolatti *et al.*, 1971). The subject's task is to decide whether test faces are or are not members of the memorised set. The other approach involves varying the interstimulus interval between target and test faces, with these varying from trial to trial (Hilliard, 1973; Moscovitch *et al.*, 1976, Expts. 3 and 4; Patterson and Bradshaw, 1975, Expt. 1).

Although we do not wish to deny the importance of these demonstrations of right hemisphere superiority for face processing, it is difficult to draw more precise conclusions. The different studies are very free in altering the nature of the processes required by varying such factors as the number of stimulus faces used, the amount of time allowed for subjects to learn the new faces, the number of repetitions of particular faces, interstimulus intervals, and the type of matching required. It should now be clear that all of these factors can affect the relative contributions of different visual processes, so that it is not at present possible to determine whether the right hemisphere is superior for all or only some of the visual processes used for unfamiliar faces. By paying careful attention to factors of the type listed above, however, it should be possible to construct tasks that investigate each of these visual processes individually and systematically (see also Hay and Ellis, 1981).

6   Is there more than one route to recognition?

An issue that is discussed extensively in this book concerns whether the reading and writing of words should be considered in terms of processes organised along a single route, or along two or more alternative routes. A related question arises as to whether face recognition normally involves one route or more than one route.

It is clear that there are multiple routes to person recognition, of which recognising the face is only one. Prosopagnosic patients become quite adept at using alternative methods of recognition such as voice, stature and clothing (Benton and Van Allen, 1972; Beyn and Knyazeva, 1962; Cohn, Neumann and Wood, 1977; Cole and Perez-Cruet, 1964; Pallis, 1955; Whiteley and Warrington, 1977). These methods are not, of course, always effective. Pevzner, Bornstein and Loewenthal (1962), for instance, describe one patient who, in order to recognise his lawyer, came to rely on the furnishings of his office. This was of no use to him in court, where he proceeded to discuss his case with his opponent's attorney.

These examples are useful in demonstrating that person information can remain relatively intact in prosopagnosic patients. They do not, however, provide evidence that *faces* are recognised by the use of such strategies. Rather, it seems that *people* are identified on the basis of deductions involving stored information concerning personal characteristics. Although these personal characteristics may in some cases be facial (Mr X has a big nose, Ms Y has small lips, and so on) such a simple use of prominent features could not serve to adequately specify all of the faces known to normal people.

We propose, then, a single route model of face recognition, whilst accepting that there are multiple routes to person recognition.

What looks like a dual route model of face recognition has, however, been put forward by Carey (1978), Carey and Diamond (1977) and Diamond and Carey (1977). They propose that faces are represented in the brain in terms of both piecemeal information concerning specific facial features (large nose, bushy eyebrows, etc.) and configurational information concerning the spatial relations of individual features. The configurational representations are seen as being orientation – sensitive and hence adversely affected by inversion of stimulus faces, whilst the piecemeal representations are seen as operating equally affectively for upright and inverted faces. In addition, Carey (1978), Carey and Diamond (1977), and Diamond and Carey (1977) argue that during development children shift from relying predominantly on piecemeal to relying on configurational encoding of faces. Although it is not the aim of the present chapter to examine the ontogeny of face recognition, it is necessary to consider some of the developmental evidence in this case as it is inextricably bound up with the other claims of Carey and her colleagues.

Although Carey puts forward interesting ideas, the evidence adduced to supprt them is not convincing. Carey and Diamond (1977) demonstrated that six-year-old children recognised upright and inverted photographs of faces equally well, whereas ten-year-olds were better with upright faces. Since it is known that adults are also better at recognising upright than inverted faces (Yin, 1969), Carey and Diamond (1977) argue that ability to use the orientation-sensitive configurational face representation develops between age 6 and age 10, and that six-year-olds tend to rely on piecemeal representations of faces, which are unaffected by orientation. This straightforward conclusion is weakened by the fact that a stimulus recognition task was used in Carey and Diamond's (1977) study, and by the curious finding in the same study that six-year-old children were poorer at recognising inverted than upright pictures of houses whereas ten-year-olds performed equally well with upright and inverted houses. Moreover, the results of studies by Young and Bion (1980, 1981) indicate that Carey and Diamond's (1977) finding of an interaction of face orientation and age only arises when a large set of unfamiliar stimulus faces is used. When sets of known faces, or a small set of initially unfamiliar faces, were used as stimuli Young and Bion (1980, 1981) found the performance of subjects of all ages tested to be equally affected by inversion of stimulus faces. Although Carey and Diamond (1977) argue that the hypothesised development of ability to use configurational representations is linked to maturational changes in the right cerebral hemisphere. Young and Bion (1980, 1981) found no evidence of any developmental changes in LVF (i.e. right hemisphere) superiority for face recognition.

It would thus seem that young children are able to use configurational representations of faces, but that when faced with tasks with a relatively demanding memory component the encoding or retrieval process involved cannot attain higher levels of performance with upright than with inverted faces.

Similar difficulties of interpretation arise in the case of the experiments reported by Diamond and Carey (1977). These used both familiar and unfamiliar faces in a difficult face recognition task. With unfamiliar faces six-year-olds were misled by changes in clothing visible in the photographs used, whereas ten-year-olds were not. Changes in the clothing of familiar people did not affect the recognition performance of either six- or ten-year-olds. These findings again demonstrate that young children can utilise configurational representations, as they do so in the familiar faces task. When faced with a difficult task, however, young children in this case clearly opt for a strategy of looking for salient nonfacial cues, such as clothing. It is not clear why such a strategy should be regarded as involving piecemeal representation of the *face*.

Our own view, then, is that the distinction of piecemeal and configurational representations made by Carey (1978), Carey and Diamond (1977) and Diamond and Carey (1977) suffers by itself failing to distinguish face and person recognition, and that the studies described do not support a dual-route model of face recognition, but are instead compatible with the multiple-route model of person recognition set out in this chapter.

7   Is there a special face processing system?

Partly because of the vast differences in theoretical formulations, a clear definition of what is to be regarded as a special face processing system has never been made. Most formulations, however, have proposed some biologically fixed function, present at or soon after birth as a result of an evolved social need to differentiate faces with speed and accuracy. The hypothesised nature of such a function has included inherent differences in coding and storage (Carey and Diamond, 1977) and utilisation of different pattern analysers (Hochberg and Galper, 1967). Other formulations envisage the special nature of faces as being a consequence of such psychological attributes as emotions, attitudes and expressions, which are closely associated with the human face (Galper, 1970; Yarmey, 1971). The notion of special face processing mechanisms has not, however, received unanimous support, and Ellis (1975) lists a number of counter-arguments and reservations.

The difficulty in establishing whether there is or is not a special face processing system is in part due to the fact that two distinct questions are often confused and conflated. The first is the question as to whether some or all of the perceptual and cognitive processes used for faces are different in nature (i.e. qualitatively different) from those used for the processing of other visual stimuli. This we will refer to as the question of the *uniqueness* to faces of the nature of the processes used. The second question concerns whether some or all of the processes used for faces are, irrespective of their nature, organised into a separate system that deals only with face stimuli. This we will refer to as the question of the *specificity* to faces of the components of the face processing system. Clearly, if the face processing system were to contain unique processes it would also contain face specific processes, but the converse is not necessarily true. A face specific system might or might not contain unique processes.

The view taken here will be that there is at present little evidence to support the idea of uniqueness (though we do not wish to deny that some of the processes may well prove to be unique when better understood), but good supporting evidence for the specificity to faces of at least some components of the face processing system.

Considering firstly the question as to the uniqueness to faces of the processes used, it is clear from the studies of Bruce (1979) that there are considerable parallels to be found between the visual and semantic processing of faces and words in search tasks. Similarly, the properties of the face recognition units in the present model were explicitly derived from those postulated for analogous processes in models of the recognition of words and objects.

If there are any processes unique to the face processing system, then, we might expect to find them among the representational processes and, perhaps, some of the visual processes used in creating new recognition units. Unfortunately it is at these points that the available evidence is the most weak and, as Ellis (1975) explains, it is difficult to adduce evidence sufficiently strong to allow rejection of the prosaic hypothesis that differences between the processing of faces and other stimuli are simply differences in efficiency arising from the greater complexity and familiarity of faces as a class of stimuli.

The principal argument used to support the idea that face processing is in some respects unique has been that inversion affects face processing more seriously than it affects the processing of other stimuli that are normally encountered in a particular orientation. Yin (1969) presented various classes of multidimensional stimuli, including faces, which are usually seen in an upright orientation. Presenting these both upright and inverted resulted in the recognition of faces being disproportionately affected by inversion. Similarly, Scapinello and Yarmey (1970) and Yarmey (1971), using faces, canine heads and architectural drawings, also found that inverting human faces produced the greatest decrement in recognition performance. The conclusion which has been drawn from such studies is that the upright human face can engage unique processing mechanisms not available for inverted faces, which are processed differently from upright faces. As Ellis (1975) explains, this is far from convincing. Moreover, Rock (1974) has in fact shown that the processing of printed words is also seriously affected by inversion, so that faces are *not* unique in this respect. Studies using inverted faces have, however, provided evidence relating to the specificity of the face processing system, which will be discussed later.

A second argument is that face processing is unique because of the need to extract emotional as well as physical information. This is also inconclusive because the processes used in 'reading' emotions from the face are themselves but poorly understood.

Turning to the question of the specificity of the face processing system it will be seen that the evidence is much stronger. The deficits seen in prosopagnosic patients provide support for the idea of face specific processing, and studies of cerebral asymmetries in normal and clinical populations also imply that at least some of the processes used for face stimuli are more asymmetrically organised than corresponding processes used with other visual stimuli.

Two main arguments have often been offered as to why case studies of prosopagnosic patients do not substantiate the face specifity hypothesis. These are:

(a) that prosopagnosia is neither a consistent nor a discrete deficit, in that it is often accompanied by a variety of other disorders;

(b) that the loci of the lesions accompanying prosopagnosia are also inconsistent.

Implicit in these arguments, however, is the view that prosopagnosia should be a unitary disorder. Sufficient evidence has already been forwarded to invalidate such a position, even for the case when the term prosopagnosia is restricted to disorders of face memory. Instead we have suggested that, as with other disorders of cognitive processes following cerebral injuries, impairments may occur at various locations in the face processing system, resulting in a range of distinct and differentiable disorders. Thus it is not to be expected that face processing disorders, which at present all tend to be labelled 'prosopagnosia' if sufficiently severe, will produce consistent symptoms or be accompanied by consistently sited lesions. For this reason we regard argument (b) as incorrect. There does, however, remain argument (a), that prosopagnosia is not a discrete deficit because of the evidence of associated disorders, such as object agnosias, disorders of colour vision and disorders of topographical orientation and memory.

Perhaps the easiest 'explanation' of prosopagnosia is that it is merely a manifestation of a more general object agnosia. Although both deficits have been known to occur together (Benson, Segarra and Albert, 1974), cases do exist in which prosopagnosia has been observed in the absence of object agnosia, and vice versa. In a review of twenty-two cases of prosopagnosia, Hécaen and Angelergues (1962), observed both deficits in only 27% of the sample, and report a case in which object agnosia was present *without* prosopagnosia. Other cases have also been described where prosopagnosia was not accompanied by object agnosia (e.g. Cole and Perez-Cruet, 1964) or where the associated object agnosia was minimal (Beyn and Knyazeva, 1962; Pallis, 1955).

The independence of the syndrome of prosopagnosia has also been challenged by the evidence that the majority of cases also appear to have associated defects of colour vision and topography. In many of the reports of disorders of colour vision, however, reliance is upon patients' descriptions without adequate testing having been done to substantiate the extent of these associated deficits. It is probably sufficient to note that discounting these cases still leaves at least one case in which the patient was prosopagnosic without suffering any disorder of colour perception (Meadows, 1974a). Moreover, in some cases where follow-up examinations have been conducted total or partial recovery of colour perception without remission of the prosopagnosia has been reported (Meadows, 1974b; Pevzner et al., 1962).

As regards disorders of a topographical nature, the above considerations also apply. That is, it is difficult to find reports in which testing has been adequate to arrive at a detailed determination of the deficits, and total recovery of function has again been noted while the prosopagnosia persisted (Pevzner et al., 1962).

What seems to be happening is that functional components involved in face, colour and topographical systems reside in adjacent cortical areas, all or some of which may be affected when gross damage results from stroke or tumour. However, the evidence of cases of dissociation of defects argues strongly for at least some forms of prosopagnosia to be considered as specific to faces.

Studies of cerebral asymmetries for face processing also support the view that at least some components of the system deal specifically with faces. Yin (1970), for instance, found that injuries to posterior areas of the right cerebral hemisphere produced a deficit in the recognition of upright stimulus faces. This deficit was not found when inverted faces were used as stimuli; nor was a comparable interaction of stimulus orientation and side of cerebral injury found for pictures of houses. An analogous phenomenon has been found in studies using brief lateral presentations of stimulus faces to normal subjects. Leehey, Carey, Diamond and Cahn (1978) and Young and Bion (1980, 1981) demonstrated that the LVF superiority for recognising upright familiar and unfamiliar faces was reduced or eliminated by inversion of the faces. Although some (but not all) of the methods used in these studies only required stimulus recognition, the consistent findings of main effects of stimulus orientation indicate that subjects were using strategies based on face recognition.

As explained previously, such studies using upright and inverted faces do not lend unequivocal support to the notion of *uniqueness* of the nature of the processing of faces. They do, however, indicate that at least one component of the right hemisphere's superiority for face recognition is *specific* to upright faces. As a face is equally complex as a visual stimulus whether upright or inverted this differential involvement of the right hemisphere cannot be due to stimulus complexity *per se*, and the findings lend support to the idea of a face processing system in which one or more components deal specifically with faces. It should be noted, however, that it cannot be deduced from the studies cited that the face specific component or components is or are located solely in the right cerebral hemisphere. The available evidence is equally consistent with the view that both cerebral hemispheres possess face specific processes but those of the right hemisphere are more effective or efficient.

Although the evidence reviewed here does not conclusively prove the existence of a specific face processing system it does provide a strong *prima facie* case. This, it should be noted, is based on evidence from studies that, because of the use of photographs, largely ignore two important properties which distinguish faces from most other multi-dimensional stimuli, namely that they are constantly changing and that they are capable of conveying mood information. Although next to nothing is known about the processes required to handle the constantly changing facial information, some recent work on how facial expressions are processed is relevant to the discussion of face specific mechanisms. This work suggests that, irrespective of whether there is a specific face processing system for the purposes of recognition, there seems to be a distinct facial affect processing mechanism.

Kurucz, Feldmar and Werner (1979) and Kurucz and Feldmar (1979) reported that some patients classed as having 'chronic organic brain syndrome' (which included patients admitted with senile or presenile dementia, schizophrenia and major affective disorder), experienced difficulty in identifying emotions represented in schematic faces or in photographs of faces, whilst still being able to identify photographs of American presidents. There was no correlation between performance on face recognition and performance on facial affect recognition.

Similarly, studies of normal subjects by Ley and Bryden (1979), Strauss and Moscovitch (1981), and Suberi and McKeever (1977) have indicated the existence of a right hemisphere superiority for identifying facial affect that is distinct from other components of the right hemisphere superiority for processing faces. Thus studies of both clinical and normal subject populations lend support to the suggestion of a specific facial affect system.

The conclusions to be drawn, then, as to whether there is a special face processing system are that there do seem to be processes that are used specifically for faces, and a specific facial affect system, but there is at present no convincing evidence of the qualitative uniqueness of the processing of faces. We would suggest, however, that the lack of evidence of uniqueness may be partly due to the fact that the perceptual and visual processes that are most likely to be unique are those that are understood least well, and that the use of static photographic stimuli in nearly all systematic studies tends to overlook the importance of the possibility of uniqueness of the more 'dynamic' aspects of face processing.

8   Summary and implications

In our endeavours to examine the properties of the face recognition system by collecting and evaluating evidence from a variety of studies of normal and clinical subject populations, we have made a number of proposals that have implications for future research which we feel deserve reiteration. These are basically of two types; first, the distinctions drawn at various points in the chapter in an effort to demarcate more clearly areas of investigation and to clarify theoretical formulations, and second, those associated with hypothesised functional components of our model of face recognition.

The distinction of face and person recognition was an attempt to emphasise that the use of face recognition units is but one method of identifying people, which in everyday circumstances will be accomplished by means of a variety of inputs from different cognitive systems. This is dramatically illustrated in the coping strategies developed by prosopagnosic patients. Although such a distinction appears obvious, in practice the decision as to whether experimental manipulations tap face or person recognition may be ambiguous. For example, supplying additional cues by dressing up targets may result in data which tell us more about the saliency of such information for person identification than about how faces are encoded in memory. Additional problems arise from the use of photographs as a stimulus medium, especially in paradigms involving the comparison of identical photographs of unfamiliar people. These studies may tell us more concerning general pattern recognition, or what we have termed here as stimulus recognition, than they do about face recognition. The same point applies to the use of 'schematic' faces.

Studies that make use of photographs or schematic faces as stimuli ignore the dynamic properties of faces which differentiate this class of verbal stimuli from so many others, and allow information as to the state of the individual to be continuously conveyed. Although there is at present no evidence that would lend unequivocal support to the suggestion that faces are processed by mechanisms employing *unique* methods of analysis, this should be distinguished from the possibility that there are face *specific* mechanisms operating in a fashion similar to those of other cognitive systems. Some support for this latter position does already exist and has been presented. In addition, we feel confident that future research, particularly investigations of the processes required for handling the dynamic properties of faces, and to determine the affective state of the individual, will add weight to this interpretation.

As regards the proposed model, several points concerning its construction deserve accentuation. First, and most important, it is not intended to be a complete model of the face processing system, since the data base on which it was built is at present limited. In fairness, it should again be pointed out that many of the studies cited, and especially those drawn from the normal experimental literature, were not primarily addressed to face recognition *per se*, employing novel faces merely because these are meaningful, complex, visual stimuli which are not easily verbally coded. This partly explains the general unsystematic fashion in which research has been conducted, the paucity of alternative models, and the difficulties faced by clinicians in deciding the exact nature of face processing deficits. What has been attempted here is to prepare a model which can adequately encompass prior findings as well as providing a framework to guide and focus future research. It is accepted that some components are specified more exactly than others. Lack of specification, however, tends to reflect areas of investigation which have either been ignored or examined in a fashion preventing clear conclusions to be drawn. As a result we have been content with merely classifying some components into clusters of interrelated processes, highlighting only those which are of particular importance. On the other hand, face recognition units have been given more detailed consideration because of their potential theoretical importance.

As regards the usefulness of the model we feel this was adequately demonstrated by its ability to predict a variety of face processing difficulties. As a result, the case reports of prosopagnosia could be classified as indicative of a number of these difficulties, thus confirming the suspicion that prosopagnosia is not a unitary disorder of face processing. In addition, types of prosopagnosia not, as yet, reported can be predicted. An example would be a deficit associated with an inability to create new recognition units. Such a patient would have no difficulty in recognising the faces of people known before the onset of the disorder but would have great difficulty with the faces of people known only after the onset of the disorder.

An analogous case has been reported by Milner (1970), who studied a patient with bilateral temporal lobe damage. The patient moved house after the onset of the injury, but even after six years in his new residence he could not recognise his neighbours, though people known before the injury were still recognised. This patient, however, suffered from additional memory difficulties not restricted to faces. We wish to suggest that an impairment of a similar type, but restricted to faces, could exist.

The model is also useful in generating a hierarchy of questions associated with each of the functional components, which are appropriate for pinpointing more exactly the nature of face processing disorders. We hope that this might prove helpful to promoting a more systematic analysis of prosopagnosic patients and patients with right hemisphere injuries, and in allowing the construction of more precise tasks for experimental studies of face processing by normal individuals.

Acknowledgements

We are very grateful to Hadyn Ellis, who offered helpful comments on a previous draft of this chapter, even though he would still disagree with most of it. The concept of face recognition units is not our own, it was appropriated from a suggestion made by Andy Ellis.

References

Anderson, J. R. and Paulson, R. (1978). Interference in memory for pictorial information. *Cognitive Psychology* 10, 178–202

Benson, D. F., Segarra, J. and Albert, M. L. (1974). Visual agnosia-prosopagnosia: a clinicopathologic correlation. *Archives of Neurology* 30, 307–310

Benton, A. L. and Van Allen, M. W. (1968). Impairment in facial recognition in patients with cerebral disease. *Cortex* 4, 344–358

Benton, A. L. and Van Allen, M. W. (1972). Prosopagnosia and facial discrimination. *Journal of Neurological Science* 15, 167–172

Bertelson, P., Vanhaelen, H. and Morais, J. (1979). Left hemifield superiority and the extraction of physiognomic information. *In* I. Steele Russell, M. W. Van Hof and G. Berlucchi (eds), *Structure and Function of Cerebral Commissures*, pp. 400–410. London: MacMillan

Beyn, E. S. and Knyazeva, G. R. (1962). The problem of prosopagnosia. *Journal of Neurology, Neurosurgery and Psychiatry* **25**, 154–158

Bodamer, J. (1947). Die Prosop-Agnosie. *Archive Psychiatrie und Zeitschrift Neurologie* **179**, 6–54

Bradshaw, J. L. and Wallace, G. (1971). Models for the processing and identification of faces. *Perception and Psychophysics* **9**, 443–448

Bruce, V. (1979). Searching for politicians: An information-processing approach to face recognition. *Quarterly Journal of Experimental Psychology* **31**, 373–395

Carey, S. (1978). A case study: face recognition. In E. Walker (ed.), *Explorations in the Biology of Language*, pp. 175–201. Vermont: Bradford Books

Carey, S. and Diamond, R. (1977). From piecemeal to configurational representation of faces. *Science* **195**, 312–314

Cohen, G. (1977). *The Psychology of Cognition*. New York: Academic Press

Cohn, R., Neumann, M. A. and Wood, D. H. (1977). Prosopagnosia: A clinicopathological study. *Annals of Neurology* **1**, 177–182

Cole, M. and Perez-Cruet, J. (1964). Prosopagnosia. *Neuropsychologia* **2**, 237–246

Davies, G. M., Ellis, H. D. and Shepherd, J. W. (1981). *Perceiving and Remembering Faces*. London: Academic Press

De Renzi, E. and Spinnler, H. (1966). Facial recognition in brain damaged patients. *Neurology* **16**, 145–152

De Renzi, E., Faglioni, P. and Spinnler, H. (1968). The performance of patients with unilateral brain damage on face recognition tasks. *Cortex* **4**, 17–34

De Renzi, E., Scotti, G. and Spinnler, H. (1969). Perceptual and associative disorders of visual recognition. *Neurology* **19**, 634–642

Diamond, R. and Carey, S. (1977). Developmental changes in the representation of faces. *Journal of Experimental Child Psychology* **23**, 1–22

Ellis, H. D. (1975). Recognising faces. *British Journal of Psychology* **66**, 409–426

Ellis, H. D. (1981). Theoretical aspects of face recognition. In G. M. Davies, H. D. Ellis and J. W. Shepherd (eds), *Perceiving and Remembering Faces*. London: Academic Press

Ellis, H. D., Davies, G. M. and Shepherd, J. W. (1977). Experimental studies of face identification. *National Journal of Criminal Defense* **3**, 219–234

Ellis, H. D., Shepherd, J. W. and Davies, G. M. (1979). Identification of familiar and unfamiliar faces from internal and external features: some implications for theories of face recognition *Perception* **8**, 431–439

Galper, R. E. (1970). Recognition of faces in photographic negative. *Psychonomic Science* **19**, 207–208

Geffen, G., Bradshaw, J. L. and Wallace, G. (1971). Interhemispheric effects on reaction time to verbal and nonverbal visual stimuli. *Journal of Experimental Psychology* **87**, 415–422

Gloning, K. and Quatember, R. (1966). Methodischer Beitrag zur Untersuchung der Prosopagnosie. *Neuropsychologia* **4**, 133–144

Gloning, I., Gloning, K., Jellinger, K. and Quatember, R. (1970). A case of prosopagnosia with necropsy findings. *Neuropsychologia* **8**, 199–204

Haith, M., Bergman, T. and Moore, M. (1977). Eye contact and face scanning in early infancy. *Science* **198**, 853–855

Hay, D. C. (1981). Asymmetries in facial recognition: Evidence for a perceptual component. *Quarterly Journal of Experimental Psychology* **33A**, 267–274

Hay, D. C. and Ellis, H. D. (1981). Asymmetries in facial recognition: Evidence for a memory component. *Cortex*

Hécaen, H. and Albert, M. (1978). *Human Neuropsychology*. Wiley and Sons: New York

Hécaen, H. and Angelergues, R. (1962). Agnosia for faces (prosopagnosia). *Archives of Neurology* **7**, 92–100

Hilliard, R. D. (1973). Hemispheric laterality effects on a facial recognition task in normal subjects. *Cortex* **9**, 246–258

Hochberg, J. and Galper, R. E. (1967). Recognition of faces, 1: An exploratory study. *Psychonomic Science* **9**, 619–620

Kurucz, J. and Feldmar, G. (1979). Prosopo-affective agnosia as a symptom of cerebral organic disease. *Journal of the American Geriatrics Society* **27**, 225–230

Kurucz, J., Feldmar, G. and Werner, W. (1979). Prosopo-affective agnosia associated with chronic organic brain syndrome. *Journal of the American Geriatrics Society* **27**, 91–95

Laughery, K. R., Fessler, P. K., Lenorovitz, D. R. and Yoblick, D. A. (1974). Time delay and similarity effects in face recognition. *Journal of Applied Psychology* **59**, 490–496

Leehey, S., Carey, S., Diamond, R. and Cahn, A. (1978). Upright and inverted faces: the right hemisphere knows the difference. *Cortex* **14**, 411–419

Ley, R. G. and Bryden, M. P. (1979). Hemispheric differences in processing emotions and faces. *Brain and Language* **7**, 127–138

Matthews, M. L. (1978). Discrimination of identikit constructions of faces: Evidence for a dual processing strategy. *Perception and Psychophysics* **23**, 153–161

Maurer, D. and Salapatek, P. (1976). Developmental changes in the scanning of faces. *Child Development* **47**, 523–527

Meadows, J. C. (1974a). The anatomical basis of prosopagnosia. *Journal of Neurology, Neurosurgery and Psychiatry* **37**, 489–501

Meadows, J. C. (1974b). Disturbed perception of colours associated with localized cerebral lesions. *Brain* **97**, 615–632

Milner, B. (1968). Visual recognition and recall after right temporal-lobe excision in man. *Neuropsychologia* **6**, 191–209

Milner, B. (1970). Memory and the medial temporal regions of the brain. *In* K. H. Pribram and D. E. Broadbent (eds), *Biology of Memory*, pp. 29–50. New York: Academic Press

Morton, J. (1969). The interaction of information in word recognition. *Psychological Review* **76**, 165–178

Morton, J. (1979). Word recognition. *In* J. Morton and J. C. Marshall (eds), *Psycholinguistics Series 2: Structures and Processes*, pp. 107–156. London: Elek

Moscovitch, M. (1979). Information processing and the cerebral hemispheres. *In* M. S. Gazzaniga (ed.), *Handbook of Behavioral Neurobiology, Vol. 2: Neuropsychology*, pp. 379–446. New York: Plenum

Moscovitch, M., Scullion, D. and Christie, D. (1976). Early versus late stages of processing and their relation to functional hemispheric asymmetries in face recognition. *Journal of Experimental Psychology: Human Perception and Performance* **3**, 401–416

Pallis, C. A. (1955). Impaired identification of faces and places with agnosia for colours. *Journal of Neurology, Neurosurgery and Psychiatry* **18**, 218–224

Patterson, K. and Bradshaw, J. L. (1975). Differential hemispheric mediation of non-verbal visual stimuli. *Journal of Experimental Psychology: Human Perception and Performance* **1**, 246–253

Pevzner, S., Bornstein, B. and Loewenthal, M. (1962). Prosopagnosia. *Journal of Neurology, Neurosurgery and Psychiatry* **25**, 336–338

Rizzolatti, G., Umilta, C. and Berlucchi, G. (1971). Opposite superiorities of left and right cerebral hemispheres in discriminative reaction time to physiognomic and alphabetic material. *Brain* **94**, 431–442

Rock, I. (1974). The perception of disoriented figures. *Scientific American* **230**, 78–85

Scapinello, K. F. and Yarmey, A. D. (1970). The role of familiarity and orientation in immediate and delayed recognition of pictorial stimuli. *Psychonomic Science* **21**, 329–330

Seymour, P. H. K. (1973). A model for reading, naming and comparison. *British Journal of Psychology* **64**, 35–49

Seymour, P. H. K. (1979). *Human Visual Cognition*. West Drayton: Collier-McMillan

Shepherd, J. W., Ellis, H. D. and Davies, G. M. (1977). Perceiving and remembering faces. *Report to the Home Office under contract POL/73/1675/24/1*

Smith, E. E. and Nielsen, G. D. (1970). Representations and retrieval processes in short-term memory: Recognition and recall of faces. *Journal of Experimental Psychology* **85**, 397–405

Strauss, E. and Moscovitch, M. (1981). Perception of facial expressions. *Brain and Language* **13**, 308–332

Suberi, M. and McKeever, W. F. (1977). Differential right hemispheric memory storage of emotional and non-emotional faces. *Neuropsychologia* **15**, 757–768

Warrington, E. K. and James, M. (1967). An experimental investigation of facial recognition in patients with unilateral cerebral lesions. *Cortex* **3**, 317–326

Whiteley, A. M. and Warrington, E. K. (1977). Prosopagnosia: a clinical, psychological and anatomical study of three patients. *Journal of Neurology, Neurosurgery and Psychiatry* **40**, 395–403

Yarmey, A. D. (1971). Recognition for familiar 'public' faces: Effects of orientation and delay. *Psychonomic Science* **24**, 286–288

Yarmey, A. D. (1973). I recognise your face but I can't remember your name: Further evidence on the tip-of-the-tongue phenomenon. *Memory and Cognition* **1**, 287–290

Yin, R. K. (1969). Looking at upside down faces. *Journal of Experimental Psychology* **81**, 141–145

Yin, R. K. (1970). Face recognition in brain injured patients: A dissociable ability? *Neuropsychologia* **8**, 395–402

Young, A. W. (1982). Methodological and theoretical bases of visual hemifield studies. *In* J. G. Beaumont (ed.), *Divided Visual Field Studies of Cerebral Organisation*. London: Academic Press

Young, A. W. and Bion, P. J. (1980). Absence of any developmental trend in right hemisphere superiority for face recognition. *Cortex* **16**, 213–221

Young, A. W. and Bion, P. J. (1981). Accuracy of naming laterally presented known faces by children and adults. *Cortex* **17**, 97–106

7

Normal and Abnormal Forgetting: Some Comments on the Human Amnesic Syndrome

PETER MEUDELL AND ANDREW MAYES
Department of Psychology, University of Manchester, England

1 Introduction

The concern of this chapter is with a dramatic memory impairment which is referred to as the amnesic syndrome or global amnesia (and sometimes loosely as Korsakoff's syndrome). Although this syndrome has several etiologies, which include chronic alchoholism, encephalitis, head injury, carbon monoxide poisoning and occlusion of the posterior cerebral artery (Whitty and Lishman, 1966), the critical damage seems to involve a small number of limbic and related brain structures. Lesions to the hippocampus, the mammillary bodies, their fornical connection, or the dorsomedial nucleus of the thalamus have been implicated (Mair, Warrington and Weiskrantz, 1979). Mishkin (1978) has suggested recently that damage to two such structures may be necessary for the occurrence of a severe amnesia on the basis of a study which only found a memory deficit in monkeys following combined hippocampal and amygdala lesions.

The amnesic syndrome is characterised psychologically by a profound difficulty in learning and remembering new information of nearly all kinds (anterograde amnesia) and a difficulty in remembering information acquired prior to the onset of the disability (retrograde amnesia) which may extend to several decades (Meudell, Northen, Snowdon and Neary, 1980). Short-term memory as assessed by the digit span or the recency effect in free recall is also usually in the normal range. Finally, dense amnesia may sometimes occur with all other cognitive functions relatively intact when these functions are assessed by tests such as the WAIS. Experimentalists have tried to select their patients so that they are 'pure' amnesics in the above sense so as to make it easier to dissociate the 'core' amnesia from memory problems arising as secondary consequences of other cognitive failures. It remains unresolved however to what extent 'impure' amnesias, such as these of dementia, share the core features of the amnesic syndrome, and indeed whether the core amnesic syndrome itself is a unitary functional complex.

2 Methodological problems

A   FLOOR, CEILING AND LEVEL OF PERFORMANCE EFFECTS

A major problem in research on amnesia is the presence of floor and ceiling effects which are ubiquitous in this area of study. The problem arises since retention intervals which get amnesics above chance performance tend to push controls to ceiling levels of performance (i.e. close to 100 percent accuracy) while, conversely, retention intervals which get controls off the ceiling tend to depress amnesics' performance to floor levels. There are two possible solutions to this problem. First, amnesics and controls could be tested at different retention intervals, amnesics being tested at relatively brief retention intervals and controls at relatively long retention intervals. Second, the retention interval could be held constant for both groups but floor or ceiling effects could be avoided by allowing the amnesic group longer exposure to the learning material than the control group. Since there may be differences in what is encoded when there are differences in the time available for learning the preferred strategy should be to hold learning time constant but to vary retention interval across the groups.

This differential testing of amnesic and control groups has another advantage apart from obviating floor and ceiling effects. If overall levels of performance are equated between the two groups as a result of, say, the use of different retention intervals, then it is possible to avoid the kind of subtle interactions which may be a function of different levels of performance (Woods and Piercy, 1974). In other words, differences in overall level of performance may cause interpretative problems because any differences in patterns of performance across the two groups might result not from qualitative differences between amnesics and controls (indicating a selective deficit in one or another stage of memory), but from the quantitative differences in levels of performance. Thus, the pattern of performance observed with amnesics and controls may be quite different when both groups are tested at the same retention interval but may be identical when the controls are tested at a (longer) retention interval which gives comparable levels of performance to the amnesics. If normal people show different patterns of performance as retention interval increases and at longer retention intervals they behave in similar ways to amnesics, it is reasonable to conclude that any interaction between amnesics and controls across an independent variable, when both groups are tested at the *same* interval, is not causally related to amnesia but is simply a consequence of it. That is, the mechanisms involved in forgetting may be identical in normal people and amnesics but amnesics very rapidly reach states of memory which are attained by normal individuals after a much longer period of time.

Why might the pattern of performance change across levels of an independent variable as retention interval increases? If the information in memory is conceived of as a multidimensional trace consisting of analysed attributes or features (Bower, 1967), and these attributes become less available over time, then if some features become unavailable more rapidly than others, those aspects of the trace which mediate the expression of memory at one retention interval may be different from those which mediate it at another. For example, since in memory tests normal peoples' ability to produce a correct response to a three letter prompt falls less rapidly than their ability to recognise that an item has been shown previously (Mayes and Meudell, 1981a), the information mediating the expression of memory when tested by prompts appears to become unavailable less rapidly than that mediating memory when tested by recognition. In this respect therefore normal people who have largely forgotten behave in similar ways to amnesics since, in comparison to controls tested at the same brief retention interval, they too are relatively better at cueing tasks than they are at recognition tasks (Warrington and Weiskrantz, 1974). The difference between amnesic memory and normal memory tested after a long retention interval thus may be simply that the same state of memory is arrived at much sooner in the former than in the latter, but in both cases the relatively better performance on cueing tasks may be a consequence of slower rates of loss of availability of the attributes mediating the expression of memory when tested by prompting than those mediating memory when tested by recognition.

While many genuine interactions may occur as a consequence of these differences in the availability of various attributes of memory over time, some may simply occur as a trivial consequence of the use of inappropriate measurement techniques. As an example of the latter consider an experiment by Miller (1977). Miller found that in comparison to a normal control group a demented amnesic group performed differentially worse, in terms of 'number correct', on 8-choice compared to 2-choice word recognition memory when both groups were tested immediately after learning. On the basis of this result Miller argued that his data supported a selective amnesic retrieval deficit. However, not only do normal people tested after a long delay show this differential impairment with 8-choice recognition when compared to normal people tested immediately after learning, the effect disappears when d' (a measure of memory independent of scoring techniques) rather than 'number correct' is used as the dependent variable (Meudell and Mayes, 1981a). Thus while some differential patterns of performance are genuinely characteristic of 'weak' normal memory and amnesic memory when compared to 'strong' normal memory and might reflect differences in feature availability, some may be consequent upon the choice of inappropriate measures of memory strength. 'Strength' here simply refers to a unidimensional variable which provides a measure of the availability of a particular memory at a given time after learning. This measure no doubt declines with retention interval and is an unknown function of its component features. Accordingly, in people with normal memory, short retention intervals lead to 'strong' memory and long ones to 'weak' memory, while in amnesics, 'weak' memory occurs even with short retention intervals. This usage of 'strength', which is not meant to do any disservice to the subtlety or complexity of the underlying trace, will be used as a shorthand throughout the rest of this chapter.

These comments on levels of performance (and memory 'strength') do not apply only to comparisons between amnesics and controls, they apply in principal to any comparisons within groups of amnesics where there may be differences in severity of amnesia. If, as seems not unreasonable, amnesics with distinct etiologies or amnesics of the same etiology but with different degrees of impairment, do differ in the severity of their memory deficit, then apparent qualitative differences in performance between different amnesic groups (e.g. Lhermitte and Signoret, 1976) might well be attributed to quantitative differences in memory 'strength'. Unfortunately, such comparisons both between and within amnesic groups are made difficult by the fact that there is no universally accepted measure of severity of memory impairment. A widely used measure, the Wechsler Memory Scale, for example, has many problems associated with it (Mair, Warrington and Weiskrantz, 1979) in that the subtests either have a strong short-term memory component (as in the 'digit span' test) or assess highly overlearned skills (as in the 'mental control' tests). Until such time as reliable, valid and commonly used memory assessment techniques are available, the claim that differences between amnesics exist is likely to remain an important theoretical issue rather than a piece of empirical evidence.

B   EXTRA-MNEMONIC IMPAIRMENT IN AMNESIC PATIENTS

Talland (1965) and more recently Butters and Cermak (1976) have reported a series of investigations on alcoholic amnesics in which they have charted not only the mnemonic difficulties of these patients but also a whole range of other impairments from disorders of mood or affect to cognitive disorders of perception, judgement and concept formation.

Disorders such as these may play one of three possible roles in organic amnesia. First, they may be the primary cause of the amnesia. Second, while not being the primary cause of the amnesia, these deficits may give rise to memory problems in their own right which are additional to, or superimposed upon, the primary deficit. Third, the disorders may be largely unrelated to memory so that they are neither responsible for the primary cause of the amnesia nor do they give rise to secondary memory deficits. How might these different roles be disentangled? If these extra deficits are solely and exclusively responsible for amnesia then they should always occur in association with memory disorders and, furthermore, the magnitude of the cognitive impairment should be proportional to the severity of the amnesia. However, if some patients with the same etiology can be shown to present with dense amnesia in the apparent absence of extra cognitive deficits, then it seems likely that the cognitive deficits found in other amnesic patients may either merely contribute towards a memory problem additional to that of the core deficit, or, the extra deficits may be simply irrelevant to memory.

Cognitive deficits which may be unrelated to memory might be, at one extreme, of little consequence for the interpretation of the basic disorder in the amnesic syndrome but at the other extreme their presence might 'cloud' the interpretation of the primary amnesic disorder. Thus, for example, the fact that mildly demented amnesics show patterns of cueing performance similar to those shown by intellectually intact amnesics (Miller, 1975), suggests that modest loss of intelligence does not necessarily prevent the appearance of an established amnesic phenomenon. On the other hand, it would seem likely that a *grossly* demented and amnesic patient might fail to show the accepted pattern of amnesic cueing performance because of profound difficulties in comprehension which are unrelated to the primary cause of the memory impairment.

Cognitive impairment which may lead to secondary memory deficits and which may be superimposed upon the primary memory deficit might lead to interpretative problems in patients with both these 'primary' and 'secondary' amnesias since, as Baddeley (1981) has pointed out, there is the danger of attributing an observed pattern of breakdown in performance to the core cause of amnesia when in fact the observed pattern is a reflection of the secondary memory impairment. In many cases this is not a serious problem since the influence of extramnemonic impairment, as in global dementia for example, is fairly obvious. At a more subtle level, however, some densely amnesic patients, who have relatively normal IQs, appear to manifest acquisitional failures and these failures have been claimed to be the cause of their 'primary' amnesia (McDowall, 1979). On the other hand, while McDowall's patients were not a demented group in the accepted sense of having widespread intellectual impairment, they did have very low 'Similarities' scores on the WAIS. Since it is known that 'Similarities' score is positively related to the employment of effective encoding strategies (Stoff and Eagle, 1971) and since dense amnesia can occur in patients in whom 'Similarities' scores are in the normal range (Mayes, Meudell and Neary, 1980), it seems likely that the inefficient acquisition shown by McDowall's patients is a secondary consequence of some extra-mnemonic impairment (indexed by the 'Similarities' score) and is not necessarily related to the primary cause of their amnesia.

In a similar vein, Butters and Cermak (1976), have argued for an encoding deficit in their alcoholic amnesics partly on the basis of the fact that their patients fail to show improved short-term memory when the semantic category of the words they must remember is changed with respect to previous trials (the Wickens, 1970, release from PI effect). These patients have normal IQ, are not demented and are densely amnesic, and thus this failure to show release from PI might appear compelling evidence for a selective amnesic acquisitional deficit. However, recently it has been reported that patients with frontal damage, who are not densely amnesic, also fail to show release from PI under similar circumstances (Moscovitch, cited by Baddeley, 1981). If failure to show release from PI occurs in patients who are not densely amnesic, its occurence in those who do have severe memory problems is probably unconnected with the primary cause of their amnesia and might simply be a secondary memory problem caused by some additional cognitive impairment.

The possible role of extra-mnemonic impairment in anterograde amnesia is being progressively documented, but its role in retrograde amnesia is somewhat less established. There are, however, two problems which might occur in examining the nature of retrograde amnesia which arise from the possibility that an amnesic's current intelligence, although maybe within normal limits, is significantly lower than it was premorbidly. First, such amnesics may be compared with control subjects whose intelligence is too low if controls are chosen to match the amnesic's postmorbid intelligence. This might well give an under-estimate of the amnesic's retrograde amnesia on the assumption that such information is better encoded and stored by more intelligent people. Second, if there has been a decline in cognitive ability, the assessment of retrograde amnesia would require the patients to access information acquired on the basis of relatively efficient cognitive processes with (currently) relatively inefficient cognitive processes and since the way in which information is encoded will determine in part what will constitute an effective retrieval strategy, patients with differences between their pre- and postmorbid IQ might produce artifactually flattened retrograde amnesia gradients. Unfortunately, although tests of premorbid intellectual level are available (e.g. Nelson and O'Connell, 1978), just as there is no commonly accepted measure of memory, there is no widely accepted measure of premorbid intellectual performance.

3 Theories and data concerning the psychological deficit in organic amnesia

A ENCODING DEFICIT THEORIES

Hasher and Zacks (1979) have recently distinguished between two types of encoding processes which they term 'automatic' and 'effortful'. Automatic encoding processes take minimal energy from limited capacity attentional systems and so they occur without effort or intention on the part of the subject and do not interfere with other ongoing cognitive activity. Hasher and Zachs argue that automatic processes are involved in the encoding of spatial, temporal and frequency of occurrence information. On the other hand, 'effortful' processing such as rehearsal and elaborative or organisational encoding strategies require considerable capacity, are thus intentionally initiated and interfere with other tasks requiring capacity.

This distinction between automatic and effortful encoding processes is a timely one since there are currently two types of encoding deficit theory which neatly fit into this dichotomy. The first of these types of theory attributes the amnesics' problem to a failure to employ the effortful processes involving 'deep' elaborative and organisational analyses of the stimulus (Butters and Cermak, 1975) while the second type attributes the cause of amnesia to a failure of those automatic processes which encode temporal and frequency information (Huppert and Piercy, 1978a). These two types of theory will be discussed in turn.

1 *Failure of effortful processing.* A most influential theory about the nature of the psychological deficit in alcoholic amnesia is the encoding deficit view of Butters and Cermak (1975). Butters and Cermak argue that the amnesics' problems with memory for both verbal and nonverbal material arise from a habitual tendency to ignore those meaningful aspects of stimuli the encoding of which are necessary for good memory. Instead amnesics tend to rely on those superficial aspects of stimuli the encoding of which, in normal subjects, gives rise to relative poor memory.

Thus, in memory for verbal material, Butters and Cermak (1975) propose that the amnesic's problem arises from a spontaneous failure to encode information to 'deep' or semantic levels during learning. In other words, if left to his own devices, he fails to employ those elaborative and organisational effortful processes which, in normal people, are spontaneously employed in verbal learning situations and which are necessary for good memory. The evidence for this position in verbal memory comes from a wide range of studies. First, under certain conditions their amnesics do not benefit as much as controls from category cues given shortly after learning a list of words comprising mixed taxonomic categories, (e.g. animals and fruits) and, accordingly, it is argued that the amnesic failed to encode the taxonomic information during learning, (Cermak and Butters, 1972). Second, the facilitatory effects such cues provide for amnesics appear to be lost more rapidly than in controls, and this, it is argued, is a consequence of poor initial semantic analysis (Cermak, Butters and Gerrein, 1973). Third, in recognition tests their amnesics chose more 'lure' items which were homonyms of target items than did controls, and this was interpreted as representing the predominance, in amnesics, of 'low' level analysis of acoustic and other similar information in memory (Butters and Cermak, 1975). Finally, as previously noted, the Boston amnesics fail to show release from PI in the Wickens' paradigm with taxonomic (category) shifts although they do show release with alphanumeric shifts (Cermak, Butters and Morreines, 1974).

Although other interpretations of each of these pieces of evidence are possible (e.g. McDowall, 1979), taken together they provide impressive support for an acquisitional deficit resulting from a spontaneous failure to encode information to 'deep' semantic levels during learning. On the other hand, the evidence is correlational or inferential in nature, there being no direct evidence for the type of encoding strategies employed by amnesics or, indeed, by controls. In an attempt to provide a more direct test of the semantic coding deficit hypothesis we have systematically varied the encoding strategies employed by our amnesics and controls by altering the instructions given in different types of orienting tasks. If the encoding deficit view is correct, then forcing amensics to analyse the semantic aspects of stimuli (by the choice of suitable orienting tasks) should differentially improve their memory, relative to ordinary 'learn' instructions, in comparison to controls. A related prediction is also possible. If amnesics habitually employ superficial analyses of stimuli without extensive analysis of the meaning of what they are trying to remember, then with an orienting task which prevents the efficient ex-traction of meaning, they should be largely unimpaired, relative to ordinary learning conditions, in comparison to controls.

We have examined these predictions across a range of different types of material to be remembered. In an early experiment (Meudell and Mayes, 1980) we investigated the specific proposal (Cermak, Naus and Reale, 1976) that the habitual mode of encoding in alcoholic amnesics was by passive rote repetition of items as they were presented for learning. Two orienting conditions were used in this first experiment, an ordinary 'learn' condition and a 'repeat' condition in which subjects had to say each to be remembered word out loud 5 times in a paced fashion before the next word was presented. This latter task was chosen so as to prevent efficient extraction of meaning from the words and also to attempt to mimic what Cermak et al. hypothesised amnesics do spontaneously. The results showed that both groups were impaired in the 'repeat' condition compared to the 'learn' condition; however, the magnitude of the impair-ment in the repeat condition, contrary to the prediction of the encoding deficit theory, was identical in both groups. This result therefore suggests that whatever processes are spontaneously engaged in during learning lists of unrelated words, they are similar in amnesics and normal people. This conclusion was reinforced by the fact that the amount of clustering in free recall over learning trials was similar in normal controls and amnesics, and if clustering in recall is a reflection of encoding processes then this too indicates normal organisational processes in our amnesics.

In this same experiment (Meudell and Mayes, 1980) we also investigated how different distractor items might effect 2-choice recognition memory of controls and amnesics after the 'learn' and 'repeat' conditions. In this particular experiment, in order to control for memory 'strength', the controls' recognition memory was tested 7 days after learning while amnesics' memory was tested shortly after learning. The lure items on the recognition tests were semantically, acoustically or graphemically related to target items. The results showed no differences in patterns of performance across the different types of lures between the two groups of subjects. In other words, there was no evidence to suggest differential patterns of performance between the two groups across distractor types as might have been expected had the amnesics been encoding in qualitatively different ways to the normal controls.

In a second experiment using verbal material as stimuli to be learned, (Mayes, Meudell and Neary, 1978) we examined both aspects of the predictions from the semantic coding deficit theory; that is, we used an orienting task which was designed to encourage the extraction of meaning (in this case giving riddles to subjects, the one word answer to which they were required to remember) and an orienting task which made extraction of meaning difficult. The results for the 'high' level orienting task were clear: far from differentially improving amnesics' recall performance as the encoding deficit theory would predict, it actually slightly impaired it. Floor effects, however, made interpretation of the effects of the counting orienting task impossible. Since from a more plausible version of the encoding deficit theory, it might be argued that semantic encoding deficits operate at retrieval as well as encoding, we gave semantic 'hints' (parts of the original riddle) following each of the three orienting tasks. If amnesics fail to employ semantic retrieval rules even after being forced to encode the meaning of stimuli, they should be differentially aided by the presence of semantic hints after the 'high' level orienting task, relative to the other orienting tasks and in comparison to controls. No such effect occurred: while semantic hints were maximally effective after the 'high' level orienting task, they were equally effective in improving recall in both amnesics and normal controls.

While the encoding deficit theory was originally developed to explain the verbal memory deficits of alcoholic amnesics, the theory has been extended recently to encompass nonverbal information such as random shapes (De Luca, Cermak and Butters, 1975), and faces (Dricker, Butters, Berman, Samuels and Carey, 1978). We have also tested the predictions from the theory in similar ways to those of Mayes, Meudell and Neary (1978) but using random shapes, photographs of faces and cartoon drawings as stimuli to be remembered. In all the experiments recognition memory was equated in amnesics and controls by testing at different retention intervals in the two groups, and subjects were reminded at the time of recognition testing of how the material had been presented in order to ensure the use of appropriate 'encoding specific' retrieval strategies. In addition, since comparisons between the memory performance of two different groups of subjects would only make sense if the two groups were executing the orienting task with the same efficiency, actual performance on the orienting task itself was also monitored.

In the first of this series of experiments (Mayes, Meudell and Neary, 1980) amnesics and controls were shown random shapes under a standard 'learn' condition, a condition in which the subjects were required to count the number of sides in the shape (a task designed to impair efficient extraction of meaning), and a condition in which the subjects were to state some action or object that the shape reminded them of (i.e. interpret the shape). The results showed that the 'interpret' condition improved memory to the same extent in amnesics and controls compared to 'learn', while the 'count' condition impaired memory equally in the two groups. In other words, there was no difference in performance patterns by the two subject groups across the orienting conditions, and thus the data provides no comfort for an encoding deficit view of amnesia.

In the second experiment of this series (Mayes, Meudell and Neary, 1980) subjects were required to remember photographs of faces, again shown under three different orienting conditions: a 'learn' condition, a condition requiring the subjects to judge the straightness of the photographed person's hair and a condition in which the subject was required to judge the 'friendliness' of the face. In comparison to the 'learn' condition and contrary to the expectations of the encoding deficit theory, both groups were equally impaired in the 'hair' condition and both were equally improved in the 'friendliness' condition.

The last experiment in this series (Meudell, Mayes and Neary, 1980a), required subjects, in one condition, to look at pairs of pictures which differed in subtle ways and find as many differences as possible. In another condition they were shown single pictures and given standard learn instructions, and in a final condition they were asked to describe out loud the content of the picture. Once again, however, the results showed that there were no differences in patterns of performance across the orienting tasks between amnesics and controls.

Across a wide range of verbal and nonverbal materials and differing orienting tasks, therefore, we have failed to obtain differences between our amnesics and our controls either in the extent of their improvement with orienting tasks which encourage the extraction of meaning, or the extent of their impairment in tasks which make the extraction of meaning difficult. Since in most experiments we equated levels of performance in the two groups of subjects, the absence of differences between groups across orienting tasks is not an artifact of differences in memory strength and, further, since we ensured that the subjects were reminded of the learning conditions at the time of testing memory, it is also improbable that our results are due to semantic deficits operating at retrieval. Cognitive slowness, which has been noted in some amnesics (Cermak, Butters and Moreines, 1974), or other inefficiencies involved in executing the orienting tasks themselves, also seem unlikely to be responsible for the absence of differences in memory across orienting tasks since not only are our amnesics as fast as controls at various reaction time tasks (Meudell, Mayes and Neary, 1980b) but also they appeared to carry out the orienting tasks in similar ways. Given these methodological points and given that there are no differences in patterns of memory across the different orienting tasks between amnesics and controls, spontaneous failure to employ 'deep' semantic coding strategies during learning or retrieval therefore appears to be an extremely unlikely cause of the dense amnesia of our patients.

The fact that our amnesics are neither slower overall than age matched controls nor differentially slower at making semantic or multiple decisions (Meudell, Mayes and Neary, 1980b) also renders implausible the hypothesis (Cermak, 1978) that encoding problems occurring secondary to slowness of information processing could be responsible for the amnesics' severe memory impairment. We believe our amnesics encode the semantic aspects of material just as rapidly, just as much and just as effectively as normal people.

The encoding deficit hypothesis owes much to Talland's (1965) original proposal that the severe anterograde and retrograde amnesias in alcoholic amnesics could both be explained in terms of 'reduced activation and premature closure of function'. He argued that reduced activation caused a range of cognitive impairments which in turn caused acquisitional and retrieval failures and he related the activation deficit directly to the often reported emotional blandness, lack of spontaneity or apathy of amnesics (Victor, Adams and Collins, 1971). If such activational deficits are responsible for amnesia then it might be possible to overcome them if amnesics are exposed to stimuli which they perceive as very significant or interesting and which thus lead to high levels of activation. Meudell, Mayes and Neary (1980a), however, found that while recognition memory for cartoons found 'very funny' by amnesics was better than for cartoons rated as 'unfunny', the effect was no greater than that seen in controls. Deficiencies in picture recognition thus cannot be overcome by exposing more arousing cartoons to amnesics and while deficient activation may still be a problem in amnesia it is not remediated by showing patients arousing stimuli. Reduced activation might also lead to impoverished attentional processes and, as Talland (1965) argued (p. 269), this might '. . . restrict their efficiency in perception and inevitably also in registration'. While both Oscar-Berman and Samuels (1977) and Parkinson (1979) have reported attentional deficits in Butters and Cermak's population of patients, we have found that our patients were not only as rapid as controls in tasks requiring attention to multiple aspects of stimuli, they also showed no greater error in these 'divided attention' tasks (Meudell, Mayes and Neary, 1980b). Accordingly the presence of attentional deficits is not a necessary factor in the cause of amnesia.

Of course in some groups of alcoholic patients, such as those described by Talland and by Cermak and Butters, it is conceivable that an apathetic state leading to attentional impairments, perceptual deficiencies, slowness of processing and generally diminished information processing capacities might contribute towards their amnesia. In other words some patients may have a primary amnesia and, in addition, a more or less severe secondary memory problem caused by some other extra-mnemonic deficit. Specifically it is possible that the apathy frequently noted in amnesics (Victor *et al.*, 1971) might be related to a tendency not to employ those encoding processes which require effort. This view receives some support from a recent experiment by Hasher and Zachs (1979) who have shown that while self-rated depressives make no more recognition errors overall than self-rated nondepressed people, the characteristic pattern of their recognition errors is different. In particular, depressed individuals tended to select lure items which were acoustically related to target items while nondepressed people tended to select lure items which were associatively related to the target item. Thus while not apparently affecting the overall level of recognition memory performance, on the assumption that recognition errors reflect encoding processes, the apathy which might be related to mild degrees of depression tended to result in a change in encoding processes compared to nonapathetic individuals.

It is conceivable therefore that the apathetic state of some alcoholic amnesics might lead to changes in encoding strategies which are unrelated to the primary cause of amnesia and whose contribution to the overall level of memory impairment may be minimal. The evidence adduced in support of an encoding deficit (Butters and Cermak, 1975) or an activation deficit (Talland, 1965) in the Boston group of patients might thus simply index the emotional state of this group of patients and may be quite unrelated to the major cause (as yet unexplained) of their profound amnesia. While it appears that changes in encoding strategies consequent upon minor degrees of depression do not inevitably lead to changes in levels of recognition performance (Hasher and Zachs, 1979), other extra-mnemonic deficits may well produce secondary memory problems in amnesics. Thus Stoff and Eagle (1971) have shown that normal subjects who report the use of 'organisational' strategies during learning not only have higher 'Similarities' scores on the WAIS than those subjects reporting the use of 'rehearsal' strategies, they also have higher free recall scores. Since dense amnesia can occur in the face of normal 'Similarities' scores (Mayes, Meudell and Neary, 1980) as noted previously, McDowall's (1979) patients who have low 'Similarities' scores might thus manifest less 'elaborative' encoding than controls and this, in turn, might lead to relatively minor additional memory problems superimposed upon the primary source of their deficit.

Finally, failure in the effortful processes involved in imagery have also been implicated as a major cause of human amnesia (Baddeley, 1973). In an early study Baddeley and Warrington (1973) showed that their amnesics were unable to take advantage of imagery instructions in order to help remember four unrelated nouns and Baddeley (1973) concluded that '. . . amnesics may be defective in their ability to utilise the imagery component of semantic memory'. On the other hand Cermak (1975) has demonstrated that when the task is made easier for amnesics by using only two nouns, then amnesics can form effective interacting images. Further, Kapur (1978) has shown that amnesics can carry out complex image requiring tasks, without a memory component, as rapidly and as accurately as normal people. It seems likely then that any apparent differences between amnesics and controls in the use of imagery in memory tests are likely to occur as a result of amnesia rather than be its cause.

2   *Failure of 'automatic' processes encoding frequency and recency information.* While elaborate encoding processes like rehearsal and organisation require attention and effort, Hasher and Zachs (1979) have argued that contextual information, like the frequency with which an item was presented and when an item was presented, are encoded automatically (without intention) and with little cognitive effort. It is a failure of the processes responsible for encoding these types of contextual information that Huppert and Piercy (1978a) have suggested may be responsible for organic amnesia. Failure to encode contextual information such as the time at which an event occurred might well have profound effects upon memory if both recall and recognition processes critically involve contextual information.

The evidence for a failure to encode contextual information in amnesics comes from an experiment in which these patients were shown to be poor at making recency judgements (judgements about when an item had been shown) relative to recognition judgements, in comparison to normal controls (Huppert and Piercy, 1976). On the basis of these results Huppert and Piercy suggested that amnesics have comparatively little difficulty in judging the familiarity of an item but a profound difficulty in assigning a temporal context to that item. In a further experiment, Huppert and Piercy (1978a) showed that amnesics differed in their patterns of performance in judgements of the recency and the frequency with which pictures had been previously presented. In particular, amnesics tended to judge recent items as having occurred frequently and frequent items as having occurred recently. Because amnesics were thus unable to discriminate between the effects of repeated as opposed to recent presentation of pictures, and *vice versa*, while normal controls largely were able to make these discriminations, Huppert and Piercy (1978a) concluded that amnesics' frequency judgements were based solely on an assessment of trace 'strength' but that controls' judgements were determined partly by an assessment of trace 'strength' but also by the availability of specific temporal and frequency information unavailable to amnesics.

However, as Huppert and Piercy (1978a) note themselves these differences between amnesics and normal people may simply be a function of differences in overall trace strength in the two groups of subjects since in both Huppert and Piercy (1976) and Huppert and Piercy (1978a) both groups were tested at the same retention intervals. In other words difficulties in determining when an item was presented and disentangling recency and frequency information may not be necessarily characteristic of amnesic memory; they might also be characteristic of 'weak' normal memory, especially if specific contextual information becomes unavailable relatively more rapidly than other attributes of memory. Without the appropriate normal control group (i.e. one tested at a longer retention interval than the amnesics) it is therefore unclear whether the different patterns of performance between amnesics and controls, when both are tested at the same retention interval, reflect differences in the efficiency with which 'automatic', contextual information is encoded or whether they reflect 'weak' memory in the amnesic group.

3   *Retrograde amnesia and encoding deficit theories.* Theories about human amnesia have been formulated largely to explain anterograde amnesia but, of course, these theories should also have implications for the retrograde amnesia normally observed in amnesic patients.

In their simplest forms, encoding deficit theories would predict that after the onset of amnesia, while there would be a more or less severe difficulty in learning new information, memories acquired before the amnesia began should be accessed normally since they were acquired and stored normally. That is, there should be no retrograde amnesia. This is clearly false: retrograde amnesia is regularly found in alcoholic amnesics (Seltzer and Benson, 1974; Marslen-Wilson and Teuber, 1975; Albert, Butters and Levin, 1979a; Meudell, Northen, Snowden and Neary, 1980) as well as in amnesia resulting from other etiologies. However, in attempts to reconcile these data with encoding deficit theories, Albert *et al.* (1979a) have suggested that there may be two possible explanations for the presence of extended retrograde amnesia in alcoholic amnesics. First, since alcoholic amnesics may not be immune from the chronic effects of prolonged alcohol abuse and malnutrition, the alcoholic amnesic may simply acquire less information over time due to an increasing deficit in information processing. In other words '. . . the retrograde amnesia of alcoholic patients with Korsakoff's disease may be considered secondary to a primary deficit in establishing new memories (i.e. anterograde amnesia)'. On the other hand, retrograde amnesias of varying duration do occur in amnesics of other etiologies where the onset is known to be acute e.g. following bilateral temporal lobectomy (Marslen-Wilson and Teuber, 1975) and electroconvulsive therapy (Squire and Chace, 1975). Genuine retrograde amnesia therefore appears to occur in patients in whom there are no relevant chronic complications and, accordingly, it is unlikely that all the observed retrograde amnesia of alcoholic amnesics can be attiributed to a progressively worsening acquisition deficit.

A genuine retrograde amnesia might be associated with a semantic coding deficit if deficient semantic processes operated at retrieval as well as at acquisition. That is, premorbid memories might well be efficiently semantically encoded but given postmorbid semantic coding deficits they would be accessed by semantically deficient retrieval processes. Just as with anterograde amnesia however, this view should predict that amnesics would be differentially aided when their memory for premorbid events is helped by giving semantic hints at retrieval. Albert *et al.* (1979a) have shown, however, that the benefits to amnesics of both phonemic and semantic hints in tests of very old memories are no greater than those seen in normal controls. Just as with anterograde amnesia therefore (Mayes, Meudell and Neary, 1978), this more subtle version of the semantic coding deficit theory appears unlikely to explain the retrograde amnesia of alcoholic amnesics.

The second type of explanation for the presence of a retrograde amnesia in the face of an acquisitional deficit is based upon the specula-tion that '. . . separate anatomical circuits . . . (*exist*) . . . for anterograde and retrograde processing' (Albert *et al.*, 1979a). In other words retrieval of already acquired memories may be mediated by a different system from that which mediates the acquisition and storage of new information. Logically, therefore, according to the hypothesis, lesions may produce one of three types of memory impairment; anterograde amnesia and retrograde amnesia (which putatively, is quite unrelated to the antero-grade amnesia), anterograde amnesia without retrograde amnesia and, finally, retrograde amnesia without anterograde amnesia. Retrograde amnesia occurring in association with anterograde amnesia is, of course, frequently noted and there is, in addition, some evidence for dissociation between retrograde and anterograde amnesias. Thus Squire and Slater (1978) have reported that a penetrating injury to the middle cranial fossa led to an anterograde amnesia but to a minimal retrograde amnesia; similarly Albert, Butters and Levin (1979b) have claimed that chronic alcoholics (not diagnosed as Korsakoff amnesics) showed no retrograde amnesia in the face of a mild anterograde amnesia. Milner, Branch and Rasmussen (1962) and Milner (1966) have reported a related effect in which an injection of sodium amytal to the contralateral side of a pre-existing temporal lobe lesion sometimes produced both an anterograde and retrograde amnesia; after the effects of the drug wore off, however, the retrograde amnesia disappeared but the patients still had little memory for information presented while under the influence of the drug. Similarly, it has been reported (Frederiks, 1979) that recovered transient global amnesics may completely regain their memory for the pre-traumatic period whilst still being unable to remember the events which occurred during the anterograde amnesia episode.

The opposite pattern of results, retrograde amnesia without antero-grade amnesia, has been claimed by Goldberg, Mathis, Hughes and Bilder (1980) who have reported a case in which recovery from antero-grade amnesia was observed in the absence of recovery from retrograde amnesia. Finally direct evidence for existence of two distinct anatomical sites for anterograde and retrograde processing has also been reported by Fedio and Van Buren (1974). In electrical stimulation studies with epileptic patients, Fedio and Van Buren found two distinct sites within the left temporal lobe, stimulation of the posterior region of which pro-duced retrograde memory deficits while stimulation of the anterior region produced anterograde memory problems.

While taken together this evidence is suggestive of separate antero-grade and retrograde processing systems, some caution must be exercised in interpreting the data for two reasons. First, it is likely that anterograde severity might be related to retrograde severity (e.g. Russell, 1959) and if the typical questionnaire techniques for the assessment of long-term memories are not especially sensitive then, at least in relatively mild amnesics, absence of retrograde amesia might reflect the relative insensitivity of long-term memory tests rather than a dissociation between anterograde and retrograde processing systems. In this connec-tion it is interesting to note that, in contrast to the finding of Albert *et al.* (1979b), a detailed examination of the data of Marslen-Wilson and Teuber (1975) who used different test material to Albert *et al.*, shows that their chronic alcoholic (non-Korsakoff) group *did* show a retrograde amnesia in comparison to controls. Second, both in the sodium amytal experiment (Milner, 1966) and in the stimulation experiment (Fedio and Van Buren, 1974), retrograde amnesia was assessed by measuring memory for in-formation presented seconds or minutes before injections or stimulation and it is therefore unclear to what extent it is possible to generalise from these studies to studies which show retrograde amnesias extending in decades. Even if, in principle, such dissociations between anterograde and retrograde amnesia could be demonstrated, the primary cause of anterograde amnesia would still remain an open issue since there is no necessary relationship between the separate origins of anterograde and retrograde amnesia, and encoding deficit explanations of anterograde amnesia.

B RETRIEVAL DEFICIT THEORIES

1 *Anterograde amnesia and retrieval deficit theories.* The best known modern protagonists of the view that amnesia represents a retrieval deficit are Warrington and Weiskrantz (1973); Weiskrantz and Warrington (1975a). They argue that encoding and consolidation/storage processes occur normally in amnesics but the patients' problem arises when memories are to be accessed. What form does the retrieval deficit take? Warrington and Weiskrantz (1973); Weiskrantz and Warrington (1975a) argued originally that at retrieval the amnesic suffers from an excessive amount of inter-ference from previously learned or other irrelevant information. This irrelevant material thus increases the amount of response competition in amnesics relative to normal people and it is argued that this excessive response competition is the source of the amnesics' deficit.

The evidence for this position depends upon three major pieces of evidence. First, while amnesics' memory for words when assessed by free recall or 'Yes/No' recognition techniques was grossly impaired in com-parison to controls, their memory for words when given partial information (the initial letters of the word or a degraded version of it) was relatively normal (Warrington and Weiskrantz, 1970, 1974). In other words while the processes underlying recall and recognition do not help the amnesic reduce excessive response competition, providing partial information or hints does help constrain the number of competing irrele-vant responses. A similar effect has been noted in paired associate learning by Winocur and Weiskrantz (1976) who showed that while amnesics were grossly impaired in learning unrelated paired associates, they were differentially improved in comparison to controls if the number of competing 'response' terms was reduced by employing semantically or phonetically related paired associates (the relationship thus constraining the range of possible responses to the 'stimulus' term).

Second, amnesics show a preponderance of intrusion errors from pre-viously learned lists when attempting to retrieve the items belonging to a current list. This effect has been noted in free recall (Warrington and Weiskrantz, 1968a), in the Peterson and Peterson paradigm (Meudell, Butters and Montegomery, 1978) and the reversal trials of 'reversal learning' experiments (Winocur and Weiskrantz, 1976; Warrington and Weiskrantz, 1974; Warrington and Weiskrantz, 1978). The presence of these prior list intrusions is cited as direct evidence for the greater pre-sence in amnesics of irrelevant, competing information which is causally related to their memory deficit.

Third, cued memory tasks are not the only conditions under which amnesics can show good learning and retention (see Baddeley, 1980, for a comprehensive review). Thus Warrington and Weiskrantz (1968b) have shown that amnesics can learn to identify fragmented pictures from the Gollin (1960) series and in addition show considerable 'savings' over long retention intervals. Similarly, Brooks and Baddeley (1976) have shown amnesics can learn and retain how to execute the Porteus Maze, how to assemble jig-saw puzzles and how to execute the pursuit rotor tracking task (see also Starr and Phillips, 1970; Corkin, 1968). Consistent with their theoretical position Warrington and Weiskrantz (1973) have argued that the common characteristic of these tasks is that, in normal people, they may be highly resistant to proactive interference. Accordingly the amnesic, who is putatively especially sensitive to such interference, might well be expected to perform well in comparison to normal people on these tasks relative to tasks which are more sensitive to the effects of proactive interference.

The notion that amnesics are especially sensitive to response competition from previously acquired information is also weakly supported by the observation that prior learning severely impedes the rate of learning by amnesic subjects of a subsequent task sharing the same recall cues. This effect occurs in paired associate learning (Winocur and Weiskrantz, 1976) and in three letter cued recall (Warrington and Weiskrantz, 1974, 1978). However, it may be simply that amnesics learn more slowly that controls (e.g. Meudell and Mayes, 1980) and the learning rates in such 'reversal' experiments are reflections of this effect rather than the effects of any prior learning. In other words an appropriate control would be to require amnesics and controls to learn a list of words, their memory being tested by prompts, in the *absence* of a previously learned list.

One additional prediction of the hypothesis that amnesics suffer excessively from competitive interference at retrieval is that, relative to normal subjects, their recall should be helped in rough proportion to the number of competing alternatives that cues render irrelevant. Thus, amnesics should gain less differential advantages from three letter cues which begin 10 or more common words as compared to cues which begin, say, 2 words. Although weak evidence for such an effect exists (Warrington and Weiskrantz, 1974), Warrington and Weiskrantz (1978) now conclude that the majority of the available evidence suggests that with retention intervals of an hour or less there is no good reason to suppose that for amnesics 'the cue operates by constraining response alternatives *per se*'. Even if the cue-constraint does not occur however it is a moot point whether this is incompatible with a response competition explanation of amnesia. Warrington and Weiskrantz (1978) themselves suggest that information may decay or extinguish abnormally slowly in amnesics so that with retention intervals presumably longer than an hour, the cue-constraint effect should operate, if this modified effect is not found it could still be argued that with short retention intervals the effective number of words to which a cue leads may be considerably less than the number of common words which it begins (Baddeley, personal communication). Thus, seeing a word already in long-term memory may 'prime' it such that the probability is increased that it will be recalled by cueing for a short period afterwards. If this 'priming' function is normal in amnesics then at short retention intervals, regardless of the number of words which a cue nominally leaves appropriate as responses, there will be, in fact, only one or two which a subject is likely to produce. Like the slow decay hypothesis, this view needs to be tested by examining the effects of cueing at more prolonged retention intervals.

In general terms, therefore, the Warrington and Weiskrantz hypothesis suggests that the amnesics' problem occurs because of a difficulty in discriminating relevant from irrelevant information in memory at retrieval. Why might this occur? What causes excessive response competition in amnesics? Three suggestions have been made. First, it has been hypothesised that previously learned information extinguishes or decays more slowly in amnesics than in normal people (Warrington and Weiskrantz, 1978). Discrimination of relevant items is thus made more difficult for amnesics than for normal people because, somewhat para-doxically, irrelevant information is still available to amnesics at times when it is unavailable to controls. The only direct evidence for slower decay in amnesics compared to controls comes from a study which showed that cued recall of words which were uniquely specified by their first three letters (e.g. juice) was actually better after a 24-hour delay in amnesics than in controls (Warrington and Weiskrantz, 1978). In this study however, as Warrington and Weiskrantz note, amnesics were rather better than controls at generating responses to three letter prompts in the absence of a memory component. The superior delayed cued recall in amnesics might therefore reflect this latter phenomenon rather than abnormally slow decay in amnesics.

A second hypothesis is that discrimination of relevant from irrelevant information is difficult for amnesics because they have difficulty in judging the 'familiarity' of information in memory (Gaffan, 1972). Thus in tasks where familiarity judgments might be critical for adequate execu-tion, amnesics should perform badly, but in tasks where familiarity judgments may not be critical they should perform relatively normally. In cueing tasks, for example, judgments of familiarity might not play an important role while in recognition tasks, where 'new' items have to be discriminated from 'old' items, judgments of familiarity may well be critically involved. Accordingly, amnesics might be relatively good at cueing tasks but relatively poor at recognition tasks in comparison to controls. Some direct evidence that familiarity judgments might be im-paired in amnesics compared to normal people tested at the same retention interval has been shown by Mayes and Meudell (1981b). Mayes and Meudell asked their amnesics and controls not only to produce a response to three letter prompts after learning a list of words but also to indicate their confidence in whether their response was, in fact, the correct one. While there was no significant difference in the number of correct responses to cues between amnesics and controls, amnesics felt confident about far fewer of their correct responses than did the controls. (A signal detection analysis on the confidence data showed that this result was not a trivial consequence of the adoption of a stricter criterion by the amnesics). If 'confidence' is an indicator of familiarity of an item then this result provides evidence that, at least in comparison to normal people tested at the *same* retention interval, amnesics do appear to have a deficiency in their ability to judge the familiarity of an item in memory. Of course the bases of judgments of familiarity are largely unknown but, apart from an assessment of overall trace strength, familiarity judgments could be conceivably based upon contextual information. Since abnormal sensitivity to learning context has been claimed in amnesics (Winocur and Kinsbourne, 1978), a related hypothesis to Gaffan's and a third way in which amnesics might have difficulty in discriminating relevant from irrelevant information at retrieval, is to hypothesise that amnesics are deficient at context retrieval. Winocur and Kinsbourne showed that after learning an initial paired associate word list, changing the environment in which a second competing list was learned significantly improved the amnesics' learning of the second list in comparison to a condition in which the second list was learned in the same environment as the first. Normal controls, on the other hand, were unaffected by the 'context' shift. On the basis of this and related results (Winocur and Olds, 1978; Winocur and Kinsbourne, 1978) Winocur and Kinsbourne argue that when 'item' information is highlighted by the presence of distinctive contextual cues, amnesics can use this information to select appropriate responses, but under ordinary learning conditions the amnesic fails to retrieve the contextual information which would, in normal people, help to discriminate relevant from irrelevant information. In other words disentangling one memory from another might critically depend upon assigning an appropriate context to items in memory. Context information might be critical in discriminating 'new' from 'old' items in recognition tests, for example, but in producing responses to prompts retrieval of the conditions under which items were originally learned may be less critical for adequate performance to occur.

A major interpretative problem with the evidence upon which each of these views is based, however, is the fact that none of the studies, so far reported, has any control for memory strength been introduced. Specifically it might be that normal individuals with 'weak' memory, in comparison to those with 'strong' memory, might also show, first, relative sparing of cued recall in comparison to recognition, second, a loss of familiarity for items that are correctly produced from memory and third, an especial sensitivity to context manipulations. In other words the phenomena which have been claimed to be the causes of amnesia may be, in fact, simply the consequences of it. Each of these three possibilities will now be discussed in turn.

First, following Woods and Piercy (1974) and Squire, Wetzel and Slater (1978), Mayes and Meudell (1981a) have examined three letter cued recall and 'Yes/No' recognition performance in groups of normal people tested 15 minutes, 7 days or 6 weeks after the original learning. With appropriate guessing controls for both cued recall and recognition, it was found that while recognition performance dropped systematically from the 15 minutes retention interval through the 7 day interval to the six week test, cued recall performance was worse at 7 days than at 15 minutes test but there was no difference in cueing performance between the 7 day test and the 6 weeks one. In other words, with very 'weak' memory, in comparison to 'stronger' memories, cued recall is a relatively effective retrieval procedure while recognition is a relatively ineffective retrieval method. It is apparent, however, that memories must be very 'weak' for this effect to occur since it does not occur with retention intervals of one day (Weiskrantz and Warrington, 1975b) nor, in our experiment, did it occur with a 7 day retention interval although Squire *et al.* (1978) did observe a cue/recognition interaction at this period. In any event it is clear that several independent studies have now shown that differential benefit from cued recall is not only a characteristic of amnesic memory, it is also a characteristic of the memories of normal people who have largely forgotten. Amnesic subjects are differentially aided by cues but so are normal people with 'weak' memory.

Second, in the same experiment (Mayes and Meudell, 1981a) in order to examine the feelings of familiarity that normal people have about their memories as these become progressively 'weaker', we also asked our normal subjects to rate their confidence about the accuracy of their responses to the three letter prompts. When tested shortly after learning these normal people felt confident about most of the responses that they had, in fact, produced correctly. However, as retention interval increased, and thus memory 'strength' decreased, the normal people progressively began to report that they felt they were guessing about most of the responses, which, nevertheless, they had correctly produced in response to the cues. Normal people with 'weak' memory thus show the same type of loss of confidence or familiarity in their (accurate) memories as do amnesics tested shortly after learning. Further, a direct comparison between amnesics' and controls' confidence judgments when both groups' memories are equivalently weak (Mayes, Meudell and Neary, 1980) showed amnesics made identical judgments in their confidence about recognition choices as did controls. Amnesics do show a loss of familiarity or confidence in their memories as Gaffan (1972) suggests but so do normal people who have largely forgotten.

Third, following the design of a study examining context effects on learning in animals (Winocur and Olds, 1978), we have investigated the effects of learning paired associates in one environment and being tested in another in groups of normal people who have 'strong' and 'weak'

memory (Mayes, Meudell and Som, 1981). In contrast to a group
with 'strong' memory, who showed little change in performance when
the environment was changed between learning and testing relative to a
condition where the acquisition and test environments were identical, a
group with 'weak' memory were significantly impaired when the context
was changed between learning and testing in comparison to the unchanged context condition. In other words just like amnesics (Winocur
and Kinsbourne, 1978), normal people who have largely forgotten are
especially sensitive to context manipulations when they are compared to
normal subjects who still have relatively intact ('strong') memory.
Deficient retrieval of contextual information may be problematical for
amnesics but it is also problematical for normal people with 'weak'
memory. In this study we also compared the retention of highly associated and relatively weakly associated paired associates in normal people
with 'weak' and 'strong' memories. People with 'strong' memories
(tested shortly after learning) showed relatively good retention of both
high and medium associate word pairs, but people with 'weak'
memory (tested 7 days after learning) showed very good retention of
highly associated paired associates but extremely poor retention of
associates that were less highly related. This effect clearly parallels the
effect observed in amnesics, namely that amnesics are relatively good at
learning highly related paired associates but are relatively poor at learning unrelated paired associates in comparison to normal controls
(Winocur and Weiskrantz, 1976; Cutting, 1978). Amnesics do retain
highly related paired associates better than weakly associated or unrelated pairs but so do normal people who have largely forgotten due to
the passage of time.

Hypotheses which attribute the amnesics' impairment to a retrieval
failure whether consequent upon slow decay, loss of familiarity or
inefficient use of contextual information, naturally explain the occurrence
of a preponderance of prior list intrusion errors in amnesics' recall performance. Indeed their excessive presence in amnesics appears to
provide critical support for the general hypothesis that discriminating
relevant from irrelevant information is the source of the amnesics'
impairment. Although Piercy (1977) has questioned whether these
intrusion errors occur to any greater extent in amnesics than in controls
and whether, numerically, they are very large, Meudell, Butters and
Montgomery (1978) showed that amnesics made almost 4 times more
prior list intrusion errors than did controls and 66 percent of all amnesics'
errors were prior list intrusion errors while this was only true of 43
percent of the controls' total errors. The greater occurrence of prior list
intrusion in amnesics' recall compared to controls therefore does appear
to be a genuine effect. Does it provide unequivocal support for retrieval
deficit hypothesis? The answer is probably negative since the occurrence
of prior list intrusion errors may simply reflect the fact that, even in

normal people, contextual information (e.g. in which list a particular word occurred) becomes unavailable more rapidly than that specifying the nature of the item itself. If amnesics arrive at states of 'weak' memory more rapidly than controls then the greater occurrence of prior list intrusion errors in amnesics compared to controls may be a consequence of 'weaker' memory in the former group in comparison to the latter. Some evidence that the occurrence of prior list intrusion errors is related to memory strength comes from the Warrington and Weiskrantz (1968a) study. Warrington and Weiskrantz gave their amnesics and controls 1, 5 or 10 learning trials on lists of words and tested memory by free recall 1, 5 or 15 minutes after learning. While there were no clear trends at the one minute test, at the 5 minute interval the normal control group showed most prior list intrusions after a single learning trial, next most after 5 learning trials and least intrusions after 10 learning trials. Similarly, at the 15 minute interval the 10 learning trial condition showed least prior list intrusion errors although at this interval the 5 learning trial condition produced fewer intrusions than did the single learning trial condition. Taken as a whole, however, these results quite strongly suggest that, if number of learning trials is directly related to memory strength, the fewer the number of learning trials normal people have (and thus the 'weaker' their memory) the more likely they are to produce intrusions from previously learned lists. Amnesics may thus produce a greater number of intrusion errors than controls, not because they have a selective retrieval deficit, but because on the whole their memories are considerably 'weaker' than controls tested at the same retention interval.

The fact that certain semantic, perceptual and motor tasks are performed relatively normally by amnesics, putatively because they involve retrieval processes which reduce or eliminate the problem of discriminating relevant from irrelevant material, might appear to provide critical support for a retrieval deficit hypothesis of amnesia. However, other hypotheses, not involving the notion of interference, can quite readily explain the relative sparing of these types of memories. First, it might be that these kinds of tasks are subserved by different parts of the brain than those damaged in the amnesic syndrome: in other words the limbic system and related structures are not involved in the mediation of these skills. Second, it is possible that the kinds of tasks on which amnesics show significant learning and retention are those tasks which normal people find particularly easy to learn and on which they show relatively large 'savings' scores over long retention intervals. In other words there may be nothing special at all about the tasks that amnesics show some acquisition and storage other than that they are easier, for unknown reasons, than, for example, free recall or recognition of unrelated lists of words. This possibility requires that while amnesics may well show significant acquisition and storage of some (putatively relatively easy) tasks, they should never show *entirely normal* learning and retention.

With the exception of one report of pursuit rotor learning (Brooks and Baddeley, 1976) which is, in fact, contradicted by an earlier study (Corkin, 1968), amnesics invariably appear to learn less rapidly and retain less over equivalent retention intervals than do normal controls whether the materials to be learned are fragmented words (Weiskrantz and Warrington, 1970a), fragmented pictures (Warrington and Weiskrantz, 1968b), the Porteus Maze test (Brooks and Baddeley, 1976) the names of inkblot figures which progressively approximated a 'proper' animal shape (Williams, 1953) or jig-saws (Brooks and Baddeley, 1976).

In this context it is worth also considering the preservation of linguistic skills and other premorbidly acquired skills such as piano playing (Starr and Phillips, 1970) or drawing skills (Zangwill, 1950) that amnesics can demonstrate in the face of dense amnesia for day-to-day events. In the case of linguistic skills, for example, Kinsbourne and Wood (1975) have argued that the preservation of these skills in amnesics might indicate the existence of separate 'semantic' and 'episodic' memory systems (crudely, memory for knowledge and memory for personal events, respectively) and that episodic but not semantic memory is impaired in amnesia. Two other explanations are however, possible. First, the preservation of some premorbid memories may simply occur for the same (unknown) reason that some 'episodic' information also appears to be preserved premorbidly (see next section). Second, and relatedly, those premorbid skills that are still retained may be those which were extensively over-rehearsed prior to the illness (Huppert and Piercy, 1981).

A further observation on these tasks for which amnesics show some learning and retention is that in some situations the amnesic can carry out a particular task with some accuracy but yet manifest no recollection of ever having done so before (Claparède, 1911; Weiskrantz and Warrington, 1979). This observation has led Baddeley (1980), following Weiskrantz (1978), to suggest that there may be something anomolous about the amnesic's 'metamemory'. That is, the amnesic patient can acquire information normally but he does not have normal conscious access to the results of his learning and, accordingly, in tasks where this conscious access is not necessary for good memory (such as certain semantic, perceptual and motor tasks) the amnesic may perform relatively normally. This hypothesis has strong similarities with Gaffan's (1972) 'familiarity' loss hypothesis and we have already seen that being able to execute cueing tasks but yet not feel any great confidence in the fact that one has done so correctly is a feature of 'weak' normal memory just as much as it is a feature of amnesic memory. Furthermore, recent results from our laboratory (Meudell and Mayes, 1981b) suggest that if normal people trained on a task requiring them to search for a hidden shape in a cartoon drawing and then are retested some time later (when their memories are 'weak') they show significant savings (in terms of reaction time) in finding the shape compared to their original performance, despite very poor ability to recognise that they have seen the actual cartoon before. Relatively poor 'metamemory' is therefore a characteristic of normal people who have largely forgotten as well as of amnesics.

We have shown therefore that the extant pieces of evidence for a retrieval failure in amnesics, including the differential benefit of cueing to amnesics which Warrington and Weiskrantz (1978) deem cruicial for any retrieval deficit hypothesis are, in fact, just as compatible with the view that amnesics simply have a 'weaker' memory than normal people tested at the same retention interval. In other words we believe that an amnesic's memory shortly after learning is probably similar to that of a normal person's after a considerable degree of forgetting. Of course in the absence of further data, this claim does not discriminate between acquisition, storage and retrieval failure explanations of amnesia since normal people could forget for any one of these reasons. Unfortunately there is no universally agreed theory for the reasons why normal people forget. Much of the evidence upon which the interference theory of forgetting has been buttressed can be shown, for example, to be quite compatible with the conception of a noisy, decaying trace (Baddeley, 1976). In the absence of an accepted theory of normal forgetting, interactions between amnesic groups and normal control groups across particular independent variables (e.g. different types of retrieval methods such as cueing and recognition) might well be *consistent* with any chosen hypothesis of the amnesics deficit but cannot provide evidence *critical* for the hypothesis.

2 *Retrograde amnesia and retrieval deficit theories.* Hypotheses which attribute the amnesics' anterograde deficit to an impairment in retrieving memories naturally predict, without additional assumptions, that premorbid memories should be inaccessible to the amnesic for the same reasons that postmorbid memories are inaccessible. Accordingly retrograde amnesia is a strong prediction from such theories. In addition to predicting the presence of retrograde amnesia, retrieval deficit views of the amnesics' impairment also predict that *all* premorbid memories, however remote in time, should be impaired with the magnitude of the impairment, in comparison to controls, being proportional to the magnitude of the retrieval deficit. This prediction, however, appears to run counter to the often reported clinical observation that amnesic patients often show extremely good recall of their own very remote past. In other words clinical impression suggests that in comparison to normal people, whose more recent memories are invariably better than their more remote memories (e.g. Warrington and Sanders, 1971), amnesics are characterised by a gradient in their memories for remote events such that relatively recent events are extremely poorly remembered but more remote events in time are rather better remembered. Such gradients, which have been demonstrated more formally in a variety of studies (e.g. Seltzer and Benson, 1974), are clearly inconsistent with current retrieval deficit explanations of amnesia.

On the other hand, the assessment of remote memories is made difficult by the fact that some remote memories might be rehearsed or
reviewed more frequently in comparison to more recently acquired
memories. In other words, some tests of memory relating to events or
people from the remote past might be easier, in that they relate to people
or events of more lasting significance, than tests of memory for more
recent happenings or individuals. Thus in amnesics, the apparent selective preservation of relatively old memories might be simply an artefact of
differences in the amount of exposure to the material involved in comparison to that of relatively recently acquired memories. On this basis
Sanders and Warrington (1971) have argued that if tests of remote
memory are designed in which the 'difficulty' of test items is equated
across recent and remote time periods, no preservation of remote
memories occurs in amnesic patients. Rather, Sanders and Warrington
have claimed that under such conditions amnesics are simply worse than
controls by a constant amount across all premorbid time periods and, of
course, this result was interpreted as being consistent with a retrieval
deficit hypothesis. Unfortunately, however, in selecting items which
were of comparable difficulty across the recent and remote past, Sanders
and Warrington (1971) chose items whose overall difficulty was such as to
depress their amnesics' recall and recognition performance to 'floor'
levels (Sanders and Warrington, 1975). Interpretations of the pattern of
amnesics' performance across the various time periods, in comparison to
that of the controls, is therefore impossible. In a later study (Sanders and
Warrington, 1975), using a 'famous face' recognition task, various
prompts were used in order to get the amnesics off the 'floor'. Under
these conditions amnesics not only scored well above floor levels but also
showed a similar pattern of performance across recent and remote
memories as a normal control group who were asked to recall the names
of the faces without prompts. Since no control group with prompts was
employed, however, and since such hints would also aid normal peoples'
memory, it still remains an open issue from this study also as to whether
the amnesics' older memories were relatively better preserved than more
recent memories in comparison to controls or whether, as retrieval deficit
views might predict, the pattern of performance across all time periods
was identical in amnesics and controls.

In a more recent attempt to control for difficulty of items in tests of
memory for remote events Albert et al. (1979a) have split their tests of
premorbid memory into those items which were 'difficult' (questions
about people or events which were famous for a brief period and then
faded into obscurity) and 'easy' (questions about people or events which
had been repeatedly exposed to the public over a number of years).
Irrespective of the ease or difficulty of the questions, irrespective of
whether memory was assessed by recall or recognition and in the absence
of floor or ceiling effects, Albert et al. (1979a) found a temporal gradient of

remote memories in amnesics such that, in relation to controls, older memories were spared more than relatively recent memories. Further support for the hypothesis that early memories are relatively resistant to manipulations which disrupt more recently acquired memories has been provided by Squire and Chace (1975). With item difficulty controlled, Squire and Chace showed that ECT given to depressed patients produced a retrograde amnesia covering 1–3 years but earlier memories were unaffected by the effects of ECT. Similarly Marslen-Wilson and Teuber (1975) have found that H.M. showed normal memory for events occurring several years prior to his temporal lobectomy. Although Marslen-Wilson and Teuber did not control for item difficulty in their tests, this result seems unlikely to be due to lack of sensitivity of the tests since head injured and alcoholic control groups both performed worse than H.M. at tests of remote time periods where he performed at least as well as a normal control group. Further since the head injured and alcoholic groups had less severe anterograde amnesia than H.M. the preservation of remote memories in the latter is unlikely to be a consequence of a mild anterograde deficit.

Taken as a whole, therefore, even when variations in item difficulty due to variations in degree of learning opportunities are controlled for, there does appear to be at least some *prima facie* evidence for the relative preservation of older memories in amnesics. If correct, this preservation of older memories presents a problem not only for retrieval deficit theories of amnesia, it is also problematical for any current hypothesis about the amnesics' deficit. The hypothesis that retrograde amnesia occurs as a secondary consequence of a learning disorder (Albert *et al.*, 1979a) might explain a long retrograde amnesia with a temporal gradient but as Albert *et al.* (1979a) note, even though remote memories were relatively spared, their amnesics never reached normal retrieval for any time period tested i.e. including those periods before an anterograde deficit could be conceivably present. The alternative hypothesis (Albert *et al.*, 1979b) that anterograde and retrograde processing are mediated by different systems within the brain has no obvious implication as to why remote memories might be relatively spared.

C   STORAGE DEFICIT THEORIES

There are two types of storage deficit explanations of the amnesic syndrome. The first are consolidation deficit hypotheses, which attribute the amnesics' impairment to a failure in those processes which occur shortly after learning and which establish or 'transfer' information in memory into a relatively permanent form, and the second are hypotheses which consider the amnesics' memory problems are a consequence of more rapid loss or decay of information from store in comparison to normal people. The efficiency of consolidation processes and subsequent rates of forgetting could be directly related or conceivably they might be independent factors in memory. There are three possibilities relating the two factors together. First, faulty consolidation may render an amnesic's memory trace 'weaker' overall than a normal person's immediately after learning but the subsequent rate of loss of information from this trace may be identical to that of a normal person's. Second, impaired consolidation may make an amnesic's trace not only 'weaker' than a control subject's initially but also, consequentially, it may affect the rate of loss of information from the trace. Finally, consolidation processes may occur normally in amnesics but for other, unknown reasons the traces might decay at an abnormally fast rate in comparison to normal people.

Weiskrantz (1978) has recently marshalled four pieces of evidence which he believes mitigates against storage deficit views of amnesia. These are the differential benefit that amnesics derive from cues, the occurrence of prior list intrusions errors in amnesics' recall protocols, the fact that amnesics can learn some tasks like identifying fragmented pictures relatively normally, and the dissociations which occur between an amnesic's ability to carry out certain memory tasks and his ability to recognise that the task had been previously learned. However, to the extent that a consolidation impairment or rapid forgetting might lead to 'weak' memory in amnesics, we have already argued that these, as well as other pieces of evidence, are readily compatible with a storage deficit. These effects, it was argued, rather than being involved causally in the amnesics' deficit, could be seen to be the *consequence* of forgetting. Of course, merely to demonstrate that extant data are consistent with a particular hypothesis is not to demonstrate that the hypothesis is, in fact, correct. Additional data are needed which provide selective support for one hypothesis but not for the others. Is there any direct evidence for a consolidation deficit and/or a more rapid rate of forgetting in amnesics?

Behavioural evidence for a consolidation failure in humans is notoriously difficult, if not impossible, to obtain, but we have recently observed some EEG abnormalities in amnesics which appeared to occur immediately after learning and which conceivably might be related to memory. Mayes, Boddy and Meudell (1980) showed amnesics and normal controls lists of words under intentional and incidental learning conditions and EEG power was measured in the 3 seconds following word offset. Both amnesics and controls showed greater overall power in the first second after word offset than they did in the following two-second period and amnesics showed less overall power than controls during the first second but not in the latter two seconds after word offset. It appears therefore that amnesics have an EEG power deficit which is confined to a very brief period following word exposure, their EEG in the resting state being in the normal range. It remains to be determined whether post stimulus EEG power is directly related to memory or not, but if it were, such an amnesic power deficit would clearly pose problems for encoding and retrieval deficit explanations of amnesia and might suggest some anomalous process occurring in amnesics at the time memories are being laid down.

Do amnesics forget faster than normal people? Since the rate of forgetting may be proportional to initial level of learning, comparisons between amnesics' and controls' rates of forgetting only make sense if the two groups are equated on initial level of performance. In two studies where this was not achieved (Williams, 1953; Warrington and Weiskrantz, 1968a) the results showed that amnesics forgot more rapidly than controls while in another (Huppert and Piercy, 1976) amnesics forgot at the same rate as controls. On the other hand, testing memory by fragmented versions of words, Weiskrantz and Warrington (1970a) showed that even when amnesics and controls were brought to the same initial level of performance, amnesics still retained less than controls at a one hour, at a 24 hour but not at a 72 hour retention interval. A similar result with a one hour retention interval, but using the initial letters of words as prompts, has been shown by Weiskrantz and Warrington (1970b). The picture is obviously not clear cut, however, since not only did Weiskrantz and Warrington (1970a) fail to observe differences in retention at 72 hours, Huppert and Piercy (1978b) failed to observe differences in retention between amnesics and controls at any interval. Huppert and Piercy showed that if amnesics and controls were equated for recognition performance by exposing pictures for 4 or 8 times as long to the amnesics, the amnesics showed an identical rate of forgetting over 7 days as did the normal individuals. Even in the much briefer retention intervals employed in the Peterson and Peterson (1959) paradigm and where performance is equated at immediate (nondistracted) test, faster forgetting than normal is observed in some studies (Cermak, Butters and Goodglass, 1971) but not in others (Baddeley and Warrington, 1970).

The issue of forgetting rates in amnesics is thus hardly clear, but, as we have already noted, it is uncertain anyway whether a consolidation deficit would predict the same or different forgetting rates in amnesics compared to normal people. Furthermore, even if there are genuinely no differences in forgetting rates between the two groups when initial performance is equated, it is not entirely clear which hypotheses this result would eliminate. On the one hand, giving eight times as long for amnesics to examine stimuli, for example, may allow an inefficient consolidation process long enough to produce a trace which is comparable in stability to that of a normal person's given the briefer exposure. On the other hand, on the assumption that amnesics' encoding processes operate normally, allowing longer for them to examine stimuli may result in them acquiring more information than controls: at least over the retention intervals so far sampled, rapid decay of a highly redundant trace in amnesics might then produce a similar observable forgetting rate to that produced by slow decay of a nonredundant trace in normal people (Brown, 1959). Finally if amnesics encode normally and lose information

at identical rates to normal people then giving amnesics extended processing time might ensure a more discriminable trace so that, if amnesics
had a retrieval deficit, their performance with many discriminable
retrieval cues might be comparable to that of a normal person's with
fewer. Similar rates of forgetting in amnesics and controls after
differential exposure of the material to be learned might well be compatible with encoding deficit hypotheses as Huppert and Piercy (1978b)
argue, but equally, they are just as compatible with consolidation deficits,
abnormally fast decay or impaired retrieval processes.

Since consolidation processes may take time to complete, some retrograde amnesia might be expected on the hypothesis of a consolidation
failure. On the other hand, since it would be unrealistic to assume that
consolidation processes take years to complete, the extended retrograde
amnesia noted in many patients can hardly be attributed to a failure to
consolidate premorbid memories acquired decades previously (though
see Wickelgren, 1979). Similarly, rapid forgetting of newly acquired information can hardly explain why premorbid memories are so grossly
impaired. Some other explanation must be sought, therefore, if storage
failure explanations of anterograde amnesia are to be made compatible
with the length of retrograde amnesia. Just as with encoding deficit
theories the most plausible hypothesis, although as yet unproved, may
be that separate circuits mediate anterograde and retrograde processes.
With both these putative systems damaged an anterograde and a retrograde amnesia would result but the factors involved in poor memory in
the former may be quite unrelated to those involved in the latter. With
such an assumption the hypothesis that anterograde amnesia is due to a
failure of storage processes, is readily compatible with the presence of
retrograde amnesia.

4   Conclusions

Many psychological theories are frequently supported by data which are
weak, in the sense that they are obtained without critical methodological
factors being considered, and ambiguous, in the sense that the data are
usually found, on reflection, to be compatible with most competing
theories. The field of amnesia, unfortunately appears to be no exception
to these considerations. Any new hypothesis about the amnesics' deficit
must be based upon experimental tests which control for the fact that
memories of different strengths are being compared in amnesics and
normal people. In addition, note must be taken of the fact that lesions
may cause multiple cognitive deficits and thus an observed cognitive
deficit may not be necessarily involved in the cause of amnesia. When
these factors are taken into account, we believe that there is no extant
evidence which unequivocally supports selective encoding or retrieval

failure in the anterograde problems of amnesic patients of any etiology. Further, although currently unfashionable, a consolidation hypothesis satisfactorily accounts for all the available data, and preliminary psychophysiological evidence appears to provide direct support for consolidation failure and not the alternative theories. Finally, a storage deficit of some description has the additional advantage that it might help to link the explanation for human memory disorders to the known functions, such as the modulation of physiological activation, of the relevant limbic system structures. Retrograde amnesia may not be an embarrassment to the view that anterograde amnesia is caused by a consolidation failure if retrieval of pretraumatic memories are mediated by different brain systems from those concerned with the acquisition and storage of posttraumatic memories.

References

Albert, M. S., Butters, N. and Levin, J. (1979a). Temporal gradients in the retrograde amnesia of patients with alcoholic Korsakoff's disease. *Archives of Neurology* **36**, 211–216

Albert, M. S., Butters, N. and Levin, J. (1979b). Memory for remote events in chronic alcoholics and alcoholic Korsakoff patients. *In* H. Begleiter and B. Kissen (eds), *Alcohol Intoxication and Withdrawal*. New York: Plenum Press

Baddeley, A. D. (1973). Theories of amnesia. *In* R. A. Kennedy and A. L. Wilkes (eds), *Studies in Long Term Memory*. London: Wiley

Baddeley, A. D. (1976). *The Psychology of Memory*. New York: Harper and Row

Baddeley, A. (1981). Amnesia: A minimal model and an interpretation. *In* L. S. Cermak (ed.), *Human Memory and Amnesia*. Hillsdale, New Jersey: Erlbaum

Baddeley, A. D. and Warrington, E. K. (1970). Amnesia and the distinction between long- and short-term memory. *Journal of Verbal Learning and Verbal Behaviour* **9**, 176–189

Baddeley, A. D. and Warrington, E. K. (1973). Memory coding and amnesia. *Neuropsychologia* **11**, 159–165

Bower, G. H. (1967). A multicomponent theory of the memory trace. *In* K. W. Spence and J. T. Spence (eds), *The Psychology of Learning and Motivation*, Vol. I. New York: Academic Press

Brooks, D. N. and Baddeley, A. D. (1976). What can amnesic patients learn? *Neuropsychologia* **14**, 111–122

Brown, J. (1959). Information, redundancy and decay of the memory trace. *In* National Physical Laboratory, Symposium No. 10, *Mechanisation of Thought Process*, Vol. 11. HMSO, London

Butters, N. and Cermak, L. (1975). Some analyses of amnesic syndromes in brain-damaged patients. *In* R. Isaacson and K. Pribram (eds), *The Hippocampus*, Vol. 2. New York: Plenum

Butters, N. and Cermak, L. S. (1976). Neuropsychological studies of alcoholic Korsakoff patients. *In* G. Goldstein and C. Neuringer (eds), *Empirical Studies of Alcoholism*. Cambridge, Mass.: Ballinger

Cermak, L. S. (1975). Imagery as an aid to retrieval for Korsakoff patients. *Cortex* **11**, 163–169

Cermak, L. S. (1978). The development and demise of verbal memory. *In* A. Caramazza and E. B. Zurif (eds), *Language Acquisition and Language Breakdown: Parallels and Divergencies*. Baltimore: John Hopkins University Press

Cermak, L. S. and Butters, N. (1972). The role of interference and encoding in the short-term memory deficits of Korsakoff patients. *Neuropsychologia* **10**, 89–95

Cermak, L., Butters, N. and Gerrein, J. (1973). The extent of the encoding ability of Korsakoff patients. *Neuropsychologia* **11**, 85–94

Cermak, L. S., Butters, N. and Goodglass, H. (1971). The extent of memory loss in Korsakoff patients. *Neuropsychologia* **9**, 307–315

Cermak, L. S., Butters, N. and Moreines, J. (1974). Some analyses of the verbal encoding deficit of alcoholic Korsakoff patients. *Brain and Language* **1**, 141–150

Cermak, L. S., Naus, M. J. and Reale, L. (1976). Rehearsal strategies of alcoholic Korsakoff patients. *Brain and Language* **3**, 375–385

Claparède, E. (1911). Récognition et moitié. *Archives of Psychology Genève* **11**, 79–90

Corkin, S. (1968). Acquisition of motor skill after bilateral temporal lobe excisions. *Neuropsychologia* **6**, 225–265

Cutting, J. (1978). A cognitive approach to Korsakoff's syndrome. *Cortex* **14**, 485–495

De Luca, D., Cermak, L. S. and Butters, N. (1975). An analysis of Korsakoff patients' recall following varying types of distractor activity. *Neuropsychologia* **13**, 271–280

Dricker, J., Butters, N., Berman, G., Samuels, I. and Carey, S. (1978). The recognition and encoding of faces by alcoholic Korsakoff and right hemisphere patients. *Neuropsychologia* **16**, 683–692

Fedio, P. and Van Buren, J. M. (1974). Memory deficits during electrical stimulation of the speech cortex in conscious man. *Brain and Language* **1**, 29–42

Frederiks, J. A. M. (1979). Transient global amnesia. *The INS Bulletin* June, 18

Gaffan, D. (1972). Loss of recognition memory in rats with lesions of the fornix. *Neuropsychologia* **10**, 327–341

Goldberg, E., Mathis, S., Hughes, J. and Bilder, R. (1980). Recovery from anterograde but not retrograde amnesia: role of reticular activation in long-term retrieval, *INS Bulletin* **5**, 18

Gollin, E. S. (1960). Developmental studies of visual recognition of incomplete objects. *Perceptual and Motor Skills* **11**, 289–298

Hasher, L. and Zacks, R. T. (1979). Automatic and effortful processes in memory. *Journal of Experimental Psychology (General)* **108**, 356–388

Huppert, F. A. and Piercy, M. (1976). Recognition memory in amnesic patients: effect of temporal context and familiarity of material. *Cortex* **12**, 3–20

Huppert, F. A. and Piercy, M. (1978a). The role of trace strength in recency and frequency judgements by amnesic and control subjects. *Quarterly Journal of Experimental Psychology* **30**, 346–354

Huppert, F. A. and Piercy, M. (1978b). Dissociation between learning and remembering in organic amnesia. *Nature* **275**, 317–318

Huppert, F. A. and Piercy, M. (1981). Learning and forgetting in amnesia. *In* L. S. Cermak (ed.), *Human Memory and Amnesia*. Hillsdale, New Jersey: Erlbaum

Kapur, N. (1978). Visual imagery capacity of alcoholic Korsakoff patients. *Neuropsychologia* **16**, 517–519

Kinsbourne, M. and Wood, F. (1975). Short-term memory processes and the amnesic syndrome. *In* D. Deutsch and J. A. Deutsch (eds), *Short Term Memory*. New York: Academic Press

Lhermitte, F. and Signoret, J. L. (1976). The amnesic syndrome and the hippocampal mammillary system. *In* M. R. Rosenzweig and E. L. Bennett (eds), *Neural Mechanisms of Learning and Memory*. Cambridge, Mass.: MIT Press

Mair, W. G. P., Warrington, E. K. and Weiskrantz, L. (1979). Memory disorders in Korsakoff's psychosis: A neuropathological and neuropsychological investigation of two cases. *Brain* **102**, 749–783

Marslen-Wilson, W. D. and Teuber, H.-L. (1975). Memory for remote events in anterograde amnesia: recognition of public figures from news-photographs. *Neuropsychologia* **13**, 353–364

Mayes, A. and Meudell, P. (1981a). How similar is the effect of cueing in amnesics and in normal subjects following forgetting? *Cortex* **17**, 113–124

Mayes, A. and Meudell, P. (1981b). How similar is immediate memory in amnesic patients to delayed memory in normal subjects? A replication, extension and reassessment of the amnesic cueing effect. *Neuropsychologia* **19**, 647–654

Mayes, A., Boddy, J. and Meudell, P. (1980). Is amnesia caused by an activational deficit? *Neuroscience Letters* **18**, 347–352

Mayes, A. R., Meudell, P. R. and Neary, D. (1978). Must amnesia be caused by either encoding or retrieval disorders? *In* M. M. Gruneberg, P. E. Morris and R. N. Sykes (eds), *Practical Aspects of Memory*. London: Academic Press

Mayes, A., Meudell, P. and Neary, D. (1980). Do amnesics adopt inefficient encoding strategies with faces and random shapes? *Neuropsychologia* **18**, 527–541

Mayes, A., Meudell, P. and Som, S. (1981). Further similarities between amnesic and normal attenuated memory: effects with paired associate learning and contextual shifts. *Neuropsychologia* **19**, 655–664

McDowall, J. (1979). Effects of encoding instructions and retrieval cueing on recall in Korsakoff patients. *Memory and Cognition* **7**, 232–239

Meudell, P. and Mayes, A. (1980). Do alcoholic amnesics passively rehearse verbal information? *Brain and Language* **10**, 189–204

Meudell, P. and Mayes, A. (1981a). A similarity between weak normal memory and amnesia with two and eight choice word recognition: a signal detection analysis. *Cortex* **17**, 19–30

Meudell, P. and Mayes, A. (1981b). The Claparède phenomenon: a further example in amnesics, a demonstration of a similar effect in controls and a reinterpretation. *Current Psychological Research* **1**, 75–88

Meudell, P., Butters, N. and Montgomery, K. (1978). The role of rehearsal in the short-term memory performance of patients with Korsakoff's and Huntington's disease. *Neuropsychologia* **16**, 507–510

Meudell, P., Mayes, A. and Neary, D. (1980a). Orienting task effects on the recognition of humorous pictures in amnesic and normal subjects. *Journal of Clinical Neuropsychology* **2**, 75–88

Meudell, P. R., Mayes, A. and Neary, D. (1980b). Amnesia is not caused by cognitive slowness. *Cortex* **16**, 413–420

Meudell, P. R., Northen, B., Snowden, J. S. and Neary, D. (1980). Long term memory for famous voices in amnesic and normal subjects. *Neuropsychologia* **18**, 133–139

Miller, E. (1975). Impaired recall and memory disturbance in presenile dementia. *British Journal of Social and Clinical Psychology* **14**, 73–79

Miller, E. (1977). *Abnormal Ageing: The Psychology of Senile and Presenile Dementia*. London: Wiley

Milner, B. (1966). Amnesia following operation on the temporal lobes. *In* C. W. M. Whitty and O. L. Zangwill (eds), *Amnesia*, 1st edn. London: Butterworths

Milner, B., Branch, C. and Rasmussen, T. (1962). Study of short-term memory after intracarotid injection of sodium amytal. *Transactions of American Neurological Association* **87**, 224–226

Mishkin, M. (1978). Memory in monkeys severely impaired by combined but not by separate removal of amygdala and hippocampus. *Nature* **273**, 297–298

Nelson, H. E. and O'Connell, A. (1978). Dementia: the estimation of premorbid intelligence levels using the new adult reading text. *Cortex* **14**, 234–244

Oscar-Berman, M. and Samuels, I. (1977). Stimulus-preference and memory factors in Korsakoff's syndrome. *Neuropsychologia* **15**, 99–106

Parkinson, S. R. (1979). The amnesic Korsakoff syndrome: a study of selective and divided attention. *Neuropsychologia* **17**, 67–75

Peterson, L. R. and Peterson, M. J. (1959). Short term retention of individual verbal items. *Journal of Experimental Psychology* **58**, 193–198

Piercy, M. F. (1977). Experimental studies of the organic amnesic syndrome. *In* C. W. M. Whitty and O. L. Zangwill (eds), *Amnesia*, 2nd edn. London: Butterworths

Russell, W. R. (1959). *Brain, Memory and Learning*. London: Oxford University Press

Sanders, H. I. and Warrington, E. K. (1971). Memory for remote events in amnesic patients. *Brain* **94**, 661–668

Sanders, H. I. and Warrington, E. K. (1975). Retrograde amnesia in organic amnesic patients. *Cortex* **11**, 397–400

Seltzer, B. and Benson, D. F. (1974). The temporal pattern of retrograde amnesia in Korsakoff's disease. *Neurology* **24**, 527–530

Squire, L. R. and Chace, P. M. (1975). Memory functions six to nine months after electro-convulsive therapy. *Archives of General Psychiatry* **32**, 1557–1564

Squire, L. R. and Slater, P. C. (1978). Anterograde and retrograde memory impairment in chronic amnesia. *Neuropsychologia* **16**, 313–322

Squire, L. R., Wetzel, C. D. and Slater, P. C. (1978). Anterograde amnesia following ECT: An analysis of the beneficial effects of partial information. *Neuropsychologia* **16**, 339–348

Starr, A. and Phillips, L. (1970). Verbal and motor memory in the amnesic syndrome. *Neurospychologia* **8**, 75–88

Stoff, D. M. and Eagle, M. N. (1971). The relationship among reported strategies, presentation rate, and verbal ability and their effects on free recall learning. *Journal of Experimental Psychology* **87**, 423–428

Talland, G. A. (1965). *Deranged Memory: A Psychonomic Study of the Amnesic Syndrome.* New York: Academic Press

Victor, M., Adams, R. D. and Collins, G. H. (1971). *The Wernicke-Korsakoff Syndrome. A Clinical and Pathological Study of 245 Patients, 82 with Post-mortem Examinations.* Oxford: Blackwell

Warrington, E. K. and Sanders, H. I. (1971). The fate of old memories. *Quarterly Journal of Experimental Psychology* **23**, 432–442

Warrington, E. K. and Weiskrantz, L. (1968a). A study of learning and retention in amnesic patients. *Neuropsychologia* **6**, 283–291

Warrington, E. K. and Weiskrantz, L. (1968b). New method of testing long-term retention with special reference to amnesic patients. *Nature* **217**, 972–974

Warrington, E. K. and Weiskrantz, L. (1970). Amnesic syndrome: consolidation or retrieval? *Nature* **228**, 628–630

Warrington, E. K. and Weiskrantz, L. (1973). An analysis of short-term and long-term memory deficits in man. *In* J. Deutsch (ed.), *The Physiological Basis of Memory.* London: Academic Press

Warrington, E. K. and Weiskrantz, L. (1974). The effect of prior learning on subsequent retention in amnesic patients. *Neuropsychologia* **12**, 419–428

Warrington, E. K. and Weiskrantz, L. (1978). Further analysis of the prior learning effect in amnesic patients. *Neuropsychologia* **16**, 169–177

Weiskrantz, L. (1978). A comparison of hippocampal pathology in man and other animals. *In Functions of the Septohippocampal System,* CIBA Foundation Symposium 58 (new series). Oxford: Elsevier

Weiskrantz, L. and Warrington, E. K. (1970a). A study of forgetting in amnesic patients. *Neuropsychologia* **8**, 281–288

Weiskrantz, L. and Warrington, E. K. (1970b). Verbal learning and retention by amnesic patients using partial information. *Psychonomic Science* **20**, 210–211

Weiskrantz, L. and Warrington, E. K. (1975a). The problem of the amnesic syndrome in man and animals. *In* R. L. Isaacson and K. H. Pribram (eds), *The Hippocampus,* Vol. 2. New York: Plenum Press

Weiskrantz, L. and Warrington, E. K. (1975b). Some comments on Woods' and Piercy's claim of a similarity between amnesic memory and normal forgetting. *Neuropsychologia* **13**, 365–368

Weiskrantz, L. and Warrington, E. K. (1979). Conditioning in amnesic patients. *Neuropsychologia* **17**, 187–194

Whitty, C. W. M. and Lishman, W. A. (1966). Amnesia in cerebral disease. *In* C. W. M. Whitty and O. L. Zangwill (eds), *Amnesia,* 1st edn. London: Butterworths

Wickens, D. D. (1970). Encoding categories of words: an empirical approach to meaning. *Psychological Review* **77**, 1–15

Wicklegren, W. A. (1979). Chunking and consolidation: a theoretical synthesis of semantic networks, configuring in conditioning, S-R versus cognitive learning, normal forgetting, the amnesic syndrome, and the hippocampal arousal system. *Psychological Review* **86**, 44–60

Williams, M. (1953). Investigation of amnesic defects by progressive prompting. *Journal of Neurology, Neurosurgery and Psychiatry* **16**, 14–18

Winocur, G. and Kinsbourne, M. (1978). Contextual cueing as an aid to Korsakoff amnesics. *Neuropsychologia* **16**, 671–682

Winocur, G. and Olds, J. (1978). Effects of context manipulation on memory and reversal learning in rats with hippocampal lesions. *Journal of Comparative and Physiological Psychology* **92**, 312–321

Winocur, G. and Weiskrantz, L. (1976). An investigation of paired associate learning in amnesic patients. *Neuropsychologia* **14**, 97–110

Woods, R. T. and Piercy, M. (1974). A similarity between amnesic memory and normal forgetting. *Neuropsychologia* **12**, 437–445

Zangwill, O. L. (1950). Amnesia and the generic image. *Quarterly Journal of Experimental Psychology* **2**, 7–12

8

Geographical Knowledge and Orientation

RICHARD W. BYRNE

Department of Psychology, University of St Andrews, Scotland

1 Introduction

A SCOPE OF THE REVIEW

When we plan a route through a busy city centre at rush-hour, decide which shops we can visit in a short lunch-break, or choose to take a new short cut through familiar woodland, we are planning and taking decisions with what is often called 'topographical knowledge' or a 'cognitive map'. We use this knowledge each time we find our way around our house or neighbourhood or give directions to a stranger. And we can use the same structure of knowledge for secondary functions; for instance, in recalling how many public houses or banks there are in our home town. We can even use a cognitive map of a building as a mnemonic (Yates, 1966), remembering an ordered sequence of objects by imagining the objects at conspicuous locations in a mental walking tour of the building. In each case we rely on a mental representation of large-scale space.

This review will be concerned with the mental organisation of such knowledge, how this leads to everyday competences and errors, and what behaviour is caused by its pathological disruption. Spatial knowledge may be thought of as forming a continuum from visual knowledge of a small object to information about world geography, but this chapter will concentrate on one part of this range. It will largely exclude information which can be gained from a *single* viewpoint (that is, 'visual perception' and 'visual imagery'); for example, knowing the arrangement of furniture within a room or the view from a mountain. At the other extreme, knowledge typically gained from words and pictures, rather than locomotor experience, will not be emphasised; for instance, the layout of countries in Africa or the knowledge that Rio de Janiero is in Brazil. So, for convenience, 'cognitive maps' are here restricted to memories of large-scale spatial areas which are typically acquired by personal experience. In addition, when we come to look at failures of performance it will become important to exclude failures due to impaired skills of communication, whether by words or by drawing maps and diagrams. To save misunderstanding, it is worth pointing out that use of the term 'cognitive map' should not be taken to imply that the mental organisation of large-scale knowledge has properties like those of a carto-graphic map; this point has been made before (e.g. Tuan, 1975; Downs and Stea, 1973). One problem in using the term 'mental map' is that it might be taken to imply the existence of 'someone in the mind' to read the map (Neisser, 1976). Of course, no such position is intended here, but the terminology will be retained as alternatives are too clumsy to be con-venient.

B   ADVANTAGES FOR STUDY

For the cognitive theorist, this topic is an exciting one. In recent years, there has been a growing awareness of the possible pitfalls of basing theories on laboratory tasks rather than everyday skills (well expressed by Neisser, 1976). By definition, cognitive maps are thoroughly ordinary and natural, and so an ideal site for study. A second advantage is that as this sort of knowledge is necessary for normal function people will always acquire it, usually by exploration and observation, though sometimes aided by verbal or graphical descriptions; its acquisition is not tied to book-learning nor to literate cultures. Also important, though harder to describe objectively, is the sheer bulk and 'complexity' of the information stored which can nevertheless be effortlessly retrieved and manipulated. Indeed, it has been argued that the need to form elaborate cognitive maps was a crucial pressure in the evolution of high intelligence in hominoid ancestors of great apes and man. McKinnon (1978), while following orang-utans in the wild, plotted the location in his study area of each durian tree, which have especially delicious fruit, in his study area. One year, the fruiting season was poor; only a very few trees had edible fruit, most were barren. At this time, he noticed the orang-utan he followed went from tree to tree among the most economical route possible until it found a tree with fruit; it did not use any familiar trails or paths. McKinnon could not have done this without his sketch map. He argued that the irregular fruiting seasons of so many tropical trees, and the extreme complexity of the rain-forest, gave a strong selective advantage to animals possessing an efficient memory for large-scale space. A final point (perhaps most useful of all) is that cognitive maps are learnt from an objectively measurable source (the real world), rather than from idiosyn-cratic education and experiences. This means that we can be sure that any errors or distortions of belief reflect, in some way, our subjects' mental apparatus. In addition, there is no need to restrict experiment to those facts which are so commonplace that they will be universally agreed.

C   A PHYSICAL ANALOGY

Physical analogies of mental faculties are often helpful, and I will use one to introduce a simple classification of the components of route-finding. I will first consider how a human navigator operates, and what 'tool kit' of apparatus he needs to avoid getting lost. Then we can later see whether our mental representations include these components. Most obvious is a *map* of some kind: a representation of places, what is found in them, and how they are spatially related to each other. As has been mentioned, the cognitive or mental map refers to *any* representation which subserves navigation, whatever its structure. Secondly, a navigator needs a *place-keeper*, a method of recording and continually updating his current position and bearing on the map; this implies a method of knowing the extent of changes in position and direction, either by monitoring movements (so-called 'deduced' or *DED reckoning*) or by noting arrival at an identifiable location predicted by the map – a *landmark*. A navigator would also expect to have a *compass*, a device for detecting orientation with respect to an effectively fixed and external frame of reference. True, with a good map and careful DED reckoning or landmark recognition he could manage without, but a compass enables both detection of small but cumulative errors in orientation, and accurate maintenance of direction of heading. Of course, with a *sextant* and *clock* as well he could establish his exact position on the earth's surface. While birds apparently do have abilities approaching this (see Keeton, 1979, for an authoritative and lucid review), it is normally assumed that we do not.

Using the above categorisation, this review will firstly consider data derived from normal subjects, chiefly using analysis of errors, and try to build up a theoretical interpretation of the abilities. Then the clinical literature will be examined in the light of this interpretation. In both cases, the literature is extensive and the papers mentioned are those which in my view are the most useful and informative.

2   Studies of normal subjects

A   THE COGNITIVE MAP

1   *Map-drawing tasks.* A straightforward way of tapping a person's topographical knowledge is to ask them to draw a physical map with pencil and paper. The geographer Lynch (1960) studied residents' knowledge of US cities in this way, and described the results in terms of the elements their maps included: *paths, landmarks, districts, nodes* and so on. In subsequent studies (summarised by Pocock and Hudson, 1978) the most general element found has been the path, a traversible route by which the city dweller gets about. Appleyard (1970) was fortunate in being able to work in a new Venezuelan city, 'uncontaminated' by published maps, and found that the great bulk of attempts at map-drawing were chain-like: very few subjects began with isolated locations and later connected

them. Shemyakin (1962) studied the development of children's maps and similarly found a great preponderance of maps drawn by tracing along familiar paths ('route maps'), with maps drawn by positioning objects in their overall configuration first ('survey maps') developing later and remaining rarer. In such tasks, maps are often drawn with a preferred orientation which is not the conventional 'north at the top'. For example, according to Anderson and Tindall (1972) the orientation is often that of the main route from home to city centre with home at the bottom of the map; however, unpublished studies in St Andrews suggest that 'sea at the bottom' (the sea is to the north and east of the town) is a popular strategy, regardless of home location. Preferences of this kind are difficult to account for, but, as Howard and Templeton (1966) note, it will be necessary to check whether subjects actually have difficulty in using other orientations, or are equally capable at several methods.

Informally attempting a map of an area one knows well can also be revealing. Comparing the results with a published map, one often finds gross distortion: complex areas, like a shopping centre, or familiar ones, like one's immediate neighbourhood, seem to grow at the expense of more monotonous parts (but perhaps this is a task artifact, and the areas are enlarged purely to 'fit in' all the information we know?). Often we draw roads as straight, intersecting at right-angles, when the reality is less simple. Griffin (1948) noticed the latter error, mentioning some Boston residents who considered its common to be straight-sided with five right-angled corners! The first cartographer of St Andrews, in the sixteenth century, was apparently prone to the same mistake (see Fig. 1).

An informal attempt at map-drawing also draws attention to some of the problems with the technique. Clearly the result is entirely limited by the drawing ability of the subject. The task is not an easy one, and it is fair to question how hard some subjects *try* to perfect their attempts: in Lynch's (1960) study, mentioned earlier, subjects were only asked for 'sketch maps', so we should be wary in using his data to make claims about mental maps. Errors are liable to be cumulative if the subject uses the strategy, shown to be commonest, of tracing along paths; and the starting point chosen will grossly affect the final configuration. Most serious of all, intuitive knowledge of simple geometry allows one to deduce and construct facts which were not initially known: the task *changes* as well as *taps* the mental representation. These limitations would seem to be fatal, and we must turn to alternative methods of investigating cognitive maps.

2   *Distance estimations.* Collecting people's systematic errors in estimation of distances between places in towns has been the most commonly used indirect technique; it has enjoyed a particular vogue with geographers as misestimation of distances might affect patterns of driving, shopping and so on. The results have often been contradictory,

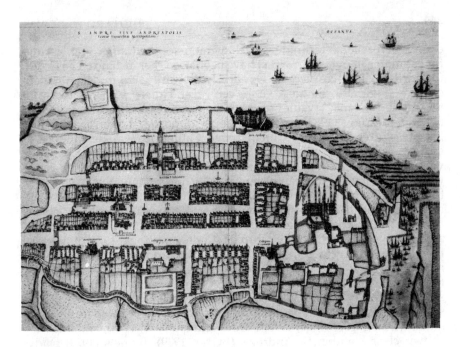

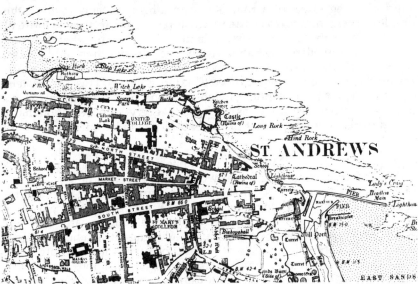

Fig. 1 *A common error of map-drawing.* The 'Bird's Eye View of St Andrews' (1530) reproduced (*top*) shows an error which is commonplace today in resident's attempts to represent the town plan. Comparison with the O.S. map (*bottom*) reveals that the three main central streets in fact form a fan, and are not parallel to each other as commonly believed

even when reliable techniques such as ratio-scaling (rather than asking for estimates in miles or metres) have been used. For instance, Lee (1970) found that distances *towards* Dundee city centre were underestimated compared with those *away* from the centre, and interpreted this as due to the higher 'valence' (value) of the city centre. Golledge and Zannaras (1973) and Briggs (1973) found the precise opposite, though argued that US city centres are relatively unattractive. Canter (1975) made a direct test of the valence idea with a single city, and found no effect of a location's value on its apparent distance. It was in any case a little hard to believe that people imagined urban distances to be noncommutative (A to B ≠ B to A). Although some studies find no effect of absolute length (Lee, 1970), others find relative overestimation of shorter routes (Cadwallader, 1973; Byrne, 1979). The change over to underestimation of 'long' routes apparently varies with the city studied (Canter and Tagg, 1975); however, Byrne (1979) suggested that the effect may be an artifact of the experimental techniques: if subjects tend to make guesses around the middle of the scale when they have no accurate knowledge, then automatically short distances are overestimated and long ones underestimated. It has several times been assumed that routes which involve more turns seem longer (Lee, 1970; Briggs, 1973; Pocock and Hudson, 1978), and this was shown clearly within St Andrews (Byrne, 1979). Byrne's (1979) study found a strong effect of a route's surroundings: distances within the complex, interesting town centre were overestimated relative to those in monotonous suburbs. Similarly, Canter (1975) found that habitual London bus travellers estimated distances as greater than did habitual Underground travellers. It would appear that the heuristic of 'how much is remembered about' a route is used to judge its length. This is consistent with the expansions of home neighbourhood and complex areas on subjects' sketch maps, as well as our frequent everyday observation that it takes surprisingly long to get to the end of a familiar but monotonous journey.

3   *Angular estimations.* Much less work has been done on estimation of angles and directions in the real world, which seems odd when one considers that Tolman (1948) first coined the term 'cognitive map' for the mental structure underlying rats' angular estimations. Tolman gave rats food rewards in a goal-box reached along a circuitous path. He then tested them with a maze like a starburst, allowing rats to choose almost any direction of travel; they chose the direction of the shortest route to the food, showing an accurate conception of the spatial relations of start and goal. Byrne (1979) showed an extraordinary *lack* of knowledge, among established residents of a city, of the angles at which familiar roads meet. With instructions emphasising accuracy of angular configuration, subjects were asked to draw plans of isolated road intersections which in reality made angles of either 60–70° or 110–120°. In almost every case,

estimates were indiscriminable from 90°, and the histograms for both groups were almost identical normal curves, centred on 90°. Evidently the bias towards 'simplification' of maps to grids of streets meeting at right-angles reflects a genuine lack of knowledge (it seems most unlikely that subjects 'really knew' the true angles but could not draw them with a ruler). Moar (personal communication) used a different technique: 'mental triangulation'. Subjects who imagined themselves at one location, were asked to point to another. This was repeated to give the bearing of each location from every other, which could then be manipulated (by computer) to plot the layout of positions best fitting the data; thus a 'mental map' could be plotted without requiring subjects to draw anything. On a very large scale (distant cities, typically learnt from an atlas and so strictly speaking excluded from this review) he found a good fit with two dimensions; for locations within a city, the fit was poor, which is not surprising from Byrne's results. Interestingly, in a very overlearned but complicated building, he was again able to obtain a three-dimensional solution, suggesting that eventually true angular configurations are learnt and heuristics become unnecessary.

4   *Studies of artificially acquired knowledge.* A few of the numerous laboratory studies of human maze-learning and orientation may be mentioned briefly. In some cases, full-scale mazes were taught and subjects were then asked about the distances and directions of places in the maze. Kosslyn, Pick and Fariello (1974) found that opaque barriers increased adults' estimation of distances, while even transparent barriers did so for children. Gärling, Böök and Lindberg (1975), using deep hospital culverts as a maze, found that blindfolded subjects systematically underestimate distances, while they do not differ from sighted subjects on angular estimates. Hintzman (1979) taught subjects the locations of objects distributed circularly about them in a room, then tested them with a response board for the ability to point towards a certain target while imagining facing towards a specified location. He found that 180° estimations were particularly fast and mirror reversal errors were common, suggesting a representation in terms of verbal propositions ('behind', 'half-left'), but it must be remembered that task specific strategies are possible with a highly-practiced laboratory task. Howard and Templeton (1966) review earlier studies, but find the results inconclusive. Kozlowski and Bryant (1977) found that those who consider they have a good 'sense of direction' are better able to learn a maze after repeated trials than those who do not, and they are also better able to point to out-of-sight buildings in a familiar environment. Tolman (1948), with his famous 'starburst' maze, showed that rats have the same ability in pointing to unseen locations.

5   *A theory of cognitive map organisation.* One way of looking at these data is to say that, for a familiar spatial area, a person has a cognitive map which is distorted. Even if we are careful to disown the implications of the

word 'map', of something flat, two-dimensional and isomorphic with the real world as viewed from above, this may be misleading. It implies a single representation for all our knowledge about any spatial area which can be used in different ways. I suspect it may be useful instead to distinguish between two radically different forms of representation which may both refer to the same spatial area, and to ask which form is tapped by a particular task rather than which of the two we use universally. The terms I have used for the two hypothetical structures are 'vector-maps' and 'network-maps' (Byrne, 1979). They differ chiefly in whether they need to encode horizontal vector distances (e.g. 'A is n units SSE of B'), or only topological connectedness (e.g. 'B is next after A on the route to C').

A NETWORK-MAP represents traversible routes as a network of *strings*, and locations along them as *nodes*. Each string is in effect a program for locomotion: each node, as well as identifying a physical location, may also contain instructions for a change of direction (see Fig. 2). So one string, encoding a route from start to finish, is rather like a set of directions; the encoding is propositional, though it may be misleading to think of it as verbal. Nodes which specify changes of direction are potentially choice-points, and if other routes are known from the choice points, the strings become branched. Linde and Labov's (1975) study of answers to the question 'could you tell me the layout of your apartment?' gives a vivid picture of the use of human network-maps. None of their subjects described their flats 'as viewed from above'; all gave 'tours'. Tours begin at the front door, and always mention one-room branches first, but do not enter them; branches leading to other rooms are always entered; at the end of a branch, the tour moves back instantaneously to its start, rather than retracing steps. With the multiple interconnections of a familiar town, strings rapidly become joined up at choice points into a complete net: duplicate representations of routes are not allowed, to avoid difficulties of searching. Nodes would necessarily exist for each branch-point, but could also encode other known locations (e.g. particular shops or houses, as well as junctions of streets) or even simply visually prominent 'landmarks'. Evidently a mechanism for accessing routes between specified pairs of locations is needed, and since part of the inspiration for this model was the computer-based theories of semantic memory (hence the terminology of 'networks' and 'nodes'), it is appropriate to suggest the 'spreading activation' concept (Collins and Loftus, 1975). In this, activation spreads out from start and end nodes at a constant rate in a metric where 'distance' corresponds to nodes, so that the 'spheres' of activation first meet on a pathway which connects the start and end with the fewest number of intervening nodes. Paris Metro displays use an electrical version of this to help travellers find their best route, and in many ways the published underground railway maps give a convenient visual model of a network-map. Anyone who has ever tried to use an underground

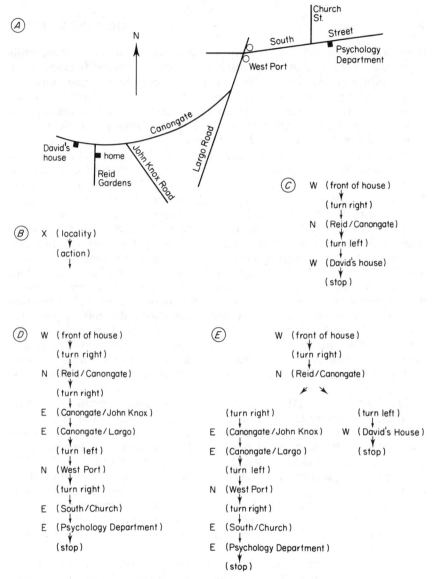

Fig. 2 *Illustration of network-map representation.* A small section of St. Andrews is shown as a rough sketch in *A* . Generalised network-map nodes can be used to represent routes on this map. One such node is shown in *B* , which can be read 'at a *locality*, when one is facing in the direction X, one should perform the *action* to reach the next node'. Two routes, sharing a common segment, are given as strings of nodes, *C* and *D* , and the routes can be traced on the sketch. A network-map is assumed to be 'economical', so in the final form *E* the routes are represented as a branched string. Notice that the directions of facing are stylised into 90° units, often deviating from reality; gradual curves, and junctions at which roads do not intersect at 90°, are not explicit on the representation

map to walk around the city streets above will readily agree that, while topological connectedness is preserved accurately, vector distance is not! The analogy breaks down when it is remembered that, unlike network-maps, underground maps are actually flat and viewed-from-above; a tangle of nodes connected by totally plastic and extensible threads gets a little closer to the concept intended. In fact, the 'links' are really no more than 'pointers' to the next node in the net.

VECTOR-MAPS, by contrast, necessarily encode horizontal information about directions and distances. They are, then, isomorphic to the real world when viewed from above. An ordinary published map, such as an Ordinance Survey map, gives a good physical analogy of a mental vector-map. The decision as to which of the two representations – network or vector – is being used on a task rests chiefly on the presence or absence of characteristic network-map distortions and failures of competence. Distance on a network-map consists of intervening nodes, so estimates should be inflated by anything which boosts the number of nodes; for instance, routes with many turns and twists, or routes in very familiar or highly memorable areas, are 'longer' on network-map metric. Direction on a network-map is quantized into propositions like 'left' or 'straight-on', so estimates of angle should show a 90° bias. Topological errors, where routes connect wrongly, should not occur with network-maps, but are quite feasible with vector-maps. On a vector-map, errors of distance and angle should be random and simply decrease in frequency with experience.

Siegel and White (1975) put forward a related distinction, based on children's map drawing. They, however, consider that drawing a 'graphic skeleton' (i.e. a net-like map, however distorted) shows use of 'survey map' knowledge, a term which is otherwise quite similar in meaning to 'vector-map'. In addition they tie the model to an implausible, quasi-physiological device which is supposed to copy the entire state of the CNS at each major landmark or change of direction. While something like this has been suggested to explain memory of the trivial circumstances in which we learn of dramatic events such as the death of President Kennedy (Brown and Kulick, 1977), such drama at every street corner seems implausible.

What concrete evidence is there in the literature reviewed so far for the occurrence of network and vector-map knowledge? There are frequent pointers to the use of network-maps, but few hints that vector-maps are used at all. In map-drawing, paths and chain-like attempts are the norm, and often show massive distortions of form, yet topological errors are a rarity: hallmarks of network-map knowledge. Children begin by tracing along familiar routes, only later and occasionally drawing a survey by placing objects in their relative locations before drawing connecting paths: so it seems that vector-maps develop later and are less used than network-maps. Estimation tasks with adults give results which can mostly be accounted for quite adequately by assuming subjects *only* possess network-map knowledge. Distance estimations of routes with many turns are inflated and routes in environmentally complex or highly familiar areas are estimated as longer. Memory for angles of intersections is strongly biassed towards 90°, indeed giving little evidence that true angles are ever noticed. Verbal descriptions of people's homes are normally tours, tracing along branches, although triangulation of direction estimates shows that vector-maps *can* be built up for very familiar buildings. And Tolman's rats clearly possessed vector-map knowledge of the location of their goal-box!

Indeed, experiments like Tolman's, in which knowledge is demonstrated of the bearing to a location which cannot be seen, constitute the best evidence for vector-maps. Wolves apparently sometimes take 'short cuts', leaving their usual network of paths (Peters, 1973), and our own ability to take novel short cuts suggests some vector-map knowledge. Asking people to point to invisible but familiar landmarks is a simple way of demonstrating the ability, and Lewis (1976) found that Australian aborigines were expert at it, with mean errors of under 5° to sacred sites.

Evidence for independent storage of distance and direction information comes from a recent study of the blind (Byrne and Scott, in prep.). No differences were found between congenitally totally blind subjects and matched controls in urban *distance* estimates, whereas the blind *were* impaired at pointing to invisible locations. The impairment was less when the home was the reference point for the bearing, compared with asking subjects to imagine themselves at one site and then to point to another. Possibly the blind compensate for their difficulty in forming vector-maps by developing a domicentric system of reference bearings: locations are remembered in terms of direction and distance from 'home', but relationships *between* locations are not known.

B MENTAL PLACE-KEEPING AND MAINTENANCE OF ORIENTATION

Few studies have investigated how we keep track of our current position and bearings during locomotion. Much the most exotic method, which clearly demonstrates the need for a mental place-keeper, has been found used by Pulawat Islanders during long canoe voyages (Gladwin, 1970). They keep track of their location on the open sea by means of the point on the horizon (described in terms of the rising and setting points of stars) under which a reference or 'etak' island lies. Each route has an etak island, situated well off the direct line from start to goal. Since the etak islands are usually too far away to be visible at any time, and the star rising and setting points can seldom be checked with the real stars, the system is highly abstract. Our everyday place-keeping is obviously very different, but is equally essential for our normal behaviour. A series of laboratory studies at Umeå in Sweden have looked at keeping track of bearings. In tasks involving learning a full-sized maze, they found that subjects learnt the shape of the maze just as quickly when they also had to perform a concurrent information-processing task (Lindberg and Gärling, 1978). However, keeping track of one's current position within the same maze does require conscious attention and is disrupted by a concurrent task (Böök and Gärling, 1978a). Linear locomotion introduces errors in estimating the distance and direction of invisible reference points, and these errors appear to be due to systematic underestimation of distance walked (Böök and Gärling, 1978b). Body rotation, on the other hand, introduces *over*compensation into estimates of the directions of fixed points (Böök and Gärling, 1978c). It will be necessary to study these kinds of ability in familiar, real-world environments before the results can be directly linked to those on cognitive maps. However, the form of representation *does* influence people's current orientation in normal surroundings. Byrne and Seaton (in prep.) asked people to orient a schematic map correctly, or to point to cardinal compass bearings. They found systematic bias which varied with the exact street location in which subjects were asked, and the errors were in directions expected from a simplified network-map representation of the town. Any attempt at drawing a town plan *consistent* with subjects' beliefs produces something more like an underground map, with straight streets meeting at right angles.

C THE MENTAL COMPASS

There has long been speculation that man might possess a special magnetic sense giving him direct awareness of compass bearing (e.g. Darwin, 1859). Travellers' tales of the remarkable abilities of 'primitive' peoples to navigate in unknown terrain are anecdotal and hard to interpret. Where abilities are well documented (e.g. Lewis, Gladwin, above) they appear to rest on excellent DED reckoning and special devices such as the 'etak' system or 'indian file' travel, which enables Saharan nomads to maintain a straight course as those at the rear immediately notice a deviation from a straight line.

An excellent review by Howard and Templeton (1966) concluded that there was no evidence that man or animals possess any special sense for magnetic orientation. For birds, just such evidence has now been produced (Merkel and Wilschko, 1965; Keeton, 1971; Walcott and Green, 1974) and repeated replication leaves no doubt that birds can detect and use the earth's magnetic field, despite scientists' initial scepticism.

Recently, Baker (1981) has tried subjecting humans to the traditional 'pigeon homing' experiments, and found that we too can orient with the earth's magnetic field – but have no conscious awareness of doing so. In several experiments, Baker took groups of blindfold student subjects by coach over winding and circuitous routes for some miles; at the destination, each subject was asked to estimate the direction of the start. Their guesses were not random but clumped, with a mean vector in error by between 1° and 44°; the subjects themselves were most surprised by their accuracy. In general, subjects could not explain how they had monitored their route. A few said they used the direction of the sun's warmth (but trials in heavy overcast were as accurate), a few reported sounds and smells which gave clues (but most clues were misidentified), and a few said they tried to keep track on a mental map, by estimating each turn of the coach by inertia, but that this was in fact almost impossible. This opinion is supported by the fact that subjects who fell asleep for intervals along the route were scarcely disadvantaged; and that estimates at intermediate points along the route do not decrease steadily in accuracy, but show a U-shaped relationship, with high accuracy up to about 3 km, then a decrease, but later another improvement. In one experiment, all subjects had metal bars strapped behind their hands, and were told that they were magnets; in fact half wore brass bars as a control, half wore bar magnets. While controls were accurately oriented, the estimates of those subjects with magnets were random. In another, subjects wore perspex helmets with coils on either side of the head. On some trials, a battery was connected to produce a magnetic field across the head, with north either to right or left. Connecting the battery had a striking effect on orientation, but not quite what was expected. For instance, with north on a subject's left throughout, they should believe they have travelled steadily west, regardless of the actual direction of movement. In fact, the errors in orientation varied with the direction of travel. For the artificial field to interact with, rather than replace, the earth's field, it would seem that the organ responsible for magnetic orientation is located near the surface of the skull. As Baker is well aware, many scientists will find these results impossible to believe. He urges all who are sceptical to replicate and try to extend his work, and we must hope that this will be done soon since there can be no more exciting topic in psychology at present than the discovery of man's magnetic 'sixth sense'.

D   SUMMARY

From this survey, it is possible to predict that certain dissociations of clinical impairments should occur, while others should not. This is tentative, since the picture of results from normal subjects is incomplete and of varied reliability. In particular, there has been a preponderance of studies in environments, real and artificial, which resemble *mazes*: areas segmented by many obstacles, allowing movement only along circuitous paths, and lacking free visibility. Where this is the case, for instance in a city, there is a selective advantage for network-map organisation of knowledge, and vector-map information may even be a *disadvantage* – as when a novel short-cut turns out to be blocked by a wall or 'no entry' sign. Our scanty knowledge of vector-maps probably reflects the lack of studies of navigation in and memory for areas which permit free movement in any direction. In addition, since vector-maps are largely defined by *absence* of typically network-map characteristics, we should expect this category to be heterogeneous, since we may be able to represent large-scale space in more than *two* alternative ways.

At the coarsest level, impairment of topographical knowledge, as shown by inabilities in following and describing familiar routes and learning new ones, should be possible in the absence of impairment to other visuospatial skills, and *vice versa*. For example, failures at object recognition, at memory for pictures and scenes, and at tasks involving imagery, should not necessarily imply a route-finding deficit. But, in practice, routes encoded as network-maps will require a recognition of landmarks for them to be *followed* correctly, though they could be *described* without. Further, topographical deficit should not always be linked to failures of memory for geographical facts (such as a country's capital or neighbours) or difficulties with tasks involving shapes which would be learnt from an atlas (such as those tasks in which subjects rate imagined and real outlines of US states for similarity of shape; Shepard and Chipman, 1970).

Impairments of topographical knowledge could presumably affect each of the three components of our analogy – compass, place-keeper and map – independently. Since clear evidence of sensitivity to the earth's magnetic field has been so elusive, it seems pointless to expect clinical symptoms from its impairment. Inability to update one's current position and bearing would make route-finding impossible, but might preserve the ability to describe or draw routes. A specific deficit of vector-map knowledge might well go unnoticed in many people, as we apparently rely so much more on network-maps; in patients, whose occupations or hobbies rely on 'good sense of direction', difficulty might be experienced when ordinary urban route-finding remained normal. Lowered ability to encode or use network-maps, on the other hand, should cause dramatic loss of everyday route-finding ability, yet leave the ability to handle large-scale directions and distances. That is, a patient with only network-map ability might recall that he 'took the third right, then second left by the bakery, and finally left again at the church' but have no idea of the general direction of his start; while a patient with only vector-map ability might know that he had come from 'over there, about a mile off' but be unable to retrace his steps exactly or describe the route. To some extent, the congenitally blind approximate the former case.

3   Studies of pathological impairments

A   LABORATORY INVESTIGATION OF THE EFFECT OF LESION SITE

One category of evidence comes from studies which attempt to relate impairment on laboratory tasks to specific lesion sites. Ideally, *patterns* of impairment are found, giving 'double dissociation' of function in which one of two tasks is affected by a lesion in one site, while the other is affected by a quite separate lesion, and not *vice versa*. Neat, circumscribed lesions, which can be precisely located, are produced by penetrating missile wounds of the brain (typically wartime schrapnel injuries); however, some studies use patients with less easily localised damage, such as is produced by tumour or vascular accident. In all cases, groups of subjects are analysed together. Numerous tasks have been invented which rely on spatial skill, but few seem particularly relevant to topographical knowledge.

Except where tasks include a need for language ability, left hemisphere damage rarely affects performance with spatial tasks. Indeed, Benton, Levin and Van Allen (1974), asking verbal questions about geographic knowledge such as 'which state is New Haven in?', found no significant difference between subjects with brain damage and controls; asking for compass bearing of one city to another, or requiring subjects to mark cities on an outline map, showed equivalent left and right hemisphere decrements. All three tasks evidently test knowledge typically acquired from books or published maps, rather than the abilities on which this review is focussed. Reitan and Tarshes (1959) used a task with two forms, an easy version in which a sequence of numbered circles were connected together with lines, and a hard version in which alternate numbers and letters (A, 1, B, 2, C, 3, etc.) had to be connected in a double staircase. Patients with right hemisphere damage found the harder version only a little more difficult, while those with left hemisphere damage found the tasks dramatically different in difficulty, having much more trouble with the more symbolic material. Most relevant to this review, a left frontal deficit was found by Butters, Soeldner and Redio (1972) on the 'Money standardised road map task'. Here, the experimenter traces a route through a fictional town-plan, and the subject has to state whether each turn is a left or a right. This ability, to imagine oneself correctly oriented at a location on a map, must be an essential component in everyday use of maps. The subjects involved experienced difficulties, although they could correctly indicate their left and right arms (and simple left/right confusion is more a feature of parietal injury; Critchley, 1953), so it seems likely that the difficulty arose from the mental changes of orientation necessary for the task.

Newcombe and Ritchie Russell (1969) found a right hemisphere decrement both for face recognition and for learning a stylus maze (where a certain path must be learnt through an array of dots on a board). Failure on the latter task was associated with low scores on Raven's matrices and on tasks involving 3-D interpretation of pictures, rather than on more typically 'visual' tasks such as pattern matching. With the same visually-guided stylus maze, Newcombe (1969) found that the right hemisphere decrement was specifically posterior and parietal (and patients with left parietal lesions were worse than other left hemisphere groups). Although superficially like a map, the stylus maze may not require similar skills to everyday navigation; only three of Newcombe's right hemisphere patients had topographical difficulties in normal life, none of these severe. Tasks involving mental rotation of visual material seem to be particularly affected by right parietal injury. Butters *et al.* (1972) required patients to copy, with sticks, a pattern made by the examiner seated opposite them (i.e. needing 180° rotation): patients with right parietal lesions were impaired relative to those with right temporal lesions, and to any left hemisphere lesions. Also, a task devised by Ratcliff (1979), in which subject must identify the marked hand of a mannikin figure, showed a right posterior deficit if the mannikin had to be mentally rotated, but not otherwise. The skill impaired would not seem to be a crucial one for topographical ability, although in our everyday use of published maps and plans we often do not rotate the map physically to align with the land, so may well be relying on mental rotation. Most people find physical rotation of the map such that it is aligned with the land reduces one's chance of error.

Finally, one laboratory task has been used which seems more closely analogous to everyday map-reading. In the Semmes, Weinskin, Ghent and Teuber (1955) 'locomotor maze', a subject has to walk around a series of marked dots on the floor of a large room, guided by a plan of the room on which a route is traced. The subject carries the plan with him and uses it like a map. One wall of the room is designed 'north', and the subject is required to keep the south side of the map towards him throughout Semmes *et al.* (1955) found patients with parietal lesions impaired relative to nonbrain damaged controls whether the task was visual or tactile, and no effect of hemisphere or impairment with other lesion sites. Weinstein, Semmes, Ghent and Teuber (1956) again found no effect of modality, so the disability is clearly not a visual one, though they found a strong association between somesthetic deficit and failure on the locomotor maze task. Presumably the coincidence of locus does not stem from a common logical stage of processing. Semmes *et al.* (1963) compared this task with that of personal orientation (above), finding that posterior left lesions affected subjects' performance on both, while anterior left lesions only affected personal orientation and posterior right lesions only affected the locomotor maze. Oddly, Ratcliff and Newcombe (1973) found no impairment on this task from any unilateral lesion, but only with *bilateral* posterior lesions. They, like Semmes and her co-workers, used missile-wound patients; the difference may arise from the longer time since the wounds were occasioned in the British subjects. One of Ratcliff and Newcombe's subjects reported that he often failed to recognise landmarks on familiar routes, and he suffered from general topographical memory loss; on the task, he memorised the path as best he could before setting out, then walked round (without consulting the map) as far as he remembered; at this point he failed, since he was unable to keep track of his current position on the map he held.

In terms of the taxonomy set up during consideration of results from normal subjects, there seems to be some association of categories with particular lesion sites. Visuospatial ability, including memorisation and mental manipulation of displays which can be seen from a single viewpoint, is closely associated with unilateral right parietal damage. On the other hand, verbal material, such as knowledge of the capitals of countries, is apparently little affected by cerebral damage. Within the focal area of this review, two laboratory tasks used appear to depend on our place-keeping and mental orientation ability, rather than the representation of information itself. Both the 'Money standardised road map' and Semmes et al.'s (1955) 'locomotor maze' are at first sight equally concerned with this ability, yet they are impaired by different lesions: left frontal, and posterior (sometimes only bilateral) lesions respectively. Although from a cognitive analysis one might well not have suspected it, this shows that the two tasks tap very different mental capabilities; it would be interesting to see this difference explored with the invention of new tasks which depend on particular aspects of map-reading skill.

None of the tasks reviewed here test the ability of patients to learn and use information about large-scale space, when acquired by locomotor experience. While this is perhaps not surprising, it is unfortunate when so much of the literature on normal subjects is devoted to cognitive maps; and when there is reason to think that there may be two fundamentally different modes of dealing with this sort of information.

B INDIVIDUAL CASE STUDIES

Although it can certainly be useful to search for characteristic patterns of performance breakdown in groups of patients with comparable lesions, there are difficulties – well recognised by neuropsychologists. 'All generalisations are suspect', and Critchley (1951) pointed out that not only do the hallmarks of parietal damage also frequently occur with prefrontal leucotomy, but many patients show none of them despite known parietal damage, in one case complete loss of parietal lobes! Probably many cases of association between lesion site and a pattern of deficits result from destruction of tissues crucial to a component skill of the several tasks impaired (i.e. a 'cognitive subsystem'), but of course there are other possibilities. That a lesion affects two or more abilities may be almost accidental, caused by a coincidence of brain evolution and implying no connection of function; the link between somesthetic deficit and map-reading skill (Weinstein et al., 1956) may be of this nature. And a lesion may simply affect a skill which is a necessary enablement for demonstrating the ability of interest, yet be otherwise unrelated; no-one would imagine that a patient impaired at drawing lacked topographical memory simply because he failed to draw a plan of his home town.

An alternative approach to that so far reviewed is the detailed examination of individual case studies, an approach long used by clinicians. The difficulty of interpreting patterns of impairment remain the same, but these studies supply an additional kind of evidence of special interest to cognitive theorists: the type of error exhibited, both in the laboratory and everyday life. Since the cognitive psychologist is chiefly concerned with the exact nature of any abberrant behaviour, and how it might have arisen from selective damage to subsystems of a cognitive model, precise localisation of damage matters less and evidence from distributed and vague damage is just as valuable. The crucial requirement is for detailed and careful descriptions of a range of behaviour, impaired and otherwise.

Benton (1969) provides a useful historical summary and review of clinical case-studies involving spatial disorders. He notes that patients with defective localisation of objects in space (inaccurate pointing, failure to bisect lines, and so on), although they usually have visual field defects as well, rarely suffer from any disturbances of topographical knowledge or exhibit route-finding difficulty. At the other extreme, Paterson and Zangwill (1944a) describe the topographical difficulties of two patients recovering from the trauma of severe head injury. Here, the error was one of *belief*: one patient, for instance, suggested that Grimsby and Scotland were the same place or very close by, that his home street was partly in both, and that his 'previous' hospitals were in Grimsby though 'this one' was in Scotland (there were no previous hospitals). Again, this is not a question of route-finding difficulty or loss of experientially acquired cognitive maps, so not central to this review. The demarcation is less straightforward from another ability which is also here tangential: visuo-constructive skill. Although constructional apraxia (inability to draw common objects from memory or copy pictures and diagrams) is a poor predictor of topographical disability, the converse is not true and patients with route-finding difficulty usually also have difficulty with any drawing or construction task. Often, constructional apraxia takes the form of 'unilateral neglect', where all the features of an object (e.g. the numerals on a clock face) are crammed onto one side of the picture. Patients who show this unilateral neglect also often show a corresponding neglect of half of their bodies; however, most patients with disorientation in external space do not show this or other defects of body schema. Critchley (1953) notes that unilateral neglect of the body, or even complete loss of awareness or paralysis of one side of the body, is more likely associated with visual defects such as hemianopia (loss of sight in one visual hemi-field); and Brain (1941) pointed out that hemianopic patients do not typically suffer from getting lost easily – they quickly learn to scan effectively with their spared hemifield.

This makes all the more striking a form of route-finding difficulty or disorientation in several patients described by Brain (1941). These patients consistently became lost, even in their own houses, because they always chose right turns when left would be correct. He suggested that they neglected all objects seen on their left, and named the disability 'agnosia for the left half of space'. They had no difficulty recognising 'left' and 'right' of themselves and the tester, but all had difficulty dressing. Case 5 was particularly clear, since he could describe all the landmarks of a route correctly (and therefore possessed an adequate network-map of it), but said 'right' each time a left turn was required – and indeed quickly became lost in practice. In Brain's cases, the symptoms were associated with neglect of the left side of the body, but in two rather similar cases described by Paterson and Zangwill (1944b), they were not. Both their patients initially showed route-finding difficulty, though not entirely due to a preference for right turns, but both recovered over time. It seems that this intriguing defect of route-finding does not fit easily into the taxonomy of abilities used to describe normal subjects' behaviour. If anything, it could be described as a specific impairment of nodes. Each node of a network-map can be seen as a [LANDMARK] → [ACTION] pair, and in Brain's patients, although each landmark was correct, the action was always 'turn right'. Nevertheless, they were not in the normal sense 'disorientated'; compare a man mentioned by Zangwill (1951) who, if he bent down to tie his shoelaces, would often think he was facing the opposite direction when he stood up.

The picture of impairment is seldom as simple as this. For instance, McFie, Piercy and Zangwill (1950) describe eight patients with right parieto-occipital lesions (as had the cases described above). They present an array of defects, all apparently partially correlated with each other; visual field defects, right-left disorientation, topographical disorientation, visuoconstructive difficulties, agnosia for the left half of space, general intellectual impairment, and so on. One case showed a clear 'lack of enablement' when he could accurately describe but not draw a plan of his house. Five had a history of 'topographical disorientation' (getting lost in normally familiar surroundings), which in four cases could be related to agnosia for the left half of space as in Brain's patients, but in one not. Three of these, and several others, also showed 'loss of topographical memory' (inability to describe routes). It is difficult to make sense of such a bewildering group, although with further study they might have been 'fractionated' (Shallice, 1979) into simpler groups.

However, some cases show clear disruption of cognitive maps. One of Hécaen, Penfield and Bertrand's (1956) seventeen patients (case 4) could not visualise the relationships between streets and consequently got lost, even in areas he had previously known well; reading the street names was of no help. Only in his own home could he get about adequately, and he claimed to be able to visualise its interior. Otherwise, Hécaen et al.'s right hemisphere parieto-occipital lesioned patients showed little if any defect of topographical knowledge. They consider that orientation disturbance may often be caused by a 'general clouding' of consciousness. Cogan's (1960) case 14 seems to be an instance of this: he frequently got lost, but his 'vision cleared' (i.e. he accessed the appropriate node in his network-map?) when a friend pointed him in the correct direction, and he could then continue. He also showed unilateral neglect, and found objects to look unreal, far off and out of focus. Cogan's series of case studies of patients with nondominant hemisphere lesions contains several examples of patients who became lost when walking, sailing or driving in familiar areas, and a rather frightening series of car accidents in several. Among these, case 12 also showed unilateral neglect, and case 11 could drive a car and describe his destination, but found all streets unfamiliar, even those between his office and normal lunching place. Interestingly, when he abandoned his car and took a taxi, he was able to recognise his destination when he arrived.

A particularly fascinating patient is described by Paterson and Zangwill (1945), again a right parietal case who was unable to find his way around his home town, Edinburgh. He was unable to recognise many distinctive and highly familiar buildings and landmarks (although this recovered slightly with time), and when he *was* able to recognise an intersection, he was quite unable to say where the roads led to. Thus network-map knowledge of the city was clearly not available. However, to a certain extent he could use street names and tram car numbers to correctly orient himself, so he evidently retained an overall idea of the general configuration of Edinburgh and the location of streets within it: vector-map knowledge. So in the terms used here, his impairment was in the recognition of topographical locations and the use of network-map representations, but there is no evidence of an impairment of vector-maps. The same may be true of a patient, reported by Spalding and Zangwill (1950), who, when walking in familiar areas, felt that all the scenery 'unfolded as if he were in a strange country', although he did not always become lost. This subject failed to learn his route from surgery to ward in a hospital after 13 days, but at the same time he *could* correctly interpret a plan of the hospital, albeit with difficulty. Whitely and Warrington (1978) report a patient with an incapacitating failure to recognise buildings, streets and other topographical landmarks. Other cognitive skills were relatively intact, and his perception was normal, but like Spalding and Zangwill's patient, he finds familiar streets seem quite novel each time he goes along them. He can use a map with ease, and in fact relies on maps for getting around; once more, the impairment concerns network-maps but apparently not vector-maps.

A deliberate strategy to compensate for loss of network-map ability was shown by one man, who memorised series of landmarks in Oxford as lists, starting from the central clock-tower, one for each main route; if the expected landmark failed to appear, he returned to the clock-tower and began again (Zangwill, 1951). Zangwill, in the same paper, distinguishes the inability to learn one's way about in novel surroundings from topographical memory loss, when knowledge of familiar areas is lost. The former may be related to deficiencies of visual learning, rather than topographical ability as such.

Deficiencies also occur which appear to reflect a specific loss of vector-map ability. Zangwill (1951) describes several patients with intact route-finding ability, who have great difficulty in indicating the bearings of nearby and well-known buildings, or in giving compass directions to routes which they could in practice follow. One patient explained 'it is not recognising buildings that gives me trouble but mastering the general lay-out': as clear an account of vector-map deficiency as one might hope for.

4 Conclusion

The suggestion made at the outset, that our knowledge, of those spatial areas which we cannot see from a single viewpoint and which instead we learn by our own locomotion, can usefully be treated as a unitary body, receives some support from the literature of pathology. Certainly it is distinct from the verbally acquired beliefs of general geographical fact; these can often persist in severe pathology and give a spurious impression of 'good topographical orientation'. Purely perceptual capabilities, such as localisation of objects in space or judgment of depth, are sharply demarcated from topographical abilities; the two are seldom impaired together. When it comes to spatial knowledge which we typically acquire from maps (the shape of the US, the road route to London, and so on), the distinction becomes hazier. Visual memory and visuospatial skill are impaired by right parietal lesions; and case studies of topographically impaired patients usually show right parietal impairment. Bilateral parietal damage affects performance on a map-reading task. But maybe we should expect a blurred distinction here, since this kind of knowledge could in principle be acquired either from maps or by locomotor experience. In normal life we can accept and learn the information in either form, even at times in both forms at once, so it is unsurprising that visuospatial skills should be partly related to topographical ability. From studies of normals, it seems that the way in which we acquire the knowledge chiefly affects the type of 'cognitive map' we form: from a published map, we will form a vector-map, while from our own locomotor experience, chiefly a network-map though also in a limited way a vector-map.

Within the area of cognitive maps, the suggestion that there are two forms of mental representation, with different strengths and weaknesses, has received support from clinical studies. Patients have been described on the one hand unable to follow or describe familiar routes but with a spared ability to appreciate relative location in large-scale space, and on the other with no impairment of route-finding skill but with a particular weakness at directions and compass bearings. It is tempting to treat this as a double dissociation of function between network-maps and vector-maps, but other patients must be found fitting this pattern, and tested specifically for network-map and vector-map aptitudes, before we can be sure. To this end, it would be helpful if clinicians could devise and use tests which separately rely on network-maps and vector-maps for their performance, and not group the two as 'topographical memory'. Tests to tap these mental representations should *not* require actual route-finding, since this would presuppose an intact ability to encode and update current location and bearing. Examples might be, on the one hand, 'tell me all the turns you would need to make on the way from here to the station, whether each one is left or right', and on the other 'turn this pointer so that it points directly towards the station' and 'is it farther as the crow flies from here to the the station or from here to the town hall?'.

The proposal, made earlier on logical grounds, to distinguish these 'updating position' and 'maintaining orientation' skills from the cognitive map *per se*, has received little support from the clinical literature. Where disorientation has occurred separately from loss of topographical memory, a general clouding of consciousness rather than loss of a particular skill has been suspected. However, no attempt seems to have been made to look specifically for such skills. Intact orientation and place-keeping might be shown by accurate navigation with a printed map, even in a subject with complete loss of cognitive maps for familiar areas. Conversely, an impairment of orientation and place-keeping would be revealed by an accurate description of routes which could not in practice be followed, provided that the inability to follow the routes was not due to the loss of a purely 'enabling' skill. It would be interesting if this dissociation could be found.

As expected, some failures at topographical tasks have been found to be caused by lack of 'enabling' skills. Most obviously, constructional apraxia impairs map-drawing, and is often manifested by a unilateral neglect, both of the map constructed and of the subject's own body. But in addition it seems that constructional apraxia and unilateral neglect are often associated with real deficiencies of topographical knowledge, though the association is asymmetrical. A remarkable disability, sometimes described as 'unilateral agnosia' (Brain, 1941), has been found in which patients with no visual field problems nevertheless persistently fail to 'notice' *left* turns, when describing or actually following a familiar route, and substitute right turns. This would not have been predicted from studies of normals, but can be described as an abnormality of the [ACTION] part of all nodes on network-maps: [turn left] is substituted by [turn right].

Finally, one finding with clinical patients suggests that the theoretical apparatus built up with normals must be extended or modified. This is that quite different lesions affect performance on two tasks which conceptually appear rather similar: the 'Money standardised road map' and the Semmes' 'locomotor maze'. Both would seem to depend on the ability to keep correctly oriented and positioned with respect to a (printed) map, and to differ chiefly on the mode of response – verbal or physical movement. The response mode *may* turn out to be the source of the difference, but until it does the possibility exists that the tasks actually tap two different aspects of orientation ability.

Several times in this account it has been suggested that clinical psychologists should follow up certain impairments, devise tasks of a certain specification, distinguish between certain different abilities, and so on. I would not wish to give the impression that cooperation between clinical and cognitive psychologists in this area is being impeded chiefly by one side. Rather, it seems to me that cognitive psychology has concentrated on the more static aspect of cognitive maps as a storehouse of fact, and neglected their use during navigation, and in particular the skill of 'keeping one's bearings'. Until more is known of this, it is not easy to suggest what symptoms clinicians might look for. In their turn, cognitive psychologists could benefit from an artificial intelligence expert turning his hand to exploring the potentialities and problems of network-maps, and the possibility of developing a workable description of a vector-map. Although the integration of the fields attempted in this chapter can only be regarded as preliminary, the extent of common ground suggests that the mutual benefit from further cooperation will be considerable: I hope so.

Acknowledgements

The Bird's Eye Plan of St Andrews is reproduced by permission of the National Library of Scotland, and part of a modern OS map by permission of the Director General of the Ordnance Survey. I am grateful to Dr Robin Baker for allowing me to read a pre-publication copy of his book, 'Human Navigation and the Sixth Sense'. And for many helpful comments and criticisms of earlier drafts of this chapter, which have considerably improved its readability, I would like to thank Andrew Ellis and in particular Alison Conning.

References

Anderson, J. and Tindall, M. (1972). The concept of home range: new data for the study of territorial behaviour. *Environmental Design Research Association* 3, 1.1–1.7
Appleyard, D. (1970). Styles and methods of structuring a city. *Environment and Behaviour* 2, 100–117
Baker, R. (1981). *Human Navigation and the Sixth Sense*. London: Hodder and Stoughton
Benton, A. L. (1969). Disorders of spatial orientation. *In* P. J. Vinken and G. W. Bruyn (eds), *Handbook of Clinical Neurology* Vol. 3. New York: Elsevier

Benton, A. L., Levin, H. S. and Van Allen, M. W. (1974). Geographic orientation in patients. *Neuropsychologia* **12**, 183–191

Böök, A. and Gärling, T. (1978a). Localisation of invisible reference points: effects of linear locomotion distance and location of reference points. *Umeå Psychological Reports* No. 139

Böök, A. and Gärling, T. (1978b). Processing of information about locomotion during locomotion: effects of concurrent task and locomotion patterns. *Umeå Psychological Reports* No. 135

Böök, A. and Gärling, T. (1978c). Localisation of invisible reference points: effects of body rotation angle and direction of reference points. *Umeå Psychological Reports* No. 140

Brain, W. R. (1941). Visual disorientation – lesions of the right hemisphere. *Brain* **64**, 244–272

Briggs, R. (1973). Urban cognitive distance. *In* R. Downs and D. Stea (eds), *Image and Environment*. Chicago: Aldine

Brown, R. and Kulik, J. (1977). Flashbulb memories. *Cognition* **5**, 73–79

Butters, N., Soeldner, C. and Redio, P. (1972). Comparison of parietal and frontal lobe deficits. *Perception and Motor Skills* **34**, 27–34

Byrne, R. W. (1979). Memory for urban geography. *Quarterly Journal of Experimental Psychology* **31**, 147–154

Byrne, R. W. and Scott, E. (in prep.). Representation of distance and direction in the blind.

Byrne, R. W. and Seaton, C. (in prep.). Human orientation in towns.

Cadwallader, M. T. (1973). A methodological analysis of cognitive distance. *In* W. F. E. Preiser (ed.), *Environmental Design Research*, Vol. 2. Stroudsburg: Dowden, Hutchinson and Ross

Canter, D. V. (1975). Distance estimation in Greater London. *S.S.R.C. Final Report*, University of Surrey

Canter, D. V. and Tagg, S. K. (1975). Distance estimation in cities. *Environment and Behaviour* **7**, 59–80

Cogan, D. G. (1960). Hemianopia and associated symptoms due to parietotemporal lobe lesions. *American Journal of Opthalmology* **50**, 1056–1066

Collins, A. M. and Loftus, E. F. (1975). A spreading-activation theory of semantic processing. *Psychological Review* **82**, 407–428

Critchley, M. (1951). Discussion on parietal lobe syndromes. *Proceedings of the Royal Society of Medicine* **44**, 337–341

Critchley, M. (1953). *The Parietal Lobes*. London: Arnold

Darwin, C. (1859). *On the Origin of Species by Means of Natural Selection*. London: J. Murray

Downs, R. and Stea, D. (1973). *Image and Environment*. Chicago: Aldine

Gärling, T., Böök, A. and Lindberg, E. (1975). Orientation performance in two-segment and three-segment route tasks during blindfolded and sighted walking. *Umeå Psychological Reports* No. 94

Gladwin, T. (1970). *East is a Big Bird*. Cambridge, Mass.: Harvard University Press

Golledge, R. G. and Zannaras, G. (1973). Cognitive approaches to the analysis of human spatial behaviour. *In* W. H. Ittleson (ed.), *Environment and Cognition*. New York: Seminar Press

Griffin, D. R. (1948). Topographical orientation. Reprinted in Downs and Stea (1973)

Hécaen, H., Penfield, W. and Bertrand, C. (1956). The syndrome of apractagnosia due to lesions of the minor cerebral hemisphere. *Archives of Neurology and Psychiatry* **75**, 400–434

Hintzman, D. L. (1979). Orientation in cognitive maps. Final Report to *National Science Foundation*

Howard, I. P. and Templeton, W. B. (1966). *Human Spatial Orientation*. London: Wiley

Keeton, W. T. (1971). Magnets interfere with pigeon homing. *Proceedings of the National Academy of Science of the U.S.A.* **68**, 102–106

Keeton, W. T. (1979). Avian orientation and navigation: a brief overview. *British Birds* **72**, 451–470

Kosslyn, S. M., Pick, H. L. and Fariello, G. R. (1974). Cognitive maps in children and men. *Child Development* **45**, 707–716

Kozlowski, L. T. and Bryant, K. J. (1977). Sense of direction, spatial orientation and cognitive maps. *Journal of Experimental Psychology* **3**, 590–598

Lee, T. R. (1970). Perceived distance as a function of direction in the city. *Environment and Behaviour* **2**, 40–51

Lewis, D. (1976). Route-finding and spatial orientation among aboriginals of Australia. *Oceania* **46**, 249–282

Lindberg, E. and Gärling, T. (1978). Acquisition of information during blind and sighted locomotion: effects of a concurrent task and locomotion paths. *Umeå Psychological Reports* No. 144

Linde, C. and Labov, W. (1975). Spatial networks as a site for the study of language and thought. *Language* **51**, 924–939

Lynch, K. (1960). *The Image of the City*. Cambridge, Mass.: MIT Press

McFie, J., Piercy, M. F. and Zangwill, O. L. (1950). Visual-spatial agnosia. *Brain* **73**, 167–190

McKinnon, J. (1978). *The Ape Within Us*. London: Collins

Merkel, F. W. and Wiltschko, W. (1965). Magnetismus und Richtungsfinden zugunruhiger Rotkehlchen. *Vogelwarte* **23**, 71–77

Neisser, U. (1976). *Cognition and Reality*. San Francisco: W. H. Freeman

Newcombe, F. (1969). *Missile Wounds of the Brain*. Milton-Keynes: Open University Press

Newcombe, F. and Ritchie Russell, W. (1969). Dissociated visual perception and spatial deficits in focal lesions of the right hemisphere. *Journal of Neurology* **32**, 73–81

Paterson, A. and Zangwill, O. L. (1944a). Recovery of spatial orientation in the post-traumatic confusional state. *Brain* **67**, 54–68

Paterson, A. and Zangwill, O. L. (1944b). Disorders of visual space perception. *Brain* **67**, 331–358

Paterson, A. and Zangwill, O. L. (1945). Topographical disorientation with unilateral lesion. *Brain* **68**, 188–212

Peters, R. (1973). Cognitive maps in wolves and men. *In* W. F. E. Preiser (ed.), *Environmental Design Research*, Vol. 2. Stroudsburg: Dowden, Hutchinson and Ross

Pocock, D. and Hudson, R. (1978). *Images of the Urban Environment*. London: Macmillan

Ratcliff, G. (1979). Spatial thought, mental rotation and the right cerebral hemisphere. *Neuropsychologia* **17**, 49–54

Ratcliff, G. and Newcombe, F. (1973). Spatial orientation in man: effects of left, right and bilateral cerebral lesions. *Journal of Neurology, Neurosurgery and Psychiatry* **36**, 448–454

Reitan, R. M. and Tarshes, E. L. (1959). Differential effects of lateralised brain lesions on the trail-making task. *Journal of Nervous and Mental Diseases* **129**, 257–262

Semmes, J., Weinstein, S., Ghent, L. and Teuber, H.-L. (1955). Spatial orientation: 1: analysis by locus of lesion. *Journal of Psychology* **39**, 227–244

Semmes, J., Weinstein, S., Ghent, L. and Teuber, H.-L. (1963). Impaired orientation in personal and extrapersonal space. *Brain* **86**, 747–772

Shallice, T. (1979). Case study approach in neuropsychological research. *Journal of Clinical Neuropsychology* **1**, 183–211

Shemyakin, F. N. (1962). Orientation in space. *In* B. G. Anan'yer *et al.* (eds), *Psychological Science in the U.S.S.R.*, Vol. 1. Washington: Report 11466 of U.S. Office of Technical Reports

Shepard, R. and Chipman, S. (1970). Second-order isomorphism of internal representations. *Cognitive Psychology* **1**, 1–17

Siegel, A. W. and White, S. H. (1975). The development of spatial representation of large-scale environments. *In* H. W. Reese (ed.), *Advances in Child Development and Behavior*, 10. New York: Academic Press

Spalding, J. M. K. and Zangwill, O. L. (1950). Disturbance of number form in a case of brain injury. *Journal of Neurology, Neurosurgery and Psychiatry* **13**, 24–29

Tolman, E. C. (1948). Cognitive maps in rats and men. *Psychological Review* **55**, 189–208

Tuan, Y. F. (1975). Images and mental maps. *Annals of the Association of American Geographers* **65**, 205–213

Walcott, C. and Green, R. P. (1974). Orientation of homing pigeons altered by a change in the direction of an applied magnetic field. *Science* **184**, 180–182

Weinstein, S., Semmes, J., Ghent, L. and Teuber, H.-L. (1956). Spatial orientation: II: Analysis by concomitant defects. *Journal of Psychology* **42**, 249–263

Whiteley, A. M. and Warrington, E. K. (1978). Selective impairment of topographical memory: a single case study. *Journal of Neurology, Neurosurgery and Psychiatry* **41**, 575–578

Yates, F. A. (1966). *The Art of Memory*. London: Routledge and Kegan Paul

Zangwill, O. L. (1951). Discussion on parietal lobe syndromes. *Proceedings of the Royal Society of Medicine* **44**, 343–346

9

Action and Performance*

ERIC A. ROY
*Department of Kinesiology, University of Waterloo, Canada
and Department of Psychology, Mount Sinai Hospital,
Toronto, Canada*

1 Introduction

Human motor performance has been the focus of much research interest in the last decade (e.g. Stelmach, 1976, 1978; Stelmach and Requin, 1980). As a result important new insights into the processes underlying learning and performance have been acquired. Much of this work has dealt with how a particular skill or action might be integrated into a coherent pattern of goal-directed movements. Emphasis has been placed on how to reduce errors, without much concern for the precise nature of the errors which occur. Careful consideration of the nature of errors may, however, provide important insights into the organization of and processes involved in the human action system.

In recent years studies of the errors made in performing actions have been made. One line of research has examined the errors which occur in the normal person, so called slips of action or actions-not-as-planned (Norman, 1979; Reason, 1977, 1979). Errors evident in the performance of brain-damaged persons have been the focus of other research (e.g. Kimura, 1977; Roy, 1978, 1981). While the errors arising in each of these states (i.e. normality and pathology) have provided insight into organizational principles in the human action system, comparisons of the errors evident in these states may be even more fruitful in this regard. The purpose of this chapter is to make such comparisons with the aim of providing further insight into the processes involved in human action. A discussion of one of the major disorders of the human action system, apraxia, is followed by a description of the nature of the errors arising in this pathological condition. These are compared with errors arising in the normal person, described by Norman (1979) and Reason (1979). The implications of these errors for the principles of organization and dynamics of control in the human action system complete the discussion.

* Preparation of this manuscript was supported through an NSERC grant.

2 Theories of motor performance in pathology: apraxia

Hughlings Jackson's (see Taylor, 1932) description of the inability of some language disordered (aphasic) patients to perform certain actions on command (e.g. coughing, protruding the tongue), in the absence of weakness in the musculature involved, was the first account of a movement disorder which later was termed apraxia (Steinthal, 1871). The term apraxia, then, refers to a variety of movement disorders where the patient is unable to successfully carry out movements, and where the inability cannot be attributed to motor paralysis, ataxia, or dementia.

The purpose of this section is to review briefly the major types of apraxia and outline the various theoretical viewpoints used to explain the mechanisms of these movement disorders. Details as to the types of errors are provided in the next section. Emphasis here is specifically on the upper limb apraxias. A broader perspective both in terms of types of apraxia and historical background can be found in several recent texts (e.g. Hécaen and Albert, 1978; Heilman, 1979).

A CLASSIFICATION OF APRAXIA

1 *Bilateral apraxias.* Hugo Liepmann (1905, 1908, 1920), a pioneer in the study of apraxia, described two forms of bilateral apraxia. The first, ideational apraxia, was associated with damage to the left posterior parietal region. Defective performance of a complex sequence of gestures characterized this movement disorder which was thought due to a dissolution of the plan or idea of the movement.

The second, ideomotor apraxia, also involved damage to the left parietal regions but in this disorder the damage was somewhat less diffuse (Brown, 1972; Hécaen, 1969). While complex motor acts were thought to be performed adequately, the components of the sequences, single gestures, were not carried out correctly. Also, a clear distinction was observed between, on the one hand, responses to verbal command and, on the other hand, imitation and those involving actual use of the object, responses in the presence of the object being better. For Liepmann the observation that the sequence of actions was performed adequately suggested, unlike ideational apraxia, that the plan or idea of the movement sequence was intact in ideomotor apraxia. The dissociation between performance to verbal command and that on imitation indicated to Liepmann that the deficit was one of a disconnection between the idea of the movement and the 'motor engram' used to execute the movement. Liepmann viewed these as distinct forms of apraxia: he felt that ideational apraxia should be applied only to those cases in which actions with objects, particularly serial actions with multiple objects, were disturbed.

Liepmann's views have been challenged on two points: the basis for the distinction between these two forms of apraxia and the view that these are distinct forms. With regard to the first point De Renzie, Pieczuro and

Vignolo (1968) concurred with the view that ideational apraxia involves the defective use of objects. They found that 33 percent of their aphasic group were apraxic according to this definition. Heilman (1973), on the other hand, considered the distinction between ideational and ideomotor apraxia was not on a continuum of object use but rather on one involving imitation. His patients while unable to perform movements to verbal command were able to perform flawlessly with the objects; such a difference in performance under these conditions characterizes the performance of the ideomotor apraxic. In contrast to ideomotor apraxia, however, there was also a marked improvement on imitation. Heilman (1973) thus proposed that the difference between ideational and ideomotor apraxia was in terms of the facilitatory effects of imitation on performance, facilitation only being apparent in ideational apraxia. Ideational apraxia was viewed as a fault in the processes intervening between language comprehension and motor performance – 'a disorder in the verbally mediated motor sequence selector' (Heilman, 1973, p. 863). Ideomotor apraxia, on the other hand, involved a 'loss of memory for motor sequences or the inability of these memories to reach the motor cortex. . .' (Heilman, 1973, p. 863).

The second challenge to Liepmann's views concerned his contention that ideational and ideomotor apraxia are distinctly different forms of apraxic disturbance. A number of investigators (e.g. Brown, 1972; DeRenzi et al., 1968; Heilman, 1973) concur with him on this point, although the explanatory basis for the distinction does not coincide with Liepmann's. Others (e.g. Hécaen, 1968; Roy, 1978; Zangwill, 1960), however, do not agree with Liepmann in that they view ideational apraxia as a severe form of ideomotor apraxia.

Luria (1966, 1973) has identified two types of bilateral apraxia, frontal and premotor apraxia. In both these forms the movement disorder is similar to that in ideational apraxia in that a sequence of actions is performed improperly, while individual movements or gestures are performed correctly. In these cases (frontal and premotor apraxia), however, there may be more disruption to the initiation of movement and a greater prevalence of perseveration. Moreover, performance does not appear to improve with imitation or object use. Frontal apraxia resulting from damage to the prefrontal areas of the cerebral cortex is thought to result from a disruption to the regulatory function of behaviour which, according to Luria (1966), involves organizing a plan or intention for action and comparing subsequent performance to this intention in order to assess whether the goal has been achieved. The goal-directed motor act is replaced by isolated movements which bear little connection to the original purpose. In contrast, premotor apraxia (also called dynamic apraxia by Luria, 1966) involving damage to the premotor areas constitutes a disruption in the organization of motor acts in time. The plan or intention is thought to be intact, but executing actions in the requisite temporal order is disturbed.

2 *Unilateral apraxias.* Several unilateral apraxias have been described. Liepmann (1905, 1908, 1920) identified three forms: limb-kinetic or melo-kinetic, sympathetic, and callosal. The first type, limb-kinetic apraxia, involved damage in the region of the sensorimotor cortex and could affect either the left or the right hand, depending on which hemisphere was damaged. The movement disorder was characterized by an ataxic-like clumsiness. The sequential ordering of movements and simple gestures were performed adequately. Liepmann viewed this apraxia as a disturbance to the motor engram itself. Luria's (1966) kinesthetic apraxia was similar in symptomology to limb-kinetic apraxia.

The second form, sympathetic apraxia, was associated with left hemisphere damage, right hemisparesis and motor aphasia and involved apraxia of the left arm and leg. Disorders in the performance of various gestures both to verbal command and on imitation were present, although there was improvement on imitation.

The third type of unilateral disorder described by Liepmann also involved defective performance in the use of the left hand. The patient was able to manipulate objects and imitate gestures with his hand; performance to verbal commands was, however, strikingly impaired. Liepmann (1920) attributed this apraxia to an anterior collosal lesion which interrupted the anatomic connections between the anterior aspects of left and the right motor cortex which controls the left hand. The right hemisphere was thought to be deprived of praxic control exerted by the left hemisphere. A variant of this was recently proposed by Geschwind (1965, 1975) who thought that this apraxia resulted because the right hemisphere, being disconnected from the left, did not have purview to the verbal commands processed in the left hemisphere.

While the latter two apraxias have received considerable study over the years and have been accepted as forms of apraxia (e.g. Geschwind, 1965, 1975; Goodglass and Kaplan, 1963), there has frequently been resistance to referring to the first form, limb-kinetic, as an apraxia. As with Luria's kinesthetic apraxia which also involves clumsy movements due to damage in the sensorimotor region, this movement disorder has been likened more to an ataxia than an apraxia (e.g. DeAjuriaguerra and Tissot, 1969).

Denny-Brown (1958; Denny-Brown and Chambers, 1958; Denny-Brown, Yanagisawa and Kirk, 1975) has identified a unilateral apraxia which he has termed kinetic apraxia. This apraxia is viewed as a disruption in equilibrium between reactions of contact and grasping and those of avoidance and withdrawal. Two subtypes were described. One type, magnetic apraxia, involves release of grasping reactions. There is an overemphasis of flexion of joints, particularly the fingers and toes, resulting in persistent grasping. The other, repellent apraxia, constitutes a release of withdrawal reactions. Here there is an overemphasis of extension, particularly of the fingers and wrist. The wrist and fingers tend to extend in response to any form of tactile stimulation in contrast to the reflexive grasping reaction seen in magnetic apraxia. As such these movement disorders tend to interfere with all gestures and movements.

In general unilateral apraxias seem to involve two forms. One relates to a disconnection between the motor centers in the right hemisphere controlling the left hand and the praxic control (Liepmann, 1920), or language control areas of the left hemisphere (Geschwind, 1975). The other types involve motor deficits which tend to interfere with the smooth, controlled execution of movements in general. Liepmann's limb-kinetic apraxia, Luria's kinesthetic apraxia and Denny-Brown's kinetic apraxia are exemplars of this type.

B   MECHANISMS OF APRAXIA

Many proposals have been put forth to explain the nature of the apraxic disorder. These seem to fall into four general categories: those which view the disorder as conceptual in nature (e.g. Ettlinger, 1969); those which consider apraxia as one of the disconnection syndromes (e.g. Geschwind, 1965, 1975), those which view apraxia as a disorder in the organization and/or execution of movement, and those which consider apraxia to involve a deficit in spatial orientation.

1   *Conceptual disorders.* One of the first notions regarding apraxia was that it was an exemplar of a more general disorder termed asymbolia – a conceptual disorder involving the inability to understand or express symbols (Finkelenburg, 1870, in Brown, 1972). This notion received impetus by the finding that, in right-handers, apraxia and aphasia are frequently coexistent symptoms as they both result from damage to the left hemisphere (Goldstein, 1942). Whereas some forms of aphasia were thought to involve a disturbance of verbal symbolization, apraxia was thought to be a defect of nonverbal symbolization (e.g. gesture and pantomime). Goldstein (1942) and Denny-Brown (1958) were early proponents of this viewpoint. The first perspective involves the concept of symbols, i.e. words or actions which stand for or represent other events or ideas. One of the lines of investigation here reasoned that if apraxia does involve a symbolic disorder, its incidence should be related to the incidence of a disorder to the language/speech system, which does involve the use of symbols. Several investigations have demonstrated little relationship between aphasia and apraxia (Goodglass and Kaplan, 1963; Liepmann, 1920) suggesting that apraxia is not a disorder of symbolic behaviour. Other investigations, however, which have employed a larger sample size and examined the nature of the language impairment have found a relationship between the severity of the two disorders (DeRenzi et al., 1968; Kertesz, 1979). Particularly strong was the relationship between severity of apraxia and the severity of the deficit in language comprehension. These findings do not necessarily support the notion

that apraxia is a symbolic disorder; rather, they imply that there may be some general comprehension-conceptual disorder which underlies both apraxia and language. This notion of a comprehension deficit in apraxia, the second major perspective on the nature of the conceptual disorder in apraxia, will be expanded on shortly.

Another approach to the study of apraxia as a symbolic disorder involves the supposition apraxics should perform symbolic gestures more poorly than non-symbolic (meaningless) ones. Evidence provided by Kimura (Kimura and Archibald, 1974; Kimura, 1977) indicates that apraxics perform poorly on both types of gesture implying that the disorder in apraxia may not be symbolically based.

The second major perspective on studying apraxia as a conceptual deficit involves the notion of comprehension. That is, apraxia may involve a disorder in understanding (1) the verbal commands outlining what the patient is to do, (2) the use to which the target object is to be put or (3) the movements which are to be employed in performing a particular action. One line of investigation here has examined the relationship between aphasia and apraxia. DeRenzi et al. (1968) noted a high correlation between ideational apraxia and receptive aphasia. They also reported aphasics to be the poorest at associating an object with the movement which is commonly required to use the object appropriately. From these findings they argued that apraxia may be a manifestation of an impairment in concept formation, an inability to associate different aspects of the same concept.

In more recent work Kertesz (1979) found evidence in support of the relationship between degree of comprehension deficit and the degree of apraxia described by DeRenzi et al. (1968). Using the western Aphasia Battery he found that aphasic groups (Isolation, Global and Wernicke's) with the lowest comprehension scores had the lowest praxis scores. Also, the correlation between performance on the praxis tests and comprehension scores (r = 0.75) was substantially higher than that between the praxis tests and verbal fluency (r = 0.60) or repetition (r = 0.57). Apparently, a majority of the patients with poor comprehension scores demonstrated that they understood the verbal command requesting them to perform an action, suggesting that the relationship between comprehension and apraxia did not arise simply because the patient could not follow the commands. This evidence seems to point to a factor in apraxia which is beyond auditory-verbal comprehension, 'a general factor of concept formation or high order cognitive function which is common to language comprehension and praxis' (Kertesz, 1979).

While both of these studies strongly suggest that there may be a conceptual component to apraxia, there are several important problems. First, in both studies, but particularly in that by Kertesz (1979), it is apparent that Broca's aphasics, who have among the highest comprehension scores, are very apraxic, at least as much so as the Wernicke's aphasics who have among the lowest scores on comprehension. The apraxia apparent in the Broca's aphasics would thus seem not to involve the same type of (comprehension) disorder as that seen in the Wernicke's aphasics. Secondly, studies indicating a relationship between deficits in comprehension and apraxia immediately raise the question as to whether the patients understood the verbal commands. Moreover, they provide no insight into the nature of the conceptual deficit. Both of these problems are solvable only if one incorporates tests of comprehension into the apraxia assessment procedures. It is to this approach that we now turn.

This approach incorporates procedures for assessing the integrity of the patient's conceptual framework for action within the apraxia test. It has the advantage of dealing with comprehension and conceptualization as they pertain specifically to the actions which are to be performed rather than with more general aspects of comprehension. This approach was originally used by Liepmann and has been adopted by others since his pioneering work (e.g. DeRenzi *et al.*, 1968; Heilman, 1973; Haaland, Porch and Delaney, 1980; Zangwill, 1960).

Several dimensions of conceptualization have been evaluated: comprehension of the verbal commands, conceptualization of the actions to be used, and knowledge of the use of the objects which are to be used. Several studies which have examined some (or all) of these dimensions indicate that apraxic patients frequently perform well on these tests of comprehension. According to these results conceptual factors would not seem to contribute to apraxia. Heilman (1979, p. 175), however, described a subtle type of conceptual deficit, one in which some ideomotor apraxics seem to have a deficit in the comprehension of pantomimed acts (e.g. flipping a coin without the coin). When shown films of pantomimed acts, these patients often selected as correct acts which were performed clumsily or ones in which the act was executed using a body part as an object (e.g. a closed fist as a hammer). This apparent defect in comprehension may be related to the fact that apraxics frequently are unable to recognize when their own performance is poor. While it is difficult to determine exactly what dimension of conceptualization Heilman's task is evaluating, it is imperative that such careful examinations be directed toward assessing these subtle conceptual defects which bear directly upon the actions to be performed.

In sum, evidence does not strongly support the notion that apraxia is a symbolic disorder. Nevertheless, some evidence does point to a subtle type of comprehension deficit which may underly some forms of apraxia. It would seem important to continue investigations into apraxia and other related disorders with the aim of more clearly delineating such subtle comprehension deficits. Several points bear consideration here. First, there is a considerable literature now concerned with the relationship between language and action (e.g. Greenfield and Westerman, 1978) which demonstrates that the structure of the sentence requesting a series of actions substantially influences the performer's conceptualization of what actions he is to perform. The structure of the sentence requesting the patient to perform an action, then, may influence his success in performance (see Brown, 1972).

The second point here relates to the patient's understanding of what the 'target' objects are used for. For example, the apraxic patient can often indicate what to do (e.g. to hammer) with an object or tool (e.g. a hammer) he is unable to use; however, it seems unclear as to whether he really 'understands' what should be done with the object. Work with anomic aphasics (Goodglass and Baker, 1976) may be instructive here. When confronted with an object and asked to name it, these aphasics very frequently indicate what the object (e.g. a hammer) is used for (e.g. hammering) rather than giving its name. In contrast to this performance, Goodglass and Baker (1976) found that when asked to indicate what words were associated with various objects, these patients made the most errors and took the longest in responding to words which described what should be done with these objects (i.e. the functional associates). Apparently, the semantic field for functional associates of objects is the most severely disturbed in these patients. These findings seem to reveal that although these patients very frequently give the function of an object in confrontation naming situations, they may not really understand what this function implies. In a similar way the apraxic patient's verbal response to the question what is the 'target' object used for may not reveal his true knowledge of what this function implies. Possibly these apraxics have a particularly profound deficit in the semantic field for functional associates suggesting that the movement disorder reflects a substantial conceptual problem.

A final point here concerns the role of context and seems relevant to observed differences between performing an action while grasping the object as opposed to a pantomimed action without the object. When the object is held by the patient, a large number of contextual cues are present – visual information regarding the orientation of the object with respect to the body and the environment and proprioceptive information associated with grasping the object. These cues are not present (i.e. they must be imagined) in the condition where the patient does not grasp the object when demonstrating its use. This contextual information may provide a link between the concept of what the object is used for and how it is to be used and the mechanisms in programming actions for using the object (see notion of descriptions in *Selection and activation*, section 4B2).

An ability to demonstrate the use of an object *only* when actually grasped may suggest that without the object in his grasp the patient is incapable of generating the contextual images necessary to relate the concept of the action to the movement system involved in programming the appropriate movements. In this situation patients often use a body part as the object (e.g. closed fist as a hammer or the fingers as the blades of a pair of scissors) indicating that they understand the concept of the action but are unable to generate the appropriate movements and/or limb postures. On the other hand, if the patient is unable to demonstrate the use of an object under either condition, it may mean that the action concept itself (what to do with and/or how to use the object) is disordered or that the contextual information involved in using the object no longer provides access to the mechanism for programming the appropriate movements.

2 *Apraxia as a disconnection syndrome.* Liepmann (1908) was the first to suggest that apraxia may result from a disconnection between control centers within the cerebral cortex. He envisaged a praxic control center in the region of the supramarginal gyrus of the left hemisphere. Praxic control over the right hand is enabled through projections to the premotor region of the left frontal area which project to the left motor hand area. Control of the left hand was thought to depend on collosal connections from the left motor hand area to homologous areas for the left hand in the right hemisphere. Lesions in these pathways were thought to result in dis-connections among these various control areas. For example, damage to the left premotor area not only resulted in right hand weakness and apraxia but also, due to the loss of control exerted by the homologous areas in the right hemisphere, resulted in 'sympathetic' apraxia in the left hand. Damage restricted to the corpus callosum was thought to result in a left-sided apraxia alone.

This 'disconnection' view of apraxia was adopted by Geschwind (1965, 1975). In his version, unlike that described by Liepmann, verbal commands and, hence, speech reception areas (Wernicke's area) are seen to be important in eliciting apraxia. Geschwind (1965, 1975) noted in studies with split-brain patients that to verbal command these patients were apraxic with their left hand, while imitating the movements or actually using the object, they were not apraxic. Geschwind argued that apraxia was only present to verbal command in these patients. According to Geschwind the right hemisphere was unable to comprehend the verbal command for action and to direct the left hand in executing the appro-priate movements, because it was disconnected, due to the collosal section, from the left hemisphere which processes the verbal command. Improvement in the praxic performance of the left hand with imitation or object use was viewed by Geschwind as evidence for the right hemi-sphere's ability for praxic control when processing verbal commands is no longer necessary.

Several problems are apparent with this view. First, recent work re-ported by Dimond and Beaumont (1974), and Zaidel and Sperry (1977) indicates that the right hemisphere is able to understand action words, a finding which brings into question Geschwind's assumption that the right hemisphere is incapable of comprehending verbal commands for action.

Secondly, if the right hemisphere is capable of praxic control when the verbal command is obviated (i.e. with imitation or object use), why is it that the intact right hemisphere of apraxic patients with left hemisphere damage is unable to exert praxic control over the left hand in the same way as Geschwind proposes that this hemisphere exerts control in split-brain patients (Kimura, 1979)? Perhaps the damaged left hemisphere exerts an inhibitory effect over the praxic control of the right hemisphere in the way that Kinsbourne has argued it inhibits the language/speech functions of the right hemisphere (Kinsbourne, 1978).

Thirdly, the length of time between the collosal section and the assessment of limb praxis is an important consideration. Sperry, Gazzaniga and Bogen (1969) noted that the unilateral (left) apraxia to verbal command initially observed in their split-brain patients had disappeared in all but one patient within one week of the commissurotomy.

Finally, the possibility for control of the left hand by the ipsilateral (left) hemisphere must be considered. Certainly, the more the praxis task requires proximal musculature, the more likely it is that the patient may be able to perform a given task to verbal command.

While there are a number of problems with Geschwind's view of verbal commands in eliciting apraxia via collosal sectioning, Heilman (1973) describes three cases which seem to involve an inability to imitate the correct sequences of movement with either hand in response to language. He suggested there was a disconnection between the cerebral areas for decoding language and those for the control of limb praxis.

In a more recent discussion Heilman (1979) has also proposed that apraxia may result from a disconnection between control centers. In this case, he argues, that apraxia may result if control centers in posterior parietal areas concerned with programming motor acts are disconnected from the anterior motor control centers. This proposal seems similar to one of Liepmann's views of disconnections in apraxia underlying ideo-motor apraxia.

3   *Apraxia as a movement disorder.* Liepmann (1905) was the first to suggest that apraxia was a movement disorder. He proposed that the left supra-marginal gyrus was the critical region for the control of limb praxis. This region was thought critical for the control of limb (or oral) movements without objects in which external (visual guidance) control is minimal. Damage to this region resulted in ideational apraxia. In this apraxia the ideational outline, an idea of the body parts as well as the rhythm, speed and sequence of movements to be used, was thought to be disturbed.

Kimura (1977, 1979) has, in recent years, elaborated upon this position. According to Kimura the supramarginal region of the left hemisphere contains a system which controls the selection and/or execution of limb positions/postures bilaterally. This control, she suggests, is not exerted over the sequence of positions/postures in an action, but rather over the transition from one position to another. This claim is based on two findings. First, tasks which required the repetition of the same response over time (e.g. single finger tapping, screw rotation) were not differentially affected by left hemisphere damage. Secondly, on limb or oral tasks which required the patient to assume different postures and/or positions, these patients tended to repeat previously executed (and correct) movements, seemingly having difficulty making the transition between limb postures. This postural selection mechanism is thought to be used within an egocentric (body-centered) spatial reference system in which external (visual primarily) guidance is thought to be minimal. This mechanism, thus, controls movements in which the external constraints are unvarying (i.e. the environmental demands do not change). Such a system, would, she suggests, be important in traditional limb praxis tasks (the use of common objects), where the movements involved are characterized by unvarying external constraints.

Heilman (1975, 1979) has proposed a scheme which also alludes to the importance of the supramarginal region of the left hemisphere (cf. Kimura, 1979). Apraxia may result from damage to this area due to the destruction of visuokinesthetic engrams used to program the motor association cortex which innervates the motor neuron pools used to execute the motor act. 'The motor association cortex programs movements (more than one muscle) and visuokinesthetic motor engrams in the parietal cortex program sequences of movements. . .' (Heilman, 1979, p. 172). While Heilman's (1979) emphasis on the importance of the posterior regions of the left hemisphere in limb praxis concurs with Kimura's viewpoint, the mechanism he alludes to may be different. The sequencing of movements and external (visual) guidance seem to be features of his scheme.

In addition to the left hemisphere's role in this 'sequential programming' mechanism, Heilman (1975) also describes a mechanism which is concerned with the finesse with which movements are performed. On a rapid finger-tapping task, his quantification of finesse or clumsiness, he found that the average rate of tapping was significantly lower in his apraxic patients than in his non-apraxic patients. Pieczuro and Vignolo (1967), Kimura (1979) and Haaland, Porch and Delaney (1980) have also addressed this problem of the clumsiness of apraxic patients. Their results, however, have not concurred with those of Heilman (1975). On manual dexterity tasks (screw rotation and/or single finger tapping) Pieczuro and Vignolo (1967) and Kimura (1979; Kimura and Archibald, 1974) found no differences between apraxic and non-apraxic left hemisphere patients, in contrast to Heilman (1975). Neither did they find differences between left and right hemisphere damaged patients.

Kimura (1979) further reported that the performance deficit was not bilateral; it tended to be greater in the hand contralateral to the damaged hemisphere and was associated with somatosensory loss as measured by a tactile two point threshold. She concluded that the performance of fine finger movements was thus not exclusively subserved by the left hemisphere. While such poor fine finger control would undoubtedly affect the apraxic patient's ability to use objects (i.e. he would be clumsy), this observed clumsiness was thought not to be the result of ineffective control by the praxis system in the left hemisphere.

Haaland, Porch and Delaney (1980) examined the performance of left-brain damaged apraxics and non-apraxics on a series of manual dexterity tasks. Their results bear upon the findings of both Kimura (1979) and Heilman (1975). Contrary to Heilman their apraxic groups did not perform differently on a finger-tapping task. They attributed this discrepancy to differences in the criteria for classifying patients as apraxic. While the apraxic groups did not differ on this simple repetitive task, there were large differences in favour of the non-apraxic group on more complex tasks (maze coordination and grooved pegboard). They argued that these differing results related to differing demands in the two types of task. The tapping task required sequencing of the same response, while the other more complex tasks involved sequencing of different responses. The apraxic patients, having incurred brain damage which was more anterior than that in the non-apraxics, possibly involving the premotor cortex, would, they argue, have very likely experienced more difficulty with the latter more complex tasks. According to Luria (1966, 1973) damage to the premotor area leads to disruption of movements which require the sequencing of *different* responses as opposed to the *same* response over time.

This notion that apraxics have particular problems in tasks which require performing a series of different responses seems similar to Kimura's (1977) proposal regarding the type of control exerted by her postural selection (praxis) system. In this case, however, the neural control center seems to be anterior, while Kimura's is posterior. While the tasks used, the locations of lesions, and criteria for classifying patients as apraxic are very different in these two studies, thus possibly precluding any valid comparisons, there seem to be two possible reasons for this apparent congruity. As suggested by Kimura (1979, figure 7.6(b)) possibly the posterior praxis system exerts control via the anterior (premotor) area. Damage to this area (Haaland *et al.*, 1980) would thus reflect disruption in control by the posterior praxis system. Alternately, anterior brain areas on the left may subserve a more or less independent system for the control of limb praxis which, however, shares the principles of control which apply to the posterior system. Kimura (1979, p. 214) doubts that praxic control is exerted by anterior areas. There are, however, numerous examples of apraxia with anterior lesions (e.g. Haaland *et al.*, 1980; Kertesz, 1979); these must be adequately accounted for in any comprehensive model.

It is apparent that apraxia may result from damage to the posterior and possibly the anterior regions of the left cerebral hemisphere. The contribution of these two regions to the control of limb praxis may, however, be somewhat different. Luria (1966, 1973) and more recently Roy (1978) have considered these differences. In this view the cerebral cortex is seen as a highly differentiated but interacting system of zones. Complex functions, such as limb praxis, are organized as functional systems which may be disturbed by lesions in any link among these systems.

For Luria apraxia could result from disorders to the input (afferent apraxia) to the system or to the output from the system (efferent apraxias). Damage in the parietal-occipital areas was thought to result in afferent apraxias. Lesions in these regions disrupt the analysis of spatial coordinates within which movement takes place. Action disintegrates primarily with respect to the spatial organization of action, impairing performance of practic activity. Damage in the anterior regions of the cerebrum was also thought to precipitate apraxia (frontal and premotor apraxia), but for different reasons. The frontal and prefrontal areas were thought to play an important role in integrating afferent information, in the regulation of action by speech and in directing the behavioral act toward the goal (i.e. planning). The premotor area of the frontal region, on the other hand, was thought important in the organization of action over time. It was thought especially important in actions which require the sequencing of *different* movements over time (cf. Haaland et al., 1980). In this case apraxia was seen more as an output disorder (Luria, 1966, 1973).

Elaborating on Luria's views; Roy (1978) considered apraxia to involve disturbances to one or more functions in a cognitive, information-processing system. Damage to the frontal or parietal-occipital areas was seen to disrupt planning, while damage to the premotor and sensorimotor regions was thought to disturb the execution of action, either in terms of the sequence of a number of movements (premotor damage) or poor control over isolated movements in a sequence (sensorimotor damage).

Kelso and Tuller (1981) provide the most recent account of apraxia as a movement disorder. Their approach derives from the notion that the motor system is organized heterarchically (i.e. there is no one executor or controller) and involves a coalitional style of control based on a dynamic interface between the performer and the environment (see Turvey, Shaw and Mace, 1978). One of the cornerstones of this view of the motor system is that of tuning, whereby supraspinal influences bias or change brain-stem and spinal organization to provide the 'postural context' in which a circumscribed class of movements may occur. In their view apraxia may result from brain insults which disrupt these supraspinal influences on brainstem and spinal organization, preventing the patient from specifying the appropriate postural context for actions he is requested to perform.

4   *Apraxia as a spatial deficit.* Apraxia has been viewed as a disruption in spatial orientation. Lhermitte (1939), DeAjuriaguerra (DeAjuriaguerra and Tissot, 1969; DeAjuriaguerra, Hécaen and Angelergues, 1960) and others (e.g. Luria, 1966; Roy, 1978) have alluded to this type of deficit in apraxia, although it is not clear precisely what the nature of the spatial deficit might be. Some view the problem as involving disruptions at a relatively low (sensory) level, others consider it to involve a disturbance to higher level integrative processes, while still others consider it to result from a distorted body image. Most recently, Kimura (1979) has proposed that apraxia may result from a disruption to an internal (body-central) spatial reference system. Although constructional apraxia is not of major concern in this chapter, work examining this type of apraxia has provided some of the most important findings for this notion of apraxia as a spatial deficit (see Warrington, 1969 for a review).

3   Errors in normality and pathology

Considering the issues presented above it is apparent that damage to the brain is associated with deficits in the control of actions. These deficits are revealed in the types of errors made. While errors in the organization and execution of actions occur in this state of pathology, they are also apparent in persons who have not incurred any apparent brain damage, i.e. in the normal state. It is to a consideration of these errors that we now turn our attention.

A   ERRORS IN NORMALITY

Both Norman (1979) and Reason (1977, 1979) have attempted to characterize the errors which occur in normality as disturbances to different stages in processing, from the formation of the intent to act and the selection of the response to the actual execution of the movements involved in the sequence. Norman (1979) suggests that errors or 'slips of action' may occur at any one of three stages: intention, activation and triggering. At the level of intention errors can result from a faulty analysis of the situation (mode error) or because the description of the desired act is not specific enough (description error), resulting in selecting an action which is inappropriate, for example, replacing the lid of the sugar container on the coffee cup. While this lack of specificity leaves the system open to make an error, the actual error which is made is determined by other factors. For example, the action which is substituted may be related in some way to the one intended.

At the stage of activation errors are seen to arise from either loss of activation which precipitates execution errors (e.g. misordering, ommissions) or unintentional activation which results in the activation and triggering of actions which are not part of the current sequence (e.g. 'On passing through the back porch on my way to get my car I stopped to put on my wellington boots and gardening jacket as if to work in the garden', from Reason, 1979). The resulting errors are termed capture errors, associative errors, and data-driven errors. Capture errors occur when a current action sequence is replaced by one which is similar to it but which is more well learned than the current one or has been more frequently associated with the present situation than the current, intended action. Associative errors occur when actions associated with the current or intended action are activated and subsequently used to control behaviour. Data-driven errors occur as a result of the interaction between the environment and action. A stimulus in the environment precipitates the intrusion of an error into performance.

At the stage of triggering Norman describes errors which result because of either false triggering which can lead to a reversal or misordering of the elements of a sequence (e.g. 'Sitting in my car about to leave my workplace, I found I had put the car into gear and released the handbrake without having started the engine', from Reason, 1979), to blending two actions together or to thought replacing or stimulating action, or failure to trigger the action schema which leads to errors in which the action sequence does not occur. This, he suggests, may be due to insufficient activation or because the conditions present at the time of the intended action were not enough like those associated with the intended schema or were not specified well enough for a match to occur so that triggering might occur.

Reason (1977) has also examined errors made in normality and has termed them 'actions not as planned', i.e. when the plan of action is satisfactory, but the actions do not go according to this plan. Central to his view is the plan (cf. Miller, Galanter and Pribram, 1960) which he considers to be a hierarchically organized set of instructions governing the sequence of actions leading to a particular goal. The errors he describes represent failures of different processes or operations involved in carrying out the action. They result in the action not going as planned. Errors, he suggests, result principally in situations where the performer's attention is not directed to the unfolding action. Accordingly, he proposes that in order for action to proceed toward the intended goal attention must be directed at key choice points, which requires a delicate balance between a closed-loop feedback-based control mode which demands attention and an open-loop mode which, he suggests, may control action with a minimum of attention and without reference to feedback information.

One type of error results from discrimination failures, (e.g. putting shaving cream on one's toothbrush), where input information is misclassified due to confusion between various attributes of the objects which are acted upon. Another type is due to program assembly failures (e.g. 'I put the butter on the drain board and the dirty dishes in the refrigerator, instead of the other way around', from Reason, 1979) where the errors result from the transposition of movement elements within or between programs. A third type, test failures, are errors which stem from a failure to verify (i.e. test) 'the progress of an action sequence at "key checkpoints" '. In some cases these errors are exemplified in undershooting or overshooting the intended end-point. In other cases, for example, branching errors, actions may proceed toward a goal other than the one originally intended. Subroutine failures, a fourth type of error, exemplified as insertions, omissions, and misordering of elements in the sequence, result from a disruption in the execution of the sequence of actions (e.g. 'While running water into a bucket from the kitchen tap, I placed the lid back onto the bucket before I had turned off the tap', from Reason, 1979). Finally, storage failures are seen resulting from poor recall of plans or actions. Forgetting previous actions resulting in 'losing one's place' in a sequence and forgetting what one intended to do are both examples of this type of error (e.g. 'I began to pour a second kettle of boiling water into a teapot full of freshly made tea. I did not recall having just made it', from Reason, 1979).

In examining the classifications made by Reason (1977, 1979) and Norman (1979) it seems that three major types of errors occur. In the first the actual production of the action sequence is disturbed so that the sequence is executed improperly: the elements of the sequence may be misordered; needed elements may be omitted or unwanted elements added; elements may be repeated; the elements of two sequences may be blended together; the action may be continued for longer than is necessary or terminated prematurely. In the other types of errors the integrity of the action sequence is unaffected. In these cases either inappropriate actions are performed or the action is omitted completely.

While both Norman (1979) and Reason (1977, 1979) have provided schemes for classifying errors, they both emphasize the point that errors may be caused by one of a number of factors; in fact in many cases they are multiply determined. That errors can originate in so many ways makes one marvel 'not that we make errors, but that we make them so comparatively rarely' (Reason, 1977). More importantly, the fact that errors are multideterminant affords a clue to ways in which the system may be organized. These will be discussed in the next section.

B   ERRORS IN PATHOLOGY

Errors in performing actions concommitant with lesions to the cerebral cortex, particularly those which occur in limb apraxia, have been described in detail (e.g. Hécaen and Albert, 1978; Heilman, 1979; Roy, 1978, 1981). One major type of error involves a disorder in performing the action itself. Errors in performing the sequence of movements are characterized as omissions, repetitions, disturbances to the order of movements in the sequence, a difficulty in terminating movements when required and a difficulty in coordinating the limbs in time and space. One of the commonest of these is the tendency to repeat (perseverate) actions (e.g. Kimura, 1977; Roy, 1981). There also appear to be errors involved in performing the movement elements which form the sequence. This has been described by Kimura (1977) and Heilman (1979) as 'clumsiness'. The movements lose the smoothness; they become jerky and ataxic-like. Fine finger control may be adversely affected (e.g. Heilman, 1975).

The second major type of error is one in which the actions are performed correctly, but they are inappropriate for the situation at hand. The patient may use an object or tool in an inappropriate way, for example, using a pencil as a comb. In this case the action of combing may be performed correctly; it is just the wrong action to be used with this implement (or the wrong implement to be used with the action of combing). In another case the patient may perform an action which for him has been associated with a particular situation, even though it may not be the one requested of him. A third example here is errors which are environmentally induced, i.e. the environmental context precipitates an error. These errors are frequent in the pathology, as brain damage often leaves the patient in a much more context-dependent state (e.g. Goldstein, 1942; Luria, 1973).

The third major type of error involves the omission of an action completely. The patient may forget what action it was he was about to perform. In other cases the patient is cognizant of what he should do with an object, for example, but he cannot demonstrate how to use it. In such cases the patient may attempt to indicate how or where the object is to be used. The use of parts of the body (body as object), of facial expressions (gestural enhancement), of verbal explanations or exclamations, or of pantomime to indicate the situational setting in which the desired movement is made may be seen (e.g. Goodglass and Kaplan, 1963). Finally, the patient may be aware of what it is he is to do and can describe how to do the action, but he cannot initiate the action on command.

C   COMPARISON OF ERRORS IN NORMALITY AND PATHOLOGY

In examining the errors made in normality and pathology it is apparent that in both states the action sequence itself may be executed improperly, the action sequence, although well executed may be inappropriate for the current situation, or the action sequence may be omitted completely. While there are these apparent commonalities, there are certain types of error which occur more frequently in pathology. First, although perseverations, sequencing errors, omissions, and problems with initiation and termination of movement occur in both states, it seems that perseverations and problems with movement initiation occur more frequently in pathology (e.g. Roy, 1981). The greater frequency of these errors in pathology may reflect pathological inertia in the motor system following cerebral damage (Luria, 1973). Secondly, problems in the actual control of movement are seldom if ever observed in normality. Such movements are characterized as clumsy, jerky or ataxic-like, although the overall order of the movement elements of the sequence may be preserved.

The errors which are common to both the normal and the pathological states would seem, therefore, to reflect a disruption in the cognitive and/or perceptual-motor processes concerned with intention, planning and response organization. Disruption to the actual execution of the movement elements of a sequence is apparently unique to the pathological state. This contrast points out the necessity for the structural integrity of the human action system in the fine control of movement; it emphasizes, on the other hand, the apparent susceptibility of the system to disruption in the early stages of response preparation and organization regardless of the state of the organism. Since these latter types of error observed in pathology are also observed (if less frequently) in normality where such errors are more likely due to processing (functional) disorders, it would seem that the errors observed in pathology may be due to processing disorders which result from the remaining intact neural structures either operating in the absence of other structures (e.g. when damaged tissue is removed) or under the inhibitory influence of the remaining damaged tissue. Such a processing approach to the study of pathology is not new (e.g. Kinsbourne, 1976; Roy, 1978); it does gain credibility, however, when such common patterns of error are observed.

These apparent commonalities suggest that functional processing disorders may underlie errors observed in normality and pathology. However, since the errors observed may have a number of determinants, what can be said about the comparability of the errors in normality and pathology? The fact that many of the same types of error occur in normality and pathology suggests that performance in these states may reveal similar information about the organization of and processes involved in the action system. Such a supposition may be rather tenuous, for two reasons. First, errors may be 'multideterminant', i.e. they may arise from a number of causes. Seemingly comparable errors in the two states may arise for markedly different reasons (see Roy, 1978). Secondly, differences in the observational base for errors in the two states also threatens interpretation. In normality reports of errors come from performance in daily life and the perpetrator is also frequently the observer who records the error. In pathology, however, clinical examinations are most often the observational source, and the person making the errors is almost never the observer. Such situation-observer differences between the two states may have a great impact upon what errors are observed and upon their comparability. Indeed situational or contextual effects are well known in the study of pathology. Errors present on clinical examination (e.g. inability to demonstrate how to use a tool such as a fork) may not be seen outside the clinic in daily life.

While these factors do at present limit the comparability of errors in the two states, it may be possible to conduct studies which might reduce their influence. Providing for comparable observational settings (e.g. the clinic or laboratory) and systematic manipulation of perceptual and response variables may afford more comparability of errors in the two states. Observing both normal and brain-injured persons in a controlled setting may be desirable. It may be equally important, however, to examine the performance of brain-injured patients in less controlled environments (e.g. at home) as has been the practice in the study of errors in normality. Observations here provide tests of the ecological validity of theories of the organization of action derived from more controlled studies.

4   The normality-pathology interface: models in transition

Acting on the world requires knowledge about the environment and about the available actions and their consequences and mechanism, a means for effecting our knowledge on the world. What do errors in normality and pathology reveal about this adaptive process? There appear to be a number of implications: for principles of organization, for mechanisms of control and for knowledge structures. Each of these will be discussed in turn.

A   IMPLICATIONS FOR PRINCIPLES OF ORGANIZATION

1   *Knowledge-mechanism dualism.* Observed errors seem to indicate that the action system is separable into knowledge and mechanism. For example, the apraxic patient is often unable to demonstrate how to use a particular tool or object despite being able to identify what it should be used for and sometimes even to indicate when someone else is using it incorrectly. Knowledge of how the object or tool should be used seems intact in this case; the processes for effecting this knowledge, however, appear to be disrupted.

Errors in normality also provide support for this knowledge-mechanism dualism. Continuing to perform an act despite having forgotten what the original intent was exemplifies the apparent dissociation between intentions and plans (knowledge – that which was forgotten) and the processes for effecting these. This dissociability of knowledge and mechanism is seen in the perspective offered by artificial intelligence (Newell and Simon, 1972).

2   *Levels of control.* The patterns of errors seen in normality and pathology reveal not only a knowledge-mechanism dualism, they also evince the dynamic quality of control. The system is controlled at a number of levels; action, thus, involves not one but a number of control systems, apparently capable of operation independently and in parallel, thus affording the potential for the *migration* of control. In pathology we noticed that some apraxic patients are unable to gesture or act appropriately upon command

but can do so when put in the appropriate context, others have difficulty in performing gestures even in the appropriate context, while others can act on command, but the movements produced lack fine control. A number of levels of control are revealed here. One is concerned with the activation of appropriate programs of action. The intentional control of this activation process seems disrupted in the first group of patients. When the appropriate context is provided for this group, intentional control of activation seems obviated; the affordances in the environment may serve to direct activation of the appropriate actions. A second level of control is thus revealed. Another level involves the sequential organization of the act itself. Patients with damage to the left hemisphere in particular seem to have a disruption at this level (e.g. Kimura, 1977; Roy, 1981). A fourth level involves the control of movement *per se*. Patients in the third group seem to exemplify a disruption at this level. Activation and sequential organization of the motor act seem unaffected, while movement control is.

Errors encountered in normality also seem indicative of the operation of a number of control systems. For example, continuing an action despite having forgotten what the original intention or plan was, performing an originally intended or planned action despite having changed one's mind about doing so, and unintentionally performing an action one only thought about are all errors which suggest that control, originally exerted by a system concerned with planning actions, has been transferred to (or captured by) a system concerned with the execution of these actions.

This notion of control systems at different levels is not a new concept (cf. Luria, 1966; Broadbent, 1977; Marteniuk, 1976; Norman, 1979). The traditional view here, which grew out of Jackson's work (Taylor, 1932), is that there is an immutable dominance relationship in which one system always exerts control over the others, a hierarchy. The errors we have described, however, indicate that it is possible for control of the action system to migrate from one level to another. Moreover, neurophysiological data (e.g. Pribram, 1971; Granit, 1977) indicate simultaneous action at a number of levels in the nervous system. Such dynamic patterns of control argue for flexible dominance relationships in which control may reside at any one level or at a number of levels concurrently. The organizing principle would then seem not to be a strict hierarchy, but rather a flexible hierarchy or a heterarchy (Turvey *et al.*, 1978).

B   IMPLICATIONS FOR MECHANISMS OF CONTROL

1   *Modes of Control.* Errors not only reveal something about the levels of control in the action system, they also indicate something about modes of control, a related concept. Two principal modes of control have been described. One mode, closed-loop, involves feedback-based control; the other, open-loop, is one in which feedback is thought not to be used. While these modes of control have been differentiated with regard to the

use of feedback, a distinction has also been made with regard to the role of attention: closed-loop control demands attention, while open-loop control allows the performer to operate with minimal attention to the actions being performed. This latter characteristic of open-loop control has been incorporated into the notions of the motor program and automaticity in skill. Motor programs are envisaged to be structured sets of commands which can be run off automatically with minimal requirements for attention on the part of the performer (Keele, 1973; Schmidt, 1976).

One of the characteristic aspects of errors in normality is that they occur most frequently at periods when the performer's attention is not directed at the ongoing action. The performer would thus seem to be operating primarily in an open-loop mode during such periods. During the period of open-loop control, Reason (1979) argues, action is directed by automatized programs in which attention is required only at critical decision points, when the performer must decide between two or more alternate programs of action. Errors arise when attention is not applied at these points or when it is applied at the wrong time, usually too late. The selective deployment of attention requires that the performer switch from the open-loop mode of control to the closed-loop mode.

Work by Reason (1979) and Norman (1979) provides clues as to when such critical choice points may occur. These points may arise under at least three circumstances: when a number of actions are associated with a given situation or with one another (associative error, Norman, 1979) and when they share common response elements (branching error, Reason, 1979). In each of these cases the performer must devote attention to the unfolding action to ensure that the appropriate action is selected. The potential for errors is accentuated in these circumstances, it seems, by the concurrent influence of the principles of recency and habit strength. According to the first principle the more recently one of the alternative actions under these circumstances has been performed, the more likely it may be performed again (see Norman, 1979, p. 14; Reason, 1979, p. 77). Such an effect would seem to be similar to the priming effect in perception (e.g. Lindsay and Norman, 1972). The second principle argues that the more frequently a particular action among these alternatives has been performed the greater is its strength and, so, the more likely it will be performed (capture error, Norman, 1979; see also Reason, 1979, p. 77). When the circumstances specified above arise, then, and one of the alternate actions is more likely to occur, the potential for error arises, providing that attention is not directed to selecting the appropriate action and, of course, assuming that the most likely action is not the correct one.

While errors arise in normality when the performer does not devote attention at critical choice points, it seems the same type of error may be encountered in pathology. The apraxic patient who is, for example, asked to light a candle may begin by correctly striking the match but instead of lighting the candle appropriately he proceeds to pick up the candle, place it in his mouth, and light it. In the context of this discussion one might envisage a critical choice occurring after the first action of lighting the match. At this point a number of actions are possible, e.g. lighting the candle (the intended one), lighting a cigarette or blowing out the match. The error which occurred may have arisen because control was captured by an action (lighting a cigarette) which is more frequently performed following match lighting or more strongly associated with match lighting than the intended action. In either case it suggests that the apraxic patient may not have been monitoring his performance at the critical point in time, when the intended action might become misdirected.

This tendency not to monitor performance (switch mode of control) when necessary seems to arise because the performer may very often be engaged in what Reason (1979) terms parallel mental activity or PMA, that is, central processes are engaged in mental activity, which may or may not be related to current action. Engaging in PMA prevents switching control modes, thus attention may not be directed at the critical points. While these errors due to faulty monitoring may be unrelated to the contents of PMA, PMA may give rise to a type of error where the contents of thought are imposed on the concurrent action such that the thought of actions replace those intended. Somewhat related types of error which arise out of PMA are ones in which thinking of an action results in the action being performed, although the person had no intention of doing so and ones in which thought replaces action, as in the case when one thinks about performing an action and later discovers that it was not actually performed.

All of these types of error indicate that the concepts of levels of control and modes of control are important principles in the organization of action. It seems that following the selection of an action control may be transferred from a system which operates primarily in a closed-loop mode to one which incorporates open-loop control. The freeing of attention which such a transfer in control may afford appears to provide the potential for errors to arise.

A system which is controlled at a number of levels must also have the capability of processing feedback at each level. Evidence from pathology supports this proposal. For example patients with limb-kinetic or kinesthetic apraxia are able to use tools and objects appropriately, although the actual movements involved lack fine control. The sequential organization of the act would seem to be relatively unimpaired, suggesting that feedback processes in the system controlling this aspect of action are intact. Motor (muscle) control, however, is disturbed, possibly because of a disruption in the motor command-feedback interface.

One of the basic tenets in the open-loop mode in addition to the freeing of attention is that in this mode sequences of action are thought to be run off independently of feedback information, thus leaving the central processor free to concentrate upon future aspects of the task (Reason, 1979, p. 75). The fact that feedback may be processed at a number of levels presents problems for this view and, indeed, for the general notion that the open-loop mode of control obviates the use of feedback (see Schmidt, 1976). While errors may indeed arise during open-loop control because the performer is no longer attending to his performance, it is undoubtedly *not* the case that feedback is not being processed. The system(s) to which control has been transferred and which direct action during these absent-minded periods use feedback appropriate for their level of operation. What apparently is not required is attention or conscious monitoring. These observations seem to bear upon notions of multiple levels of control within the nervous system (e.g. Schneider, 1967; Trevarthen, 1978) and of the heterarchical organization of action (e.g. Turvey *et al.*, 1978).

Work by Trevarthen (e.g. Trevarthen, 1978) and others suggests that a number of systems (e.g. vision) are represented and controlled at at least two levels in the central nervous system, cortical and subcortical. Control at the cortical level has been described as intensive and discriminative and demands attention, while that at the subcortical level is extensive and integrative and may operate largely below the level of consciousness. Processes at the cortical level might be envisaged, then, as intentional and goal-directed which involve planning and organizing action, while those at the subcortical level subserve, in conjunction with the relevant cortical areas, the execution of the actions selected. These subcortical control systems seem to provide the potential for automatization of skilled actions (e.g. Eccles, 1967). Also, the neural mechanisms for a dynamic interface between the performer and the environment, recently described by Turvey (Turvey *et al.*, 1978) as a coalitional style of control, may also be afforded.

These observations suggest, then, that the feedback aspect of open-loop control which provides the potential for errors is not that feedback is not processed, but rather that it is processed and that these processes apparently do not demand attention. Through the operation of sub-cortical and spinal brain mechanisms actions, even those which are unin-tended (especially these in this case), may be executed appropriately. This idea is consistent with Schmidt's (1976) proposal that despite having selected the wrong action (a selection error) errors encountered during the execution of this erroneous action (execution errors) can be corrected using feedback involving existing neural systems, with minimal attention demands.

While the reduced attention demand in processing feedback enables the potential for a variety of errors, it seems one type of error may be more or less directly ascribed to this factor. These are termed data-driven errors, environmentally induced errors whereby information in the en-vironment intrudes upon the course of action. Both Norman (1979, p. 14–

15) and Reason (1979) provide examples of these types of errors. One of particular interest involves what Reason (1979, p. 73) calls multiple side-tracking. Here the intended action (e.g. to sort out and collect the dirty washing) is side-tracked into another (e.g. cleaning the bathroom) when visual information (e.g. the bathroom looked like it needed cleaning) indicated that the latter action should be taken.

While the environment may induce errors in the normal state, it seems to have both a negative (reduces performance) and positive (improves performance) effect in pathology. Damage to the cortex characteristically induces two states. One is a state of increased susceptibility to the environment in which the patient is often highly distractible; his attention is easily diverted from the task at hand. The other is a tendency to be very concrete, very context-dependent. The first state would seem to lead to the negative effect. Actions are easily diverted by the demands of the environment. The latter, on the other hand, may lead, somewhat para-doxically, to the positive effect in which apraxic patients, for example, are sometimes unable to use a tool, except in the appropriate environmental context. The context seems in some way to facilitate the patient's per-formance. Consideration of this facilitatory effect in pathology in con-junction with the errors (i.e. data-driven errors) apparent in normality affords clues to the activation processes involved in action. These will be discussed in detail in a later section. Suffice to say at this point that these observations strongly support the proposal that there are dynamic inter-actions between the performer and the environment (e.g. Turvey et al., 1978) such that under certain conditions the environment may very effectively direct action.

Other aspects of feedback processing also seem to lead to errors. It might be envisaged that the information used at these various levels of control may be different, i.e. the various control systems use different languages. Such a principle would seem desirable since the specifications at one level (e.g. planning or selecting actions according to the goal) are very different from those at other levels (e.g. motor commands for move-ment). If this were indeed the case, errors might well arise when the performer attempts to correct errors through one system using the commands (i.e. the language) of another. Such errors do, in fact, seem to arise in normality, supporting this notion of different languages (see Norman, 1979, p. 20).

Another source of error concerned with feedback relates to the type of feedback the performer is monitoring. At least two sources of feedback information would seem to be important in action: one concerns whether the goal has been achieved (knowledge of results), the other whether the action or movements specified have been performed adequately (know-ledge of performance, see Gentile, 1972; Marteniuk, 1976). Patterns of monitoring these sources of information may lead to errors as well as to varying delays in catching errors. Monitoring information concerning the achievement of the goal may allow errors to arise in the process of activation (e.g. the wrong action may be triggered) and/or production (e.g. intrusion errors – actions similar to the one being performed intrude upon it), while monitoring information about the adequacy of the actions performed may lead to the wrong action being selected. In this latter case the performer is informed about whether the action is performed well, but not necessarily whether it is the correct one.

2   *Selection and activation.* Actions which were not intended do occur. More than one action, then, must have been activated, and the error arises because the wrong one is selected and triggered (Norman, 1979). Norman and Bobrow (1976, 1979) suggest that activation in memory may involve employing a set of descriptions which provide a means for activating the schemata in memory fitting them. These descriptions may be context-dependent in that they identify a set of conditions in which a particular class of actions may be correct. Perceptual (i.e. shape, size) and contextual (e.g. in the kitchen) information provides descriptions of objects and situations which may be used to activate the associated actions.

A subset of the actions activated in this process are the appropriate ones in that they most clearly meet the description. While the correct action is usually performed when these appropriate actions are selected, there are situations when this is not so. In some cases the description may not be specific enough or is in some way confused (discrimination failure, Reason, 1979) resulting in an inappropriate action being performed. In other cases the description may be adequate, but the action elicited was not the one originally intended (data-driven error, Reason, 1979).

While a subset of the activated actions do most clearly meet the description, it would seem that there must also be an additional subset which is activated at the same time. These actions would seem to be associated in some way with those in the first set, since errors arise in which such associated actions are performed instead of the appropriate one(s). The basis for the association would seem to be contextual (e.g. both subsets of actions are performed in the same spatial location or the same time) and procedural (e.g. they share some common action components). Such actions, rather than the intended ones, may be selected because of a lack of discriminability among the activated actions. Discriminability may be afforded by providing further specifications as to precisely which action is the 'target' of retrieval (cf. Norman and Bobrow, 1976, 1979). If these further specifications are not provided the action which has most recently been performed or which has the greatest strength (e.g. Reason, 1979), may be selected and performed.

The role of such context-dependent descriptions seems further exemplified in pathology where the patient is often able to perform an appropriate action (e.g. using a spoon) only in the associated context.

While there are a number of explanations for this observation, from the standpoint of activation and selection the context would seem to provide the further specification necessary to select the appropriate action. Context (see Kelso and Tuller, 1981) in this case seems to be both tactual-motor (the patient can only perform the action when actually holding the object) and environmental (the situation usually associated with using the object).

The processes of selection and activation described here seem to be intimately related to the notions of levels and modes of control. First, many of the errors seem to arise when attention is not directed at per-formance, seemingly when control has been transferred from a level which demands attention to one which does not. Whenever a number of objects or situations and their associated actions share common per-ceptual, contextual or procedural features, discrimination among the activated target actions to be selected or among the target objects to be incorporated into the action becomes difficult. Accordingly, the potential for selecting the wrong action or the wrong object to be incorporated into an intended action is increased. That diversion of attention increases the potential for these errors suggests that the description processes whereby actions are activated, selected and triggered may require minimal, if any, attention. Attention would seem required principally to monitor per-formance and correct for errors in the event that an incorrect action is selected.

The second clue that these notions of levels of control and activation are intimately related is provided in errors in which an intended or thought-of action is performed, despite having changed one's mind. Activation would seem to be applied at a number of levels in the system. Although it subsides at one level (e.g. the person changes his mind), other possibly lower levels would seem to remain activated providing the potential to respond, given the necessary set of conditions. This notion of activation at different levels is consistent with MacKay's (1980) idea of cotemporal activation in speech, whereby activation is thought to occur at all the levels of representation (e.g. propositional, phonological).

3   *Execution processes.* Evidence on the nature of errors would suggest that the execution of sequences of action involve operations at a number of levels in the system. Lower level operations may proceed with minimal attention in a top-down fashion through the operation of motor programs and/or in a bottom-up fashion through the environment directing action. Motor programs which may exert top-down control have been the subject of study for many years. While much work has been carried out on determining the nature of representation of these programs (e.g. Keele, 1968; Keele and Summers, 1976), considerable evidence suggests that under certain circumstances, the array of movements or actions (events) comprising the sequence are organized as a chain of event-to-event

associations. Errors in which unwanted actions are inserted into the sequence or in which a sequence other than the one intended is performed suggest that while a program may involve these event-to-event associations, there may also be numerous other associations between the events or actions in one program and those in other programs. Since control at this level demands minimal attention, it is possible for these other associations to draw the sequence away from the intended goal, resulting in an error. The circumstances leading to such errors have been outlined more fully above (see p. 285).

Bottom-up or data-driven (Norman, 1979) control of action has been described by Turvey and his colleagues (e.g. Turvey *et al.*, 1978), whereby cues in the environment serve to direct action. Research has revealed a number of dynamic environmental cues to which the human action system seems responsive (e.g. optic flow patterns). There may, however, be other more static perceptual information to which the system learns to respond. For example, the performer may learn that certain perceptual attributes afford certain actions (e.g. an object which shares perceptual attributes with say, a hammer, would afford hammering). Knowledge about action, then, may become *externalized* as these perceptual attributes which afford certain actions. The environment, then, operating through lower level systems could conceivably play a role in directing action (see the notion of descriptions, p. 289). As with top-down control described above, this type of control may involve only minimal attention demands. As a result the system seems susceptible to particular types of error (i.e. data-driven errors).

For both top-down and bottom-up control, then, it would appear that the action system is capable of programming sequences of actions which may be run off with minimal attention. It would seem to be this very capability, however, which leads to errors. Attention needs to be directed at certain critical points during action to prevent such errors from occurring.

While action may become diverted from the intended goal if attention is not directed at the critical point in time, it may likewise be disrupted if attention is directed at the wrong time. A number of reports (e.g. Adams, 1971; Reason, 1977) have been made of the deterioration in performance which arises when the expert performer attends too closely to his actions. In this regard Freud (1922) once wrote that many acts are best performed when they are not the objects of 'particularly concentrated attention'. Mistakes may arise when 'one is most eager to be accurate'. This suggests, then, that the execution of actions involves a very delicate balance between the attention-demanding processes of higher level systems and the largely autonomous operations subserved by those at lower levels. This balance of control among levels is similar to that described by Schmidt (1976), although at a much more global level. The operations at higher levels attempt to keep the action directed toward the intended goal and correct for selection (goal-directed) errors. Those at lower levels subserve programs which, when selected, direct action with minimal attention demands for a period of time.

This description would suggest that sequences of action are probably not prepacked units waiting to be run off like a tape recording. Rather, it seems that at a number of critical choice points in the sequence several possible actions may be activated. The conditions or context present at the time (the description), the associations between the activated actions which fit this description, the association between these actions and ones next in the sequence, and the relative recency and habit strength of these actions all seem to influence the process of selecting which one will be triggered (see *Selection and activation*, section 4B2). Attention needs to be directed at these points to ensure that the action sequence continues toward the intended goal.

How do these notions relate to the concept of planning? Planning might be thought of as a recursive checking process in which the unfolding action pattern is monitored periodically to ensure that the goal state will be achieved (e.g. Miller *et al.*, 1960). Such a process would seem to require periodic attention demands. The view espoused here that action sequencing involves such recursive attention demands seems related to this planning process. Performing sequences of actions does not always require attention, however. As we have seen, lower levels in the system seem to afford this type of control, albeit at some cost (i.e. increased potential for errors). Action sequences performed in this way either through the operation of motor programs or through the environment directing action would not seem to require planning (cf. Roy, 1978). It would appear, then, that planning may be necessary primarily when intended actions *depart from* the pattern(s) controlled at these lower levels. For example, if one intends to purchase beer on the way home from the office, planning (i.e. directing attention at critical choice points) is required to prevent the well-learned 'driving-home-from-the-office' sequence from prevailing, which would result in arriving home without the beer (cf. Norman, 1979). Alternatively, when asked to demonstrate how to light a candle the patient who after striking the match put the candle in his mouth and lit it may not have been able to direct his attention at the critical point (i.e. planned the candle lighting sequence) so as to prevent the well-learned 'cigarette-lighting' sequence from being performed. Envisaged in this way planning would seem to require a substantial degree of selective inhibition.

C IMPLICATIONS FOR KNOWLEDGE STRUCTURES

Errors observed in normality and pathology reveal several aspects about the nature of knowledge which forms a basis for action. Discrimination failures are errors which arise because the performer confuses perceptual or contextual aspects of objects or situations (Norman, 1979). The fact that such confusions occur suggests that the performer may be using both perceptual and contextual information to determine what action to perform. Two objects which share some features may be confused and, so, used or acted upon inappropriately. One aspect of knowledge, then would appear to represent sets of perceptual (e.g. shape, size) and contextual (e.g. time of day, spatial location) features which are associated with or mapped on to sets of procedures (what to do) defining various actions. Together these form active memory structures which encompass descriptions of actions performed on various tools or objects or in various situations (cf. Norman and Bobrow, 1979).

The fact that actions-not-as-planned do occur suggests that more than one action must have been activated. Such multiple activation would imply that there are networks of these memory structures which are formed on the basis of common or shared features. The description of the particular event or object encountered in the environment activates these networks. Situations or objects encompassed by these networks may be easily confused, thus increasing the potential for discrimination failure (see *Selection and activation*, section 4B2). An examination of the nature of these errors provides a clue as to what information may be incorporated into these descriptions. Such errors arise from a number of confusions (Reason, 1979) – perceptual (e.g. objects are physically similar), functional/procedural (e.g. objects are functionally similar), spatial (e.g. objects are in close spatial proximity) and temporal (e.g. time is misperceived) – suggesting that all of these aspects may provide information within these descriptions.

Procedures, part of the description of the object and situations stored in these memory networks, afford a conceptualization of what to do with these objects or in these situations. These may be verbalized, imagined both visually and kinesthetically, or translated into action. That these procedures can be put 'into action' suggests that there is another level of knowledge, more sensorimotor in form, which serves as a basis for action.

Various forms of errors reveal something of the nature of this knowledge. Branching errors are of particular interest here. When two actions share a common initial segment, the wrong action may be continued beyond the end of this common point. These errors suggest that knowledge structures at this level involve a set of descriptions which may define actions as sensorimotor patterns. The descriptions here may be in a language relevant to movement, for example, force/time relationships and direction. Context as well may play an important part in these descriptions. One aspect of context may be body-centered as reflected in the pattern of spinal tuning which biases or constrains the system so that a particular class of actions (e.g. hammering) is afforded (cf. Kelso and Tuller, 1981; Turvey *et al.*, 1978). The grasp associated with the tool or object which is used in the action may provide another aspect of this context. Actions which share some of these movement/contextual features may be associated with one another and, so, form sets of networks. These associations may provide the basis for errors in which intended actions are replaced by others which 'possess elements in common with the intended ones' (Reason, 1979, p. 78).

So far these observations suggest that there may be two levels of knowledge, one conceptual and the other sensorimotor in form. An examination of errors suggests that these may be separable (see *Knowledge-mechanism dualism*, section 4A1). Gibson (1977) and more recently Turvey and his colleagues (e.g. Fowler and Turvey, 1978), however, have stressed the interface between perception and action in acquiring knowledge about the world. A dramatic example of how experience with objects in the world may affect one's conceptualization of how they may be used is provided by the concept of functional fixedness, 'the inhibition in discovering an appropriate use of an object due to the subject's previous use of the object in a function dissimilar to that required by the present situation' (Duncker, 1945).

The sensorimotor levels of knowledge described above may be utilized in an open-loop style of control either through the environment driving action or through the operation of motor programs. Access to this knowledge and its use in action may demand little attention. As we have seen, however, this style of control provides the potential for errors. When these arise there must be another type or level of knowledge which is used to correct them. This knowledge may provide an awareness of and memory for the goal of a series of actions, a concatenation of single action events, which is invoked at the outset of an act in the form of an intent or plan and during its course whenever the act diverts from what was intended. In addition to being used to correct for errors this knowledge would seem important in keeping track of where one is in the sequence. Various types of error in normality, particularly those due to storage failure (Reason, 1977, 1979), seem to arise if there are disruptions associated with this knowledge. Forgetting the intended goal and forgetting one's place in a sequence are two examples of these types of errors. In pathology damage to the frontal lobes may result in a disruption in this level of knowledge. The patient may be unable to formulate and/or sustain an organized plan for his actions (Roy, 1978).

5 Summary

Errors in normality and pathology appear to have some implications for descriptions of the organizational principles and control dynamics of the action system. Action might be envisaged as driven or controlled in two ways: conceptually-driven and data-driven (cf. Norman and Bobrow, 1976). Conceptually-driven control incorporates abstract, higher level processes involving the selection and planning of courses of action. Knowledge about what actions are appropriate for various tools or objects and in various situations plays a role in this control. Some aspects of conceptually-driven control would seem to involve conscious, attention-demanding processes, for example, intending and planning to perform a series of actions. Following considerable experience action may still be conceptually-driven; however, it is now more or less automatized, attention demands are reduced. In both these situations some knowledge (conceptual) component may be important; the nature of this knowledge is different, however. In the former case knowledge about the nature of action is represented at a conscious level and may involve a significant verbal component. In the latter it is much more sensorimotor in nature, possibly involving schema-like programs for generating action (e.g. Schmidt, 1975). In essence, these represent different levels of knowing with regard to action.

Data-driven control involves the interface between the performer and the environment. It may involve some of the same processes (and neural systems) as in conceptually-driven, automatized control in that attention demands may be minimal; in this case, however, the control is not exerted from the top (conceptual) down but rather from the bottom up – information in the environment serves to direct action. Such a mode of control has been described by Turvey and his colleagues (e.g. Turvey, 1977; Turvey *et al.*, 1978).

While comparing errors made in these two states seems to reveal something about action, it may be just as important to make comparisons of seemingly correct performance. Recent work concerned with recovery of function following brain injury (e.g. Finger, 1979) reveals that while patients who have recovered from brain injury may be able to achieve the goal of an action, the *means* of achieving it may be fundamentally different from those used by them prior to injury. By carefully comparing the performance of such patients with that of normal persons we may acquire even more clues as to the neurobehavioral correlates of action.

References

Adams, J. A. (1971). A closed-loop theory of motor learning. *Journal of Motor Behavior* **3**, 111–149

Broadbent, D. E. (1977). Levels, hierarchies and the locus of control. *Quarterly Journal of Experimental Psychology* **29**, 181–201

Brown, J. (1972). *Aphasia, Apraxia and Agnosia*. Springfield, Ill.: Thomas

DeAjuriaguerra, J., Hécaen, H. and Angelergues, R. (1960). Les apraxies: variété cliniques et lateralisation lésionelle. *Revue Neurologique* **102**, 566–594

DeAjuriaguerra, J. and Tissot, R. (1969). The apraxias. *In* P. J. Vinken and G. W. Bruyn (eds), *Handbook of Clinical Neurology*, Vol. 4, *Disorders of Speech, Perception and Symbolic Behavior*. Amsterdam: North-Holland

Denny-Brown, D. (1958). The nature of apraxia. *Journal of Nervous and Mental Disease* **126**, 9–32

Denny-Brown, D. and Chambers, R. A. (1958). The parietal lobe and behavior. *Research Publications of the Association for Nervous and Mental Disease* **36**, 35–117

Denny-Brown, D., Yanagisawa, N. and Kirk, E. J. (1975). The localization of hemispheric mechanisms of visually directed reaching and grasping. *In* K. J. Zulch, O. Creutzfeldt and Cr. C. Galbraith (eds), *Cerebral Localization*. New York: Springer

DeRenzi, R. E., Pieczuro, A. and Vignolo, L. A. (1968). Ideational apraxia: A quantitative study. *Neuropsychologia* **6**, 41–52

Dimond, S. J. and Beaumont, J. G. (1974). *Hemispheric Function in the Human Brain*. London: Elek

Duncker, K. (1945). On problem solving. *Psychological Monographs* 58:5, Whole No. 270

Eccles, J. C. (1967). Circuits in the cerebellar control of movement. *Proceedings of the National Academy of Sciences* **58**, 336–343

Ettlinger, G. (1969). Apraxia considered as a disorder of movements that are language-dependent: Evidence from cases of brain bi-section. *Cortex* **2**, 285–289

Finger, S. (1979). *Recovery from Brain Damage*. New York: Plenum

Fowler, C. A. and Turvey, M. T. (1978). Skill acquisition: An event approach with special reference to searching for the optimum of a function of several variables. *In* G. E. Stelmach (ed.), *Information Processing in Motor Control and Learning*. New York: Academic Press

Freud, S. (1922). *Introductory Lectures on Psychoanalysis*. London: George Allen and Unwin

Gentile, A. M. (1972). A working model of skill acquisition with application to teaching. *Quest* **17**, 3–23

Geschwind, N. (1965). Disconnexion syndromes in animals and man. *Brain* **88**, 237–294; 585–644

Geschwind, N. (1975). The apraxias: Neural mechanisms of disorders of learned movements. *American Scientist* **63**, 188–195

Gibson, J. J. (1977). The theory of affordances. *In* R. Shaw and J. Bransford (eds), *Perceiving, Acting and Knowing*. New Jersey: Erlbaum

Goldstein, K. (1942). *Aftereffects of Brain Injuries in War*. New York: Grune and Stratton

Goodglass, H. and Baker, E. (1976). Semantic field, naming, and auditory comprehension in aphasis. *Brain and Language* **3**, 359–394

Goodglass, H. and Kaplan, E. (1963). Disturbances of gesture and pantomime in aphasia. *Brain* **86**, 703–720

Granit, R. (1977). *The Purposive Brain*. Cambridge, Mass.: MIT Press

Greenfield, P. M. and Westerman, M. A. (1978). Some psychological relations between action and language structure. *Journal of Psycholinguistic Research* **7**, 453–475

Haaland, K. Y., Porch, B. E. and Delaney, H. D. (1980). Limb apraxia and motor performance. *Brain and Language* **9**, 315–323

Hécaen, H. (1968). Suggestions of a typology of apraxia. *In* M. L. Simmal (ed.), *The Reach of Mind: Essays in Memory of Kurk Goldstein*. New York: Springer

Hécaen, H. (1969). Aphasic, apraxic and agnosic syndromes in right and left hemisphere lesions. *In* P. J. Vinken and G. W. Bruyn (eds), *Handbook of Clinical Neurology*, Vol. 4, *Disorders of Speech, Perception and Symbolic Behavior*. New York: Elsevier

Hécaen, H. and Albert, M. L. (1978). *Human Neuropsychology*. New York: Wiley

Heilman, K. M. (1973). Ideational apraxia – a redefinition. *Brain* **96**, 861–864

Heilman, K. M. (1975). A tapping test in apraxia. *Cortex* **11**, 259–263

Heilman, K. M. (1979). Apraxia. *In* K. M. Heilman and E. Valenstein (eds), *Clinical Neuropsychology*. New York: Oxford University Press

Keele, S. W. (1973). *Attention and Human Performance*. Pacific Palisades: Goodyear

Keele, S. W. and Summers, J. J. (1976). The structure of motor programs. *In* G. E. Stelmach (ed.), *Motor Control: Issues and Trends*. New York: Academic Press

Kelso, J. A. S. and Tuller, B. (1981). Towards a theory of apractic syndromes. *Brain and Language* **12**, 224–245

Kertesz, A. (1979). *Aphasia and Associated Disorders: Taxonomics, Localization and Recovery*. New York: Grune and Stratton

Kimura, D. (1977). Acquisition of a motor skill after left hemisphere damage. *Brain* **100**, 527–542

Kimura, D. (1979). Neuromotor mechanisms in the evolution of human communication. *In* H. D. Steklis and M. J. Raleigh (eds), *Neurobiology of Social Communication in Primates*. New York: Academic Press

Kimura, D. and Archibald, Y. (1974). Motor functions of the left hemisphere. *Brain* **97**, 337–350

Kinsbourne, M. (1976). Cognitive deficit: An experimental analysis. *In* J. L. McGaugh (ed.), *Psychobiology*. New York: Academic Press

Kinsbourne, M. (1978). *Asymmetrical Function of the Brain*. New York: Cambridge University Press

Lhermitte, J. (1939). *L'image de Notre Corps. Nouvelle Revue Critique*. Paris

Liepmann, H. (1905). Die linke Hemisphare und das Handelm. *Munch. Med. Wschr.* **49**, 2375–2378

Liepmann, H. (1908). *Drei Aulsatje aus dem Apraxiegebiet*. Berlin: Karger

Liepmann, H. (1920). Apraxie. *Ergon der ges Med.* **1**, 516–543

Lindsay, P. H. and Norman, D. A. (1972). *Human Information Processing*. New York: Academic Press

Luria, A. R. (1966). *Higher Cortical Functions in Man*. New York: Basic Books

Luria, A. R. (1973). *The Working Brain*. New York: Basic Books

Marteniuk, R. G. (1976). *Information Processing in Motor Skills*. New York: Holt, Rinehart and Winston

MacKay, D. G. (1980). A general theory of serial order in behavior. Unpublished manuscript, Department of Psychology, University of California, Los Angeles, California

Miller, G. A., Galanter, E. and Pribram, K. H. (1960). *Plans and the Structure of Behavior*. New York: Holt, Rinehart and Winston

Newell, A. and Simon, H. A. (1972). *Human Problem Solving*. Englewood Cliffs, New Jersey: Prentice Hall

Norman, D. A. (1979). Steps of the mind and an outline for a theory of action. Unpublished manuscript, Center for Human Information Processing, University of California, San Diego, California

Norman, D. A. and Bobrow, D. G. (1976). On the role of active memory processes in perception and cognition. *In* C. N. Cofer (ed.), *The Structure of Human Memory*. San Francisco: W.H. Freeman

Norman, D. A. and Bobrow, D. G. (1979). Descriptions: An intermediate stage in memory retrieval. *Cognitive Psychology* **11**, 107–123

Pieczuro, A. and Vignolo, L. A. (1967). Studio sperimentale sul' aprassia ideomotoria. *Sistema Nervoso* **19**, 131–143

Pribram, K. H. (1971). *Languages of the Brain*. New Jersey: Prentice-Hall

Reason, J. T. (1977). Skill and error in everyday life. *In* M. Howe (ed.), *Adult Learning*. London: Wiley

Reason, J. T. (1979). Actions not as planned. *In* G. Underwood and R. Stevens (eds), *Aspects of Consciousness*. London: Academic Press

Roy, E. A. (1978). Apraxia: A new look at an old syndrome. *Journal of Human Movement Studies* **4**, 191–210

Roy, E. A. (1981). Action sequences and lateralized cerebral damage. Evidence for asymmetries in control. *In* J. Long and A. Baddeley (eds), *Attention and Performance IX*. New Jersey: Erlbaum

Schneider, G. E. (1967). Contrasting visuomotor functions of the tectum and cortex in the golden hamster. *Psychologische Forschung* **31**, 52–62

Schmidt, R. A. (1975). A schema theory of discrete motor skill learning. *Psychological Review* **4**, 229–261

Schmidt, R. A. (1976). Control processes in motor skills. *In* J. Keogh and R. S. Hutton (eds), *Exercise and Sport Sciences Review*, Vol. 4. Santa Barbara, California: Journal Publishing Associates

Sperry, R. W., Gazzaniga, M. S. and Bogen, J. E. (1969). Interhemispheric relationships:

The neocortical commissures, syndromes of hemispheric disconnection. *In* P. J. Vinken and G. W. Bruyn (eds), *Handbook of Clinical Neurology*, Vol. 4, *Disorders of Speech, Perception and Symbolic Behavior*. New York: Elsevier

Steinthal, P. (1871). *Abriss der Sprachwissenschaft*. Berlin

Stelmach, G. E. (1976). *Motor Control: Issues and Trends*. New York: Academic Press

Stelmach, G. E. (1978). *Information Processing in Motor Control and Learning*. New York: Academic Press

Stelmach, G. E. and Requin, J. (1980). *Tutorials in Motor Behavior*. Amsterdam: North-Holland

Taylor, J. (1932). *Selected Writings of John Hughlings Jackson*. London: Hodder & Stoughton

Trevarthen, C. (1978). Manipulative strategies of baboons and origins of cerebral asymmetrics. *In* M. Kinsbourne (ed.), *Asymmetrical Function of the Brain*. New York: Cambridge University Press

Turvey, M. T. (1977). Preliminaries to a theory of action with reference to vision. *In* R. Shaw and J. Brandsford (eds), *Perceiving, Acting and Knowing: Toward an Ecological Psychology*. Hillsdale, New Jersey: Erlbaum

Turvey, M. T., Shaw, R. E. and Mace, W. (1978). Issues in the theory of action: Degrees of freedom, coordinative structures and coalitions. *In* J. Requin (ed.), *Attention and Performance*, VII. New Jersey: Erlbaum

Warrington, E. (1969). Constructional apraxia. *In* P. J. Vinken and G. W. Bruyn (eds), *Handbook of Clinical Neurology*, Vol. 4, *Disorders of Speech, Perception and Symbolic Behavior*. New York: Elsevier

Zaidel, D. and Sperry, R. W. (1977). Some long term motor effects of cerebral commissurotomy. *Neuropsychologia* **15**, 193–204

Zangwill, O. (1960). Le problème de l'apraxie idéatoire. *Revue Neurologique* **102**, 595–603

10

Artistry following Damage to the Human Brain

HOWARD GARDNER

Psychology Service, Boston Veterans Administration Hospital, Boston, USA

1   Introduction: why a neuropsychology of the arts?

When probing human cognition, most psychologists have had in mind a
paradigmatic form of thought – that logical problem-solving activity
characteristic of the Western scientist (Bruner, Goodnow and Austin,
1956; Newell and Simon, 1972; Piaget, 1950). This focus is understandable, in view of the importance of such deductive thought for the working
scientist, and its susceptibility to coherent theorizing and experimentation. Yet, it seems probable that, for most of humanity, and throughout
most of human history, the processes and products involved in artistic
creation and perception have been far more pervasive than those en-
shrined in the sciences. In fact, logical scientific thought can be considered an invention of the West in the wake of the Renaissance – an
invention which is still restricted to a small enclave of thinkers; participation in the literary, musical, or graphic arts, on the other hand, has
been widespread for thousands of years.

The arts constitute a central aspect of human experience, one which
merits careful examination on the part of the scientific community. The
arts feature a number of roles – e.g. performer, creator, audience
member, critic – which individuals can assume; they entail a unique, and
potentially instructive amalgam of cognitive, affective, and motivational
features (Gardner, 1973; Goodman, 1968; Perkins and Leondar, 1977).
Indeed, many outstanding psychologists have at least attempted to construct a psychology of the arts (e.g. Fechner, 1876; Freud, 1958; Skinner,
1961): and if few have been notably successful, this state of affairs simply
underscores the difficulty of the undertaking. There is, in fact, no area of
psychology in which a vaster distance prevails between what should be
known, and what has in fact been established.

There are objective reasons why a psychology of the arts has proved so
elusive. Artistic activities are exceedingly complex; they involve a variety
of roles as well as an intricate amalgam of psychological processes; vast

differences in competence can be achieved in each of the principal art forms; the relationship among skills within each art form, and the nature of the relations among the several art forms, remain unresolved; questions about artistic standards and value judgments vex even the most committed aesthetician. Finally, as regards those accomplishments of greatest interest – the artistic creations of incomparable masters – the skills involved may themselves be so highly articulated and differentiated as to render them virtually invisible to the typical (or even the extraordinary) psychological researcher.

Undaunted by these obstacles, a number of researchers have in recent years sought to place the psychology of art on firmer footing. The processes underlying normal artistic ability (Arnheim, 1974; Berlyne, 1971; Child, 1969), artistic ability possessed by the highly talented individual (Arnheim, 1962; Meyer, 1956; Perkins, 1977; Rothenberg, 1979), and the processes underlying artistic development (Gardner, 1973, 1977, 1980a) have each undergone scrutiny (see Kreitler and Kreitler, 1974; Perkins, 1981; Winner, 1982, for reviews of current research in the psychology of art). Yet the nature of artistic thinking as a whole, particularly as manifest in the most gifted practitioners of the arts, has remained mysterious. It was in fact as a consequence of the difficulties entailed in modelling the behavior of the accomplished artist that I turned several years ago to the study of the brain-damaged individual. I hoped that, through an examination of disintegrating skill, I might receive insight into the nature of intact artistry. My original desire was to study only gifted artists, but very few artists came to my attention. And so, making a virtue of necessity, I have broadened by inquiry to encompass the artistic abilities of normal individuals. The present essay may be viewed as an early 'progress report' from the field.

2   Methodological preliminaries

Neurosurgical investigations of basic cognitive processes have generally taken one of a number of tracks. In some instances the approach has been largely inductive (cf. Benson, 1979): fascinating if perplexing cases have been reported, with explanations arising primarily from the facts concerning particular brain-damaged individuals. An opposing approach has stressed deduction: the brain-damaged population has been studied primarily for its relevance to a model of the psychological process under investigation: thus, in a typical example, models of normal speaking or reading processes have been 'tested' through the presence or absence of predicted clusters of symptoms (Arbib and Caplan, 1979; Coltheart, 1980; Marshall and Newcombe, 1973; Morton, 1969; Patterson, 1979 – see also Garrett, Patterson and Ellis, this volume).

A third approach might be termed 'local theory testing'. In such instances, a particular case or subject population has been examined with an eye toward a specific issue. For instance, an interest in whether language ordinarily plays a constitutive role in the drawing of an object can be pursued through the study of drawing practices among anomic patients (i.e. aphasics with a primary naming order), and, correlatively, through a study of linguistic capacities of individuals suffering from constructional apraxia (i.e. patients with primary disorders of drawing). In this latter instance, case studies are examined primarily in terms of the light they may shed on a specific scientific issue.

Reflecting the paucity of work in the 'normal' psychology of art, the literature on the neuropsychology of the arts is scanty. Published work falls almost entirely in the first and third of the above described categories. There have been a number of instructive case reports of artists who have suffered brain damage (cf. e.g. Alajouanine, 1948; Luria *et al.*, 1965; Wapner, Judd and Gardner, 1978) as well as several studies which test 'local theories' (e.g. Ustvedt, 1937; Warrington, 1969). In contradistinction to other areas discussed in this volume, virtually no efforts have been undertaken to test general models of artistry, nor, for that matter, models of perceptual or performatory competence in specific art forms. The reason for this dearth can be simply stated: there are few such general models in the 'normal psychology' of the arts, and a 'neuropsychology of the arts' has yet to be founded.

This very dearth, however, harbors an opportunity. In most fields of psychology, neuropsychologists have arrived late and so they have, almost inevitably, begun merely as 'testers' of what has been established in the 'normal literature' (cf. Cermak and Craik, 1979). Not infrequently, the very expectation that the 'brain-injured' is but an inferior instance of the normal has impeded progress, even as the neuropsychologist's urge to prove his worth to 'mainstream' psychologists has often dissipated resources which might have been better deployed in carrying out original studies. In my own view, 'normal' individuals (usually operationalized as college sophomores) are no more privileged a population that any other group, be it seven-year-olds, seventy-year-olds, retarded individuals, or geniuses: each population can elucidate fundamental psychological issues. Thus, in a field where the prevailing wisdom has yet to be established, the first emerging syntheses may properly incorporate all relevant populations and skills.

3 An approach to the psychology of art

Before any such investigative program can be launched, it is desirable to establish a way of thinking about artistic activities – a point of departure for theory building, design of experiments, and collection of case materials. Work in my laboratory has been heavily influenced by a point of view first put forward by the philosopher Nelson Goodman (1968, 1972, 1979) and developed over the past decade at Harvard Project Zero (Gardner, 1976, 1979; Gardner, Howard and Perkins, 1974; Perkins and Leondar, 1977). The principal lines of this approach should therefore be sketched.

Involvement in the arts entails the ability to process symbols. Symbols – the vehicles of thought – exist in a variety of forms and formats: they may be verbal, pictorial, gestural, numerical, musical, or some combination drawn from these or other symbol systems. Symbols and symbol systems are not, by their nature, artistic or nonartistic; rather a symbol enters into the arts to the extent that it presents certain kinds of messages, and is interpreted by certain kinds of mental processes. Thus, if a squiggle on a piece of paper designates the fluctuating price of gold over the last three years, it is not functioning in an aesthetic way; in contrast, should the same line of jagged points designate Mt Fuji – as rendered say, in a Japanese scroll of the late 17th century – interpretation of the mark marshalls quite separate skills of discrimination, of the sort featured in aesthetic activity. By the same token, a string of words can function (as in this very sentence) principally for the communication of certain concepts: susceptible to translation, or even to presentation in some other kind of symbolic scheme (for example, a diagram), such verbal units are not functioning as an aesthetic symbol. Another verbal string – featuring some of the very same words – becomes an aesthetic message if its constituent units call attention to themselves, and have been selected and combined in such a way that they invite processes of discrimination, comparison, figurative interpretation, and the like.

A number of conceptual consequences follow from this seemingly simple distinction. To begin with, the arts are seen as fundamentally cognitive: mental processes are needed to make sense of (or interpret) artistic symbols to the same extent as they are needed to interpret symbols functioning in a scientific, journalistic, or conventional vein. One must 'read' a work of art – be it musical or pictorial – to the same degree that one reads a tome of science. And, to pursue the analogy, literacy in the constructive or creative processes of art is as demanding as literacy in the creative aspects of science or humanistic scholarship.

Thus viewed, artistry emerges as an arena where skills must be developed, often over a long period of time, and often with the need for explicit or implicit instruction on the part of the community. The unreflective (if widespread) view of the arts as chiefly an arena of play, leisure, amusement, or emotional inspiration is supplanted by a conception of artistic involvement and accomplishment which stresses serious, and fully engaged cognitive activity. Even as the emphasis on emotions or amusement is played down as in no way exclusive to the arts, so, too, the assumption that the arts are a domain restricted to value and value judgments is discarded. To be sure, it is possible to make value judgments across art objects, even as one continually makes judgments about the importance of specific scientific works, or the significance of rival scientific theories. However, the purpose of the arts is not simply to make value judgments, which after all can be assumed to change over time. If anything, the attribution of value to a specific art object should serve as a *means:* to call the attention of the perceiver to properties of an art object which he might not ordinarily have noticed; far from fostering a religious spirit, an attribution of artistic value should stimulate cognitive processes and enhance understanding of the world of art, and the many worlds to which it makes reference.

As symbols, artistic objects most typically communicate from their creators to the audience to which they have been directed. In ordinary life, symbols generally serve a *referential* or *denotational* purpose: words or diagrams designate states of affairs in the world. Certainly artistic communication can serve this mundane referential purpose: Picasso's portrait of Gertrude Stein denotes Gertrude Stein; a Hemingway short story recounts the activities of a prize fighter or a news reporter.

But artistic symbols also exhibit another kind of communicative function, one which may be termed *expressive*: they convey moods, affects, emotions, or allied properties. A Renoir nude does not just represent, or denote, a person; it also may express a mood of serenity, peace, and calm. These properties must be 'read' by one literate in Western impressionist art, just as the referential aspects of the picture (such as color of hair, shape of nose) must be read. Moreover, once one shifts from representational to nonrepresentational art, the expressive functions of the symbol come to dominate. Hence any psychology of art must take into account these two principal aspects of symbolic communication – the processes whereby the artist is able to imbue his symbols with these properties and the complementary processes whereby the audience member succeeds in decoding such symbols.

Goodman's approach, as elaborated upon by researchers at Project Zero, has provided a means of orientation in a forbidding area of research and has led to some provocative findings in several specialities of psychology (Gardner, 1973, 1980a; Perkins and Leondar, 1977; Perkins, 1981). But it is primarily a way of thinking about the arts, a philosophical approach to symbol systems, rather than a program for psychological research. Indeed, Goodman's approach can be usefully considered as a point of departure; for instance, it becomes worth investigating whether the differences among symbol systems (notations *vs* non-notational) and among properties of symbolic communication (denotation *vs* expression) have psychological validity and force (cf. Gardner, 1974; Gardner, Howard and Perkins, 1974). Left completely untouched by Goodman's approach is a raft of issues which would immediately suggest themselves to psychologically trained investigators as suitable subjects for research.

A psychology of art (and, by extension, a neuropsychology of art) should be responsive to the following issues:

1 To what extent is the psychology of art a separate domain? Are there in fact processes which are involved exclusively, or primarily, in the arts or are the arts composed chiefly of psychological processes found across diverse human activities? If the latter is the case, do the arts nonetheless involve a peculiar combination of psychological processes, which, whenever they are combined in a certain way, yield artistic activity?

2 Can certain psychological processes be usefully construed as 'pan-artistic'? For example, can sensitivities to style, expressiveness, or nuance, be brought to bear upon a variety of aesthetic media?

3 Is it useful to posit skills at a number of different levels of complexity – e.g. technical skills (ability to sing a scale), skills exclusive to one art form (pitch discrimination), organizational skills (ability to play and write a complete short story), and holistic skills (sensitivity to harmony, composition, 'the work as a whole')?

4 Do distinct neurological processes figure in each of the aforementioned artistic skills? Does brain organization more faithfully reflect particular art forms (with form A mediated in zone A), particular artistic processes (with process A mediated in zone A), or some combination of these two lines of analysis?

5 What relationship obtains between particular roles and processes in the arts? To what extent are overlapping skills involved in the roles of perceiver, creator, critic, and audience member within and across the several art forms? By extension, to what extent is there a confluence between technical skills, organizational skills, and holistic skills in the attainment of artistic competence?

6 How much is entailed in the achievement of virtuosity? Are the skills of the accomplished artistic producer or consumer merely a more developed version of the skills of the novice? Or are fundamental reorganizations involved in the attainment of higher levels of skills? Is such attainment within the purview of every individual or does it presuppose a certain level of genetic and neurological endowment?

Lengthening this list of questions would prove easy but the point has already been made: even armed with a promising way to approach questions in aesthetics, the list of psychological topics for investigation is virtually endless. And, it must be confessed at the outset that our knowledge about these questions is dismayingly scanty. Nonetheless, in possession of such an orientation, and equipped with questions of this sort, it is at least possible to begin the lengthy process of constructing a neuropsychology of art.

4 The plan of this paper

In what follows, I will review certain lines of evidence about the nature of artistry. For a number of reasons, to be set forth shortly, I have chosen to focus on the art form of music. My treatment begins with a brief consideration of some ways of thinking about music which have proved useful to investigators in the field. Then, building upon work with normal and brain-damaged subjects, I indicate a few of the general findings which have emerged about the nature of musical representation in the human organism. Proceeding from the skills of the average individual to the performance of the gifted individual, I consider the ways in which our knowledge of artistry has been enhanced by studies of individuals who have achieved significant artistic stature.

The examination of musical abilities is followed by brief accounts of artistry in the visual-graphic and literary areas. In each case I review evidence gleaned from normal individuals without special training in the arts as well as evidence from individuals whose premorbid level of performance was noteworthy. In conclusion, I consider some ways in which this neuropsychological review has helped to elucidate the place of the arts in human cognition.

5 Introduction to a neuropsychology of music

A PRELIMINARY CONSIDERATIONS

Music is a logical candidate for initial consideration in any neuropsychology of the arts. Some form of music is evident in all human cultures; musical performance and rites date back thousands of years. Beyond its universality, music also highlights 'purely aesthetic' features. Because music is almost entirely nonrepresentational, it stands apart from nonaesthetic symbol systems: in contrast, literature, as a verbal art form, cannot dispense with ordinary semantic content. Similarly, representational visual art has an immediately obvious relation to the world of daily experience and so it, too, has less of a free-standing existence than nonrepresentational music. Indeed, the survival of music, in the face of the 'triumph' of language, poses a riddle for evolutionary theorists, even as it is a helpful reminder to psychologists that an apparently 'nonadaptive' form may continue to figure importantly in human culture.

Other reasons motivating a neuropsychology of music merit brief mention. Music offers a particularly rich set of roles – in addition to audience member and critic, individuals can partake through singing, playing works produced by others or creating works of their own, for voice, for instrument, or even for electronic realization by a computer. There is a vast and rich literature of music, ranging from folk music to high art, a myriad of styles, and a complex notation which is understood, at least in part, by many literate individuals. This variegated field instantly raises a multitude of questions about how competence can be organized in the human mind, and the human brain.

Even to mention the many approaches to music developed over the centuries by musicians, scholars, and, most recently, behavioral scientists, would take many pages (for reviews, see Cooper and Meyer, 1960; Langer, 1953; Lerdahl and Jackendoff, forthcoming; Meyer, 1956). Moreover, much of the discussion of music, whatever merit it possesses within that domain, has relatively little relevance to contemporary psychology of music. Hence, rather than offering a necessarily superficial review of what has been said before, it seems preferable to announce those organizing principles which have most often cropped up in current efforts to study music.

To begin with, one may (following current terminology in the cognitive sciences) distinguish two primary approaches to conceptualizing the domain of music. Taking a 'bottom-up' approach, one may focus on the elementary components of music – pitch, rhythm, timbre – and gradually build up from these individual components to that complex interplay which constitutes a musical composition. Adopting the contrasting 'top-down' approach, one takes as a point of departure the organized piece of music. It is assumed that musical analysis, like the perception of a musical work, should begin by approaching the organized musical form, or gestalt, with subsequent analysis into components an optional (and possibly advisable) ploy on the part of the analyst or the observer.

Strategies of research often reflect the conceptualization of the analyst. Researchers who adopt the 'top-down' approach are prone to stress the importance of musical schemata – those abstract representational frameworks into which particular musical works can be 'slotted'; thus particular symphonic compositions are considered instances of a general schema for classical symphonies. Such analysts, accordingly, present subjects entire works and solicit global judgments (Bamberger, 1977, 1979; Meyer, 1956). Individuals are often distinguished from one another in terms of their abilities to proceed from global impressions (or figural understandings) to more analytic or 'particularistic' forms of understanding.

In contrast, researchers who adopt a 'bottom-up' approach are likely to stress the identity of particular elements – specific pitches, harmonic relations or rhythms, and to view particular works as exemplars which either possess, or deviate from, certain combinations of these elements. And, accordingly, researchers from this tradition present subjects with specific musical tones, fragments, or phrases and solicit specific judgments of sameness or difference (Deutsch, 1973; E. Gordon, 1979; Seashore, 1967).

Neither approach is wholly adequate. Those researchers who adopt a 'top-down' approach often have difficulty specifying the components of music which contribute to understanding; those who embrace a 'bottom-up' approach are often unable to effect the bridge from artificial musical stimuli to more naturalistic 'whole pieces' of music.

It should be noted that a few researchers have exhibited ingenuity in bridging the gap between the building blocks of music and more holistic patterns of perception and production. The most effective methods have utilized a strategy whereby a specific musical fragment is viewed as an instance within a more general musical vocabulary. Thus Krumhansl (1979) has provided musical contexts to subjects and then asked them to judge the similarity of stimuli presented within these contexts; and Dowling (1978, 1979; Bartlett and Dowling, 1980) has studied the abilities of individuals to discern similarities and differences among musical passages which differ systematically in the kinds of tonal relationships which are featured. While such efforts still lean heavily on judgment of brief, somewhat contrived stimuli, their incorporation of musical contexts and their focus on musical (as opposed to straight acoustic) modes of analysis suggest a fruitful way of integrating the two approaches sketched above.

While the aforementioned strategies characterize the range of investigations, certain issues have proved particularly germane for those researchers working in the neuropsychological tradition. In what follows, we will focus on three organizing issues:

1 *The relationship between linguistic and musical processing.* At least in certain superficial aspects (e.g. the processing of sequential materials over time, the existence of a basic syntactic component, division into perceptual and productive capacities), music can be analogized to natural language (cf. Kleist, 1962). But the utility of this comparison remains to be demonstrated.

2 *The predominant mode of musical processing.* Echoing the distinctions raised above, it is possible to view the apprehension of music primarily in terms of gestalt or holistic processes, primarily in terms of elementary or atomistic factors, or through some amalgam of these two approaches. This issue assumes particular aptness in view of current discussions about processing strategies favored by the two cerebral hemispheres.

3 *Contrasting pattern of skills across levels of talent or accomplishment.* Because of the enormous range of competence in the music domain, courtesy of differences in genetic endowment and/or training, it becomes crucial to establish whether superior performances by subjects are due simply to a greater facility in processing musical elements, or whether they reflect qualitatively different strategies.

B THE COMPONENTS OF MUSIC

Most studies in the neuropsychology of music have focused on the extent to which specific musical capacities and skills can be dissociated by brain damage (cf. Benton, 1977). A pioneering study was published in 1962 by Milner. Subtests of the Seashore-Battery were administered both pre- and postoperatively to epileptic patients who underwent the removal of one of their temporal lobes. Following removal of the right temporal lobe, there was a significant drop in scores on subtests measuring sensitivity to timbre, sensitivity to intensity, and tonal memory. Other sub-test scores revealed no significant drop. Of greater importance, the performances of patients with left temporal lobe removal were generally comparable to their preoperative levels. Here, then, was early documentation of the relatively greater importance of the right hemisphere in the processing of musical stimuli, as well as a provisional demonstration that musical abilities could be dissociated on a neurological basis.

Subsequent studies utilizing different patient populations and testing techniques have validated the greater importance of the right hemisphere in the processing of musical stimuli, and have documented an important split in the organization of musical skills. As summarized in a major review article by Gates and Bradshaw (1977), rhythmic processing, a time-dependent sequencing task, draws particularly on intact left hemisphere structures. In contrast, the processing of pitch presupposes major participation on the part of the right hemisphere (H. Gordon, 1970; Kimura, 1973; Shankweiler, 1966; Zattore, 1979). Recent evidence suggests further a decisive role played by the anterior portions of the right frontal lobes in the processing of tonal material (Shapiro, Grossman and Gardner, 1981).

While most experimental research has focused on the perception of musical components, there is some documentation of lateralization in the production of musical entities. Injecting sodium amytal into the carotid arteries of presurgical patients, Bogen and Gordon (1971) were able to mimic (in a reversible manner) the effects of hemispherectomies. After paralysis of the right hemisphere, singing was reduced to a monotone. Following injection of the left hemisphere, words were omitted and the melody was distorted, but still recognizable. Contrary to what might have been expected, rhythm remained relatively intact under both procedures.

These findings are consistent with scattered clinical impressions. Many aphasiologists have reported a relative sparing of singing capacities following severe aphasia (Goodglass and Kaplan, 1972) and one promising form of aphasia therapy in fact exploits this preserved singing ability as a basis for reconstructing propositional speech (Sparks, Helm and Albert, 1974). My own observations indicate that, in left hemisphere patients, production of a melody aids in the production of articulated words; in contrast, among right hemisphere patients, it is the production of the verbal components of music which actually aids in the accurate rendition of melodies (see also Ross and Mesulam, 1979).

Some researchers have queried whether musical capacities may be organized differently in talented or trained individuals. While the data are still far from conclusive, some intriguing possibilities have been suggested. Thus Bever and Chiarello (1974) devised a task which required the analysis of the internal structure of musical fragments. Individuals with musical training not only performed better on this task but also displayed a stronger right ear (left hemisphere) advantage than musically naïve subjects. In a supporting study, Shanon (1980) documented greater amount of left hemisphere involvement in tasks requiring complex musical decisions. However, another study, in which patients were required to recognize dichotically presented chords yielded a contrasting pattern of results (H. Gordon, 1970): here musicians demonstrated a right hemisphere advantage, while non-musicians exhibited no ear preference. This latter study dictates caution in inferring a universal pattern in the performances of musically trained (as against musically naïve) subjects: effects may prove specific to certain stimuli, tasks, or subject groups.

Occasional efforts have been undertaken to examine the 'meaning' of musical fragments. In one study Gardner, Silverman et al. (1977) asked patients to match a simple musical fragment with one of two contrasting geometric patterns. The sets of pictures were varied systematically on a number of graphic dimensions hypothesized to reflect different connotative aspects of musical patterns. Thus, for example, an ascending passage should be paired with an up-pointing line, while a descending passage should be paired with a descending line; a continuous tone 'matches' an intact circle, while a broken tone 'matches' a fragmented circle.

Though levels of performance varied considerably across groups of organic patients, a revealing dichotomy emerged: right hemisphere patients proved better able to link a musical passage to a pattern which portrayed the temporal course of the piece (such as regularity-irregularity), than to a pattern which captured gestalt aspects (such as continuity-discontinuity). In contrast, left anterior patients proved better able to match sounds to pictures which captured holistic properties of the piece, while performing less adequately on those stimuli which depicted temporal aspects. Here, then, is evidence that understanding of the connotative (or expressive) aspects of a piece of music is consistent with certain hypotheses about preferred modes of information processing in the two hemispheres (Galin, 1974; Kaplan, 1980; Nebes, 1974).

C STUDIES OF LARGER MUSICAL FRAGMENTS

A few investigators have asked subjects to make judgments about actual musical works. For instance, in an effort to document comprehension of the denotative meanings of familiar pieces, Gardner, Silverman et al. (1977) asked patients to pick out that picture from a set of four which 'went with' a familiar piece of music. In half the instances, the correct answer was based upon the lyrics (not given) of a song; for example, in order to match a musical selection with the correct illustration (a boat), a patient would have had to know the lyrics ('Row, row, row your boat'). For the other half of items, knowledge of lyrics was unnecessary: thus, to match a selection with the correct illustration (the President), a patient merely had to know that the piece was usually played at official cere- monies – he did not have to know its unfamiliar title 'Hail to the Chief'.

Results documented the extent to which musical performance by right hemisphere injured patients depend upon verbal information. On those items where correct performance necessitated knowledge of lyrics, right hemisphere patients outperformed those with left hemisphere damage: on the other hand, on those items where knowledge of lyrics was irrele- vant and identification could proceed simply on the basis of knowledge of the situation in which such a piece was ordinarily heard, left hemisphere patients surpassed those with injury to the right hemisphere. Here, then, is further documentation that purely musical components cohere, and can be dissociated from verbal aspects of musical stimuli.

Following another line of investigation, Shapiro et al. (1981) asked whether the effects found with atomistic musical stimuli are also in evidence with familiar compositions. Experimenters played familiar pieces and asked subjects merely to judge whether they sounded 'right' or 'wrong'. Groups of subjects proved differentially skilled at this task. Thus, left anterior patients evinced skill at detecting the major kinds of errors, having slight difficulty only with those pieces which were played unusually rapidly, or unusually slowly. Left posterior and left central patients performed somewhat more poorly, particularly on items probing sensitivity to tempi.

Patients with right anterior damage performed at the lowest level: they evinced difficulty with all items, performing at chance on every kind of item save the control pieces (pieces that were correctly performed). Counter to the current notion that the left hemisphere is dominant for rhythmic processing, it was the right hemisphere patients who proved poor at detecting rhythmic errors.

This pattern of results may be interpreted as evidence that right hemi- sphere patients have a fragile, or impaired internal representation of all aspects of the melody. In the absence of such an internal representation, which indicates what the piece is supposed to sound like, it would of necessity prove difficult to determine whether or not it had been per- formed correctly. Further evidence for a possible deficit in the overall internal representation (or auditory imagery) of musical material comes from a recent case study at the Aphasia Research Center. An amateur musician suffering from auditory agnosia, secondary to major right hemi- sphere involvement, proved able to answer challenging theoretical questions about music; yet the same patient could not indicate whether the first note of a piece of music was higher, or lower than the second. From such evidence, my colleagues and I concluded that his internal auditory imagery for known melodies had been severely degraded.

D CASE STUDIES

By far the richest and most important information about the organization of artistic skills has so far been acquired through the study of talented individuals who have sustained brain damage. Only through such a population is it possible to examine the organization of the highest level of skill. Moreover, in cases where examples of premorbid art can be examined, it proves possible to make crucial comparisons which may illuminate the effect of the brain damage on the organization of artistry.

In this review of case studies, I will cite the organizing themes which have guided review of more traditional empirical investigations. I will examine the effect of linguistic competence on artistic achievement: the kinds of strategies used by individuals who have suffered brain disease, and the fate of various discrete and holistic capacities in the light of brain damage. In addition it will be possible, in the case of the most talented creative artists, to comment upon the fate of originality, creativeness, and overall sense of form, in their artistic achievements following injury to the brain.

A well-known pair of case studies has highlighted the relationship between models of language competence and models of musical competence. Botez and Wertheim (1959) studied on accordian player who, following removal of a tumor in the second right frontal convolution, suffered several severe amusic disturbances. While able to sing individual pitches, he could not combine them into a song. His repetition of rhythmic and melodic material was poor and, most importantly, he was unable to play his accordion. Despite these difficulties, the subject had perfectly preserved perceptual and receptive capacities for music. He recognized pieces, caught deliberate errors introduced in them, and was highly critical of his own performance. Suggesting an anology to expressive aphasia, Botez and Wertheim spoke of their patient as exhibiting expressive amusia secondary to damage in the right frontal lobe.

Wertheim and Botez (1961) also reported a case of receptive amusia in a concert violinist who became severely aphasic. In contrast to their other patient, this violinist lost his absolute pitch, had difficulty in appreciating tempo changes, was unable to analyze chord structure, and could not name familiar pieces. His performance was far from perfect but he was able to pick out pieces on the violin with his nonparetic hand. Moreover, when accompanied on the piano, his performance improved. Thus, pursuing the analogy to the aphasias, here was a patient whose receptive problems were more striking than his expressive ones. Yet, while this dichotomy may aid in an effort to organize complex sets of findings, the distinction between receptive and expressive remains problematic, particularly with reference to the violin player.

A second topic which can be probed only with case studies of musically talented individuals is the fate of music reading following damage to the brain. Intuitively, it might seem that linguistic and musical alexia should be closely allied. In fact, however, these two forms of reading have been dissociated from one another in a number of instances. Thus Soukes' and Baruk's (1930) patient, a severe Wernicke's aphasic, was totally unable to read text while still able to read music at the piano. In contrast, Dorgueille (1966) reported a patient who, after a left hemisphere stroke, was no longer able to read music but could still read text.

A few other generalizations can be made on the basis of the case studies carried out over the past eighty years. It is very rare to encounter individuals who have sustained significant aphasia without some loss in musical competence (Feuchtwanger, 1930; Ustvedt, 1937), even though the overlap between aphasia and amusia is very far from being complete. There may be a rough association between receptive factors on the one hand and expressive on the other, but in general no set of factors is completely impaired without there being correlative difficulty with other factors. In nearly all cases, individuals prove better able to handle old and over-learned material than new or unfamiliar materials. In fact, in some cases, patients perform almost perfectly with well-known material, while showing little capacity at all to master new material (Judd, Gardner and Geschwind, 1980). This result may simply reflect the well-documented phonemenon that brain-damaged individuals have an inordinate amount of difficulty learning to master any new kinds of material.

Of the numerous case studies which have been conducted with competent musicians, several stand out in terms of the detail of reporting and the significance of the results.

In the five reviewed here, relatively good information existed about the premorbid level of skill; moreover, the examiners posed relevant issues about the organization of artistic capacities.

In three cases, a major composer suffered a stroke in the posterior region of the left hemisphere, thereby developing a significant aphasic disturbance. The first, the renowned Russian composer Shebalin, became severely aphasic following a stroke; nonetheless, he continued his composing and teaching activities as before and was considered by critics to be as brilliant a composer as ever (Luria *et al.*, 1965). A second individual was a major American composer of choral works; he initially suffered a fluent aphasia which later cleared to the level of a moderate anomia. Like Shebalin, this musician's capacities to compose and to criticize performances of music returned rather quickly to a level approaching that of his premorbid skills (Judd *et al.*, 1980).

The condition of this American composer is instructive in that he remained completely alexic for written language. As a result he had to institute various innovations to permit him to set text to music; for example, memorizing the text or having it read aloud frequently. His ability to read and write musical notation was much less severely impaired. Often, when unable to identify exact notes, he was still able to make shrewd guesses about what was wanted in a particular circumstance; and he could readily recognize scores, even when he could name neither the pitches nor the compositions. Here, then, is an instructive instance where the mechanics of musical performance and composition were impaired, due to particular difficulty in the processing of visual symbols, while underlying musical intelligence was spared.

The well-known French composer Maurice Ravel had a tumor in the left hemisphere which left him with a permanent Wernicke's aphasia (Alajouanine, 1948). Ravel presented an interesting pattern of musical breakdown. He was able to recognize pieces he had known before his illness and could detect even minor faults in a performance. He still enjoyed listening to music after his illness and remained able to evaluate new pieces critically. However, he was never able to write or compose another piece and he had great difficulty in playing the piano. Whether Ravel's inability to compose was due to mechanical difficulties of the sort which obtain in the Judd et al. (1980) case or to a more fundamental impairment of musical intelligence, could not be determined with assuredness, though it seems likely that his musical intelligence was at least compromised to a certain extent.

Another case provides further information on the relationship between left hemisphere disease and amusia. A Swiss pianist presented at age 64 with a form of a Wernicke's aphasia in which word deafness was particularly pronounced. Despite this difficulty with language, his musical capacities remained essentially intact. He could recognize instantly pieces of music and make all necessary corrections in a performance. Moreover, he was able to play pieces and melodies including new ones with no noticeable defects. Only when tasks involved a linguistic capacity, for example the identification of notes by name, did the patient exhibit difficulties (Assal, 1973).

A final and highly instructive contrasting case is presented by A.A., a composer studied recently by T. Judd and co-workers who suffered a stroke involving the right frontal-parieto, and temporal regions. Following his stroke, A.A.'s musical understanding clearly remained intact. In fact, he authored a musical textbook and also mastered two foreign languages. While musical testing uncovered some subtle perceptual defects, he was able to continue teaching at a school of music.

In sharp contrast to the other musicians reviewed, however, A.A. lost his interest in the creative process. He no longer felt motivated to compose; as he put it, he could no longer conjure up the appropriate atmosphere. He even reported that he could no longer 'conceive of a whole piece'. He stated, moreover, that he didn't listen to music for enjoyment as much as he had in the past and that he no longer experienced that rich set of associations while listening to music. His own postmorbid compositions he correctly judged as uninspired and uninspiring.

The case of A.A. helps to clarify results obtained from individuals who have suffered an aphasia. With the possible exception of Ravel, musicians with language impairment caused by left hemisphere disease retain the capacity and the desire to engage in creative musical activity. In contrast, an individual with significant right hemisphere disease, whose language remains on an extraordinarily high level and whose musical technique and technical skill have been largely spared, seems to have undergone an alteration in his relationship to musical material and proves able to compose only in a very limited and uninspiring way. On the basis of this review, then, it seems possible to distinguish, on the one hand, between a capacity to carry out various technical musical capacities (for example naming pitch, reading notation) and a proclivity, on the other hand, to engage in musical creation and to sustain certain kinds of emotional gratification from a relationship with works of music.

6   Other art forms

We turn now to brief reviews of major findings obtained in the areas of graphic and literary artistic competence.

A   DRAWING

The bulk of research conducted with both normal and gifted individuals documents a high degree of dissociation between graphic and linguistic capacity. Indeed, with the exception of Bay (1962), nearly all authorities agree that graphic competence can exist at a high level despite a significant aphasia, and, correlatively, that graphic competence can be compromised even in the face of linguistic sparing.

A more promising way of conceptualizing graphic competence highlights the different contributions made to the graphic process by each cerebral hemisphere. As formulated by Kaplan (1980) the left hemisphere seems particularly important for providing the details in a copied or original graphic production; in contrast, the right hemisphere assumes a significant role in providing the overall form, or external configuration, of a target object. Thus, individuals with left hemisphere disease are prone to make drawings whose overall configuration is correct or at least recognizable, but whose internal detailed structure is impoverished: in contrast, individuals with unilateral right hemisphere disease are prone to fashion drawings with rich internal detail but with an impaired external configuration and, not infrequently, a relative neglect of the left side of space.

Other lateralized dissociations have also been reported. For instance, according to Jones-Gotman and Milner (1977), the right hemisphere seems to play a particular importance in the relative ease or fluency with which drawings are produced. And, when asked to draw an instance of a category (e.g. to draw a vegetable), injury to the right hemisphere leads to bizarre drawings which include incorrect or extraneous information (e.g. a picture of a potato with a stem when asked to draw a vegetable). In contrast, individuals with left anterior injury are able to draw prototypical members of a category, though various defects may also attend the performance by these language impaired patients. Fluent aphasics, despite profound word finding deficits, encounter little difficulty producing large numbers of pictures. Often, these patients cannot name the perfectly recognizable pictures which they have drawn (Grossman, 1980).

It is important to indicate that, while these differences in drawing performance can be documented in certain clear-cut instances, in many other cases, overall level of drawing deteriorates to such an extent that the site of damage and the kind of drawing deterioration becomes difficult to specify.

On the receptive side, there is ample evidence to suggest that the right hemisphere plays a principal role in the 'reading of pictorial information' including paintings and drawings. Little information has been gathered on the abilities of brain-damaged patients to attend to those aspects of graphic symbols which contribute to their specifically aesthetic significance, such as composition, balance, or expressiveness. However, one study (Gardner, 1975a) does document a particular difficulty in right-hemisphere patients in detecting the styles of works of art, with a correlative focus on the subject matter as a sole basis for classifying works of art. Aphasic (left hemispheric) patients, in contrast, show a normal or even a super normal capacity to sort paintings by style, quite possibly because their orientation to the major subject matter has been diminished by their pathology.

A study of skilled artists who have suffered brain disease uncovers a number of suggestive phenomena. An investigation of a visually agnosic artist documented a striking dissociation of capacities (Wapner, Judd and Gardner, 1978). This individual was unable to recognize objects which were presented to him, although he remained able to draw quite accurately from memory those objects as he had once known them. When asked to copy an object or picture placed in front of him, he was able to make exceedingly slavish copies of that object, ones of almost photographic accuracy, despite the fact that he was unable to identify or name the object in question. In those rare cases where identification was possible or where the name was provided, he drew the objects in a very different, more schematic and less slavish way.

This patient documents two separate forms of graphic competence in an artist: (1) a 'photographic' copying mechanism, in which every detail of an object is rendered just in the way that it is perceived, even at the cost of distortion (cf. Goodman, 1968); (2) a more schematic way of rendering, in which the patient exploits some established patterns for representing an object. In the latter instance, the painter is prepared to sacrifice particular identifying features of the object in question in order to produce a more generally recognizable and more readily elicited version of that object. Further confirmation of this dissociation can be found in the remarkable drawings by the autistic girl Nadia (Selfe, 1977). This young child could produce slavishly realistic representations of objects and drawings, but had no apparent understanding of the concepts involved, and no generalized schema which could be used to denote an entire class of objects.

The small amount of research carried out with major visual artists who have suffered strokes permits certain tentative generalizations. If a gifted artist suffers a left hemisphere stroke, and is not completely paralyzed, he should be able to continue to draw in the same style and also exhibit the same skills as in his permorbid state. If there is a regression, the style of depiction is likely to be more primitive but still recognizable. Indeed, the literature contains several descriptions of individuals who became aphasic and who were allegedly able to draw better than before; however, a certain romanticism may stimulate such claims (Gardner, 1975b).

It has proved possible to study the paintings of a few individuals who suffered significant right hemisphere disease and yet still continued to paint (Jung, 1974). Two German expressionists, Lovis Corinth and Anton Räderscheidt, both resumed painting after partial recovery from significant right hemisphere strokes. Initially, their paintings included neglect on the left side of the space, irregular contours, misplaced detail, and general fuzziness in depiction. With recovery, the neglect of space was reduced; however the drawings continued to exhibit fundamental differences in style. Specifically, the drawings became much more emotional, primitive and bizarre, featuring rough lines, grotesque affects and the like (Gardner, 1975b). At the time these drawings were first produced, art historians and critics spoke of a general change in style, one perhaps reflecting the patient's reaction to his severe illness. However, it is possible to put forward an alternative explanation. Suppose, as several studies have suggested, that the right hemisphere is essential for emotional appropriateness; it may be that, as a result of their significant pathology, these patients were now affected by a different set of emotional concerns. Reflecting these concerns, they went on to produce paintings which were much more sensual and 'raw' in appearance.

It is important to ascertain which account of the changed style of these painters is correct. If it is the case that painters, irrespective of their variety of brain damage, begin to paint in anomalous styles, then the 'general reactive' interpretation gains in persuasiveness. If, however, as this author believes, such painting changes will only occur in individuals with significant right hemisphere pathology, then the style alteration can be traced directly to a certain form of brain damage.

In summary, then, studies with both normal and gifted brain-damaged artists indicate little relationship between linguistic capacities and the ability to produce competent graphic works. Significant brain damage will affect the work of the artist but, quite possibly in ways reflecting the nature and extent of brain lesion. Moreover, these effects may include not only shifts in the representational quality of an individual's work but also in its organizing emotional tone.

B LANGUAGE AND LITERARY CREATIVITY

The major findings about literary talent following aphasia can be sharply, if tentatively, put: both oral and written language will break down to the same extent in the gifted as in the normal individual. Literary talent in no way protects against the ravages of aphasia. This is poignantly brought out by the case of Baudelaire who, after suffering a major stroke, was able only to utter the phrase 'cré nom'. Possibly, in selected cases of recovery from aphasia, some writing ability may be preserved. For example, the poet William Carlos Williams was apparently able to write some poetry after he had recovered from an anterior aphasia (Plimpton, 1977); and Jakobson and Halle (1956) describes a Wernicke's aphasic who may have been able to continue writing, though with a distorted style. However, even if these exceptional cases are more fully documented, the validity of the above generalization about the indissociability of aphasia and literary creativity seems likely.

Unfortunately, no direct evidence exists about the effect upon literary creativity of significant injury to the right hemisphere. Zangwill (1973, personal communication) does report one actor who because of visual-spatial problems was unable to return to the stage, but still able to perform on the radio. There are also scattered cases of verbally-oriented intellectuals (like historians or lawyers) who are able to continue some work in the wake of a significant right hemisphere disease (Lezak, 1979). However, in these latter cases, the performance seemed normal only with familiar, overlearned materials. Once the individual was expected to talk or write about new topics, the customary difficulties with novel materials emerged (Gardner, 1980b).

In an effort to build a bridge to creative language capacities, my colleagues and I are probing the ability to process complex linguistic materials following significant injury to the right hemisphere (Wapner, Hamby and Gardner, 1981). We have found, for instance, that right hemisphere patients perform as poorly or even more poorly than matched sets of left hemisphere patients in tasks requiring the appreciation of humorous material or figurative language (Gardner, Ling, Flamm and Silverman, 1975; Winner and Gardner, 1977). It appears that an underlying appreciation of these linguistic forms remains in aphasic patients, even though the patients may lack the linguistic competence to perform at a high level. In striking contrast, while right hemisphere patients seem sensitive to literal meanings of jokes and metaphors, they often indicate an inability to understand the underlying meaning embedded in these figures of speech. The right hemisphere patient seems to have difficulty both in appreciating or providing the context of a given remark and in probing beneath the surface of the remark to discern the spirit or attitude with which it was uttered.

These findings have been further underscored by studies of narrative competence in right hemisphere patients. Patients have been asked to read or to view narrative materials and then to answer questions about the meanings and implications of such narratives. The patients prove able to recall literal information in the text even when such information has to do with emotional or spatial types of information. However, whenever a broader task is posed to such patients, their behavior is significantly compromised. Patients with right hemisphere pathology have difficulty in drawing inferences from text, in figuring out the moral of a story, and perhaps most instructively, in determining which points in the story are major, which extraneous, and which may even run counter to the overall themes of a story (Wapner, Hamby and Gardner, 1981).

Research currently underway should help to answer whether these symptoms reflect difficulties in remembering or integrating information, in assessing the significance of certain kinds of information, in relating information to its context, or in some other combination of these deficits. In the meantime, however, the recurrent finding that right hemisphere patients exhibit difficulties in handling literary materials beyond the simplest level of analysis provides suggestive, if only tentative, information that literary creativity requires the intact right as well as the intact left hemisphere. Indeed, it is only in the most 'context-free' phonological, syntactic, and semantic processes that the individual with a damaged right hemisphere may still remain competent.

7 Conclusion

This review of artistic creativity in a number of symbolic domains has yielded few conclusive generalizations. Nonetheless, some closing remarks about the various organizing themes may be appropriate.

To begin with, except in the realm of literary creativity, artistic skills can be exercised in relative independence of linguistic competence. In the case of music, high levels of skill can be manifest despite a significant aphasia; in the case of drawing (assuming no paralysis), aphasia may have little or no effect. Nonetheless, when more conceptual aspects of artistic creation are involved, an aphasia can have a debilitating effect. However, such effects have yet to be convincingly documented in the literature of artistry following brain damage.

A second organizing theme – the contrast between gestalt and detailed features – does not adequately account for the data in the several art forms. Only in the graphic realm can one find regular and clear-cut dissociations between the mastery of individual, particular components and the ability to deal with overall contour gestalt of a work. It is true that certain holistic capacities may play an important role in the conceptualization and execution of work in the literary and musical realms, and these may tend to be represented in the right hemisphere. However, until now, there has been no convincing demonstration of a generalized dissociation between two modes of information processing in normal or talented individuals.

Instead, on the basis of neuropsychological evidence concerning the gamut of cognitive capacities, a more differentiated view of the organization of artistic skills seems warranted. The brain seems better conceived of as a set of complex, multifaceted computational devices: included are specific mechanisms for dealing with linguistic, graphic, musical and other forms of symbolic information ranging from the numerical to the interpersonal. Each of these domains involves its own neurological substrate or substrata; each can break down or be spared at least to some extent independently of the other symbolic domains.

To be sure, there may be certain general skills – for example, those involving planning – which cut across symbolic domains. Moreover, because high levels of achievement, including those in artistry, depend on an extremely intricate orchestration of intellectual and emotional facilities, almost any significant form of brain damage is likely to compromise artistic skills. However, as an overall picture of human cognition, the present survey suggests that it is more fruitful to focus within each artistic symbolic domain: one can then separate out those technical skills which may depend upon very specific brain loci, as well as those more general forms of understanding necessary for competence with a specific artistic symbol system, from the most generalized skills of planning, organization, and conception, which may well depend not only on considerable training, but also on much more pervasive neural mechanisms.

Clearly, the neuropsychology of art sketched in our opening pages has yet to be born. What is needed are more careful studies of individuals of undisputed artistic competence who have sustained brain injury; their behavior should be reviewed in the light of neuroanatomical evidence and contrasted with the behavior of other artists of similar competence. Only in this way will it be possible to tease out the 'natural kinds' of artistic competence which must figure in any dynamic model of artistry. This task may seem overwhelming, quite possibly beyond our current research skill. However, if one examines the progress made over the past two decades in the understanding of linguistic skills, it seems at least possible that a similar level of progress can be hoped for in the understanding of artistic competences. After all, if understanding of our major mode of communication has been enhanced, how desirable it would be to attain a comparable level of understanding of a full range of human symbolic competences.

Acknowledgements

Preparation of this chapter was supported by the Veterans Administration, the National Institute of Neurological Diseases, Communication Disorders, and Stroke (MS 11408), and Harvard Project Zero. I would like to thank Hiram Brownell, Andrew Ellis, Dee Michel, and Ellen Winner for their thoughtful comments on an earlier version. Anne T. Berg assisted with the early preparation of the manuscript.

References

Alajouanine, T. (1948). Aphasia and artistic realization. *Brain* **71**, 229–241
Arbib, M. and Caplan, D. (1979). Neurolinguistics must be computational. *Behavioral and Brain Sciences* **2**, (3), 449–483
Arnheim, R. (1962). *Picasso's Guernica*. Berkeley: University of California Press
Arnheim, R. (1974). *Art and Visual Perception*. Berkeley: University of California Press
Assal, G. (1973). Aphasie de Wernicke chez un pianiste. *Revue Neurologique* **29**, 251–255
Bamberger, J. (1977). In search of a tune. *In* D. Perkins and B. Leondar (eds), *The Arts and Cognition*. Baltimore: Johns Hopkins University Press
Bamberger, J. (1979). Intuitive and formal musical knowing: Parables of cognitive dissonance. *In* S. Madeja (ed.), *The Arts, Cognition, and Basic Skills*. St. Louis: CEMREL
Bartlett, J. C. and Dowling, W. J. (1980). Recognition of transposed melodies: A key distance effect in developmental perspective. *Journal of Experimental Psychology: Human Perception and Performance* **6**, 505–515
Bay, E. (1962). Aphasia and non-verbal disorders of language. *Brain* **85**, 411–426
Benson, D. F. (1979). *Aphasia, Alexia and Agraphia*. London: Churchill, Livingstone
Benton, A. L. (1977). The amusias. *In* M. Critchley and R. A. Henson (eds), *Music and the Brain*. London: Heinemann
Berlyne, D. E. (1971). *Aesthetics and Psychobiology*. New York: Appleton Century Crofts
Bever, R. and Chiarello, R. (1974). Cerebral dominance in musicians and non-musicians. *Science* **185**, 357–359
Bogen, J. and Gordon, H. (1971). Musical tests for functional lateralization with intra-carotid armabarbital. *Nature* **230**, 524–525
Botez, M. I. and Wertheim, N. (1959). Expressive aphasia and amusia following right frontal lesion in a right handed man. *Brain* **82**, 186–201
Bruner, J. S., Goodnow, J. and Austin, G. A. (1956). *A Study of Thinking*. New York: Wiley
Cermak, L. and Craik, F. (eds) (1979). *Levels of Processing in Human Memory*. Hillside, New Jersey: Erlbaum
Child, I. L. (1969). Esthetics. *In* G. Lindzey and E. Aronson (eds), *Handbook of Social Psychology*. Reading, Mass.: Addison-Wesley
Coltheart, M. (1980). Reading, phonological coding and deep dyslexia. *In* Coltheart, M., Patterson, K. E. and Marshall, J. C. (eds), *Deep Dyslexia*. London: Routledge and Kegan Paul
Cooper, G. and Meyer, L. (1960). *The Rhythmic Structure of Music*. Chicago: University of Chicago Press
Deutsch, D. (1973). Octave generalization of specific interference effects in memory for tonal pitch. *Perception and Psychophysics* **13**, 271–275
Dorgeuille, C. (1966). Introduction a l'étude des amusies. Unpublished doctoral dissertation, Paris. (Cited in Benton, 1977)
Dowling, W. J. (1978). Scale and contour. Two components of a theory of memory for melodies. *Psychological Review* **85**, 341–354
Dowling, W. J. (1979). Mental structures through which music is perceived. Paper pre-

sented at the National Symposium on the Applications of Psychology to the Teaching and Learning of Music. Ann Arbor, Michigan

Fechner, G. (1876). *Vorschule der Aestetik*. Leipzig: Breitkopft and Hartel

Feuchtwanger, E. (1930). *Amusie*. Berlin: Springer

Freud, S. (1958). *On Creativity and the Unconscious*. (Ed. Benjamin Nelson). New York: Harper and Row

Galin, D. (1974). Implications for psychiatry of left and right cerebral specialization. *Archives of General Psychiatry* **35**, 572–583

Gardner, H. (1973). *The Arts and Human Development*. New York: Wiley

Gardner, H. (1974). A psychological examination of Nelson Goodman's theory of symbols. *The Monist* **58**, 319–326

Gardner, H. (1975a). Artistry following aphasia. Paper presented at the Academy of Aphasia, Victoria, British Columbia, October 1975

Gardner, H. (1975b). *The Shattered Mind*. New York: Knopf

Gardner, H. (1976). Promising paths to knowledge. *Journal of Aesthetic Education* **10**, 201–207

Gardner, H. (1977). Senses, symbols, operations: an organization of artistry. *In* D. Perkins and B. Leondar (eds), *The Arts and Cognition*. Baltimore: Johns Hopkins University Press

Gardner, H. (1979). Developmental psychology after Piaget: An approach in terms of symbolization. *Human Development* **22**, 73–88

Gardner, H. (1980a). *Artful Scribbles: the Significance of Children's Drawings*. New York: Basic Books

Gardner, H. (1980b). The laws of the brain. (Unpublished paper)

Gardner, H., Howard, V. and Perkins, D. (1974). Symbol systems: philosophical, psychological and educational investigation. *In* D. Olson (ed.), *Media and Symbols*. Chicago: University of Chicago Press

Gardner, H., Ling, K., Flamm, L. and Silverman, J. (1975). Comprehension and appreciation of humor in brain-damaged patients. *Brain* **98**, 399–412

Gardner, H., Silverman, J., Denes, G., Semenza, C. and Rosenstiel, A. (1977). Sensitivity to musical denotation and connotation in organic patients. *Cortex* **13**, 243–256

Gates, A. and Bradshaw, J. (1977). The role of the cerebral hemisphere in music. *Brain and Language* **4**, 403–431

Goodglass, H. and Kaplan, E. (1972). *Assessment of Aphasia*. Philadelphia: Lea and Febiger

Goodman, N. (1968). *Languages of Art*. Indianapolis: Bobbs-Merrill

Goodman, N. (1972). *Problems and Projects*. Indianapolis: Bobbs-Merrill

Goodman, N. (1979). *Ways of Worldmaking*. Indianapolis: Hackett

Gordon, E. (1979). *Primary Measures of Music Audiation*. Chicago: G & A

Gordon, H. (1970). Hemispheric asymmetries in the perception of musical chords. *Cortex* **6**, 387–398

Grossman, M. (1980). Figurative referential skills after brain damage. Paper presented at the International Neuropsychological Society, San Diego, February 1980

Jakobson, R. and Halle, M. (1956). *Fundamentals of Language*. Hague: Mouton

Jones-Gotman, M. and Milner, B. (1977). Design fluency: The invention of nonsense drawings after local cortical lesions. *Neuropsychologia* **15**, 653–674

Judd, T., Gardner, H. and Geschwind, N. (1980). Alexia without agraphia in a composer. Project Zero Technical Report No. 15

Jung, R. (1974). Neuropsychologie und Neurophysiologie des Kontur- und Formensehens in Zeichnung und Malerei. *In* H. M. Wieck (ed.), *Psychopathologie musischer Gestaltungen*. Stuttgart: Schattauer-Verlag

Kaplan, E. (1980). Presidential address, International Neuropsychology Society, San Diego, February 1980

Kimura, D. (1973). The asymmetry of the human brain. *Scientific American* **228**, 70–78

Kleist, K. (1962). *Sensory Aphasia and Amusia*. Oxford: Pergamon

Kreitler, H. and Kreitler, S. (1974). *Psychology of the Arts*. Durham, North Carolina: Duke University Press

Krumhansl, C. (1979). The psychological representation of musical pitch in a tonal context. *Cognitive Psychology* **11**, 346–374

Langer, S. (1953). *Feeling and Form*. New York: Scribner's

Lerdahl, F. and Jackendoff, R. (forthcoming). *A Formal Theory of Music*

Lezak, M. D. (1979). Behavioral concomitants of configurational disorganization in right hemisphere damaged patients. Unpublished paper, Portland, Oregon

Lindauer, M. (1974). *Psychological Study of Literature*. Chicago: Nelson Hall

Luria, A. R., Tsvetkova, L. S. and Futer, D. S. (1965). Aphasia in a composer. *Journal of Neurological Science* **2**, 288–292

Marshall, J. C. and Newcombe, F. (1973). Patterns of paralexia: A psycholinguistic approach. *Journal of Psycholinguistic Research*, **2**, 175–199

Meyer, L. (1956). *Emotion and Meaning in Music*. Chicago: University of Chicago Press

Milner, B. (1962). Laterality effects in audition. *In* V. B. Mountcastle (ed.), *Interhemispheric Relations and Cerebral Dominance*. Baltimore: Johns Hopkins University Press

Morton, J. (1969). The interaction of information in word recognition. *Psychological Review* **76**, 165–178

Nebes, R. (1974). Hemispheric specialization in commisurotized man. *Psychological Bulletin* **81**, 1–14

Newell, A. and Simon, H. (1972). *Human Problem Solving*. Englewood Cliffs, New Jersey: Prentice-Hall

Patterson, K. E. (1979). What is right with 'deep' dyslexia patients? *Brain and Language* **8**, 111–129

Perkins, D. (1977). A better word. *In* D. Perkins and B. Leondar (eds), *The Arts and Cognition*. Baltimore: Johns Hopkins University Press

Perkins, D. (1981). *The Mind's Best Work*. Cambridge: Harvard University Press

Perkins, D. and Leondar, B. (eds) (1977). *The Arts and Cognition*. Baltimore: Johns Hopkins University Press

Piaget, J. (1950). *The Psychology of Intelligence*. London: Routledge and Kegan Paul

Plimpton, G. (ed.) (1977). *Writers at Work*, Vol. 3. New York: Penguin

Ross, E. and Mesulam, M. (1979). Dominant language functions of the right hemisphere: Prosody and emotional gesturing. *Archives of Neurology* **36**, 144–148

Rothenberg, A. (1979). *The Emerging Goddess: The Creative Process in Art Science and Other Fields*. Chicago: University of Chicago Press

Seashore, C. (1967). *The Psychology of Music*. New York: Dover

Selfe, L. (1977). *Nadia*. New York: Academic Press

Shankweiler, D. (1966). Effects of temporal lobe damage on perception of dichotically presented melodies. *Journal of Comparative and Physiological Psychology* **62**, 115

Shanon, B. (1980). Lateralization effects in musical decision tasks. *Neuropsychologia* **18**, 21–31

Shapiro, B. J., Grossman, M. and Gardner, H. (1981). Selective musical processing deficits in brain damaged populations. *Neuropsychologia* **19**, 161–170

Skinner, B. F. (ed.) (1961). *Cumulative Record. A Selection of Papers*, (3rd edn.) New York: Century Psychology Series

Soukes, A. and Baruk, H. (1930). Autopsie d'un cas d'amusie (avec aphasie) chez un professeur de piano. *Revue Neurologique* **1**, 545–556

Sparks, R., Helm, N. and Albert, M. (1974). Aphasia rehabilitation resulting from melodic intonation therapy. *Cortex* **10**, 303–316

Ustvedt, H. (1937). Über die Untersuchung der musikalischen Funktionen bei Patienten mit Gerhirnleiden, besonders bei Patienten mit Aphasie. *Acta Medica Scandinavia Supplement* **86**

Wapner, W., Hamby, S. and Gardner, H. (1981). The role of the right hemisphere in the organization of complex linguistic materials. *Brain and Language* **14**, 15–33

Wapner, W., Judd, T. and Gardner, H. (1978). Visual agnosia in an artist. *Cortex* **14**, 343–364

Warrington, E. (1969). Constructional apraxia. *In* P. J. Winken and G. W. Bruyn (eds), *Handbook of Clinical Neurology*, Vol. 4. Amsterdam: North-Holland

Wertheim, N. and Botez, M. (1961). Receptive amusia. *Brain* **84**, 19–30
Winner, E. (1982). *Invented Worlds: An Introduction to the Psychology of Art*. Cambridge: Harvard University Press
Winner, E. and Gardner, H. (1977). The comprehension of metaphor in brain damaged patients. *Brain* **100**, 719–727
Zattore, R. J. (1979). Recognition of dichotic melodies by musicians and non-musicians. *Neuropsychologia* **17**, 607–617

Subject Index